Streaming Systems

The *What*, *Where*, *When*, *and How* *of*
Large-Scale Data Processing

Tyler Akidau, Slava Chernyak, and Reuven Lax

Beijing · Boston · Farnham · Sebastopol · Tokyo

Streaming Systems

by Tyler Akidau, Slava Chernyak, and Reuven Lax

Published by O'Reilly Media, Inc., 1005 Gravenstein Highway North, Sebastopol, CA 95472.

O'Reilly books may be purchased for educational, business, or sales promotional use. Online editions are also available for most titles (*http://oreilly.com*). For more information, contact our corporate/institutional sales department: 800-998-9938 or *corporate@oreilly.com*.

Editors: Rachel Roumeliotis and Jeff Bleiel	**Indexer:** Ellen Troutman-Zaig
Production Editor: Nicholas Adams	**Interior Designer:** David Futato
Copyeditor: Octal Publishing, Inc.	**Cover Designer:** Karen Montgomery
Proofreader: Kim Cofer	**Illustrator:** Rebecca Demarest

August 2018:   First Edition

Revision History for the First Edition
2018-07-12:   First Release
2019-12-13:   Second Release

See *http://oreilly.com/catalog/errata.csp?isbn=9781491983874* for release details.

978-1-491-98387-4

[LSI]

Table of Contents

Preface Or: What Are You Getting Yourself Into Here?. vii

Part I.   The Beam Model

1. Streaming 101. 3
Terminology: What Is Streaming?   4
On the Greatly Exaggerated Limitations of Streaming   6
Event Time Versus Processing Time   9
Data Processing Patterns   12
Bounded Data   12
Unbounded Data: Batch   13
Unbounded Data: Streaming   14
Summary   22

2. The *What*, *Where*, *When*, and *How* of Data Processing. 25
Roadmap   26
Batch Foundations: *What* and *Where*   28
What: Transformations   28
Where: Windowing   32
Going Streaming: *When* and *How*   34
When: The Wonderful Thing About Triggers Is Triggers Are Wonderful
    Things!   34
When: Watermarks   39
When: Early/On-Time/Late Triggers FTW!   44
When: Allowed Lateness (i.e., Garbage Collection)   47
How: Accumulation   51
Summary   55

3. Watermarks. **59**
  Definition   59
  Source Watermark Creation   62
    Perfect Watermark Creation   64
    Heuristic Watermark Creation   65
  Watermark Propagation   67
    Understanding Watermark Propagation   69
    Watermark Propagation and Output Timestamps   75
    The Tricky Case of Overlapping Windows   80
  Percentile Watermarks   81
  Processing-Time Watermarks   84
  Case Studies   86
    Case Study: Watermarks in Google Cloud Dataflow   87
    Case Study: Watermarks in Apache Flink   88
    Case Study: Source Watermarks for Google Cloud Pub/Sub   90
  Summary   93

4. Advanced Windowing. **95**
  When/*Where*: Processing-Time Windows   95
    Event-Time Windowing   97
    Processing-Time Windowing via Triggers   98
    Processing-Time Windowing via Ingress Time   100
  Where: Session Windows   103
  Where: Custom Windowing   107
    Variations on Fixed Windows   108
    Variations on Session Windows   115
    One Size Does Not Fit All   119
  Summary   119

5. Exactly-Once and Side Effects. **121**
  Why Exactly Once Matters   121
  Accuracy Versus Completeness   122
    Side Effects   123
    Problem Definition   123
  Ensuring Exactly Once in Shuffle   125
  Addressing Determinism   126
  Performance   127
    Graph Optimization   127
    Bloom Filters   128
    Garbage Collection   129
  Exactly Once in Sources   130
  Exactly Once in Sinks   131

Use Cases   133
    Example Source: Cloud Pub/Sub   133
    Example Sink: Files   134
    Example Sink: Google BigQuery   135
Other Systems   136
    Apache Spark Streaming   136
    Apache Flink   136
Summary   138

Part II.   Streams and Tables

6. Streams and Tables. **141**
Stream-and-Table Basics Or: a Special Theory of Stream and Table Relativity 142
    Toward a General Theory of Stream and Table Relativity   143
Batch Processing Versus Streams and Tables   144
    A Streams and Tables Analysis of MapReduce   144
    Reconciling with Batch Processing   150
What, *Where*, *When*, and *How* in a Streams and Tables World   150
    What: Transformations   150
    Where: Windowing   154
    When: Triggers   157
    How: Accumulation   165
    A Holistic View of Streams and Tables in the Beam Model   166
A General Theory of Stream and Table Relativity   171
Summary   172

7. The Practicalities of Persistent State. **175**
Motivation   175
    The Inevitability of Failure   176
    Correctness and Efficiency   177
Implicit State   178
    Raw Grouping   179
    Incremental Combining   181
Generalized State   184
    Case Study: Conversion Attribution   186
    Conversion Attribution with Apache Beam   189
Summary   199

8. Streaming SQL. **201**
What Is Streaming SQL?   201
    Relational Algebra   202

Time-Varying Relations   203
Streams and Tables   207
Looking Backward: Stream and Table Biases   214
The Beam Model: A Stream-Biased Approach   214
The SQL Model: A Table-Biased Approach   218
Looking Forward: Toward Robust Streaming SQL   226
Stream and Table Selection   227
Temporal Operators   228
Summary   249

9. Streaming Joins. **253**
All Your Joins Are Belong to Streaming   253
Unwindowed Joins   254
FULL OUTER   255
LEFT OUTER   258
RIGHT OUTER   259
INNER   259
ANTI   261
SEMI   262
Windowed Joins   266
Fixed Windows   267
Temporal Validity   269
Summary   282

10. The Evolution of Large-Scale Data Processing. **283**
MapReduce   284
Hadoop   288
Flume   289
Storm   294
Spark   297
MillWheel   300
Kafka   304
Cloud Dataflow   307
Flink   309
Beam   313
Summary   316

Index. **319**

Preface Or: What Are You Getting Yourself Into Here?

Hello adventurous reader, welcome to our book! At this point, I assume that you're either interested in learning more about the wonders of stream processing or hoping to spend a few hours reading about the glory of the majestic brown trout. Either way, I salute you! That said, those of you in the latter bucket who don't also have an advanced understanding of computer science should consider how prepared you are to deal with disappointment before forging ahead; *caveat piscator*, and all that.

To set the tone for this book from the get go, I wanted to give you a heads up about a couple of things. First, this book is a little strange in that we have multiple authors, but we're not pretending that we somehow all speak and write in the same voice like we're weird identical triplets who happened to be born to different sets of parents. Because as interesting as that sounds, the end result would actually be less enjoyable to read. Instead, we've opted to each write in our own voices, and we've granted the book just enough self-awareness to be able to make reference to each of us where appropriate, but not so much self-awareness that it resents us for making it only into a book and not something cooler like a robot dinosaur with a Scottish accent.[1]

As far as voices go, there are three you'll come across:

Tyler

> That would be me. If you haven't explicitly been told someone else is speaking, you can assume that it's me, because we added the other authors somewhat late in the game, and I was basically like, "hells no" when I thought about going back and updating everything I'd already written. I'm the technical lead for the Data

---

1 Which incidentally is what we requested our animal book cover be, but O'Reilly felt it wouldn't translate well into line art. I respectfully disagree, but a brown trout is a fair compromise.

Processing Languages ands Systems[2] group at Google, responsible for Google Cloud Dataflow, Google's Apache Beam efforts, as well as Google-internal data processing systems such as Flume, MillWheel, and MapReduce. I'm also a founding Apache Beam PMC member.

Slava

Slava was a long-time member of the MillWheel team at Google, and later an original member of the Windmill team that built MillWheel's successor, the heretofore unnamed system that powers the Streaming Engine in Google Cloud Dataflow. Slava is the foremost expert on watermarks and time semantics in stream processing systems the world over, period. You might find it unsurprising then that he's the author of Chapter 3, *Watermarks*.

Reuven

Reuven is at the bottom of this list because he has more experience with stream processing than both Slava and me combined and would thus crush us if he were placed any higher. Reuven has created or led the creation of nearly all of the interesting systems-level magic in Google's general-purpose stream processing engines, including applying an untold amount of attention to detail in providing high-throughput, low-latency, exactly-once semantics in a system that nevertheless utilizes fine-grained checkpointing. You might find it unsurprising that he's the author of Chapter 5, *Exactly-Once and Side Effects*. He also happens to be an Apache Beam PMC member.

Figure P-1. The cover that could have been...

Navigating This Book

Now that you know who you'll be hearing from, the next logical step would be to find out what you'll be hearing about, which brings us to the second thing I wanted to

---

2 Or DataPLS, pronounced Datapals—get it?

mention. There are conceptually two major parts to this book, each with four chapters, and each followed up by a chapter that stands relatively independently on its own.

The fun begins with Part I, *The Beam Model* (Chapters 1–4), which focuses on the high-level batch plus streaming data processing model originally developed for Google Cloud Dataflow, later donated to the Apache Software Foundation as Apache Beam, and also now seen in whole or in part across most other systems in the industry. It's composed of four chapters:

- Chapter 1, *Streaming 101*, which covers the basics of stream processing, establishing some terminology, discussing the capabilities of streaming systems, distinguishing between two important domains of time (processing time and event time), and finally looking at some common data processing patterns.

- Chapter 2, *The What, Where, When, and How of Data Processing*, which covers in detail the core concepts of robust stream processing over out-of-order data, each analyzed within the context of a concrete running example and with animated diagrams to highlight the dimension of time.

- Chapter 3, *Watermarks* (written by Slava), which provides a deep survey of temporal progress metrics, how they are created, and how they propagate through pipelines. It ends by examining the details of two real-world watermark implementations.

- Chapter 4, *Advanced Windowing*, which picks up where Chapter 2 left off, diving into some advanced windowing and triggering concepts like processing-time windows, sessions, and continuation triggers.

Between Parts I and II, providing an interlude as timely as the details contained therein are important, stands Chapter 5, *Exactly-Once and Side Effects* (written by Reuven). In it, he enumerates the challenges of providing end-to-end exactly-once (or effectively-once) processing semantics and walks through the implementation details of three different approaches to exactly-once processing: Apache Flink, Apache Spark, and Google Cloud Dataflow.

Next begins Part II, *Streams and Tables* (Chapters 6–9), which dives deeper into the conceptual and investigates the lower-level "streams and tables" way of thinking about stream processing, recently popularized by some upstanding citizens in the Apache Kafka community but, of course, invented decades ago by folks in the database community, because wasn't everything? It too is composed of four chapters:

- Chapter 6, *Streams and Tables*, which introduces the basic idea of streams and tables, analyzes the classic MapReduce approach through a streams-and-tables lens, and then constructs a theory of streams and tables sufficiently general to encompass the full breadth of the Beam Model (and beyond).

- Chapter 7, *The Practicalities of Persistent State*, which considers the motivations for persistent state in streaming pipelines, looks at two common types of implicit state, and then analyzes a practical use case (advertising attribution) to inform the necessary characteristics of a general state management mechanism.

- Chapter 8, *Streaming SQL*, which investigates the meaning of streaming within the context of relational algebra and SQL, contrasts the inherent stream and table biases within the Beam Model and classic SQL as they exist today, and proposes a set of possible paths forward toward incorporating robust streaming semantics in SQL.

- Chapter 9, *Streaming Joins*, which surveys a variety of different join types, analyzes their behavior within the context of streaming, and finally looks in detail at a useful but ill-supported streaming join use case: temporal validity windows.

Finally, closing out the book is Chapter 10, *The Evolution of Large-Scale Data Processing*, which strolls through a focused history of the MapReduce lineage of data processing systems, examining some of the important contributions that have evolved streaming systems into what they are today.

Takeaways

As a final bit of guidance, if you were to ask me to describe the things I most want readers to take away from this book, I would say this:

- The single most important thing you can learn from this book is the theory of streams and tables and how they relate to one another. Everything else builds on top of that. No, we won't get to this topic until Chapter 6. That's okay; it's worth the wait, and you'll be better prepared to appreciate its awesomeness by then.

- Time-varying relations are a revelation. They are stream processing incarnate: an embodiment of everything streaming systems are built to achieve and a powerful connection to the familiar tools we all know and love from the world of batch. We won't learn about them until Chapter 8, but again, the journey there will help you appreciate them all the more.

- A well-written distributed streaming engine is a magical thing. This arguably goes for distributed systems in general, but as you learn more about how these systems are built to provide the semantics they do (in particular, the case studies from Chapters 3 and 5), it becomes all the more apparent just how much heavy lifting they're doing for you.

- LaTeX/Tikz is an amazing tool for making diagrams, animated or otherwise. A horrible, crusty tool with sharp edges and tetanus, but an incredible tool nonetheless. I hope the clarity the animated diagrams in this book bring to the complex topics we discuss will inspire more people to give LaTeX/Tikz a try (in

"Figures" on page xii, we provide for a link to the full source for the animations from this book).

Conventions Used in This Book

The following typographical conventions are used in this book:

Italic
Indicates new terms, URLs, email addresses, filenames, and file extensions.

`Constant width`
Used for program listings, as well as within paragraphs to refer to program elements such as variable or function names, databases, data types, environment variables, statements, and keywords.

`Constant width bold`
Shows commands or other text that should be typed literally by the user.

`Constant width italic`
Shows text that should be replaced with user-supplied values or by values determined by context.

 This element signifies a tip or suggestion.

 This element signifies a general note.

 This element indicates a warning or caution.

Online Resources

There are a handful of associated online resources to aid in your enjoyment of this book.

Figures

All the of the figures in this book are available in digital form on the book's website. This is particularly useful for the animated figures, only a few frames of which appear (comic-book style) in the non-Safari formats of the book:

- Online index: *http://www.streamingbook.net/figures*
- Specific figures may be referenced at URLs of the form:

  http://www.streamingbook.net/fig/<FIGURE-NUMBER>

  For example, for Figure 2-5: *http://www.streamingbook.net/fig/2-5*

The animated figures themselves are LaTeX/Tikz drawings, rendered first to PDF, then converted to animated GIFs via ImageMagick. For the more intrepid among you, full source code and instructions for rendering the animations (from this book, the "Streaming 101" (*http://oreil.ly/1p1AKux*) and "Streaming 102" (*http://oreil.ly/1TV7YGU*) blog posts, and the original Dataflow Model paper (*http://bit.ly/2sXgVJ3*)) are available on GitHub at *http://github.com/takidau/animations*. Be warned that this is roughly 14,000 lines of LaTeX/Tikz code that grew very organically, with no intent of ever being read and used by others. In other words, it's a messy, intertwined web of archaic incantations; turn back now or abandon all hope ye who enter here, for there be dragons.

Code Snippets

Although this book is largely conceptual, there are are number of code and psuedo-code snippets used throughout to help illustrate points. Code for the more functional core Beam Model concepts from Chapters 2 and 4, as well as the more imperative state and timers concepts in Chapter 7, is available online at *http://github.com/takidau/streamingbook*. Since understanding semantics is the main goal, the code is provided primarily as Beam PTransform/DoFn implementations and accompanying unit tests. There is also a single standalone pipeline implementation to illustrate the delta between a unit test and a real pipeline. The code layout is as follows:

src/main/java/net/streamingbook/BeamModel.java
: Beam PTransform implementations of Examples 2-1 through 2-9 and Example 4-3, each with an additional method returning the expected output when executed over the example datasets from those chapters.

src/test/java/net/streamingbook/BeamModelTest.java
: Unit tests verifying the example PTransforms in *BeamModel.java* via generated datasets matching those in the book.

src/main/java/net/streamingbook/Example2_1.java
Standalone version of the Example 2-1 pipeline that can be run locally or using a distributed Beam runner.

src/main/java/net/streamingbook/inputs.csv
Sample input file for *Example2_1.java* containing the dataset from the book.

src/main/java/net/streamingbook/StateAndTimers.java
Beam code implementing the conversion attribution example from Chapter 7 using Beam's state and timers primitives.

src/test/java/net/streamingbook/StateAndTimersTest.java
Unit test verifying the conversion attribution DoFns from *StateAndTimers.java*.

src/main/java/net/streamingbook/ValidityWindows.java
Temporal validity windows implementation.

src/main/java/net/streamingbook/Utils.java
Shared utility methods.

This book is here to help you get your job done. In general, if example code is offered with this book, you may use it in your programs and documentation. You do not need to contact us for permission unless you're reproducing a significant portion of the code. For example, writing a program that uses several chunks of code from this book does not require permission. Selling or distributing a CD-ROM of examples from O'Reilly books does require permission. Answering a question by citing this book and quoting example code does not require permission. Incorporating a significant amount of example code from this book into your product's documentation does require permission.

We appreciate, but do not require, attribution. An attribution usually includes the title, author, publisher, and ISBN. For example: "*Streaming Systems* by Tyler Akidau, Slava Chernyak, and Reuven Lax (O'Reilly). Copyright 2018 O'Reilly Media, Inc., 978-1-491-98387-4."

If you feel your use of code examples falls outside fair use or the permission given above, feel free to contact us at *permissions@oreilly.com*.

O'Reilly Safari

 *Safari* (formerly Safari Books Online) is a membership-based training and reference platform for enterprise, government, educators, and individuals.

Members have access to thousands of books, training videos, Learning Paths, interactive tutorials, and curated playlists from over 250 publishers, including O'Reilly Media, Harvard Business Review, Prentice Hall Professional, Addison-Wesley Professional, Microsoft Press, Sams, Que, Peachpit Press, Adobe, Focal Press, Cisco Press, John Wiley & Sons, Syngress, Morgan Kaufmann, IBM Redbooks, Packt, Adobe Press, FT Press, Apress, Manning, New Riders, McGraw-Hill, Jones & Bartlett, and Course Technology, among others.

For more information, please visit *http://www.oreilly.com/safari*.

How to Contact Us

Please address comments and questions concerning this book to the publisher:

O'Reilly Media, Inc.
1005 Gravenstein Highway North
Sebastopol, CA 95472
800-998-9938 (in the United States or Canada)
707-829-0515 (international or local)
707-829-0104 (fax)

We have a web page for this book, where we list errata, examples, and any additional information. You can access this page at *http://bit.ly/streaming-systems*.

To comment or ask technical questions about this book, send email to *bookquestions@oreilly.com*.

For more information about our books, courses, conferences, and news, see our website at *http://www.oreilly.com*.

Find us on Facebook: *http://facebook.com/oreilly*

Follow us on Twitter: *http://twitter.com/oreillymedia*

Watch us on YouTube: *http://www.youtube.com/oreillymedia*

Acknowledgments

Last, but certainly not least: many people are awesome, and we would like to acknowledge a specific subset of them here for their help in creating this tome.

The content in this book distills the work of an untold number of extremely smart individuals across Google, the industry, and academia at large. We owe them all a sincere expression of gratitude and regret that we could not possibly list them all here, even if we tried, which we will not.

Among our colleagues at Google, much credit goes to everyone in the DataPLS team (and its various ancestor teams: Flume, MillWheel, MapReduce, et al.), who've helped bring so many of these ideas to life over the years. In particular, we'd like to thank:

- Paul Nordstrom and the rest of the MillWheel team from the Golden Age of MillWheel: Alex Amato, Alex Balikov, Kaya Bekiroğlu, Josh Haberman, Tim Hollingsworth, Ilya Maykov, Sam McVeety, Daniel Mills, and Sam Whittle for envisioning and building such a comprehensive, robust, and scalable set of low-level primitives on top of which we were later able to construct the higher-level models discussed in this book. Without their vision and skill, the world of massive-scale stream processing would look very different.

- Craig Chambers, Frances Perry, Robert Bradshaw, Ashish Raniwala, and the rest of the Flume team of yore for envisioning and creating the expressive and powerful data processing foundation that we were later able to unify with the world of streaming.

- Sam McVeety for lead authoring the original MillWheel paper, which put our amazing little project on the map for the very first time.

- Grzegorz Czajkowski for repeatedly supporting our evangelization efforts, even as competing deadlines and priorities loomed.

Looking more broadly, a huge amount of credit is due to everyone in the Apache Beam, Calcite, Kafka, Flink, Spark, and Storm communities. Each and every one of these projects has contributed materially to advancing the state of the art in stream processing for the world at large over the past decade. Thank you.

To shower gratitude a bit more specifically, we would also like to thank:

- Martin Kleppmann, for leading the charge in advocating for the streams-and-tables way of thinking, and also for investing a huge amount of time providing piles of insightful technical and editorial input on the drafts of every chapter in this book. All this in addition to being an inspiration and all-around great guy.

- Julian Hyde, for his insightful vision and infectious passion for streaming SQL.

- Jay Kreps, for fighting the good fight against Lambda Architecture tyranny; it was your original "Questioning the Lambda Architecture" (*https://www.oreilly.com/ideas/questioning-the-lambda-architecture*) post that got Tyler pumped enough to go out and join the fray, as well.

- Stephan Ewen, Kostas Tzoumas, Fabian Hueske, Aljoscha Krettek, Robert Metzger, Kostas Kloudas, Jamie Grier, Max Michels, and the rest of the data Artisans extended family, past and present, for always pushing the envelope of what's possible in stream processing, and doing so in a consistently open and collaborative way. The world of streaming is a much better place thanks to all of you.

- Jesse Anderson, for his diligent reviews and for all the hugs. If you see Jesse, give him a big hug for me.

- Danny Yuan, Sid Anand, Wes Reisz, and the amazing QCon developer conference, for giving us our first opportunity to talk publicly within the industry about our work, at QCon San Francisco 2014.

- Ben Lorica at O'Reilly and the iconic Strata Data Conference, for being repeatedly supportive of our efforts to evangelize stream processing, be it online, in print, or in person.

- The entire Apache Beam community, and in particular our fellow committers, for helping push forward the Beam vision: Ahmet Altay, Amit Sela, Aviem Zur, Ben Chambers, Griselda Cuevas, Chamikara Jayalath, Davor Bonaci, Dan Halperin, Etienne Chauchot, Frances Perry, Ismaël Mejía, Jason Kuster, Jean-Baptiste Onofré, Jesse Anderson, Eugene Kirpichov, Josh Wills, Kenneth Knowles, Luke Cwik, Jingsong Lee, Manu Zhang, Melissa Pashniak, Mingmin Xu, Max Michels, Pablo Estrada, Pei He, Robert Bradshaw, Stephan Ewen, Stas Levin, Thomas Groh, Thomas Weise, and James Xu.

No acknowledgments section would be complete without a nod to the otherwise faceless cohort of tireless reviewers whose insightful comments helped turn garbage into awesomeness: Jesse Anderson, Cosmin Arad, Grzegorz Czajkowski, Marián Dvorský, Stephan Ewen, Rafael J. Fernández-Moctezuma, Martin Kleppmann, Kenneth Knowles, Sam McVeety, Mosha Pasumansky, Frances Perry, Jelena Pjesivac-Grbovic, Jeff Shute, and William Vambenepe. You are the Mr. Fusion to our DeLorean Time Machine. That had a nicer ring to it in my head—see, this is what I'm talking about.

And of course, a big thanks to our authoring and production support team:

- Marie Beaugureau, our original editor, for all of her help and support in getting this project off the ground and her everlasting patience with my persistent desire to subvert editorial norms. We miss you!

- Jeff Bleiel, our editor 2.0, for taking over the reins and helping us land this monster of a project and his everlasting patience with our inability to meet even the most modest of deadlines. We made it!

- Bob Russell, our copy editor, for reading our book more closely than anyone should ever have to. I tip my hat to your masterful command of grammar, punctuation, vocabulary, and Adobe Acrobat annotations.

- Nick Adams, our intrepid production editor, for helping tame a mess of totally sketchy HTMLBook code into a print-worthy thing of beauty and for not getting mad at me when I asked him to manually ignore Bob's many, many individual suggestions to switch our usage of the term "data" from plural to singular. You've managed to make this book look even better than I'd hoped for, thank you.

- Ellen Troutman-Zaig, our indexer, for somehow weaving a tangled web of off-hand references into a useful and comprehensive index. I stand in awe at your attention to detail.
- Rebecca Panzer, our illustrator, for beautifying our static diagrams and for assuring Nick that I didn't need to spend more weekends figuring out how to refactor my animated LaTeX diagrams to have larger fonts. Phew x2!
- Kim Cofer, our proofreader, for pointing out how sloppy and inconsistent we were so others wouldn't have to.

Tyler would like to thank:

- My coauthors, Reuven Lax and Slava Chernyak, for bringing their ideas and chapters to life in ways I never could have.
- George Bradford Emerson II, for the Sean Connery inspiration. That's my favorite joke in the book and we haven't even gotten to the first chapter yet. It's all downhill from here, folks.
- Rob Schlender, for the amazing bottle of scotch he's going to buy me shortly before robots take over the world. Here's to going down in style!
- My uncle, Randy Bowen, for making sure I discovered just how much I love computers and, in particular, that homemade POV-Ray 2.x floppy disk that opened up a whole new world for me.
- My parents, David and Marty Dauwalder, without whose dedication and unbelievable perseverance none of this would have ever been possible. You're the best parents ever, for reals!
- Dr. David L. Vlasuk, without whom I simply wouldn't be here today. Thanks for everything, Dr. V.
- My wonderful family, Shaina, Romi, and Ione Akidau for their unwavering support in completing this levianthantine effort, despite the many nights and weekends we spent apart as a result. I love you always.
- My faithful writing partner, Kiyoshi: even though you only slept and barked at postal carriers the entire time we worked on the book together, you did so flawlessly and seemingly without effort. You are a credit to your species.

Slava would like to thank:

- Josh Haberman, Sam Whittle, and Daniel Mills for being codesigners and cocreators of watermarks in MillWheel and subsequently Streaming Dataflow as well as many other parts of these systems. Systems as complex as these are never designed in a vacuum, and without all of the thoughts and hard work that each of you put in, we would not be here today.

- Stephan Ewen of data Artisans for helping shape my thoughts and understanding of the watermark implementation in Apache Flink.

Reuven would like to thank:

- Paul Nordstrom for his vision, Sam Whittle, Sam McVeety, Slava Chernyak, Josh Haberman, Daniel Mills, Kaya Bekiroğlu, Alex Balikov, Tim Hollingsworth, Alex Amato, and Ilya Maykov for all their efforts in building the original MillWheel system and writing the subsequent paper.
- Stephan Ewen of data Artisans for his help reviewing the chapter on exactly-once semantics, and valuable feedback on the inner workings of Apache Flink.

Lastly, we would all like to thank *you*, glorious reader, for being willing to spend real money on this book to hear us prattle on about the cool stuff we get to build and play with. It's been a joy writing it all down, and we've done our best to make sure you'll get your money's worth. If for some reason you don't like it...well hopefully you bought the print edition so you can at least throw it across the room in disgust before you sell it at a used bookstore. Watch out for the cat.[3]

---

3 Or don't. I actually don't like cats.

PART I

The Beam Model

CHAPTER 1

Streaming 101

Streaming data processing is a big deal in big data these days, and for good reasons; among them are the following:

- Businesses crave ever-more timely insights into their data, and switching to streaming is a good way to achieve lower latency

- The massive, unbounded datasets that are increasingly common in modern business are more easily tamed using a system designed for such never-ending volumes of data.

- Processing data as they arrive spreads workloads out more evenly over time, yielding more consistent and predictable consumption of resources.

Despite this business-driven surge of interest in streaming, streaming systems long remained relatively immature compared to their batch brethren. It's only recently that the tide has swung conclusively in the other direction. In my more bumptious moments, I hope that might be in small part due to the solid dose of goading I originally served up in my "Streaming 101" (*http://oreil.ly/1p1AKux*) and "Streaming 102" (*http://oreil.ly/1TV7YGU*) blog posts (on which the first few chapters of this book are rather obviously based). But in reality, there's also just a lot of industry interest in seeing streaming systems mature and a lot of smart and active folks out there who enjoy building them.

Even though the battle for general streaming advocacy has been, in my opinion, effectively won, I'm still going to present my original arguments from "Streaming 101" more or less unaltered. For one, they're still very applicable today, even if much of industry has begun to heed the battle cry. And for two, there are a lot of folks out there who still haven't gotten the memo; this book is an extended attempt at getting these points across.

To begin, I cover some important background information that will help frame the rest of the topics I want to discuss. I do this in three specific sections:

Terminology

To talk precisely about complex topics requires precise definitions of terms. For some terms that have overloaded interpretations in current use, I'll try to nail down exactly what I mean when I say them.

Capabilities

I remark on the oft-perceived shortcomings of streaming systems. I also propose the frame of mind that I believe data processing system builders need to adopt in order to address the needs of modern data consumers going forward.

Time domains

I introduce the two primary domains of time that are relevant in data processing, show how they relate, and point out some of the difficulties these two domains impose.

Terminology: What Is Streaming?

Before going any further, I'd like to get one thing out of the way: what is streaming? The term streaming is used today to mean a variety of different things (and for simplicity I've been using it somewhat loosely up until now), which can lead to misunderstandings about what streaming really is or what streaming systems are actually capable of. As a result, I would prefer to define the term somewhat precisely.

The crux of the problem is that many things that ought to be described by *what* they are (unbounded data processing, approximate results, etc.), have come to be described colloquially by *how* they historically have been accomplished (i.e., via streaming execution engines). This lack of precision in terminology clouds what streaming really means, and in some cases it burdens streaming systems themselves with the implication that their capabilities are limited to characteristics historically described as "streaming," such as approximate or speculative results.

Given that well-designed streaming systems are just as capable (technically more so) of producing correct, consistent, repeatable results as any existing batch engine, I prefer to isolate the term "streaming" to a very specific meaning:

Streaming system

A type of data processing engine that is designed with infinite datasets in mind.[1]

---

1 For completeness, it's perhaps worth calling out that this definition includes both true streaming as well as microbatch implementations. For those of you who aren't familiar with microbatch systems, they are streaming systems that use repeated executions of a batch processing engine to process unbounded data. Spark Streaming is the canonical example in the industry.

If I want to talk about low-latency, approximate, or speculative results, I use those specific words rather than imprecisely calling them "streaming."

Precise terms are also useful when discussing the different types of data one might encounter. From my perspective, there are two important (and orthogonal) dimensions that define the shape of a given dataset: *cardinality* and *constitution*.

The cardinality of a dataset dictates its size, with the most salient aspect of cardinality being whether a given dataset is finite or infinite. Here are the two terms I prefer to use for describing the coarse cardinality in a dataset:

Bounded data
> A type of dataset that is finite in size.

Unbounded data
> A type of dataset that is infinite in size (at least theoretically).

Cardinality is important because the unbounded nature of infinite datasets imposes additional burdens on data processing frameworks that consume them. More on this in the next section.

The constitution of a dataset, on the other hand, dictates its physical manifestation. As a result, the constitution defines the ways one can interact with the data in question. We won't get around to deeply examining constitutions until Chapter 6, but to give you a brief sense of things, there are two primary constitutions of importance:

Table
> A holistic view of a dataset at a specific point in time. SQL systems have traditionally dealt in tables.

Stream[2]
> An element-by-element view of the evolution of a dataset over time. The Map-Reduce lineage of data processing systems have traditionally dealt in streams.

We look quite deeply at the relationship between streams and tables in Chapters 6, 8, and 9, and in Chapter 8 we also learn about the unifying underlying concept of *time-varying relations* that ties them together. But until then, we deal primarily in streams because that's the constitution pipeline developers directly interact with in most data processing systems today (both batch and streaming). It's also the constitution that most naturally embodies the challenges that are unique to stream processing.

---

2 Readers familiar with my original "Streaming 101" (*https://oreil.ly/2JBfN7X*) article might recall that I rather emphatically encouraged the abandonment of the term "stream" when referring to datasets. That never caught on, which I initially thought was due to its catchiness and pervasive existing usage. In retrospect, however, I think I was simply wrong. There actually is great value in distinguishing between the two different types of dataset constitutions: tables and streams. Indeed, most of the second half of this book is dedicated to understanding the relationship between those two.

On the Greatly Exaggerated Limitations of Streaming

On that note, let's next talk a bit about what streaming systems can and can't do, with an emphasis on can. One of the biggest things I want to get across in this chapter is just how capable a well-designed streaming system can be. Streaming systems have historically been relegated to a somewhat niche market of providing low-latency, inaccurate, or speculative results, often in conjunction with a more capable batch system to provide eventually correct results; in other words, the Lambda Architecture (*http://nathanmarz.com/blog/how-to-beat-the-cap-theorem.html*).

For those of you not already familiar with the Lambda Architecture, the basic idea is that you run a streaming system alongside a batch system, both performing essentially the same calculation. The streaming system gives you low-latency, inaccurate results (either because of the use of an approximation algorithm, or because the streaming system itself does not provide correctness), and some time later a batch system rolls along and provides you with correct output. Originally proposed by Twitter's Nathan Marz (creator of Storm (*http://storm.apache.org*)), it ended up being quite successful because it was, in fact, a fantastic idea for the time; streaming engines were a bit of a letdown in the correctness department, and batch engines were as inherently unwieldy as you'd expect, so Lambda gave you a way to have your proverbial cake and eat it too. Unfortunately, maintaining a Lambda system is a hassle: you need to build, provision, and maintain two independent versions of your pipeline and then also somehow merge the results from the two pipelines at the end.

As someone who spent years working on a strongly consistent streaming engine, I also found the entire principle of the Lambda Architecture a bit unsavory. Unsurprisingly, I was a huge fan of Jay Kreps' "Questioning the Lambda Architecture" (*https://oreil.ly/2LSEdqz*) post when it came out. Here was one of the first highly visible statements against the necessity of dual-mode execution. Delightful. Kreps addressed the issue of repeatability in the context of using a replayable system like Kafka as the streaming interconnect, and went so far as to propose the Kappa Architecture, which basically means running a single pipeline using a well-designed system that's appropriately built for the job at hand. I'm not convinced that notion requires its own Greek letter name, but I fully support the idea in principle.

Quite honestly, I'd take things a step further. I would argue that well-designed streaming systems actually provide a strict superset of batch functionality. Modulo perhaps an efficiency delta, there should be no need for batch systems as they exist today. And kudos to the Apache Flink (*http://flink.apache.org*) folks for taking this idea to heart and building a system that's all-streaming-all-the-time under the covers, even in "batch" mode; I love it.

Batch and Streaming Efficiency Differences

One which I propose is not an inherent limitation of streaming systems, but simply a consequence of design choices made in most streaming systems thus far. The efficiency delta between batch and streaming is largely the result of the increased bundling and more efficient shuffle transports found in batch systems. Modern batch systems go to great lengths to implement sophisticated optimizations that allow for remarkable levels of throughput using surprisingly modest compute resources. There's no reason the types of clever insights that make batch systems the efficiency heavyweights they are today couldn't be incorporated into a system designed for unbounded data, providing users flexible choice between what we typically consider to be high-latency, higher-efficiency "batch" processing and low-latency, lower-efficiency "streaming" processing. This is effectively what we've done at Google with Cloud Dataflow by providing both batch and streaming runners under the same unified model. In our case, we use separate runners because we happen to have two independently designed systems optimized for their specific use cases. Long term, from an engineering perspective, I'd love to see us merge the two into a single system that incorporates the best parts of both while still maintaining the flexibility of choosing an appropriate efficiency level. But that's not what we have today. And honestly, thanks to the unified Dataflow Model, it's not even strictly necessary; so it may well never happen.

The corollary of all this is that broad maturation of streaming systems combined with robust frameworks for unbounded data processing will in time allow for the relegation of the Lambda Architecture to the antiquity of big data history where it belongs. I believe the time has come to make this a reality. Because to do so—that is, to beat batch at its own game—you really only need two things:

Correctness

This gets you parity with batch. At the core, correctness boils down to consistent storage. Streaming systems need a method for checkpointing persistent state over time (something Kreps has talked about in his "Why local state is a fundamental primitive in stream processing" (*https://oreil.ly/2l8asqf*) post), and it must be well designed enough to remain consistent in light of machine failures. When Spark Streaming first appeared in the public big data scene a few years ago, it was a beacon of consistency in an otherwise dark streaming world. Thankfully, things have improved substantially since then, but it is remarkable how many streaming systems still try to get by without strong consistency.

To reiterate—because this point is important: strong consistency is required for exactly-once processing,[3] which is required for correctness, which is a requirement for any system that's going to have a chance at meeting or exceeding the capabilities of batch systems. Unless you just truly don't care about your results, I implore you to shun any streaming system that doesn't provide strongly consistent state. Batch systems don't require you to verify ahead of time if they are capable of producing correct answers; don't waste your time on streaming systems that can't meet that same bar.

If you're curious to learn more about what it takes to get strong consistency in a streaming system, I recommend you check out the MillWheel (*http://bit.ly/2Muob70*), Spark Streaming (*http://bit.ly/2Mrq8Be*), and Flink snapshotting (*http://bit.ly/2t4DGK0*) papers. All three spend a significant amount of time discussing consistency. Reuven will dive into consistency guarantees in Chapter 5, and if you still find yourself craving more, there's a large amount of quality information on this topic in the literature and elsewhere.

Tools for reasoning about time

This gets you beyond batch. Good tools for reasoning about time are essential for dealing with unbounded, unordered data of varying event-time skew. An increasing number of modern datasets exhibit these characteristics, and existing batch systems (as well as many streaming systems) lack the necessary tools to cope with the difficulties they impose (though this is now rapidly changing, even as I write this). We will spend the bulk of this book explaining and focusing on various facets of this point.

To begin with, we get a basic understanding of the important concept of time domains, after which we take a deeper look at what I mean by unbounded, unordered data of varying event-time skew. We then spend the rest of this chapter looking at common approaches to bounded and unbounded data processing, using both batch and streaming systems.

---

3 If you're unfamiliar with what I mean when I say *exactly-once*, it's referring to a specific type of consistency guarantee that certain data processing frameworks provide. Consistency guarantees are typically bucketed into three main classes: at-most-once processing, at-least-once processing, and exactly-once processing. Note that the names in use here refer to the effective semantics as observed within the outputs generated by the pipeline, not the actual number of times a pipeline might process (or attempt to process) any given record. For this reason, the term *effectively-once* is sometimes used instead of exactly-once, since it's more representative of the underlying nature of things. Reuven covers these concepts in much more detail in Chapter 5.

Event Time Versus Processing Time

To speak cogently about unbounded data processing requires a clear understanding of the domains of time involved. Within any data processing system, there are typically two domains of time that we care about:

Event time
> This is the time at which events actually occurred.

Processing time
> This is the time at which events are observed in the system.

Not all use cases care about event times (and if yours doesn't, hooray! your life is easier), but many do. Examples include characterizing user behavior over time, most billing applications, and many types of anomaly detection, to name a few.

In an ideal world, event time and processing time would always be equal, with events being processed immediately as they occur. Reality is not so kind, however, and the skew between event time and processing time is not only nonzero, but often a highly variable function of the characteristics of the underlying input sources, execution engine, and hardware. Things that can affect the level of skew include the following:

- Shared resource limitations, like network congestion, network partitions, or shared CPU in a nondedicated environment
- Software causes such as distributed system logic, contention, and so on
- Features of the data themselves, like key distribution, variance in throughput, or variance in disorder (i.e., a plane full of people taking their phones out of airplane mode after having used them offline for the entire flight)

As a result, if you plot the progress of event time and processing time in any real-world system, you typically end up with something that looks a bit like the red line in Figure 1-1.

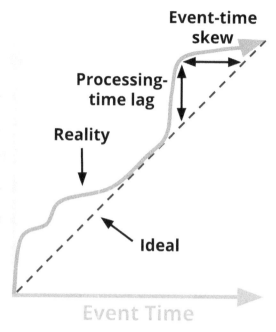

Figure 1-1. Time-domain mapping. The x-axis represents event-time completeness in the system; that is, the time X in event time up to which all data with event times less than X have been observed. The y-axis[4] represents the progress of processing time; that is, normal clock time as observed by the data processing system as it executes.

In Figure 1-1, the black dashed line with slope of 1 represents the ideal, where processing time and event time are exactly equal; the red line represents reality. In this example, the system lags a bit at the beginning of processing time, veers closer toward the ideal in the middle, and then lags again a bit toward the end. At first glance, there are two types of skew visible in this diagram, each in different time domains:

Processing time

The vertical distance between the ideal and the red line is the lag in the processing-time domain. That distance tells you how much delay is observed (in processing time) between when the events for a given time occurred and when

---

4 Since the original publication of "Streaming 101," numerous individuals have pointed out to me that it would have been more intuitive to place processing time on the x-axis and event time on the y-axis. I do agree that swapping the two axes would initially feel more natural, as event time seems like the dependent variable to processing time's independent variable. However, because both variables are monotonic and intimately related, they're effectively interdependent variables. So I think from a technical perspective you just have to pick an axis and stick with it. Math is confusing (especially outside of North America, where it suddenly becomes plural and gangs up on you).

they were processed. This is the perhaps the more natural and intuitive of the two skews.

Event time

The horizontal distance between the ideal and the red line is the amount of event-time skew in the pipeline at that moment. It tells you how far behind the ideal (in event time) the pipeline is currently.

In reality, processing-time lag and event-time skew at any given point in time are identical; they're just two ways of looking at the same thing.[5] The important takeaway regarding lag/skew is this: Because the overall mapping between event time and processing time is not static (i.e., the lag/skew can vary arbitrarily over time), this means that you cannot analyze your data solely within the context of when they are observed by your pipeline if you care about their event times (i.e., when the events actually occurred). Unfortunately, this is the way many systems designed for unbounded data have historically operated. To cope with the infinite nature of unbounded datasets, these systems typically provide some notion of windowing the incoming data. We discuss windowing in great depth a bit later, but it essentially means chopping up a dataset into finite pieces along temporal boundaries. If you care about correctness and are interested in analyzing your data in the context of their event times, you cannot define those temporal boundaries using processing time (i.e., processing-time windowing), as many systems do; with no consistent correlation between processing time and event time, some of your event-time data are going to end up in the wrong processing-time windows (due to the inherent lag in distributed systems, the online/offline nature of many types of input sources, etc.), throwing correctness out the window, as it were. We look at this problem in more detail in a number of examples in the sections that follow, as well as the remainder of the book.

Unfortunately, the picture isn't exactly rosy when windowing by event time, either. In the context of unbounded data, disorder and variable skew induce a completeness problem for event-time windows: lacking a predictable mapping between processing time and event time, how can you determine when you've observed all of the data for a given event time *X*? For many real-world data sources, you simply can't. But the vast majority of data processing systems in use today rely on some notion of completeness, which puts them at a severe disadvantage when applied to unbounded datasets.

I propose that instead of attempting to groom unbounded data into finite batches of information that eventually become complete, we should be designing tools that allow us to live in the world of uncertainty imposed by these complex datasets. New data will arrive, old data might be retracted or updated, and any system we build should be able to cope with these facts on its own, with notions of completeness being

---

5 This result really shouldn't be surprising (but was for me, hence why I'm pointing it out), because we're effectively creating a right triangle with the ideal line when measuring the two types of skew/lag. Maths are cool.

a convenient optimization for specific and appropriate use cases rather than a semantic necessity across all of them.

Before getting into specifics about what such an approach might look like, let's finish up one more useful piece of background: common data processing patterns.

Data Processing Patterns

At this point, we have enough background established that we can begin looking at the core types of usage patterns common across bounded and unbounded data processing today. We look at both types of processing and, where relevant, within the context of the two main types of engines we care about (batch and streaming, where in this context, I'm essentially lumping microbatch in with streaming because the differences between the two aren't terribly important at this level).

Bounded Data

Processing bounded data is conceptually quite straightforward, and likely familiar to everyone. In Figure 1-2, we start out on the left with a dataset full of entropy. We run it through some data processing engine (typically batch, though a well-designed streaming engine would work just as well), such as MapReduce (*http://bit.ly/ 2sZNfuA*), and on the right side end up with a new structured dataset with greater inherent value.

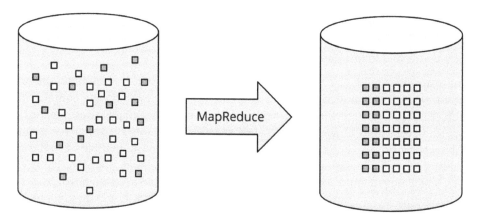

Figure 1-2. Bounded data processing with a classic batch engine. A finite pool of unstructured data on the left is run through a data processing engine, resulting in corresponding structured data on the right.

Though there are of course infinite variations on what you can actually calculate as part of this scheme, the overall model is quite simple. Much more interesting is the task of processing an unbounded dataset. Let's now look at the various ways unbounded data are typically processed, beginning with the approaches used with traditional batch engines and then ending up with the approaches you can take with a system designed for unbounded data, such as most streaming or microbatch engines.

Unbounded Data: Batch

Batch engines, though not explicitly designed with unbounded data in mind, have nevertheless been used to process unbounded datasets since batch systems were first conceived. As you might expect, such approaches revolve around slicing up the unbounded data into a collection of bounded datasets appropriate for batch processing.

Fixed windows

The most common way to process an unbounded dataset using repeated runs of a batch engine is by windowing the input data into fixed-size windows and then processing each of those windows as a separate, bounded data source (sometimes also called *tumbling windows*), as in Figure 1-3. Particularly for input sources like logs, for which events can be written into directory and file hierarchies whose names encode the window they correspond to, this sort of thing appears quite straightforward at first blush because you've essentially performed the time-based shuffle to get data into the appropriate event-time windows ahead of time.

In reality, however, most systems still have a completeness problem to deal with (What if some of your events are delayed en route to the logs due to a network partition? What if your events are collected globally and must be transferred to a common location before processing? What if your events come from mobile devices?), which means some sort of mitigation might be necessary (e.g., delaying processing until you're sure all events have been collected or reprocessing the entire batch for a given window whenever data arrive late).

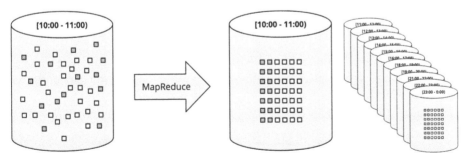

Figure 1-3. Unbounded data processing via ad hoc fixed windows with a classic batch engine. An unbounded dataset is collected up front into finite, fixed-size windows of bounded data that are then processed via successive runs a of classic batch engine.

Sessions

This approach breaks down even more when you try to use a batch engine to process unbounded data into more sophisticated windowing strategies, like sessions. Sessions are typically defined as periods of activity (e.g., for a specific user) terminated by a gap of inactivity. When calculating sessions using a typical batch engine, you often end up with sessions that are split across batches, as indicated by the red marks in Figure 1-4. We can reduce the number of splits by increasing batch sizes, but at the cost of increased latency. Another option is to add additional logic to stitch up sessions from previous runs, but at the cost of further complexity.

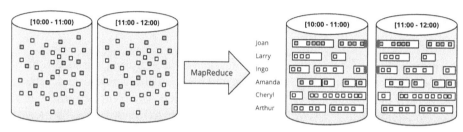

Figure 1-4. Unbounded data processing into sessions via ad hoc fixed windows with a classic batch engine. An unbounded dataset is collected up front into finite, fixed-size windows of bounded data that are then subdivided into dynamic session windows via successive runs a of classic batch engine.

Either way, using a classic batch engine to calculate sessions is less than ideal. A nicer way would be to build up sessions in a streaming manner, which we look at later on.

Unbounded Data: Streaming

Contrary to the ad hoc nature of most batch-based unbounded data processing approaches, streaming systems are built for unbounded data. As we talked about earlier, for many real-world, distributed input sources, you not only find yourself dealing with unbounded data, but also data such as the following:

- Highly unordered with respect to event times, meaning that you need some sort of time-based shuffle in your pipeline if you want to analyze the data in the context in which they occurred.

- Of varying event-time skew, meaning that you can't just assume you'll always see most of the data for a given event time X within some constant epsilon of time Y.

There are a handful of approaches that you can take when dealing with data that have these characteristics. I generally categorize these approaches into four groups: time-agnostic, approximation, windowing by processing time, and windowing by event time.

Let's now spend a little bit of time looking at each of these approaches.

Time-agnostic

Time-agnostic processing is used for cases in which time is essentially irrelevant; that is, all relevant logic is data driven. Because everything about such use cases is dictated by the arrival of more data, there's really nothing special a streaming engine has to support other than basic data delivery. As a result, essentially all streaming systems in existence support time-agnostic use cases out of the box (modulo system-to-system variances in consistency guarantees, of course, if you care about correctness). Batch systems are also well suited for time-agnostic processing of unbounded data sources by simply chopping the unbounded source into an arbitrary sequence of bounded datasets and processing those datasets independently. We look at a couple of concrete examples in this section, but given the straightforwardness of handling time-agnostic processing (from a temporal perspective at least), we won't spend much more time on it beyond that.

Filtering.   A very basic form of time-agnostic processing is filtering, an example of which is rendered in Figure 1-5. Imagine that you're processing web traffic logs and you want to filter out all traffic that didn't originate from a specific domain. You would look at each record as it arrived, see if it belonged to the domain of interest, and drop it if not. Because this sort of thing depends only on a single element at any time, the fact that the data source is unbounded, unordered, and of varying event-time skew is irrelevant.

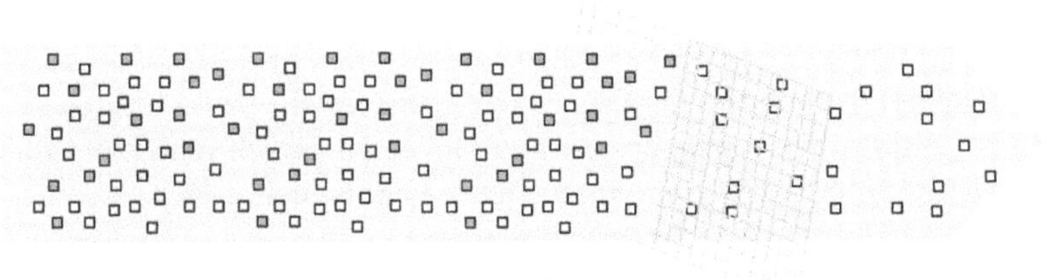

Figure 1-5. Filtering unbounded data. A collection of data (flowing left to right) of varying types is filtered into a homogeneous collection containing a single type.

Inner joins.   Another time-agnostic example is an inner join, diagrammed in Figure 1-6. When joining two unbounded data sources, if you care only about the results of a join when an element from both sources arrive, there's no temporal element to the logic. Upon seeing a value from one source, you can simply buffer it up in persistent state; only after the second value from the other source arrives do you need to emit the joined record. (In truth, you'd likely want some sort of garbage collection policy for unemitted partial joins, which would likely be time based. But for a use case with little or no uncompleted joins, such a thing might not be an issue.)

Figure 1-6. Performing an inner join on unbounded data. Joins are produced when matching elements from both sources are observed.

Switching semantics to some sort of outer join introduces the data completeness problem we've talked about: after you've seen one side of the join, how do you know whether the other side is ever going to arrive or not? Truth be told, you don't, so you need to introduce some notion of a timeout, which introduces an element of time. That element of time is essentially a form of windowing, which we'll look at more closely in a moment.

Approximation algorithms

The second major category of approaches is approximation algorithms, such as approximate Top-N (*http://bit.ly/2JLcOG9*), streaming k-means (*http://bit.ly/2JLQE6O*), and so on. They take an unbounded source of input and provide output data that, if you squint at them, look more or less like what you were hoping to get, as in Figure 1-7. The upside of approximation algorithms is that, by design, they are low overhead and designed for unbounded data. The downsides are that a limited set of them exist, the algorithms themselves are often complicated (which makes it difficult to conjure up new ones), and their approximate nature limits their utility.

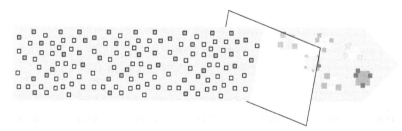

Figure 1-7. Computing approximations on unbounded data. Data are run through a complex algorithm, yielding output data that look more or less like the desired result on the other side.

It's worth noting that these algorithms typically do have some element of time in their design (e.g., some sort of built-in decay). And because they process elements as they arrive, that time element is usually processing-time based. This is particularly important for algorithms that provide some sort of provable error bounds on their approximations. If those error bounds are predicated on data arriving in order, they mean essentially nothing when you feed the algorithm unordered data with varying event-time skew. Something to keep in mind.

Approximation algorithms themselves are a fascinating subject, but as they are essentially another example of time-agnostic processing (modulo the temporal features of the algorithms themselves), they're quite straightforward to use and thus not worth further attention, given our current focus.

Windowing

The remaining two approaches for unbounded data processing are both variations of windowing. Before diving into the differences between them, I should make it clear exactly what I mean by windowing, insomuch as we touched on it only briefly in the previous section. Windowing is simply the notion of taking a data source (either unbounded or bounded), and chopping it up along temporal boundaries into finite chunks for processing. Figure 1-8 shows three different windowing patterns.

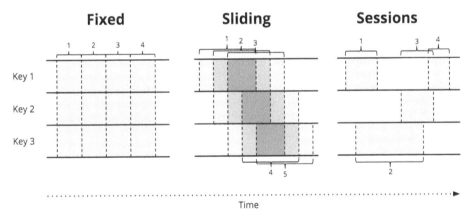

Figure 1-8. Windowing strategies. Each example is shown for three different keys, highlighting the difference between aligned windows (which apply across all the data) and unaligned windows (which apply across a subset of the data).

Let's take a closer look at each strategy:

Fixed windows (aka tumbling windows)
> We discussed fixed windows earlier. Fixed windows slice time into segments with a fixed-size temporal length. Typically (as shown in Figure 1-9), the segments for fixed windows are applied uniformly across the entire dataset, which is an exam-

ple of *aligned* windows. In some cases, it's desirable to phase-shift the windows for different subsets of the data (e.g., per key) to spread window completion load more evenly over time, which instead is an example of *unaligned* windows because they vary across the data.[6]

Sliding windows (aka hopping windows)
A generalization of fixed windows, sliding windows are defined by a fixed length and a fixed period. If the period is less than the length, the windows overlap. If the period equals the length, you have fixed windows. And if the period is greater than the length, you have a weird sort of sampling window that looks only at subsets of the data over time. As with fixed windows, sliding windows are typically aligned, though they can be unaligned as a performance optimization in certain use cases. Note that the sliding windows in Figure 1-8 are drawn as they are to give a sense of sliding motion; in reality, all five windows would apply across the entire dataset.

Sessions
An example of dynamic windows, sessions are composed of sequences of events terminated by a gap of inactivity greater than some timeout. Sessions are commonly used for analyzing user behavior over time, by grouping together a series of temporally related events (e.g., a sequence of videos viewed in one sitting). Sessions are interesting because their lengths cannot be defined a priori; they are dependent upon the actual data involved. They're also the canonical example of unaligned windows because sessions are practically never identical across different subsets of data (e.g., different users).

The two domains of time we discussed earlier (processing time and event time) are essentially the two we care about.[7] Windowing makes sense in both domains, so let's look at each in detail and see how they differ. Because processing-time windowing has historically been more common, we'll start there.

Windowing by processing time. When windowing by processing time, the system essentially buffers up incoming data into windows until some amount of processing time has passed. For example, in the case of five-minute fixed windows, the system would buffer data for five minutes of processing time, after which it would treat all of the data it had observed in those five minutes as a window and send them downstream for processing.

---

6 We look at aligned fixed windows in detail in Chapter 2, and unaligned fixed windows in Chapter 4.

7 If you poke around enough in the academic literature or SQL-based streaming systems, you'll also come across a third windowing time domain: *tuple-based windowing* (i.e., windows whose sizes are counted in numbers of elements). However, tuple-based windowing is essentially a form of processing-time windowing in which elements are assigned monotonically increasing timestamps as they arrive at the system. As such, we won't discuss tuple-based windowing in detail any further.

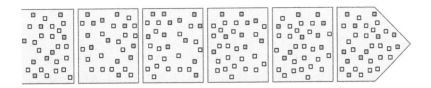

Figure 1-9. Windowing into fixed windows by processing time. Data are collected into windows based on the order they arrive in the pipeline.

There are a few nice properties of processing-time windowing:

- It's simple. The implementation is extremely straightforward because you never worry about shuffling data within time. You just buffer things as they arrive and send them downstream when the window closes.

- Judging window completeness is straightforward. Because the system has perfect knowledge of whether all inputs for a window have been seen, it can make perfect decisions about whether a given window is complete. This means there is no need to be able to deal with "late" data in any way when windowing by processing time.

- If you're wanting to infer information about the source *as it is observed*, processing-time windowing is exactly what you want. Many monitoring scenarios fall into this category. Imagine tracking the number of requests per second sent to a global-scale web service. Calculating a rate of these requests for the purpose of detecting outages is a perfect use of processing-time windowing.

Good points aside, there is one very big downside to processing-time windowing: *if the data in question have event times associated with them, those data must arrive in event-time order if the processing-time windows are to reflect the reality of when those events actually happened.* Unfortunately, event-time ordered data are uncommon in many real-world, distributed input sources.

As a simple example, imagine any mobile app that gathers usage statistics for later processing. For cases in which a given mobile device goes offline for any amount of time (brief loss of connectivity, airplane mode while flying across the country, etc.), the data recorded during that period won't be uploaded until the device comes online again. This means that data might arrive with an event-time skew of minutes, hours, days, weeks, or more. It's essentially impossible to draw any sort of useful inferences from such a dataset when windowed by processing time.

As another example, many distributed input sources might *seem* to provide event-time ordered (or very nearly so) data when the overall system is healthy. Unfortunately, the fact that event-time skew is low for the input source when healthy does not mean it will always stay that way. Consider a global service that processes data collected on multiple continents. If network issues across a bandwidth-constrained trans-continental line (which, sadly, are surprisingly common) further decrease bandwidth and/or increase latency, suddenly a portion of your input data might begin arriving with much greater skew than before. If you are windowing those data by processing time, your windows are no longer representative of the data that actually occurred within them; instead, they represent the windows of time as the events arrived at the processing pipeline, which is some arbitrary mix of old and current data.

What we really want in both of those cases is to window data by their event times in a way that is robust to the order of arrival of events. What we really want is event-time windowing.

Windowing by event time.   Event-time windowing is what you use when you need to observe a data source in finite chunks that reflect the times at which those events actually happened. It's the gold standard of windowing. Prior to 2016, most data processing systems in use lacked native support for it (though any system with a decent consistency model, like Hadoop or Spark Streaming 1.x, could act as a reasonable substrate for building such a windowing system). I'm happy to say that the world of today looks very different, with multiple systems, from Flink to Spark to Storm to Apex, natively supporting event-time windowing of some sort.

Figure 1-10 shows an example of windowing an unbounded source into one-hour fixed windows.

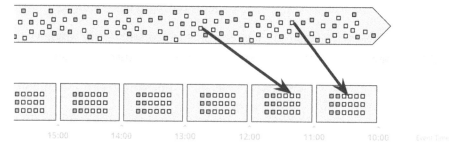

Figure 1-10. Windowing into fixed windows by event time. Data are collected into windows based on the times at which they occurred. The black arrows call out example data that arrived in processing-time windows that differed from the event-time windows to which they belonged.

The black arrows in Figure 1-10 call out two particularly interesting pieces of data. Each arrived in processing-time windows that did not match the event-time windows to which each bit of data belonged. As such, if these data had been windowed into processing-time windows for a use case that cared about event times, the calculated results would have been incorrect. As you would expect, event-time correctness is one nice thing about using event-time windows.

Another nice thing about event-time windowing over an unbounded data source is that you can create dynamically sized windows, such as sessions, without the arbitrary splits observed when generating sessions over fixed windows (as we saw previously in the sessions example from "Unbounded Data: Streaming" on page 14), as demonstrated in Figure 1-11.

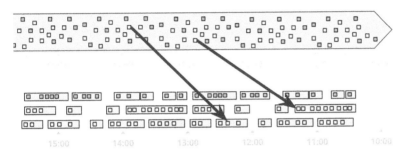

Figure 1-11. Windowing into session windows by event time. Data are collected into session windows capturing bursts of activity based on the times that the corresponding events occurred. The black arrows again call out the temporal shuffle necessary to put the data into their correct event-time locations.

Of course, powerful semantics rarely come for free, and event-time windows are no exception. Event-time windows have two notable drawbacks due to the fact that windows must often live longer (in processing time) than the actual length of the window itself:

Buffering
Due to extended window lifetimes, more buffering of data is required. Thankfully, persistent storage is generally the cheapest of the resource types most data processing systems depend on (the others being primarily CPU, network bandwidth, and RAM). As such, this problem is typically much less of a concern than you might think when using any well-designed data processing system with strongly consistent persistent state and a decent in-memory caching layer. Also, many useful aggregations do not require the entire input set to be buffered (e.g., sum or average), but instead can be performed incrementally, with a much smaller, intermediate aggregate stored in persistent state.

Completeness
Given that we often have no good way of knowing when we've seen all of the data for a given window, how do we know when the results for the window are ready

to materialize? In truth, we simply don't. For many types of inputs, the system can give a reasonably accurate heuristic estimate of window completion via something like the watermarks found in MillWheel, Cloud Dataflow, and Flink (which we talk about more in Chapters 3 and 4). But for cases in which absolute correctness is paramount (again, think billing), the only real option is to provide a way for the pipeline builder to express when they want results for windows to be materialized and how those results should be refined over time. Dealing with window completeness (or lack thereof) is a fascinating topic but one perhaps best explored in the context of concrete examples, which we look at next.

Summary

Whew! That was a lot of information. If you've made it this far, you are to be commended! But we are only just getting started. Before forging ahead to looking in detail at the Beam Model approach, let's briefly step back and recap what we've learned so far. In this chapter, we've done the following:

- Clarified terminology, focusing the definition of "streaming" to refer to systems built with unbounded data in mind, while using more descriptive terms like approximate/speculative results for distinct concepts often categorized under the "streaming" umbrella. Additionally, we highlighted two important dimensions of large-scale datasets: cardinality (i.e., bounded versus unbounded) and constitution (i.e., table versus stream), the latter of which will consume much of the second half of the book.

- Assessed the relative capabilities of well-designed batch and streaming systems, positing streaming is in fact a strict superset of batch, and that notions like the Lambda Architecture, which are predicated on streaming being inferior to batch, are destined for retirement as streaming systems mature.

- Proposed two high-level concepts necessary for streaming systems to both catch up to and ultimately surpass batch, those being correctness and tools for reasoning about time, respectively.

- Established the important differences between event time and processing time, characterized the difficulties those differences impose when analyzing data in the context of when they occurred, and proposed a shift in approach away from notions of completeness and toward simply adapting to changes in data over time.

- Looked at the major data processing approaches in common use today for bounded and unbounded data, via both batch and streaming engines, roughly categorizing the unbounded approaches into: time-agnostic, approximation, windowing by processing time, and windowing by event time.

Next up, we dive into the details of the Beam Model, taking a conceptual look at how we've broken up the notion of data processing across four related axes: what, where, when, and how. We also take a detailed look at processing a simple, concrete example dataset across multiple scenarios, highlighting the plurality of use cases enabled by the Beam Model, with some concrete APIs to ground us in reality. These examples will help drive home the notions of event time and processing time introduced in this chapter while additionally exploring new concepts such as watermarks.

CHAPTER 2

The *What*, *Where*, *When*, and *How* of Data Processing

Okay party people, it's time to get concrete!

Chapter 1 focused on three main areas: *terminology*, defining precisely what I mean when I use overloaded terms like "streaming"; *batch versus streaming*, comparing the theoretical capabilities of the two types of systems, and postulating that only two things are necessary to take streaming systems beyond their batch counterparts: correctness and tools for reasoning about time; and *data processing patterns*, looking at the conceptual approaches taken with both batch and streaming systems when processing bounded and unbounded data.

In this chapter, we're now going to focus further on the data processing patterns from Chapter 1, but in more detail, and within the context of concrete examples. By the time we're finished, we'll have covered what I consider to be the core set of principles and concepts required for robust out-of-order data processing; these are the tools for reasoning about time that truly get you beyond classic batch processing.

To give you a sense of what things look like in action, I use snippets of Apache Beam (*https://beam.apache.org/*) code, coupled with time-lapse diagrams[1] to provide a visual representation of the concepts. Apache Beam is a unified programming model and portability layer for batch and stream processing, with a set of concrete SDKs in various languages (e.g., Java and Python). Pipelines written with Apache Beam can

---

1 If you're fortunate enough to be reading the Safari version of the book, you have full-blown time-lapse animations just like in "Streaming 102" (*http://oreil.ly/1TV7YGU*). For print, Kindle, and other ebook versions, there are static images with a link to animated versions on the web.

then be portably run on any of the supported execution engines (Apache Apex, Apache Flink, Apache Spark, Cloud Dataflow, etc.).

I use Apache Beam here for examples not because this is a Beam book (it's not), but because it most completely embodies the concepts described in this book. Back when "Streaming 102" (*http://oreil.ly/1TV7YGU*) was originally written (back when it was still the Dataflow Model from Google Cloud Dataflow and not the Beam Model from Apache Beam), it was literally the only system in existence that provided the amount of expressiveness necessary for all the examples we'll cover here. A year and a half later, I'm happy to say much has changed, and most of the major systems out there have moved or are moving toward supporting a model that looks a lot like the one described in this book. So rest assured that the concepts we cover here, though informed through the Beam lens, as it were, will apply equally across most other systems you'll come across.

Roadmap

To help set the stage for this chapter, I want to lay out the five main concepts that will underpin all of the discussions therein, and really, for most of the rest of Part I. We've already covered two of them.

In Chapter 1, I first established the critical distinction between event time (the time that events happen) and processing time (the time they are observed during processing). This provides the foundation for one of the main theses put forth in this book: if you care about both correctness and the context within which events actually occurred, you must analyze data relative to their inherent event times, not the processing time at which they are encountered during the analysis itself.

I then introduced the concept of *windowing* (i.e., partitioning a dataset along temporal boundaries), which is a common approach used to cope with the fact that unbounded data sources technically might never end. Some simpler examples of windowing strategies are *fixed* and *sliding* windows, but more sophisticated types of windowing, such as *sessions* (in which the windows are defined by features of the data themselves; for example, capturing a session of activity per user followed by a gap of inactivity) also see broad usage.

In addition to these two concepts, we're now going to look closely at three more:

Triggers
  A trigger is a mechanism for declaring when the output for a window should be materialized relative to some external signal. Triggers provide flexibility in choosing when outputs should be emitted. In some sense, you can think of them as a flow control mechanism for dictating when results should be materialized. Another way of looking at it is that triggers are like the shutter-release on a cam-

era, allowing you to declare when to take a snapshots in time of the results being computed.

Triggers also make it possible to observe the output for a window multiple times as it evolves. This in turn opens up the door to refining results over time, which allows for providing speculative results as data arrive, as well as dealing with changes in upstream data (revisions) over time or data that arrive late (e.g., mobile scenarios, in which someone's phone records various actions and their event times while the person is offline and then proceeds to upload those events for processing upon regaining connectivity).

Watermarks

A watermark is a notion of input completeness with respect to event times. A watermark with value of time X makes the statement: "all input data with event times less than X have been observed." As such, watermarks act as a metric of progress when observing an unbounded data source with no known end. We touch upon the basics of watermarks in this chapter, and then Slava goes super deep on the subject in Chapter 3.

Accumulation

An accumulation mode specifies the relationship between multiple results that are observed for the same window. Those results might be completely disjointed; that is, representing independent deltas over time, or there might be overlap between them. Different accumulation modes have different semantics and costs associated with them and thus find applicability across a variety of use cases.

Also, because I think it makes it easier to understand the relationships between all of these concepts, we revisit the old and explore the new within the structure of answering four questions, all of which I propose are critical to every unbounded data processing problem:

- *What* results are calculated? This question is answered by the types of transformations within the pipeline. This includes things like computing sums, building histograms, training machine learning models, and so on. It's also essentially the question answered by classic batch processing

- *Where* in event time are results calculated? This question is answered by the use of event-time windowing within the pipeline. This includes the common examples of windowing from Chapter 1 (fixed, sliding, and sessions); use cases that seem to have no notion of windowing (e.g., time-agnostic processing; classic batch processing also generally falls into this category); and other, more complex types of windowing, such as time-limited auctions. Also note that it can include processing-time windowing, as well, if you assign ingress times as event times for records as they arrive at the system.

- *When* in processing time are results materialized? This question is answered by the use of triggers and (optionally) watermarks. There are infinite variations on this theme, but the most common patterns are those involving repeated updates (i.e., materialized view semantics), those that utilize a watermark to provide a single output per window only after the corresponding input is believed to be complete (i.e., classic batch processing semantics applied on a per-window basis), or some combination of the two.

- *How* do refinements of results relate? This question is answered by the type of accumulation used: discarding (in which results are all independent and distinct), accumulating (in which later results build upon prior ones), or accumulating and retracting (in which both the accumulating value plus a retraction for the previously triggered value(s) are emitted).

We look at each of these questions in much more detail throughout the rest of the book. And, yes, I'm going to run this color scheme thing into the ground in an attempt to make it abundantly clear which concepts relate to which question in the *What*/*Where*/*When*/*How* idiom. You're welcome <winky-smiley/>.[2]

Batch Foundations: *What* and *Where*

Okay, let's get this party started. First stop: batch processing.

What: Transformations

The transformations applied in classic batch processing answer the question: "*What* results are calculated?" Even though you are likely already familiar with classic batch processing, we're going to start there anyway because it's the foundation on top of which we add all of the other concepts.

In the rest of this chapter (and indeed, through much of the book), we look at a single example: computing keyed integer sums over a simple dataset consisting of nine values. Let's imagine that we've written a team-based mobile game and we want to build a pipeline that calculates team scores by summing up the individual scores reported by users' phones. If we were to capture our nine example scores in a SQL table named "UserScores," it might look something like this:

```
> SELECT * FROM UserScores ORDER BY EventTime;
-------------------------------------------------
| Name  | Team  | Score | EventTime | ProcTime |
-------------------------------------------------
| Julie | TeamX |     5 | 12:00:26  | 12:05:19 |
```

---

2 Bear with me here. Fine-grained emotional expressions via composite punctuation (i.e., emoticons) are strictly forbidden in O'Reilly publications <winky-smiley/>.

```
| Frank | TeamX |    9 |  12:01:26 |  12:08:19 |
| Ed    | TeamX |    7 |  12:02:26 |  12:05:39 |
| Julie | TeamX |    8 |  12:03:06 |  12:07:06 |
| Amy   | TeamX |    3 |  12:03:39 |  12:06:13 |
| Fred  | TeamX |    4 |  12:04:19 |  12:06:39 |
| Naomi | TeamX |    3 |  12:06:39 |  12:07:19 |
| Becky | TeamX |    8 |  12:07:26 |  12:08:39 |
| Naomi | TeamX |    1 |  12:07:46 |  12:09:00 |
-----------------------------------------------------
```

Note that all the scores in this example are from users on the same team; this is to keep the example simple, given that we have a limited number of dimensions in our diagrams that follow. And because we're grouping by team, we really just care about the last three columns:

Score
> The individual user score associated with this event

EventTime
> The event time for the score; that is, the time at which the score occurred

ProcTime
> The processing for the score; that is, the time at which the score was observed by the pipeline

For each example pipeline, we'll look at a time-lapse diagram that highlights how the data evolves over time. Those diagrams plot our nine scores in the two dimensions of time we care about: event time in the x-axis, and processing time in the y-axis. Figure 2-1 illustrates what a static plot of the input data looks like.

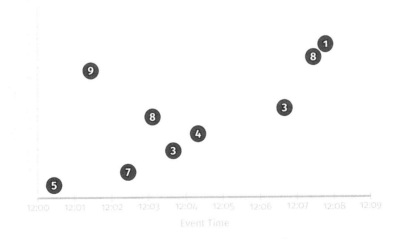

Figure 2-1. Nine input records, plotted in both event time and processing time

Subsequent time-lapse diagrams are either animations (Safari) or a sequence of frames (print and all other digital formats), allowing you to see how the data are processed over time (more on this shortly after we get to the first time-lapse diagram).

Preceding each example is a short snippet of Apache Beam Java SDK pseudocode to make the definition of the pipeline more concrete. It is pseudocode in the sense that I sometime bend the rules to make the examples clearer, elide details (like the use of concrete I/O sources), or simplify names (the trigger names in Beam Java 2.x and earlier are painfully verbose; I use simpler names for clarity). Beyond minor things like those, it's otherwise real-world Beam code (and real code is available on GitHub (*http://bit.ly/2KMsDwR*) for all examples in this chapter).

If you're already familiar with something like Spark or Flink, you should have a relatively easy time understanding what the Beam code is doing. But to give you a crash course in things, there are two basic primitives in Beam:

PCollections
These represent datasets (possibly massive ones) across which parallel transformations can be performed (hence the "P" at the beginning of the name).

PTransforms
These are applied to PCollections to create new PCollections. PTransforms may perform element-wise transformations, they may group/aggregate multiple elements together, or they may be a composite combination of other PTransforms, as depicted in Figure 2-2.

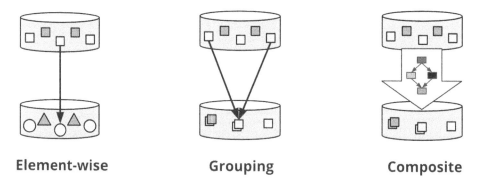

Element-wise   **Grouping**   **Composite**

Figure 2-2. Types of transformations

For the purposes of our examples, we typically assume that we start out with a preloaded PCollection<KV<Team, Integer>> named "input" (that is, a PCollection composed of key/value pairs of Teams and Integers, where the Teams are just something like Strings representing team names, and the Integers are scores from any individual on the corresponding team). In a real-world pipeline, we would've acquired input by reading in a PCollection<String> of raw data (e.g., log records) from an I/O source and then transforming it into a PCollection<KV<Team, Integer>> by parsing the log records into appropriate key/value pairs. For the sake of clarity in this first example, I include pseudocode for all of those steps, but in subsequent examples, I elide the I/O and parsing.

Thus, for a pipeline that simply reads in data from an I/O source, parses team/score pairs, and calculates per-team sums of scores, we'd have something like that shown in Example 2-1.

Example 2-1. Summation pipeline

```
PCollection<String> raw = IO.read(...);
PCollection<KV<Team, Integer>> input = raw.apply(new ParseFn());
PCollection<KV<Team, Integer>> totals =
  input.apply(Sum.integersPerKey());
```

Key/value data are read from an I/O source, with a Team (e.g., String of the team name) as the key and an Integer (e.g., individual team member scores) as the value. The values for each key are then summed together to generate per-key sums (e.g., total team score) in the output collection.

For all the examples to come, after seeing a code snippet describing the pipeline that we're analyzing, we'll then look at a time-lapse diagram showing the execution of that pipeline over our concrete dataset for a single key. In a real pipeline, you can imagine that similar operations would be happening in parallel across multiple machines, but for the sake of our examples, it will be clearer to keep things simple.

As noted previously, Safari editions present the complete execution as an animated movie, whereas print and all other digital formats use a static sequence of key frames that provide a sense of how the pipeline progresses over time. In both cases, we also provide a URL to a fully animated version on *www.streamingbook.net*.

Each diagram plots the inputs and outputs across two dimensions: event time (on the x-axis) and processing time (on the y-axis). Thus, real time as observed by the pipeline progresses from bottom to top, as indicated by the thick horizontal black line that ascends in the processing-time axis as time progresses. Inputs are circles, with the number inside the circle representing the value of that specific record. They start out light gray, and darken as the pipeline observes them.

As the pipeline observes values, it accumulates them in its intermediate state and eventually materializes the aggregate results as output. State and output are represented by rectangles (gray for state, blue for output), with the aggregate value near the top, and with the area covered by the rectangle representing the portions of event time and processing time accumulated into the result. For the pipeline in

Example 2-1, it would look something like that shown in Figure 2-3 when executed on a classic batch engine.

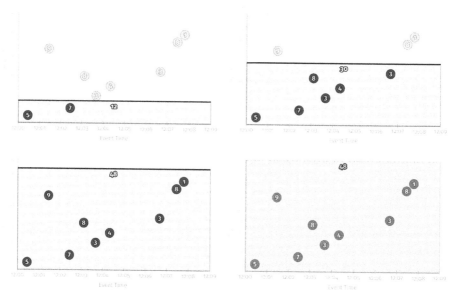

Figure 2-3. Classic batch processing (http://streamingbook.net/fig/2-3)

Because this is a batch pipeline, it accumulates state until it's seen all of the inputs (represented by the dashed green line at the top), at which point it produces its single output of 48. In this example, we're calculating a sum over all of event time because we haven't applied any specific windowing transformations; hence the rectangles for state and output cover the entirety of the x-axis. If we want to process an unbounded data source, however, classic batch processing won't be sufficient; we can't wait for the input to end, because it effectively never will. One of the concepts we want is windowing, which we introduced in Chapter 1. Thus, within the context of our second question—"*Where* in event time are results calculated?"—we'll now briefly revisit windowing.

Where: Windowing

As discussed in Chapter 1, windowing is the process of slicing up a data source along temporal boundaries. Common windowing strategies include fixed windows, sliding windows, and sessions windows, as demonstrated in Figure 2-4.

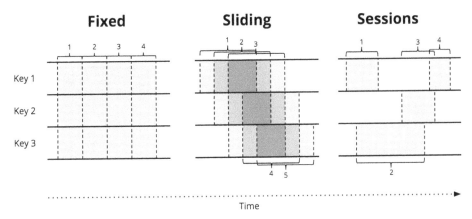

Figure 2-4. Example windowing strategies. Each example is shown for three different keys, highlighting the difference between aligned windows (which apply across all the data) and unaligned windows (which apply across a subset of the data).

To get a better sense of what windowing looks like in practice, let's take our integer summation pipeline and window it into fixed, two-minute windows. With Beam, the change is a simple addition of a `Window.into` transform, which you can see highlighted in Example 2-2.

Example 2-2. Windowed summation code

```
PCollection<KV<Team, Integer>> totals = input
  .apply(Window.into(FixedWindows.of(TWO_MINUTES)))
  .apply(Sum.integersPerKey());
```

Recall that Beam provides a unified model that works in both batch and streaming because semantically batch is really just a subset of streaming. As such, let's first execute this pipeline on a batch engine; the mechanics are more straightforward, and it will give us something to directly compare against when we switch to a streaming engine. Figure 2-5 presents the result.

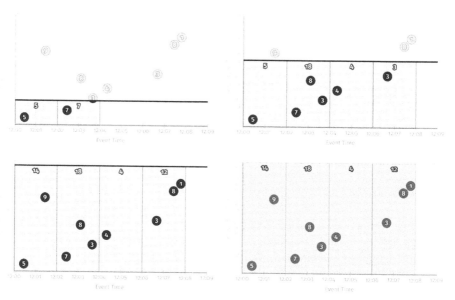

Figure 2-5. Windowed summation on a batch engine (http://streamingbook.net/fig/2-5)

As before, inputs are accumulated in state until they are entirely consumed, after which output is produced. In this case, however, instead of one output, we get four: a single output, for each of the four relevant two-minute event-time windows.

At this point we've revisited the two main concepts that I introduced in Chapter 1: the relationship between the event-time and processing-time domains, and windowing. If we want to go any further, we'll need to start adding the new concepts mentioned at the beginning of this section: triggers, watermarks, and accumulation.

Going Streaming: *When* and *How*

We just observed the execution of a windowed pipeline on a batch engine. But, ideally, we'd like to have lower latency for our results, and we'd also like to natively handle unbounded data sources. Switching to a streaming engine is a step in the right direction, but our previous strategy of waiting until our input has been consumed in its entirety to generate output is no longer feasible. Enter triggers and watermarks.

When: The Wonderful Thing About Triggers Is Triggers Are Wonderful Things!

Triggers provide the answer to the question: "*When* in processing time are results materialized?" Triggers declare when output for a window should happen in processing time (though the triggers themselves might make those decisions based on things that happen in other time domains, such as watermarks progressing in the event-time domain, as we'll see in a few moments). Each specific output for a window is referred to as a *pane* of the window.

Though it's possible to imagine quite a breadth of possible triggering semantics,[3] conceptually there are only two generally useful types of triggers, and practical applications almost always boil down using either one or a combination of both:

Repeated update triggers
    These periodically generate updated panes for a window as its contents evolve. These updates can be materialized with every new record, or they can happen after some processing-time delay, such as once a minute. The choice of period for a repeated update trigger is primarily an exercise in balancing latency and cost.

Completeness triggers
    These materialize a pane for a window only after the input for that window is believed to be complete to some threshold. This type of trigger is most analogous to what we're familiar with in batch processing: only after the input is complete do we provide a result. The difference in the trigger-based approach is that the notion of completeness is scoped to the context of a single window, rather than always being bound to the completeness of the entire input.

Repeated update triggers are the most common type of trigger encountered in streaming systems. They are simple to implement and simple to understand, and they provide useful semantics for a specific type of use case: repeated (and eventually consistent) updates to a materialized dataset, analogous to the semantics you get with materialized views in the database world.

Completeness triggers are less frequently encountered, but provide streaming semantics that more closely align with those from the classic batch processing world. They also provide tools for reasoning about things like missing data and late data, both of which we discuss shortly (and in the next chapter) as we explore the underlying primitive that drives completeness triggers: watermarks.

But first, let's start simple and look at some basic repeated update triggers in action. To make the notion of triggers a bit more concrete, let's go ahead and add the most straightforward type of trigger to our example pipeline: a trigger that fires with every new record, as shown in Example 2-3.

---

3 And indeed, we did just that with the original triggers feature in Beam. In retrospect, we went a bit overboard. Future iterations will be simpler and easier to use, and in this book I focus only on the pieces that are likely to remain in some form or another.

Example 2-3. Triggering repeatedly with every record

```
PCollection<KV<Team, Integer>> totals = input
  .apply(Window.into(FixedWindows.of(TWO_MINUTES))
              .triggering(Repeatedly(AfterCount(1))));
  .apply(Sum.integersPerKey());
```

If we were to run this new pipeline on a streaming engine, the results would look something like that shown in Figure 2-6.

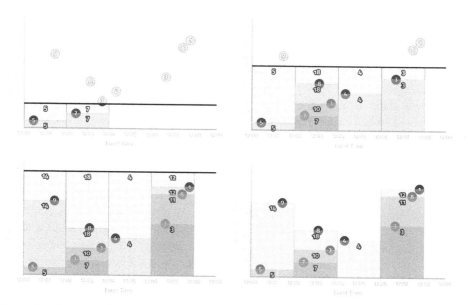

Figure 2-6. Per-record triggering on a streaming engine (http://streamingbook.net/fig/ 2-6)

You can see how we now get multiple outputs (panes) for each window: once per corresponding input. This sort of triggering pattern works well when the output stream is being written to some sort of table that you can simply poll for results. Any time you look in the table, you'll see the most up-to-date value for a given window, and those values will converge toward correctness over time.

One downside of per-record triggering is that it's quite chatty. When processing large-scale data, aggregations like summation provide a nice opportunity to reduce the cardinality of the stream without losing information. This is particularly noticeable for cases in which you have high-volume keys; for our example, massive teams with lots of active players. Imagine a massively multiplayer game in which players are split into one of two factions, and you want to tally stats on a per-faction basis. It's probably unnecessary to update your tallies with every new input record for every player in a given faction. Instead, you might be happy updating them after some processing-time delay, say every second, or every minute. The nice side effect of using processing-time delays is that it has an equalizing effect across high-volume keys or windows: the resulting stream ends up being more uniform cardinality-wise.

There are two different approaches to processing-time delays in triggers: *aligned delays* (where the delay slices up processing time into fixed regions that align across keys and windows) and *unaligned delays* (where the delay is relative to the data observed within a given window). A pipeline with aligned delays might look like Example 2-4, the results of which are shown in Figure 2-7.

Example 2-4. Triggering on aligned two-minute processing-time boundaries

```
PCollection<KV<Team, Integer>> totals = input
  .apply(Window.into(FixedWindows.of(TWO_MINUTES))
                .triggering(Repeatedly(AlignedDelay(TWO_MINUTES))))
  .apply(Sum.integersPerKey());
```

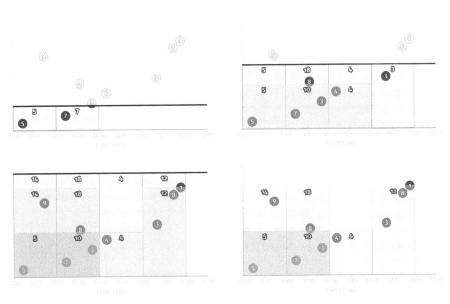

Figure 2-7. Two-minute aligned delay triggers (i.e., microbatching) (http://streaming book.net/fig/2-7)

This sort of aligned delay trigger is effectively what you get from a microbatch streaming system like Spark Streaming. The nice thing about it is predictability; you get regular updates across all modified windows at the same time. That's also the downside: all updates happen at once, which results in bursty workloads that often require greater peak provisioning to properly handle the load. The alternative is to use an unaligned delay. That would look something Example 2-5 in Beam. Figure 2-8 presents the results.

Example 2-5. Triggering on unaligned two-minute processing-time boundaries

```
PCollection<KV<Team, Integer>> totals = input
  .apply(Window.into(FixedWindows.of(TWO_MINUTES))
               .triggering(Repeatedly(UnalignedDelay(TWO_MINUTES))))
  .apply(Sum.integersPerKey());
```

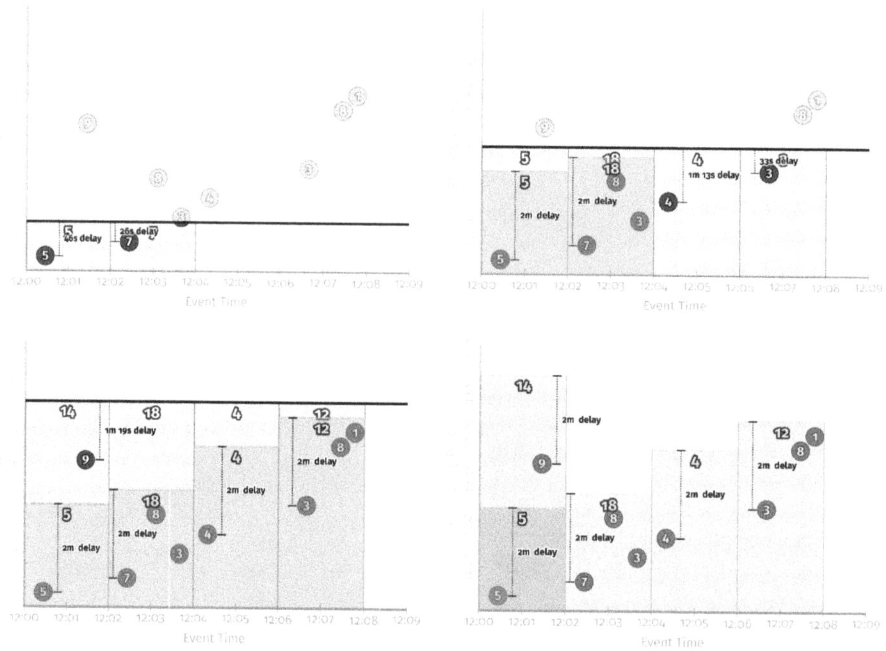

Figure 2-8. Two-minute unaligned delay triggers (http://streamingbook.net/fig/2-8)

Contrasting the unaligned delays in Figure 2-8 to the aligned delays in Figure 2-6, it's easy to see how the unaligned delays spread the load out more evenly across time. The actual latencies involved for any given window differ between the two, sometimes more and sometimes less, but in the end the average latency will remain essentially the same. From that perspective, unaligned delays are typically the better choice for large-scale processing because they result in a more even load distribution over time.

Repeated update triggers are great for use cases in which we simply want periodic updates to our results over time and are fine with those updates converging toward correctness with no clear indication of when correctness is achieved. However, as we discussed in Chapter 1, the vagaries of distributed systems often lead to a varying level of skew between the time an event happens and the time it's actually observed by your pipeline, which means it can be difficult to reason about when your output presents an accurate and complete view of your input data. For cases in which input completeness matters, it's important to have some way of reasoning about completeness rather than blindly trusting the results calculated by whichever subset of data happen to have found their way to your pipeline. Enter watermarks.

When: Watermarks

Watermarks are a supporting aspect of the answer to the question: "*When* in processing time are results materialized?" Watermarks are temporal notions of input completeness in the event-time domain. Worded differently, they are the way the system measures progress and completeness relative to the event times of the records being processed in a stream of events (either bounded or unbounded, though their usefulness is more apparent in the unbounded case).

Recall this diagram from Chapter 1, slightly modified in Figure 2-9, in which I described the skew between event time and processing time as an ever-changing function of time for most real-world distributed data processing systems.

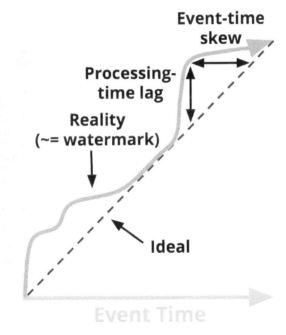

Figure 2-9. Event-time progress, skew, and watermarks

That meandering red line that I claimed represented reality is essentially the watermark; it captures the progress of event-time completeness as processing time progresses. Conceptually, you can think of the watermark as a function, $F(P) \rightarrow E$, which takes a point in processing time and returns a point in event time.[4] That point in event time, E, is the point up to which the system believes all inputs with event times less than E have been observed. In other words, it's an assertion that no more data with event times less than E will ever be seen again. Depending upon the type of watermark, perfect or heuristic, that assertion can be a strict guarantee or an educated guess, respectively:

Perfect watermarks

> For the case in which we have perfect knowledge of all of the input data, it's possible to construct a perfect watermark. In such a case, there is no such thing as late data; all data are early or on time.

Heuristic watermarks

> For many distributed input sources, perfect knowledge of the input data is impractical, in which case the next best option is to provide a heuristic watermark. Heuristic watermarks use whatever information is available about the inputs (partitions, ordering within partitions if any, growth rates of files, etc.) to provide an estimate of progress that is as accurate as possible. In many cases, such watermarks can be remarkably accurate in their predictions. Even so, the use of a heuristic watermark means that it might sometimes be wrong, which will lead to late data. We show you about ways to deal with late data soon.

Because they provide a notion of completeness relative to our inputs, watermarks form the foundation for the second type of trigger mentioned previously: *completeness triggers*. Watermarks themselves are a fascinating and complex topic, as you'll see when you get to Slava's watermarks deep dive in Chapter 3. But for now, let's look at them in action by updating our example pipeline to utilize a completeness trigger built upon watermarks, as demonstrated in Example 2-6.

Example 2-6. Watermark completeness trigger

```
PCollection<KV<Team, Integer>> totals = input
  .apply(Window.into(FixedWindows.of(TWO_MINUTES))
             .triggering(AfterWatermark()))
  .apply(Sum.integersPerKey());
```

---

4 More accurately, the input to the function is really the state at time *P* of everything upstream of the point in the pipeline where the watermark is being observed: the input source, buffered data, data actively being processed, and so on; but conceptually it's simpler to think of it as a mapping from processing time to event time.

Now, an interesting quality of watermarks is that they are a class of functions, meaning there are multiple different functions $F(P) \rightarrow E$ that satisfy the properties of a watermark, to varying degrees of success. As I noted earlier, for situations in which you have perfect knowledge of your input data, it might be possible to build a perfect watermark, which is the ideal situation. But for cases in which you lack perfect knowledge of the inputs or for which it's simply too computationally expensive to calculate the perfect watermark, you might instead choose to utilize a heuristic for defining your watermark. The point I want to make here is that the given watermark algorithm in use is independent from the pipeline itself. We're not going to discuss in detail what it means to implement a watermark here (Slava does that in Chapter 3). For now, to help drive home this idea that a given input set can have different watermarks applied to it, let's take a look at our pipeline in Example 2-6 when executed on the same dataset but using two distinct watermark implementations (Figure 2-10): on the left, a perfect watermark; on the right, a heuristic watermark.

In both cases, windows are materialized as the watermark passes the end of the window. The perfect watermark, as you might expect, perfectly captures the event-time completeness of the pipeline as time progresses. In contrast, the specific algorithm used for the heuristic watermark on the right fails to take the value of 9 into account,[5] which drastically changes the shape of the materialized outputs, both in terms of output latency and correctness (as seen by the incorrect answer of 5 that's provided for the [12:00, 12:02) window).

The big difference between the watermark triggers from Figure 2-10 and the repeated update triggers we saw in Figures 2-6 through 2-8 is that the *watermarks give us a way to reason about the completeness of our input*. Until the system materializes an output for a given window, we know that the system does not yet believe the inputs to be complete. This is especially important for use cases in which you want to reason about a *lack of data* in the input, or *missing data*.

---

5 Note that I specifically chose to omit the value of 9 from the heuristic watermark because it will help me to make some important points about late data and watermark lag. In reality, a heuristic watermark might be just as likely to omit some other value(s) instead, which in turn could have significantly less drastic effect on the watermark. If winnowing late-arriving data from the watermark is your goal (which is very valid in some cases, such as abuse detection, for which you just want to see a significant majority of the data as quickly as possible), you don't necessarily want a heuristic watermark rather than a perfect watermark. What you really want is a percentile watermark, which explicitly drops some percentile of late-arriving data from its calculations. See Chapter 3.

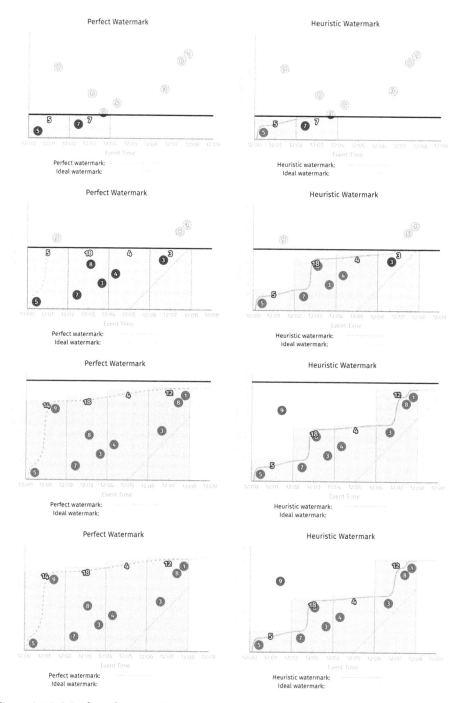

Figure 2-10. Windowed summation on a streaming engine with perfect (left) and heuristic (right) watermarks (http://streamingbook.net/fig/2-10)

A great example of a missing-data use case is outer joins. Without a notion of completeness like watermarks, how do you know when to give up and emit a partial join rather than continue to wait for that join to complete? You don't. And basing that decision on a processing-time delay, which is the common approach in streaming systems that lack true watermark support, is not a safe way to go, because of the variable nature of event-time skew we spoke about in Chapter 1: as long as skew remains smaller than the chosen processing-time delay, your missing-data results will be correct, but any time skew grows beyond that delay, they will suddenly become *incorrect*. From this perspective, event-time watermarks are a critical piece of the puzzle for many real-world streaming use cases which must reason about a lack of data in the input, such as outer joins, anomaly detection, and so on.

Now, with that said, these watermark examples also highlight two *shortcomings* of watermarks (and any other notion of completeness), specifically that they can be one of the following:

Too slow

When a watermark of any type is correctly delayed due to known unprocessed data (e.g., slowly growing input logs due to network bandwidth constraints), that translates directly into delays in output if advancement of the watermark is the only thing you depend on for stimulating results.

This is most obvious in the left diagram of Figure 2-10, for which the late arriving 9 holds back the watermark for all the subsequent windows, even though the input data for those windows become complete earlier. This is particularly apparent for the second window, [12:02, 12:04), for which it takes nearly seven minutes from the time the first value in the window occurs until we see any results for the window whatsoever. The heuristic watermark in this example doesn't suffer the same issue quite so badly (five minutes until output), but don't take that to mean heuristic watermarks never suffer from watermark lag; that's really just a consequence of the record I chose to omit from the heuristic watermark in this specific example.

The important point here is the following: Although watermarks provide a very useful notion of completeness, depending upon completeness for producing output is often not ideal from a latency perspective. Imagine a dashboard that contains valuable metrics, windowed by hour or day. It's unlikely you'd want to wait a full hour or day to begin seeing results for the current window; that's one of the pain points of using classic batch systems to power such systems. Instead, it would be much nicer to see the results for those windows refine over time as the inputs evolve and eventually become complete.

Too fast

When a heuristic watermark is incorrectly advanced earlier than it should be, it's possible for data with event times before the watermark to arrive some time later, creating late data. This is what happened in the example on the right: the watermark advanced past the end of the first window before all the input data for that window had been observed, resulting in an incorrect output value of 5 instead of 14. This shortcoming is strictly a problem with heuristic watermarks; their heuristic nature implies they will sometimes be wrong. As a result, relying on them alone for determining when to materialize output is insufficient if you care about correctness.

In Chapter 1, I made some rather emphatic statements about notions of completeness being insufficient for most use cases requiring robust out-of-order processing of unbounded data streams. These two shortcomings—watermarks being too slow or too fast—are the foundations for those arguments. You simply cannot get both low latency and correctness out of a system that relies solely on notions of completeness.[6] So, for cases for which you do want the best of both worlds, what's a person to do? Well, if repeated update triggers provide low-latency updates but no way to reason about completeness, and watermarks provide a notion of completeness but variable and possible high latency, why not combine their powers together?

When: Early/On-Time/Late Triggers FTW!

We've now looked at the two main types of triggers: repeated update triggers and completeness/watermark triggers. In many case, neither of them alone is sufficient, but the combination of them together is. Beam recognizes this fact by providing an extension of the standard watermark trigger that also supports repeated update triggering on either side of the watermark. This is known as the early/on-time/late trigger because it partitions the panes that are materialized by the compound trigger into three categories:

- Zero or more *early panes*, which are the result of a repeated update trigger that periodically fires up until the watermark passes the end of the window. The panes generated by these firings contain speculative results, but allow us to observe the evolution of the window over time as new input data arrive. This compensates for the shortcoming of watermarks sometimes being *too slow*.

- At most one *on-time pane*, which is the result of the completeness/watermark trigger firing after the watermark passes the end of the window. This firing is special because it provides an assertion that the system now believes the input for

---

6 Which isn't to say there aren't use cases that care primarily about correctness and not so much about latency; in those cases, using an accurate watermark as the sole driver of output from a pipeline is a reasonable approach.

this window to be complete.[7] This means that it is now safe to reason about *missing data*; for example, to emit a partial join when performing an outer join.

- Zero or more *late panes*, which are the result of another (possibly different) repeated update trigger that periodically fires any time late data arrive after the watermark has passed the end of the window. In the case of a perfect watermark, there will always be zero late panes. But in the case of a heuristic watermark, any data the watermark failed to properly account for will result in a late firing. This compensates for the shortcoming of watermarks being *too fast*.

Let's see how this looks in action. We'll update our pipeline to use a periodic processing-time trigger with an aligned delay of one minute for the early firings, and a per-record trigger for the late firings. That way, the early firings will give us some amount of batching for high-volume windows (thanks to the fact that the trigger will fire only once per minute, regardless of the throughput into the window), but we won't introduce unnecessary latency for the late firings, which are hopefully somewhat rare if we're using a reasonably accurate heuristic watermark. In Beam, that looks Example 2-7 (Figure 2-11 shows the results).

Example 2-7. Early, on-time, and late firings via the early/on-time/late API

```
PCollection<KV<Team, Integer>> totals = input
  .apply(Window.into(FixedWindows.of(TWO_MINUTES))
             .triggering(AfterWatermark()
                          .withEarlyFirings(AlignedDelay(ONE_MINUTE))
                          .withLateFirings(AfterCount(1))))
  .apply(Sum.integersPerKey());
```

---

7 And, as we know from before, this assertion is either guaranteed, in the case of a perfect watermark being used, or an educated guess, in the case of a heuristic watermark.

Figure 2-11. Windowed summation on a streaming engine with early, on-time, and late firings (http://streamingbook.net/fig/2-11)

This version has two clear improvements over Figure 2-10:

- For the "watermarks too slow" case in the second window, [12:02, 12:04): we now provide periodic early updates once per minute. The difference is most stark in the perfect watermark case, for which time-to-first-output is reduced from almost seven minutes down to three and a half; but it's also clearly improved in the heuristic case, as well. Both versions now provide steady refinements over time (panes with values 7, 10, then 18), with relatively minimal latency between the input becoming complete and materialization of the final output pane for the window.

- For the "heuristic watermarks too fast" case in the first window, [12:00, 12:02): when the value of 9 shows up late, we immediately incorporate it into a new, corrected pane with value of 14.

One interesting side effect of these new triggers is that they effectively normalize the output pattern between the perfect and heuristic watermark versions. Whereas the two versions in Figure 2-10 were starkly different, the two versions here look quite similar. They also look much more similar to the various repeated update version from Figures 2-6 through 2-8, with one important difference: thanks to the use of the watermark trigger, we can also reason about input completeness in the results we generate with the early/on-time/late trigger. This allows us to better handle use cases that care about *missing data*, like outer joins, anomaly detection, and so on.

The biggest remaining difference between the perfect and heuristic early/on-time/late versions at this point is window lifetime bounds. In the perfect watermark case, we know we'll never see any more data for a window after the watermark has passed the end of it, hence we can drop all of our state for the window at that time. In the heuristic watermark case, we still need to hold on to the state for a window for some amount of time to account for late data. But as of yet, our system doesn't have any good way of knowing just how long state needs to be kept around for each window. That's where *allowed lateness* comes in.

When: Allowed Lateness (i.e., Garbage Collection)

Before moving on to our last question ("*How* do refinements of results relate?"), I'd like to touch on a practical necessity within long-lived, out-of-order stream processing systems: garbage collection. In the heuristic watermarks example in Figure 2-11, the persistent state for each window lingers around for the entire lifetime of the example; this is necessary to allow us to appropriately deal with late data when/if they arrive. But while it would be great to be able to keep around all of our persistent state until the end of time, in reality, when dealing with an unbounded data source, it's often not practical to keep state (including metadata) for a given window indefinitely;

we'll eventually run out of disk space (or at the very least tire of paying for it, as the value for older data diminishes over time).

As a result, any real-world out-of-order processing system needs to provide some way to bound the lifetimes of the windows it's processing. A clean and concise way of doing this is by defining a horizon on the allowed lateness within the system; that is, placing a bound on how late any given *record* may be (relative to the watermark) for the system to bother processing it; any data that arrives after this horizon are simply dropped. After you've bounded how late individual data may be, you've also established precisely how long the state for windows must be kept around: until the watermark exceeds the lateness horizon for the end of the window. But in addition, you've also given the system the liberty to immediately drop any data later than the horizon as soon as they're observed, which means the system doesn't waste resources processing data that no one cares about.

Measuring Lateness

It might seem a little odd to be specifying a horizon for handling late data using the very metric that resulted in the late data in the first place (i.e., the heuristic watermark). And in some sense it is. But of the options available, it's arguably the best. The only other practical option would be to specify the horizon in processing time (e.g., keep windows around for 10 minutes of processing time after the watermark passes the end of the window), but using processing time would leave the garbage collection policy vulnerable to issues within the pipeline itself (e.g., workers crashing, causing the pipeline to stall for a few minutes), which could lead to windows that didn't actually have a chance to handle late data that they otherwise should have. By specifying the horizon in the event-time domain, garbage collection is directly tied to the actual progress of the pipeline, which decreases the likelihood that a window will miss its opportunity to handle late data appropriately.

Note however, that not all watermarks are created equal. When we speak of watermarks in this book, we generally refer to *low* watermarks, which pessimistically attempt to capture the event time of the *oldest* unprocessed record the system is aware of. The nice thing about dealing with lateness via low watermarks is that they are resilient to changes in event-time skew; no matter how large the skew in a pipeline may grow, the low watermark will always track the oldest outstanding event known to the system, providing the best guarantee of correctness possible.

In contrast, some systems may use the term "watermark" to mean other things. For example, watermarks in Spark Structured Streaming (*http://bit.ly/2yhCHMm*) are *high* watermarks, which optimistically track the event time of the *newest* record the system is aware of. When dealing with lateness, the system is free to garbage collect any window older than the high watermark adjusted by some user-specified lateness threshold. In other words, the system allows you to specify the maximum amount of event-time skew you expect to see in your pipeline, and then throws away any data

---

outside of that skew window. This can work well if skew within your pipeline remains within some constant delta, but is more prone to incorrectly discarding data than low watermarking schemes.

Because the interaction between allowed lateness and the watermark is a little subtle, it's worth looking at an example. Let's take the heuristic watermark pipeline from Example 2-7/Figure 2-11 and add in Example 2-8 a lateness horizon of one minute (note that this particular horizon has been chosen strictly because it fits nicely into the diagram; for real-world use cases, a larger horizon would likely be much more practical):

Example 2-8. Early/on-time/late firings with allowed lateness

```
PCollection<KV<Team, Integer>> totals = input
  .apply(Window.into(FixedWindows.of(TWO_MINUTES))
              .triggering(
                AfterWatermark()
                  .withEarlyFirings(AlignedDelay(ONE_MINUTE))
                  .withLateFirings(AfterCount(1))
              .withAllowedLateness(ONE_MINUTE))
  .apply(Sum.integersPerKey());
```

The execution of this pipeline would look something like Figure 2-12, in which I've added the following features to highlight the effects of allowed lateness:

- The thick black line denoting the current position in processing time is now annotated with ticks indicating the lateness horizon (in event time) for all active windows.
- When the watermark passes the lateness horizon for a window, that window is closed, which means that all state for the window is discarded. I leave around a dotted rectangle showing the extent of time (in both domains) that the window covered when it was closed, with a little tail extending to the right to denote the lateness horizon for the window (for contrasting against the watermark).
- For this diagram only, I've added an additional late datum for the first window with value 6. The 6 is late, but still within the allowed lateness horizon and thus is incorporated into an updated result with value 11. The 9, however, arrives beyond the lateness horizon, so it is simply dropped.

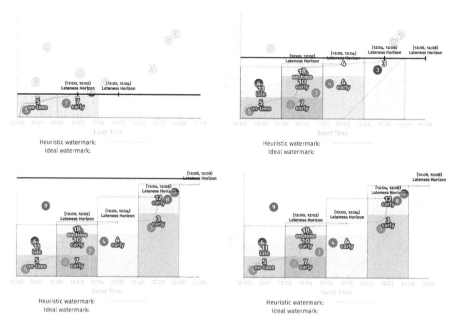

Figure 2-12. Allowed lateness with early/on-time/late firings (http://streamingbook.net/fig/2-12)

Two final side notes about lateness horizons:

- To be absolutely clear, if you happen to be consuming data from sources for which perfect watermarks are available, there's no need to deal with late data, and an allowed lateness horizon of zero seconds will be optimal. This is what we saw in the perfect watermark portion of Figure 2-10.

- One noteworthy exception to the rule of needing to specify lateness horizons, even when heuristic watermarks are in use, would be something like computing global aggregates over all time for a tractably finite number of keys (e.g., computing the total number of visits to your site over all time, grouped by web browser family). In this case, the number of active windows in the system is bounded by the limited keyspace in use. As long as the number of keys remains manageably low, there's no need to worry about limiting the lifetime of windows via allowed lateness.

Practicality sated, let's move on to our fourth and final question.

How: Accumulation

When triggers are used to produce multiple panes for a single window over time, we find ourselves confronted with the last question: "*How* do refinements of results relate?" In the examples we've seen so far, each successive pane is built upon the one immediately preceding it. However, there are actually three[8] different modes of accumulation:[9]

Discarding

Every time a pane is materialized, any stored state is discarded. This means that each successive pane is independent from any that came before. Discarding mode is useful when the downstream consumer is performing some sort of accumulation itself; for example, when sending integers into a system that expects to receive deltas that it will sum together to produce a final count.

Accumulating

As in Figures 2-6 through 2-11, every time a pane is materialized, any stored state is retained, and future inputs are accumulated into the existing state. This means that each successive pane builds upon the previous panes. Accumulating mode is useful when later results can simply overwrite previous results, such as when storing output in a key/value store like HBase or Bigtable.

Accumulating and retracting

This is like accumulating mode, but when producing a new pane, it also produces independent retractions for the previous pane(s). Retractions (combined with the new accumulated result) are essentially an explicit way of saying "I previously told you the result was *X*, but I was wrong. Get rid of the *X* I told you last time, and replace it with *Y*." There are two cases for which retractions are particularly helpful:

- When consumers downstream are *regrouping data by a different dimension*, it's entirely possible the new value may end up keyed differently from the previous value and thus end up in a different group. In that case, the new

---

8 You might note that there should logically be a fourth mode: discarding and retracting. That mode isn't terribly useful in most cases, so I don't discuss it further here.

9 In retrospect, it probably would have been clearer to choose a different set of names that are more oriented toward the observed nature of data in the materialized stream (e.g., "output modes") rather than names describing the state management semantics that yield those data. Perhaps: discarding mode → delta mode, accumulating mode → value mode, accumulating and retracting mode → value and retraction mode? However, the discarding/accumulating/accumulating and retracting names are enshrined in the 1.x and 2.x lineages of the Beam Model, so I don't want to introduce potential confusion in the book by deviating. Also, it's very likely accumulating modes will blend into the background more with Beam 3.0 and the introduction of sink triggers (*https://s.apache.org/beam-sink-triggers*); more on this when we discuss SQL in Chapter 8.

value can't just overwrite the old value; you instead need the retraction to remove the old value

- When *dynamic windows* (e.g., sessions, which we look at more closely in a few moments) are in use, the new value might be replacing more than one previous window, due to window merging. In this case, it can be difficult to determine from the new window alone which old windows are being replaced. Having explicit retractions for the old windows makes the task straightforward. We see an example of this in detail in Chapter 8.

The different semantics for each group are somewhat clearer when seen side-by-side. Consider the two panes for the fourth window (the one with event-time range [12:06, 12:08)) in Figure 2-11 (the one with early/on-time/late triggers). Table 2-1 shows what the values for each pane would look like across the three accumulation modes (with *accumulating* mode being the specific mode used in Figure 2-11 itself).

Table 2-1. Comparing accumulation modes using the fourth window from Figure 2-11

	Discarding	Accumulating	Accumulating & Retracting
Pane 1: inputs=[3]	3	3	3
Pane 2: inputs=[8, 1]	9	12	12, −3
Value of final normal pane	9	12	12
Sum of all panes	12	15	12

Let's take a closer look at what's happening:

Discarding

Each pane incorporates only the values that arrived during that specific pane. As such, the final value observed does not fully capture the total sum. However, if you were to sum all of the independent panes themselves, you would arrive at a correct answer of 12. This is why discarding mode is useful when the downstream consumer itself is performing some sort of aggregation on the materialized panes.

Accumulating

As in Figure 2-11, each pane incorporates the values that arrived during that specific pane, plus all of the values from previous panes. As such, the final value observed correctly captures the total sum of 12. If you were to sum up the individual panes themselves, however, you'd effectively be double-counting the inputs from pane 1, giving you an incorrect total sum of 15. This is why accumulating mode is most useful when you can simply overwrite previous values with new values: the new value already incorporates all of the data seen thus far.

Accumulating and retracting

Each pane includes both a new accumulating mode value as well as a retraction of the previous pane's value. As such, both the last value observed (excluding retractions) as well as the total sum of all materialized panes (including retractions) provide you with the correct answer of 12. This is why retractions are so powerful.

Example 2-9 demonstrates discarding mode in action, illustrating the changes we would make to Example 2-7:

Example 2-9. Discarding mode version of early/on-time/late firings

```
PCollection<KV<Team, Integer>> totals = input
  .apply(Window.into(FixedWindows.of(TWO_MINUTES))
              .triggering(
                 AfterWatermark()
                   .withEarlyFirings(AlignedDelay(ONE_MINUTE))
                   .withLateFirings(AtCount(1))
              .discardingFiredPanes())
  .apply(Sum.integersPerKey());
```

Running again on a streaming engine with a heuristic watermark would produce output like that shown in Figure 2-13.

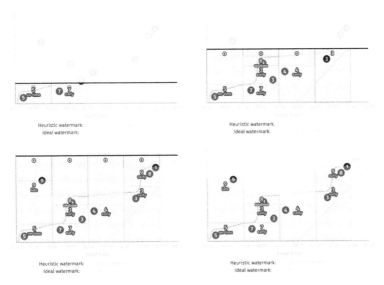

Figure 2-13. Discarding mode version of early/on-time/late firings on a streaming engine (http://streamingbook.net/fig/2-13)

Even though the overall shape of the output is similar to the accumulating mode version from Figure 2-11, note how none of the panes in this discarding version overlap. As a result, each output is independent from the others.

If we want to look at retractions in action, the change would be similar, as shown in Example 2-10. Figure 2-14 depicts the results.

Example 2-10. Accumulating and retracting mode version of early/on-time/late firings

```
PCollection<KV<Team, Integer>> totals = input
  .apply(Window.into(FixedWindows.of(TWO_MINUTES))
               .triggering(
                 AfterWatermark()
                   .withEarlyFirings(AlignedDelay(ONE_MINUTE))
                   .withLateFirings(AtCount(1))
               .accumulatingAndRetractingFiredPanes())
  .apply(Sum.integersPerKey());
```

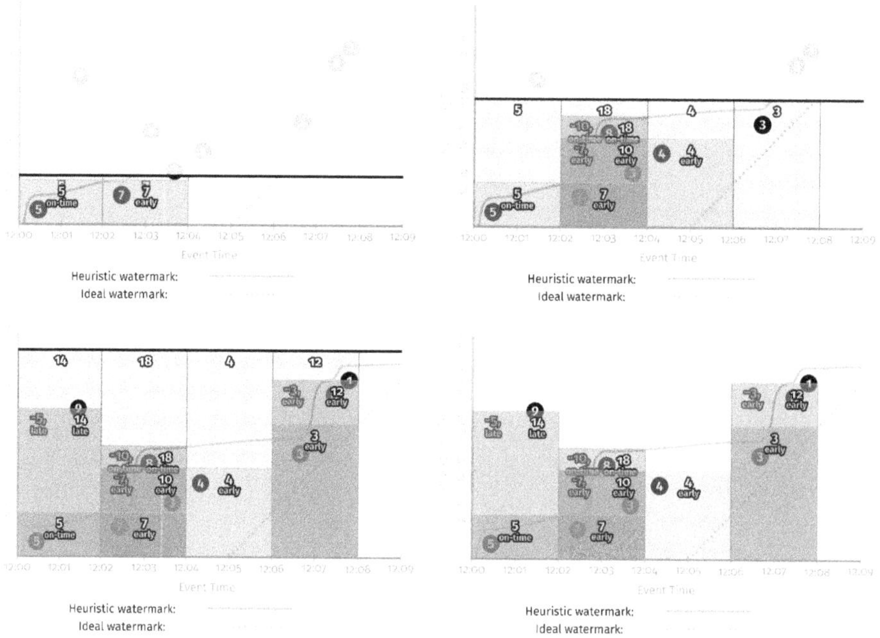

Figure 2-14. Accumulating and retracting mode version of early/late firings on a streaming engine (http://streamingbook.net/fig/2-14)

Because the panes for each window all overlap, it's a little tricky to see the retractions clearly. The retractions are indicated in red, which combines with the overlapping blue panes to yield a slightly purplish color. I've also horizontally shifted the values of the two outputs within a given pane slightly (and separated them with a comma) to make them easier to differentiate.

Figure 2-15 combines the final frames of Figures 2-11 (heuristic only), 2-13, and 2-14 side-by-side, providing a nice visual contrast of the three modes.

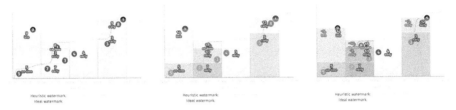

Figure 2-15. Side-by-side comparison of accumulation modes

As you can imagine, the modes in the order presented (discarding, accumulating, accumulating and retracting) are each successively more expensive in terms of storage and computation costs. To that end, choice of accumulation mode provides yet another dimension for making trade-offs along the axes of correctness, latency, and cost.

Summary

With this chapter complete, you now understand the basics of robust stream processing and are ready to go forth into the world and do amazing things. Of course, there are eight more chapters anxiously waiting for your attention, so hopefully you won't go forth like right now, this very minute. But regardless, let's recap what we've just covered, lest you forget any of it in your haste to amble forward. First, the major concepts we touched upon:

Event time versus processing time
   The all-important distinction between when events occurred and when they are observed by your data processing system.

Windowing
   The commonly utilized approach to managing unbounded data by slicing it along temporal boundaries (in either processing time or event time, though we narrow the definition of windowing in the Beam Model to mean only within event time).

Triggers
   The declarative mechanism for specifying precisely when materialization of output makes sense for your particular use case.

Watermarks

The powerful notion of progress in event time that provides a means of reasoning about completeness (and thus missing data) in an out-of-order processing system operating on unbounded data.

Accumulation

The relationship between refinements of results for a single window for cases in which it's materialized multiple times as it evolves.

Second, the four questions we used to frame our exploration:

- *What* results are calculated? = transformations.
- *Where* in event time are results calculated? = windowing.
- *When* in processing time are results materialized? = triggers plus watermarks.
- *How* do refinements of results relate? = accumulation.

Third, to drive home the flexibility afforded by this model of stream processing (because in the end, that's really what this is all about: balancing competing tensions like correctness, latency, and cost), a recap of the major variations in output we were able to achieve over the same dataset with only a minimal amount of code change:

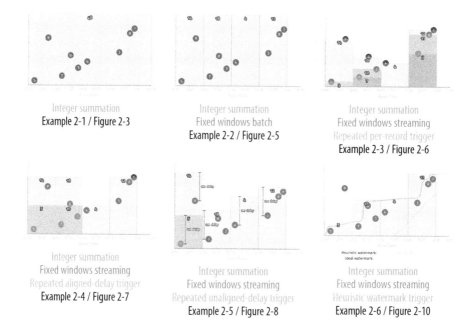

Integer summation
Example 2-1 / Figure 2-3

Integer summation
Fixed windows batch
Example 2-2 / Figure 2-5

Integer summation
Fixed windows streaming
Repeated per-record trigger
Example 2-3 / Figure 2-6

Integer summation
Fixed windows streaming
Repeated aligned-delay trigger
Example 2-4 / Figure 2-7

Integer summation
Fixed windows streaming
Repeated unaligned-delay trigger
Example 2-5 / Figure 2-8

Integer summation
Fixed windows streaming
Heuristic watermark trigger
Example 2-6 / Figure 2-10

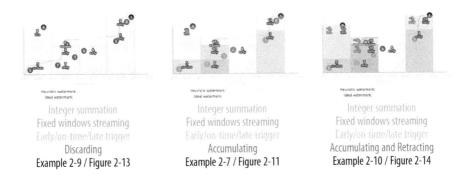

Heuristic watermark: Ideal watermark:	Heuristic watermark: Ideal watermark:	Heuristic watermark: Ideal watermark:
Integer summation	Integer summation	Integer summation
Fixed windows streaming	Fixed windows streaming	Fixed windows streaming
Early/on-time/late trigger	Early/on-time/late trigger	Early/on-time/late trigger
Discarding	Accumulating	Accumulating and Retracting
Example 2-9 / Figure 2-13	Example 2-7 / Figure 2-11	Example 2-10 / Figure 2-14

All that said, at this point, we've really looked at only one type of windowing: fixed windowing in event time. As we know, there are a number of dimensions to windowing, and I'd like to touch upon at least two more of those before we call it a day with the Beam Model. First, however, we're going to take a slight detour to dive deeper into the world of watermarks, as this knowledge will help frame future discussions (and be fascinating in and of itself). Enter Slava, stage right...

CHAPTER 3

Watermarks

So far, we have been looking at stream processing from the perspective of the pipeline author or data scientist. Chapter 2 introduced watermarks as part of the answer to the fundamental questions of *where* in event-time processing is taking place and *when* in processing time results are materialized. In this chapter, we approach the same questions, but instead from the perspective of the underlying mechanics of the stream processing system. Looking at these mechanics will help us motivate, understand, and apply the concepts around watermarks. We discuss how watermarks are created at the point of data ingress, how they propagate through a data processing pipeline, and how they affect output timestamps. We also demonstrate how watermarks preserve the guarantees that are necessary for answering the questions of *where* in event-time data are processed and *when* it is materialized, while dealing with unbounded data.

Definition

Consider any pipeline that ingests data and outputs results continuously. We wish to solve the general problem of when it is safe to call an event-time window closed, meaning that the window does not expect any more data. To do so we would like to characterize the progress that the pipeline is making relative to its unbounded input.

One naive approach for solving the event-time windowing problem would be to simply base our event-time windows on the current processing time. As we saw in Chapter 1, we quickly run into trouble—data processing and transport is not instantaneous, so processing and event times are almost never equal. Any hiccup or spike in our pipeline might cause us to incorrectly assign messages to windows. Ultimately, this strategy fails because we have no robust way to make any guarantees about such windows.

Another intuitive, but ultimately incorrect, approach would be to consider the rate of messages processed by the pipeline. Although this is an interesting metric, the rate may vary arbitrarily with changes in input, variability of expected results, resources available for processing, and so on. Even more important, rate does not help answer the fundamental questions of completeness. Specifically, rate does not tell us when we have seen all of the messages for a particular time interval. In a real-world system, there will be situations in which messages are not making progress through the system. This could be the result of transient errors (such as crashes, network failures, machine downtime), or the result of persistent errors such as application-level failures that require changes to the application logic or other manual intervention to resolve. Of course, if lots of failures are occurring, a rate-of-processing metric might be a good proxy for detecting this. However a rate metric could never tell us that a single message is failing to make progress through our pipeline. Even a single such message, however, can arbitrarily affect the correctness of the output results.

We require a more robust measure of progress. To arrive there, we make one fundamental assumption about our streaming data: *each message has an associated logical event timestamp*. This assumption is reasonable in the context of continuously arriving unbounded data because this implies the continuous generation of input data. In most cases, we can take the time of the original event's occurrence as its logical event timestamp. With all input messages containing an event timestamp, we can then examine the distribution of such timestamps in any pipeline. Such a pipeline might be distributed to process in parallel over many agents and consuming input messages with no guarantee of ordering between individual shards. Thus, the set of event timestamps for active in-flight messages in this pipeline will form a distribution, as illustrated in Figure 3-1.

Messages are ingested by the pipeline, processed, and eventually marked completed. Each message is either "in-flight," meaning that it has been received but not yet completed, or "completed," meaning that no more processing on behalf of this message is required. If we examine the distribution of messages by event time, it will look something like Figure 3-1. As time advances, more messages will be added to the "in-flight" distribution on the right, and more of those messages from the "in-flight" part of the distribution will be completed and moved into the "completed" distribution.

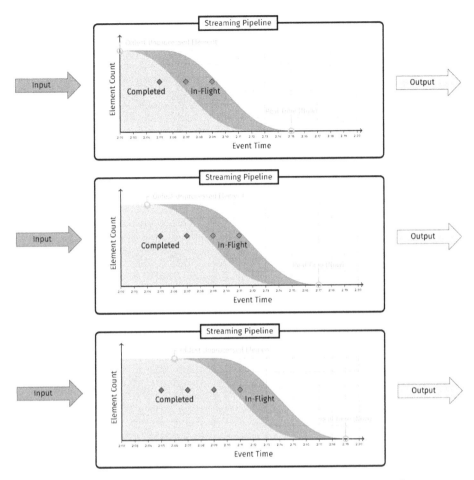

Figure 3-1. Distribution of in-flight and completed message event times within a streaming pipeline. New messages arrive as input and remain "in-flight" until processing for them completes. The leftmost edge of the "in-flight" distribution corresponds to the oldest unprocessed element at any given moment. (http://streamingbook.net/fig/3-1)

There is a key point on this distribution, located at the leftmost edge of the "in-flight" distribution, corresponding to the oldest event timestamp of any unprocessed message of our pipeline. We use this value to define the watermark:

The watermark is a monotonically[1] increasing timestamp of the oldest work not yet completed.

There are two fundamental properties that are provided by this definition that make it useful:

Completeness

If the watermark has advanced past some timestamp T, we are guaranteed by its monotonic property that no more processing will occur for on-time (nonlate data) events at or before T. Therefore, we can correctly emit any aggregations at or before T. In other words, the watermark allows us to know when it is correct to materialize a window.

Visibility

If a message is stuck in our pipeline for any reason, the watermark cannot advance. Furthermore, we will be able to find the source of the problem by examining the message that is preventing the watermark from advancing.

Source Watermark Creation

Where do these watermarks come from? To establish a watermark for a data source, we must assign a logical event timestamp to every message entering the pipeline from that source. As Chapter 2 informs us, all watermark creation falls into one of two broad categories: *perfect* or *heuristic*. To remind ourselves about the difference between perfect and heuristic watermarks, let's look at Figure 3-2, which presents the windowed summation example from Chapter 2.

---

1 Note the additional mention of monotonicity; we have not yet discussed how to achieve this. Indeed the discussion thus far makes no mention of monotonicity. If we considered exclusively the oldest in-flight event time, the watermark would not always be monotonic, as we have made no assumptions about our input. We return to this discussion later on.

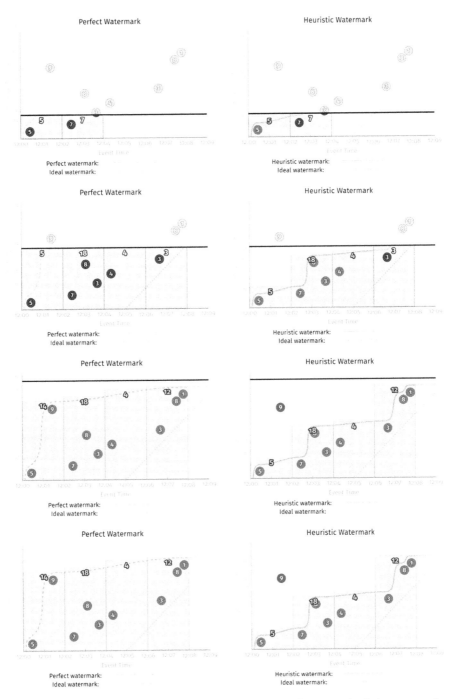

Figure 3-2. Windowed summation with perfect (left) and heuristic (right) watermarks (http://streamingbook.net/fig/3-2)

Notice that the distinguishing feature is that perfect watermarks ensure that the watermark accounts for *all* data, whereas heuristic watermarks admit some late-data elements.

After the watermark is created as either perfect or heuristic, watermarks remain so throughout the rest of the pipeline. As to what makes watermark creation perfect or heuristic, it depends a great deal on the nature of the source that's being consumed. To see why, let's look at a few examples of each type of watermark creation.

Perfect Watermark Creation

Perfect watermark creation assigns timestamps to incoming messages in such a way that the resulting watermark is a *strict guarantee* that no data with event times less than the watermark will ever be seen again from this source. Pipelines using perfect watermark creation never have to deal with late data; that is, data that arrive after the watermark has advanced past the event times of newly arriving messages. However, perfect watermark creation requires perfect knowledge of the input, and thus is impractical for many real-world distributed input sources. Here are a couple of examples of use cases that can create perfect watermarks:

Ingress timestamping

A source that assigns ingress times as the event times for data entering the system can create a perfect watermark. In this case, the source watermark simply tracks the current processing time as observed by the pipeline. This is essentially the method that nearly all streaming systems supporting windowing prior to 2016 used.

Because event times are assigned from a single, monotonically increasing source (actual processing time), the system thus has perfect knowledge about which timestamps will come next in the stream of data. As a result, event-time progress and windowing semantics become vastly easier to reason about. The downside, of course, is that the watermark has no correlation to the event times of the data themselves; those event times were effectively discarded, and the watermark instead merely tracks the progress of data relative to its arrival in the system.

Static sets of time-ordered logs

A statically sized[2] input source of time-ordered logs (e.g., an Apache Kafka topic with a static set of partitions, where each partition of the source contains monot-

---

2 To be precise, it's not so much that the number of logs need be static as it is that the number of logs at any given time be known a priori by the system. A more sophisticated input source composed of a dynamically chosen number of inputs logs, such as Pravega (*http://pravega.io*), could just as well be used for constructing a perfect watermark. It's only when the number of logs that exist in the dynamic set at any given time is unknown (as in the example in the next section) that one must fall back on a heuristic watermark.

onically increasing event times) would be a relatively straightforward source atop which to create a perfect watermark. To do so, the source would simply track the minimum event time of unprocessed data across the known and static set of source partitions (i.e., the minimum of the event times of the most recently read record in each of the partitions).

Similar to the aforementioned ingress timestamps, the system has perfect knowledge about which timestamps will come next, thanks to the fact that event times across the static set of partitions are known to increase monotonically. This is effectively a form of bounded out-of-order processing; the amount of disorder across the known set of partitions is bounded by the minimum observed event time among those partitions.

Typically, the only way you can guarantee monotonically increasing timestamps within partitions is if the timestamps within those partitions are assigned as data are written to it; for example, by web frontends logging events directly into Kafka. Though still a limited use case, this is definitely a much more useful one than ingress timestamping upon arrival at the data processing system because the watermark tracks meaningful event times of the underlying data.

Heuristic Watermark Creation

Heuristic watermark creation, on the other hand, creates a watermark that is merely an *estimate* that no data with event times less than the watermark will ever be seen again. Pipelines using heuristic watermark creation might need to deal with some amount of *late data*. Late data is any data that arrives after the watermark has advanced past the event time of this data. Late data is only possible with heuristic watermark creation. If the heuristic is a reasonably good one, the amount of late data might be very small, and the watermark remains useful as a completion estimate. The system still needs to provide a way for the user to cope with late data if it's to support use cases requiring correctness (e.g., things like billing).

For many real-world, distributed input sources, it's computationally or operationally impractical to construct a perfect watermark, but still possible to build a highly accurate heuristic watermark by taking advantage of structural features of the input data source. Following are two example for which heuristic watermarks (of varying quality) are possible:

Dynamic sets of time-ordered logs
   Consider a dynamic set of structured log files (each individual file containing records with monotonically increasing event times relative to other records in the same file but with no fixed relationship of event times between files), where the full set of expected log files (i.e., partitions, in Kafka parlance) is not known at runtime. Such inputs are often found in global-scale services constructed and managed by a number of independent teams. In such a use case, creating a per-

fect watermark over the input is intractable, but creating an accurate heuristic watermark is quite possible.

By tracking the minimum event times of unprocessed data in the existing set of log files, monitoring growth rates, and utilizing external information like network topology and bandwidth availability, you can create a remarkably accurate watermark, even given the lack of perfect knowledge of all the inputs. This type of input source is one of the most common types of unbounded datasets found at Google, so we have extensive experience with creating and analyzing watermark quality for such scenarios and have seen them used to good effect across a number of use cases.

Google Cloud Pub/Sub

Cloud Pub/Sub is an interesting use case. Pub/Sub currently makes no guarantees on in-order delivery; even if a single publisher publishes two messages in order, there's a chance (usually small) that they might be delivered out of order (this is due to the dynamic nature of the underlying architecture, which allows for transparent scaling up to very high levels of throughput with zero user intervention). As a result, there's no way to guarantee a perfect watermark for Cloud Pub/Sub. The Cloud Dataflow team has, however, built a reasonably accurate heuristic watermark by taking advantage of what knowledge *is* available about the data in Cloud Pub/Sub. The implementation of this heuristic is discussed at length as a case study later in this chapter.

Consider an example where users play a mobile game, and their scores are sent to our pipeline for processing: you can generally assume that for any source utilizing mobile devices for input it will be generally impossible to provide a perfect watermark. Due to the problem of devices that go offline for extended periods of time, there's just no way to provide any sort of reasonable estimate of absolute completeness for such a data source. You can, however, imagine building a watermark that accurately tracks input completeness for devices that are currently online, similar to the Google Pub/Sub watermark described a moment ago. Users who are actively online are likely the most relevant subset of users from the perspective of providing low-latency results anyway, so this often isn't as much of a shortcoming as you might initially think.

With heuristic watermark creation, broadly speaking, the more that is known about the source, the better the heuristic, and the fewer late data items will be seen. There is no one-size-fits-all solution, given that the types of sources, distributions of events, and usage patterns will vary greatly. But in either case (perfect or heuristic), after a watermark is created at the input source, the system can propagate the watermark through the pipeline perfectly. This means perfect watermarks will remain perfect downstream, and heuristic watermarks will remain strictly as heuristic as they were when established. This is the benefit of the watermark approach: you can reduce the complexity of tracking completeness in a pipeline entirely to the problem of creating a watermark at the source.

Watermark Propagation

So far, we have considered only the watermark for the inputs within the context of a single operation or stage. However, most real-world pipelines consist of multiple stages. Understanding how watermarks propagate across independent stages is important in understanding how they affect the pipeline as a whole and the observed latency of its results.

Pipeline Stages

Different stages are typically necessary every time your pipeline groups data together by some new dimension. For example, if you had a pipeline that consumed raw data, computed some per-user aggregates, and then used those per-user aggregates to compute some per-team aggregates, you'd likely end up with a three-stage pipeline:

- One consuming the raw, ungrouped data
- One grouping the data by user and computing per-user aggregates
- One grouping the data by team and computing per-team aggregates

We learn more about the effects of grouping on pipeline shapes in Chapter 6.

Watermarks are created at input sources, as discussed in the preceding section. They then conceptually flow through the system as data progress through it.[3] You can track watermarks at varying levels of granularity. For pipelines comprising multiple distinct stages, each stage likely tracks its own watermark, whose value is a function of all the inputs and stages that come before it. Therefore, stages that come later in the pipeline will have watermarks that are further in the past (because they've seen less of the overall input).

We can define watermarks at the boundaries of any single operation, or stage, in the pipeline. This is useful not only in understanding the relative progress that each stage in the pipeline is making, but for dispatching timely results independently and as soon as possible for each individual stage. We give the following definitions for the watermarks at the boundaries of stages:

---

3 Note that by saying "flow through the system," I don't necessarily imply they flow along the same path as normal data. They might (as in Apache Flink), but they might also be transmitted out-of-band (as in MillWheel/Cloud Dataflow).

- An *input watermark*, which captures the progress of everything upstream of that stage (i.e., how complete the input is for that stage). For sources, the input watermark is a source-specific function creating the watermark for the input data. For nonsource stages, the input watermark is defined as the minimum of the output watermarks of all shards/partitions/instances of all of its upstream sources and stages.

- An *output watermark*, which captures the progress of the stage itself, and is essentially defined as the minimum of the stage's input watermark and the event times of all nonlate data active messages within the stage. Exactly what "active" encompasses is somewhat dependent upon the operations a given stage actually performs, and the implementation of the stream processing system. It typically includes data buffered for aggregation but not yet materialized downstream, pending output data in flight to downstream stages, and so on.

One nice feature of defining an input and output watermark for a specific stage is that we can use these to calculate the amount of event-time latency introduced by a stage. Subtracting the value of a stage's output watermark from the value of its input watermark gives the amount of event-time latency or *lag* introduced by the stage. This lag is the notion of how far delayed behind real time the output of each stage will be. As an example, a stage performing 10-second windowed aggregations will have a lag of 10 seconds or more, meaning that the output of the stage will be at least that much delayed behind the input and real time. Definitions of input and output watermarks provide a recursive relationship of watermarks throughout a pipeline. Each subsequent stage in a pipeline delays the watermark as necessary, based on event-time lag of the stage.

Processing within each stage is also not monolithic. We can segment the processing within one stage into a flow with several conceptual components, each of which contributes to the output watermark. As mentioned previously, the exact nature of these components depends on the operations the stage performs and the implementation of the system. Conceptually, each such component serves as a buffer where active messages can reside until some operation has completed. For example, as data arrives, it is buffered for processing. Processing might then write the data to state for later delayed aggregation. Delayed aggregation, when triggered, might write the results to an output buffer awaiting consumption from a downstream stage, as shown in Figure 3-3.

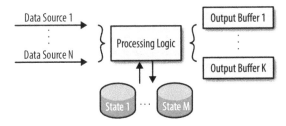

Figure 3-3. Example system components of a streaming system stage, containing buffers of in-flight data. Each will have associated watermark tracking, and the overall output watermark of the stage will be the minimum of the watermarks across all such buffers.

We can track each such buffer with its own watermark. The minimum of the watermarks across the buffers of each stage forms the output watermark of the stage. Thus the output watermark could be the minimum of the following:

- *Per-source* watermark—for each sending stage.
- *Per-external input* watermark—for sources external to the pipeline
- *Per-state component* watermark—for each type of state that can be written
- *Per-output buffer* watermark—for each receiving stage

Making watermarks available at this level of granularity also provides better visibility into the behavior of the system. The watermarks track locations of messages across various buffers in the system, allowing for easier diagnosis of stuckness.

Understanding Watermark Propagation

To get a better sense for the relationship between input and output watermarks and how they affect watermark propagation, let's look at an example. Let's consider gaming scores, but instead of computing sums of team scores, we're going to take a stab at measuring user engagement levels. We'll do this by first calculating per-user session lengths, under the assumption that the amount of time a user stays engaged with the game is a reasonable proxy for how much they're enjoying it. After answering our four questions once to calculate sessions lengths, we'll then answer them a second time to calculate average session lengths within fixed periods of time.

To make our example even more interesting, lets say that we are working with two datasets, one for Mobile Scores and one for Console Scores. We would like to perform identical score calculations via integer summation in parallel over these two independant datasets. One pipeline is calculating scores for users playing on mobile devices, whereas the other is for users playing on home gaming consoles, perhaps due to different data collection strategies employed for the different platforms. The important point is that these two stages are performing the same operation but over different data, and thus with very different output watermarks.

To begin, let's take a look at Example 3-1 to see what the abbreviated code for what the first section of this pipeline might be like.

Example 3-1. Calculating session lengths

```
PCollection<Double> mobileSessions = IO.read(new MobileInputSource())
    .apply(Window.into(Sessions.withGapDuration(Duration.standardMinutes(1)))
             .triggering(AtWatermark())
             .discardingFiredPanes())
    .apply(CalculateWindowLength());

PCollection<Double> consoleSessions = IO.read(new ConsoleInputSource())
    .apply(Window.into(Sessions.withGapDuration(Duration.standardMinutes(1)))
             .triggering(AtWatermark())
             .discardingFiredPanes())
    .apply(CalculateWindowLength());
```

Here, we read in each of our inputs independently, and whereas previously we were keying our collections by team, in this example we key by user. After that, for the first stage of each pipeline, we window into sessions and then call a custom PTransform named CalculateWindowLength. This PTransform simply groups by key (i.e., User) and then computes the per-user session length by treating the size of the current window as the value for that window. In this case, we're fine with the default trigger (AtWatermark) and accumulation mode (discardingFiredPanes) settings, but I've listed them explicitly for completeness. The output for each pipeline for two particular users might look something like Figure 3-4.

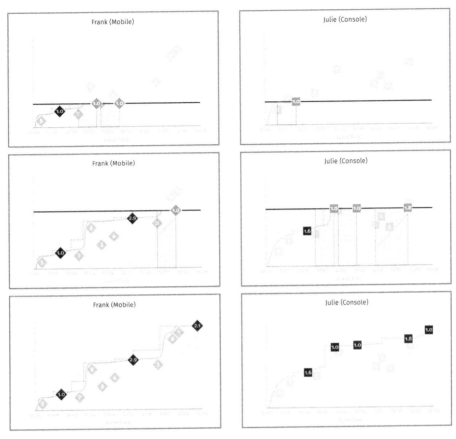

Figure 3-4. Per-user session lengths across two different input pipelines (http://streaming book.net/fig/3-4)

Because we need to track data across multiple stages, we track everything related to Mobile Scores in red, everything related to Console Scores in blue, while the watermark and output for Average Session Lengths in Figure 3-5 are yellow.

We have answered the four questions of *what*, *where*, *when*, and *how* to compute individual session lengths. Next we'll answer them a second time to transform those session lengths into global session-length averages within fixed windows of time. This requires us to first flatten our two data sources into one, and then re-window into fixed windows; we've already captured the important essence of the session in the session-length value we computed, and we now want to compute a global average of those sessions within consistent windows of time over the course of the day. Example 3-2 shows the code for this.

Example 3-2. Calculating session lengths

```
PCollection<Double> mobileSessions = IO.read(new MobileInputSource())
  .apply(Window.into(Sessions.withGapDuration(Duration.standardMinutes(1)))
            .triggering(AtWatermark())
            .discardingFiredPanes())
  .apply(CalculateWindowLength());

PCollection<Double> consoleSessions = IO.read(new ConsoleInputSource())
  .apply(Window.into(Sessions.withGapDuration(Duration.standardMinutes(1)))
            .triggering(AtWatermark())
            .discardingFiredPanes())
  .apply(CalculateWindowLength());

PCollection<Float> averageSessionLengths = PCollectionList
  .of(mobileSessions).and(consoleSessions)
  .apply(Flatten.pCollections())
  .apply(Window.into(FixedWindows.of(Duration.standardMinutes(2)))
            .triggering(AtWatermark())
  .apply(Mean.globally());
```

If we were to see this pipeline in action, it would look something like Figure 3-5. As before, the two input pipelines are computing individual session lengths for mobile and console players. Those session lengths then feed into the second stage of the pipeline, where global session-length averages are computed in fixed windows.

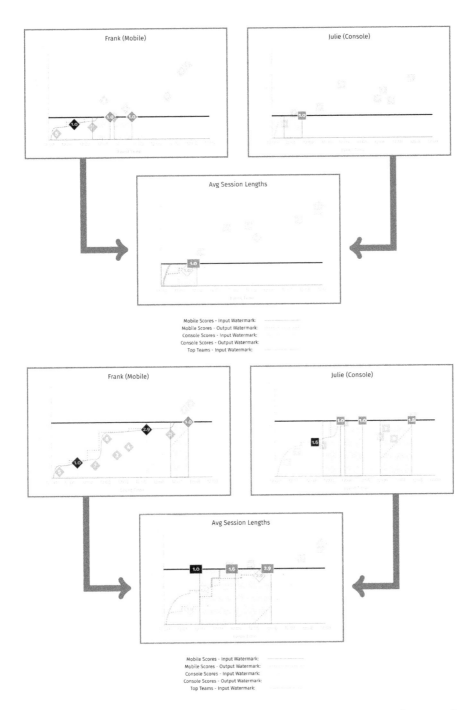

Figure 3-5. Average session lengths of mobile and console gaming sessions (continued next) (http://streamingbook.net/fig/3-5)

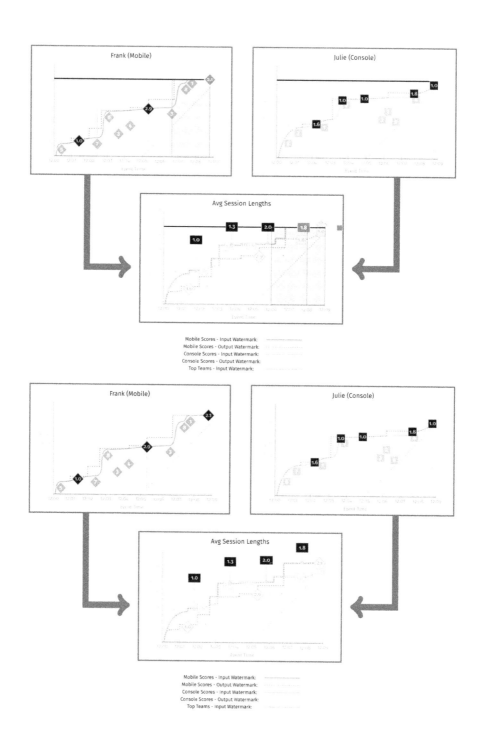

Let's walk through some of this example, given that there's a lot going on. The two important points here are:

- The *output watermark* for each of the Mobile Sessions and Console Sessions stages is at least as old as the corresponding input watermark of each, and in reality a little bit older. This is because in a real system computing answers takes time, and we don't allow the output watermark to advance until processing for a given input has completed.

- The *input watermark* for the Average Session Lengths stage is the minimum of the output watermarks for the two stages directly upstream.

The result is that the downstream input watermark is an alias for the minimum composition of the upstream output watermarks. Note that this matches the definitions for those two types of watermarks earlier in the chapter. Also notice how watermarks further downstream are further in the past, capturing the intuitive notion that upstream stages are going to be further ahead in time than the stages that follow them.

One observation worth making here is just how cleanly we were able to ask the questions again in Example 3-1 to substantially alter the results of the pipeline. Whereas before we simply computed per-user session lengths, we now compute two-minute global session-length averages. This provides a much more insightful look into the overall behaviors of the users playing our games and gives you a tiny glimpse of the difference between simple data transformations and real data science.

Even better, now that we understand the basics of how this pipeline operates, we can look more closely at one of the more subtle issues related to asking the four questions over again: *output timestamps*.

Watermark Propagation and Output Timestamps

In Figure 3-5, I glossed over some of the details of output timestamps. But if you look closely at the second stage in the diagram, you can see that each of the outputs from the first stage was assigned a timestamp that matched the end of its window. Although that's a fairly natural choice for output timestamps, it's not the only valid choice. As you know from earlier in this chapter, watermarks are never allowed to move backward. Given that restriction, you can infer that the range of valid timestamps for a given window begins with the timestamp of the earliest nonlate record in the window (because only nonlate records are guaranteed to hold a watermark up) and extends all the way to positive infinity. That's quite a lot of options. In practice, however, there tend to be only a few choices that make sense in most circumstances:

End of the window[4]

Using the end of the window is the only safe choice if you want the output time-stamp to be representative of the window bounds. As we'll see in a moment, it also allows the smoothest watermark progression out of all of the options.

Timestamp of first nonlate element

Using the timestamp of the first nonlate element is a good choice when you want to keep your watermarks as conservative as possible. The trade-off, however, is that watermark progress will likely be more hindered, as we'll also see shortly.

Timestamp of a specific element

For certain use cases, the timestamp of some other arbitrary (from the system's perspective) element is the right choice. Imagine a use case in which you're join-ing a stream of queries to a stream of clicks on results for that query. After per-forming the join, some systems will find the timestamp of the query to be more useful; others will prefer the timestamp of the click. Any such timestamp is valid from a watermark correctness perspective, as long as it corresponded to an ele-ment that did not arrive late.

Having thought a bit about some alternate options for output timestamps, let's look at what effects the choice of output timestamp can have on the overall pipeline. To make the changes as dramatic as possible, in Example 3-3 and Figure 3-6, we'll switch to using the earliest timestamp possible for the window: the timestamp of the first non-late element as the timestamp for the window.

Example 3-3. Average session lengths pipeline, that output timestamps for session windows set at earliest element

```
PCollection<Double> mobileSessions = IO.read(new MobileInputSource())
  .apply(Window.into(Sessions.withGapDuration(Duration.standardMinutes(1)))
                .triggering(AtWatermark())
                .withTimestampCombiner(EARLIEST)
                .discardingFiredPanes())
  .apply(CalculateWindowLength());

PCollection<Double> consoleSessions = IO.read(new ConsoleInputSource())
  .apply(Window.into(Sessions.withGapDuration(Duration.standardMinutes(1)))
                .triggering(AtWatermark())
                .withTimestampCombiner(EARLIEST)
                .discardingFiredPanes())
  .apply(CalculateWindowLength());
```

---

4 The *start* of the window is not a safe choice from a watermark correctness perspective because the first ele-ment in the window often comes *after* the beginning of the window itself, which means that the watermark is not guaranteed to have been held back as far as the start of the window.

```
PCollection<Float> averageSessionLengths = PCollectionList
  .of(mobileSessions).and(consoleSessions)
  .apply(Flatten.pCollections())
  .apply(Window.into(FixedWindows.of(Duration.standardMinutes(2)))
            .triggering(AtWatermark())
  .apply(Mean.globally());
```

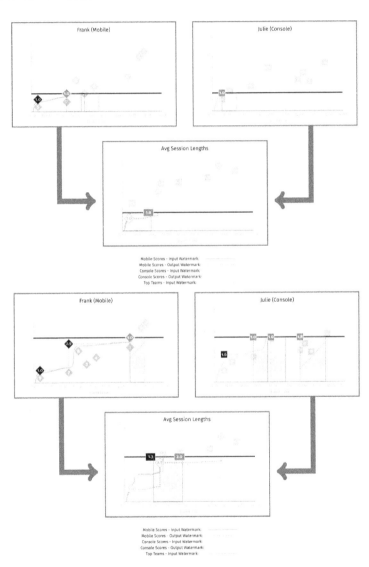

Figure 3-6. Average session lengths for sessions that are output at the timestamp of the earliest element (continued next) (http://streamingbook.net/fig/3-6)

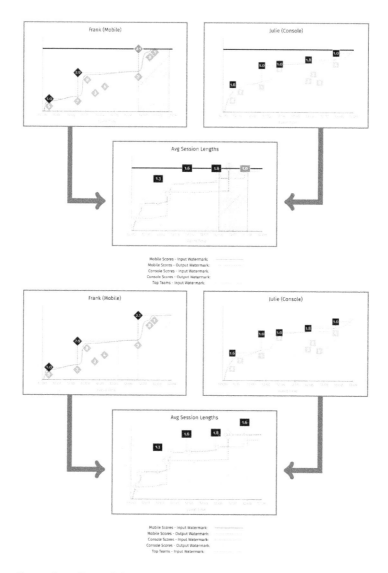

To help call out the effect of the output timestamp choice, look at the dashed lines in the first stages showing what the output watermark for each stage is being held to. The output watermark is delayed by our choice of timestamp, as compared to Figures 3-7 and 3-8, in which the output timestamp was chosen to be the end of the window. You can see from this diagram that the input watermark of the second stage is thus subsequently also delayed.

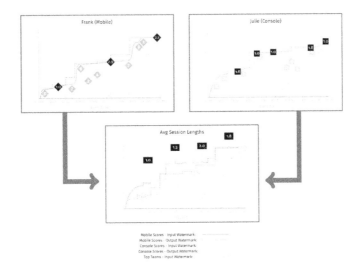

Figure 3-7. Comparison of watermarks and results with different choice of window output timestamps. The watermarks in this figure correspond to output timestamps at the end of the session windows (i.e., Figure 3-5).

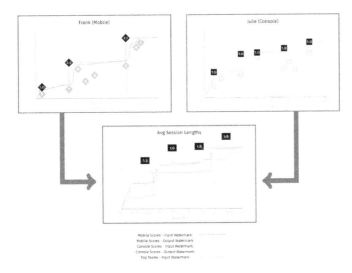

Figure 3-8. In this figure, the watermarks are at the beginning of the session windows (i.e., Figure 3-6). We can see that the watermark line in this figure is more delayed, and the resulting average session lengths are different.

As far as differences in this version compared to Figure 3-7, two are worth noting:

Watermark delay

Compared to Figure 3-5, the watermark proceeds much more slowly in Figure 3-6. This is because the output watermark for the first stage is held back to the timestamp of the first element in every window until the input for that window becomes complete. Only after a given window has been materialized is the output watermark (and thus the downstream input watermark) allowed to advance.

Semantic differences

Because the session timestamps are now assigned to match the earliest nonlate element in the session, the individual sessions often end up in different fixed window buckets when we then calculate the session-length averages in the next stage. There's nothing inherently right or wrong about either of the two options we've seen so far; they're just different. But it's important to understand that they *will* be different as well as have an intuition for the way in which they'll be different so that you can make the correct choice for your specific use case when the time comes.

The Tricky Case of Overlapping Windows

One additional subtle but important issue regarding output timestamps is how to handle sliding windows. The naive approach of setting the output timestamp to the earliest element can very easily lead to delays downstream due to watermarks being (correctly) held back. To see why, consider an example pipeline with two stages, each using the same type of sliding windows. Suppose that each element ends up in three successive windows. As the input watermark advances, the desired semantics for sliding windows in this case would be as follows:

- The first window completes in the first stage and is emitted downstream.
- The first window then completes in the second stage and can also be emitted downstream.
- Some time later, the second window completes in the first stage… and so on.

However, if output timestamps are chosen to be the timestamp of the first nonlate element in the pane, what actually happens is the following:

- The first window completes in the first stage and is emitted downstream.
- The first window in the second stage remains unable to complete because its input watermark is being held up by the output watermark of the second and third windows upstream. Those watermarks are rightly being held back because

the earliest element timestamp is being used as the output timestamp for those windows.

- The second window completes in the first stage and is emitted downstream.
- The first and second windows in the second stage remain unable to complete, held up by the third window upstream.
- The third window completes in the first stage and is emitted downstream.
- The first, second, and third windows in the second stage are now all able to complete, finally emitting all three in one swoop.

Although the results of this windowing are correct, this leads to the results being materialized in an unnecessarily delayed way. Because of this, Beam has special logic for overlapping windows that ensures the output timestamp for window $N+1$ is always greater than the end of window N.

Percentile Watermarks

So far, we have concerned ourselves with watermarks as measured by the minimum event time of active messages in a stage. Tracking the minimum allows the system to know when all earlier timestamps have been accounted for. On the other hand, we could consider the entire distribution of event timestamps for active messages and make use of it to create finer-grained triggering conditions.

Instead of considering the minimum point of the distribution, we could take any percentile of the distribution and say that we are guaranteed to have processed this percentage of all events with earlier timestamps.[5]

What is the advantage of this scheme? If for the business logic "mostly" correct is sufficient, percentile watermarks provide a mechanism by which the watermark can advance more quickly and more smoothly than if we were tracking the minimum event time by discarding outliers in the long tail of the distribution from the watermark. Figure 3-9 shows a compact distribution of event times where the 90th percentile watermark is close to the 100th percentile. Figure 3-10 demonstrates a case where the outlier is further behind, so the 90th percentile watermark is significantly ahead of the 100th percentile. By discarding the outlier data from the watermark, the percentile watermark can still keep track of the bulk of the distribution without being delayed by the outliers.

---

5 The percentile watermark triggering scheme described here is not currently implemented by Beam; however, other systems such as MillWheel implement this.

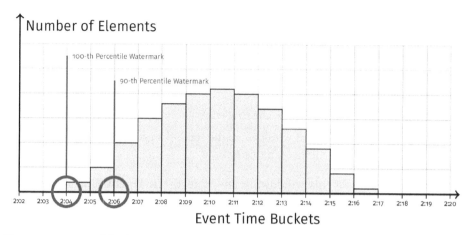

Figure 3-9. Normal-looking watermark histogram

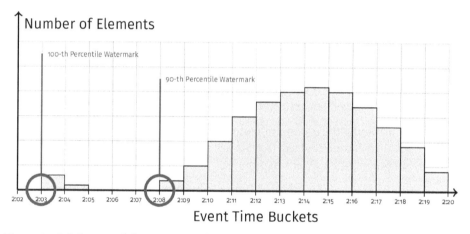

Figure 3-10. Watermark histogram with outliers

Figure 3-11 shows an example of percentile watermarks used to draw window boundaries for two-minute fixed windows. We can draw early boundaries based on the percentile of timestamps of arrived data as tracked by the percentile watermark.

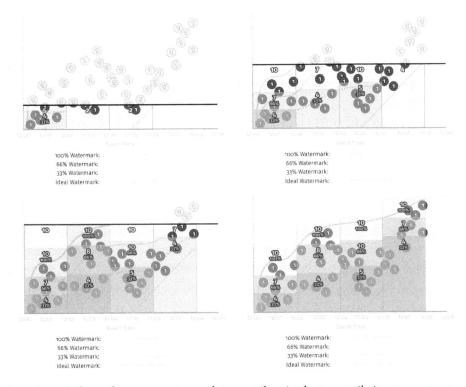

100% Watermark:
66% Watermark:
33% Watermark:
Ideal Watermark:

100% Watermark:
66% Watermark:
33% Watermark:
Ideal Watermark:

100% Watermark:
66% Watermark:
33% Watermark:
Ideal Watermark:

100% Watermark:
66% Watermark:
33% Watermark:
Ideal Watermark:

Figure 3-11. Effects of varying watermark percentiles. As the percentile increases, more events are included in the window: however, the processing time delay to materialize the window also increases. (http://streamingbook.net/fig/3-11)

Figure 3-11 shows the 33rd percentile, 66th percentile, and 100th percentile (full) watermark, tracking the respective timestamp percentiles in the data distribution. As expected, these allow boundaries to be drawn earlier than tracking the full 100th percentile watermark. Notice that the 33rd and 66th percentile watermarks each allow earlier triggering of windows but with the trade-off of marking more data as late. For example, for the first window, [12:00, 12:02), a window closed based on the 33rd percentile watermark would include only four events and materialize the result at 12:06 processing time. If we use the 66th percentile watermark, the same event-time window would include seven events, and materialize at 12:07 processing time. Using the 100th percentile watermark includes all ten events and delays materializing the results until 12:08 processing time. Thus, percentile watermarks provide a way to tune the trade-off between latency of materializing results and precision of the results.

Processing-Time Watermarks

Until now, we have been looking at watermarks as they relate to the data flowing through our system. We have seen how looking at the watermark can help us identify the overall delay between our oldest data and real time. However, this is not enough to distinguish between old data and a delayed system. In other words, by only examining the event-time watermark as we have defined it up until now, we cannot distinguish between a system that is processing data from an hour ago quickly and without delay, and a system that is attempting to process real-time data and has been delayed for an hour while doing so.

To make this distinction, we need something more: processing-time watermarks. We have already seen that there are two time domains in a streaming system: processing time and event time. Until now, we have defined the watermark entirely in the event-time domain, as a function of timestamps of the data flowing through the system. This is an event-time watermark. We will now apply the same model to the processing-time domain to define a processing-time watermark.

Our stream processing system is constantly performing operations such as shuffling messages between stages, reading or writing messages to persistent state, or triggering delayed aggregations based on watermark progress. All of these operations are performed in response to previous operations done at the current or upstream stage of the pipeline. Thus, just as data elements "flow" through the system, a cascade of operations involved in processing these elements also "flows" through the system.

We define the processing-time watermark in the exact same way as we have defined the event-time watermark, except instead of using the event-time timestamp of oldest work not yet completed, we use the processing-time timestamp of the oldest operation not yet completed. An example of delay to the processing-time watermark could be a stuck message delivery from one stage to another, a stuck I/O call to read state or external data, or an exception while processing that prevents processing from completing.

The processing-time watermark, therefore, provides a notion of processing delay separate from the data delay. To understand the value of this distinction, consider the graph in Figure 3-12 where we look at the event-time watermark delay.

We see that the data delay is monotonically increasing, but there is not enough information to distinguish between the cases of a stuck system and stuck data. Only by looking at the processing-time watermark, shown in Figure 3-13, can we distinguish the cases.

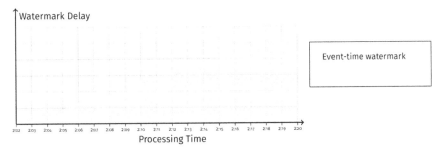

Figure 3-12. Event-time watermark increasing. It is not possible to know from this information whether this is due to data buffering or system processing delay.

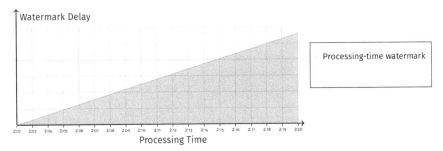

Figure 3-13. Processing-time watermark also increasing. This indicates that the system processing is delayed.

In the first case (Figure 3-12), when we examine the processing-time watermark delay we see that it too is increasing. This tells us that an operation in our system is stuck, and the stuckness is also causing the data delay to fall behind. Some real-world examples of situations in which this might occur are when there is a network issue preventing message delivery between stages of a pipeline or if a failure has occurred and is being retried. In general, a growing processing-time watermark indicates a problem that is preventing operations from completing that are necessary to the system's function, and often involves user or administrator intervention to resolve.

In this second case, as seen in Figure 3-14, the processing-time watermark delay is small. This tells us that there are no stuck operations. The event-time watermark delay is still increasing, which indicates that we have some buffered state that we are waiting to drain. This is possible, for example, if we are buffering some state while waiting for a window boundary to emit an aggregation, and corresponds to a normal operation of the pipeline, as in Figure 3-15.

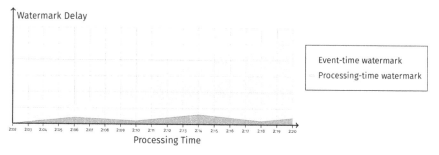

Figure 3-14. Event-time watermark delay increasing, processing-time watermark stable. This is an indication that data are buffered in the system and waiting to be processed, rather than an indication that a system operation is preventing data processing from completing.

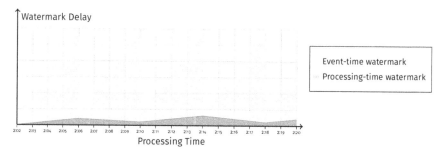

Figure 3-15. Watermark delay for fixed windows. The event-time watermark delay increases as elements are buffered for each window, and decreases as each window's aggregate is emitted via an on-time trigger, whereas the processing-time watermark simply tracks system-level delays (which remain relatively steady in a healthy pipeline).

Therefore, the processing-time watermark is a useful tool in distinguishing system latency from data latency. In addition to visibility, we can use the processing-time watermark at the system-implementation level for tasks such as garbage collection of temporary state (Reuven talks more about an example of this in Chapter 5).

Case Studies

Now that we've laid the groundwork for how watermarks ought to behave, it's time to take a look at some real systems to understand how different mechanisms of the watermark are implemented. We hope that these shed some light on the trade-offs that are possible between latency and correctness as well as scalability and availability for watermarks in real-world systems.

Case Study: Watermarks in Google Cloud Dataflow

There are many possible approaches to implementing watermarks in a stream processing system. Here, we present a quick survey of the implementation in Google Cloud Dataflow, a fully managed service for executing Apache Beam pipelines on Google Cloud Platform resources.

Dataflow stripes (shards) each of the data processing steps in its data processing graph across multiple physical workers by splitting the available keyspace of each stage into key ranges and assigning each range to a worker. Whenever a GroupByKey operation with distinct keys is encountered, data must be shuffled to corresponding keys.

Figure 3-16 depicts a logical representation of the processing graph with a GroupBy Key.

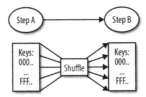

Figure 3-16. A GroupByKey step consumes data from another DoFn. This means that there is a data shuffle between the keys of the first step and the keys of the second step.

Whereas the physical assignment of key ranges to workers might look like Figure 3-17.

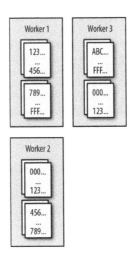

Figure 3-17. Key ranges of both steps are assigned (striped) across the available workers.

In the watermark propagation section, we discussed that the watermark is maintained for multiple subcomponents of each step. Dataflow keeps track of the per-range watermarks of each of these components. Watermark aggregation then involves computing the minimum of each watermark across all ranges, ensuring that the following guarantees are met:

- All ranges must be reporting a watermark. If a watermark is not present for a range, we cannot advance the watermark, because a range not reporting must be treated as unknown.

- Ensure that the watermark is monotonically increasing. Because late data is possible, we must not update the watermark if it would cause the watermark to move backward.

Google Cloud Dataflow performs aggregation via a centralized aggregator agent. We can shard this agent for efficiency. From a correctness standpoint, the watermark aggregator serves as a "single source of truth" about the watermark.

Ensuring correctness in distributed watermark aggregation poses certain challenges. It is paramount that watermarks are not advanced prematurely because advancing the watermark prematurely will turn on-time data into late data. Specifically, as physical assignments are actuated to workers, the workers maintain leases on the persistent state attached to the key ranges, ensuring that only a single worker may mutate the persistent state for a key. To guarantee watermark correctness, we must ensure that each watermark update from a worker process is admitted into the aggregate only if the worker process still maintains a lease on its persistent state; therefore, the watermark update protocol must take state ownership lease validation into account.

Case Study: Watermarks in Apache Flink

Apache Flink is an open source stream processing framework for distributed, high-performing, always-available, and accurate data streaming applications. It is possible to run Beam programs using a Flink runner. In doing so, Beam relies on the implementation of stream processing concepts such as watermarks within Flink. Unlike Google Cloud Dataflow, which implements watermark aggregation via a centralized watermark aggregator agent, Flink performs watermark tracking and aggregation in-band.[6]

To understand how this works, let's look at a Flink pipeline, as shown in Figure 3-18.

---

6 For more information on Flink watermarks, see the Flink documentation on the subject. (*https://ci.apache.org/projects/flink/flink-docs-release-1.3/dev/event_time.html*)

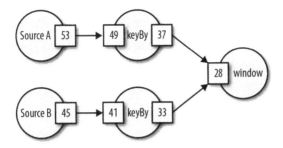

Figure 3-18. A Flink pipeline with two sources and event-time watermarks propagating in-band

In this pipeline data is generated at two sources. These sources also both generate watermark "checkpoints" that are sent synchronously in-band with the data stream. This means that when a watermark checkpoint from source A for timestamp "53" is emitted, it guarantees that no nonlate data messages will be emitted from source A with timestamp behind "53". The downstream "keyBy" operators consume the input data and the watermark checkpoints. As new watermark checkpoints are consumed, the downstream operators' view of the watermark is advanced, and a new watermark checkpoint for downstream operators can be emitted.

This choice to send watermark checkpoints in-band with the data stream differs from the Cloud Dataflow approach that relies on central aggregation and leads to a few interesting trade-offs.

Following are some advantages of in-band watermarks:

Reduced watermark propagation latency, and very low-latency watermarks
  Because it is not necessary to have watermark data traverse multiple hops and await central aggregation, it is possible to achieve very low latency more easily with the in-band approach.

No single point of failure for watermark aggregation
  Unavailability in the central watermark aggregation agent will lead to a delay in watermarks across the entire pipeline. With the in-band approach, unavailability of part of the pipeline cannot cause watermark delay to the entire pipeline.

Inherent scalability
  Although Cloud Dataflow scales well in practice, more complexity is needed to achieve scalability with a centralized watermark aggregation service versus implicit scalability with in-band watermarks.

Here are some advantages of out-of-band watermark aggregation:

Single source of "truth"
> For debuggability, monitoring, and other applications such as throttling inputs based on pipeline progress, it is advantageous to have a service that can vend the values of watermarks rather than having watermarks implicit in the streams, with each component of the system having its own partial view.

Source watermark creation
> Some source watermarks require global information. For example, sources might be temprarily idle, have low data rates, or require out-of-band information about the source or other system components to generate the watermarks. This is easier to achieve in a central service. For an example see the case study that follows on source watermarks for Google Cloud Pub/Sub.

Case Study: Source Watermarks for Google Cloud Pub/Sub

Google Cloud Pub/Sub is a fully managed real-time messaging service that allows you to send and receive messages between independent applications. Here, we discuss how to create a reasonable heuristic watermark for data sent into a pipeline via Cloud Pub/Sub.

First, we need to describe a little about how Pub/Sub works. Messages are published on Pub/Sub *topics*. A particular topic can be subscribed to by any number of Pub/Sub *subscriptions*. The same messages are delivered on all subscriptions subscribed to a given topic. The method of delivery is for clients to *pull* messages off the subscription, and to ack the receipt of particular messages via provided IDs. Clients do not get to choose which messages are pulled, although Pub/Sub does attempt to provide oldest messages first, with no hard guarantees around this.

To build a heuristic, we make some assumptions about the source that is sending data into Pub/Sub. Specifically, we assume that the timestamps of the original data are "well behaved"; in other words, we expect a bounded amount of out-of-order time-stamps on the source data, before it is sent to Pub/Sub. Any data that are sent with timestamps outside the allowed out-of-order bounds will be considered late data. In our current implementation, this bound is at least 10 seconds, meaning reordering of timestamps up to 10 seconds before sending to Pub/Sub will not create late data. We call this value the *estimation band*. Another way to look at this is that when the pipe-pline is perfectly caught up with the input, the watermark will be 10 seconds behind real time to allow for possible reorderings from the source. If the pipeline is backlog-ged, all of the backlog (not just the 10-second band) is used for estimating the water-mark.

What are the challenges we face with Pub/Sub? Because Pub/Sub does not guarantee ordering, we must have some kind of additional metadata to know enough about the backlog. Luckily, Pub/Sub provides a measurement of backlog in terms of the "oldest unacknowledged publish timestamp." This is not the same as the event timestamp of our message, because Pub/Sub is agnostic to the application-level metadata being sent through it; instead, this is the timestamp of when the message was ingested by Pub/Sub.

This measurement is not the same as an event-time watermark. It is in fact the processing-time watermark for Pub/Sub message delivery. The Pub/Sub publish timestamps are not equal to the event timestamps, and in the case that historical (past) data are being sent, it might be arbitrarily far away. The ordering on these time-stamps might also be different because, as mentioned earlier, we allow a limited amount of reordering.

However, we can use this as a measure of backlog to learn enough information about the event timestamps present in the backlog so that we can create a reasonable water-mark as follows.

We create two subscriptions to the topic containing the input messages: a *base sub-scription* that the pipeline will actually use to read the data to be processed, and a *tracking subscription*, which is used for metadata only, to perform the watermark esti-mation.

Taking a look at our base subscription in Figure 3-19, we see that messages might arrive out of order. We label each message with its Pub/Sub publish timestamp "pt" and its event-time timestamp "et." Note that the two time domains can be unrelated.

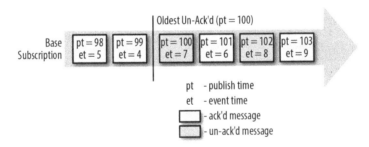

Figure 3-19. Processing-time and event-time timestamps of messages arriving on a Pub/Sub subscription

Some messages on the base subscription are unacknowledged forming a backlog. This might be due to them not yet being delivered or they might have been delivered but not yet processed. Remember also that pulls from this subscription are dis-tributed across multiple shards. Thus, it is not possible to say just by looking at the base subscription what our watermark should be.

The tracking subscription, seen in Figure 3-20, is used to effectively inspect the backlog of the base subscription and take the minimum of the event timestamps in the backlog. By maintaining little or no backlog on the tracking subscription, we can inspect the messages ahead of the base subsciption's oldest unacknowledged message.

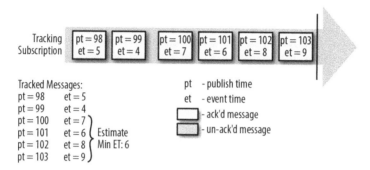

Figure 3-20. An additional "tracking" subscription receiving the same messages as the "base" subscription

We stay caught up on the tracking subscription by ensuring that pulling from this subscription is computationally inexpensive. Conversely, if we fall sufficiently behind on the tracking subscription, we will stop advancing the watermark. To do so, we ensure that at least one of the following conditions is met:

- The tracking subscription is sufficiently ahead of the base subscription. Sufficiently ahead means that the tracking subscription is ahead by at least the estimation band. This ensures that any bounded reorder within the estimation band is taken into account.

- The tracking subscription is sufficiently close to real time. In other words, there is no backlog on the tracking subscription.

We acknowledge the messages on the tracking subscription as soon as possible, after we have durably saved metadata about the publish and event timestamps of the messages. We store this metadata in a sparse histogram format to minimize the amount of space used and the size of the durable writes.

Finally, we ensure that we have enough data to make a reasonable watermark estimate. We take a band of event timestamps we've read from our tracking subscription with publish timestamps newer than the oldest unacknowledged of the base subscription, or the width of the estimation band. This ensures that we consider all event timestamps in the backlog, or if the backlog is small, the most recent estimation band, to make a watermark estimate.

Finally, the watermark value is computed to be the minimum event time in the band.

This method is correct in the sense that all timestamps within the reordering limit of 10 seconds at the input will be accounted for by the watermark and not appear as late data. However, it produces possibly an overly conservative watermark, one that advances "too slowly" in the sense described in Chapter 2. Because we consider all messages ahead of the base subscription's oldest unacknowledged message on the tracking subscription, we can include event timestamps in the watermark estimate for messages that have already been acknowledged.

Additionally, there are a few heuristics to ensure progress. This method works well in the case of dense, frequently arriving data. In the case of sparse or infrequent data, there might not be enough recent messages to build a reasonable estimate. In the case that we have not seen data on the subscription in more than two minutes (and there's no backlog), we advance the watermark to near real time. This ensures that the watermark and the pipeline continue to make progress even if no more messages are forthcoming.

All of the above ensures that as long as source data-event timestamp reordering is within the estimation band, there will be no additional late data.

Summary

At this point, we have explored how we can use the event times of messages to give a robust definition of progress in a stream processing system. We saw how this notion of progress can subsequently help us answer the question of *where* in event time processing is taking place and *when* in processing time results are materialized. Specifically, we looked at how watermarks are created at the sources, the points of data ingestion into a pipeline, and then propagated throughout the pipeline to preserve the essential guarantees that allow the questions of *where* and *when* to be answered. We also looked at the implications of changing the output window timestamps on watermarks. Finally, we explored some real-world system considerations when building watermarks at scale.

Now that we have a firm footing in how watermarks work under the covers, we can take a dive into what they can do for us as we use windowing and triggering to answer more complex queries in Chapter 4.

CHAPTER 4

Advanced Windowing

Hello again! I hope you enjoyed Chapter 3 as much as I did. Watermarks are a fascinating topic, and Slava knows them better than anyone on the planet. Now that we have a deeper understanding of watermarks under our belts, I'd like to dive into some more advanced topics related to the *what*, *where*, *when*, and *how* questions.

We first look at *processing-time windowing*, which is an interesting mix of both where and when, to understand better how it relates to event-time windowing and get a sense for times when it's actually the right approach to take. We then dive into some more advanced event-time windowing concepts, looking at *session windows* in detail, and finally making a case for why generalized *custom windowing* is a useful (and surprisingly straightforward) concept by exploring three different types of custom windows: *unaligned* fixed windows, *per-key* fixed windows, and *bounded* sessions windows.

When/*Where*: Processing-Time Windows

Processing-time windowing is important for two reasons:

- For certain use cases, such as usage monitoring (e.g., web service traffic QPS), for which you want to analyze an incoming stream of data as it's observed, processing-time windowing is absolutely the appropriate approach to take.
- For use cases for which the time that events happened is important (e.g., analyzing user behavior trends, billing, scoring, etc.), processing-time windowing is absolutely the wrong approach to take, and being able to recognize these cases is critical.

As such, it's worth gaining a solid understanding of the differences between processing-time windowing and event-time windowing, particularly given the prevalence of processing-time windowing in many streaming systems today.

When working within a model for which windowing as a first-class notion is strictly event-time based, such as the one presented in this book, there are two methods that you can use to achieve processing-time windowing:

Triggers

> Ignore event time (i.e., use a global window spanning all of event time) and use triggers to provide snapshots of that window in the processing-time axis.

Ingress time

> Assign ingress times as the event times for data as they arrive, and use normal event-time windowing from there on. This is essentially what something like Spark Streaming 1.x does.

Note that the two methods are more or less equivalent, although they differ slightly in the case of multistage pipelines: in the triggers version, a multistage pipeline will slice the processing-time "windows" independently at each stage, so, for example, data in window N for one stage might instead end up in window $N-1$ or $N+1$ in the following stage; in the ingress-time version, after a datum is incorporated into window N, it will remain in window N for the duration of the pipeline due to synchronization of progress between stages via watermarks (in the Cloud Dataflow case), microbatch boundaries (in the Spark Streaming case), or whatever other coordinating factor is involved at the engine level.

As I've noted to death, the big downside of processing-time windowing is that the contents of the windows change when the observation order of the inputs changes. To drive this point home in a more concrete manner, we're going to look at these three use cases: *event-time* windowing, *processing-time* windowing via triggers, and *processing-time* windowing via ingress time.

Each will be applied to two different input sets (so six variations total). The two inputs sets will be for the exact same events (i.e., same values, occurring at the same event times), but with different observation orders. The first set will be the observation order we've seen all along, colored gray; the second one will have all the values shifted in the processing-time axis as in Figure 4-1, colored purple. You can simply imagine that the purple example is another way reality could have happened if the winds had been blowing in from the east instead of the west (i.e., the underlying set of complex distributed systems had played things out in a slightly different order).

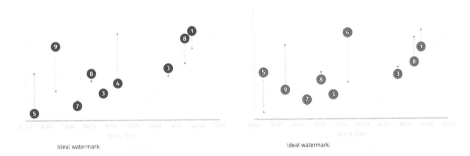

Ideal watermark: Ideal watermark:

Figure 4-1. Shifting input observation order in processing time, holding values, and event-times constant (http://streamingbook.net/fig/4-1)

Event-Time Windowing

To establish a baseline, let's first compare fixed windowing in event time with a heuristic watermark over these two observation orderings. We'll reuse the early/late code from Example 2-7/Figure 2-10 to get the results shown in Figure 4-2. The lefthand side is essentially what we saw before; the righthand side is the results over the second observation order. The important thing to note here is that even though the overall shape of the outputs differs (due to the different orders of observation in processing time), *the final results for the four windows remain the same*: 14, 18, 4, and 12.

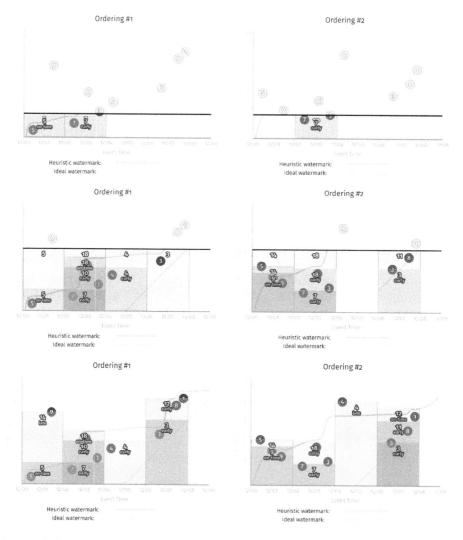

Figure 4-2. Event-time windowing over two different processing-time orderings of the same inputs (http://streamingbook.net/fig/4-2)

Processing-Time Windowing via Triggers

Let's now compare this to the two processing-time methods just described. First, we'll try the triggers method. There are three aspects to making processing-time "windowing" work in this manner:

Windowing

We use the global event-time window because we're essentially emulating processing-time windows with event-time panes.

Triggering

We trigger periodically in the processing-time domain based on the desired size of the processing-time windows.

Accumulation

We use discarding mode to keep the panes independent from one another, thus letting each of them act like an independent processing-time "window."

The corresponding code looks something like Example 4-1; note that global windowing is the default in Beam, hence there is no specific override of the windowing strategy.

Example 4-1. Processing-time windowing via repeated, discarding panes of a global event-time window

```
PCollection<KV<Team, Integer>> totals = input
  .apply(Window.triggering(Repeatedly(AlignedDelay(TWO_MINUTES)))
              .discardingFiredPanes())
  .apply(Sum.integersPerKey());
```

When executed on a streaming runner against our two different orderings of the input data, the results look like Figure 4-3. Here are some interesting notes about this figure:

- Because we're emulating processing-time windows via event-time panes, the "windows" are delineated in the processing-time axis, which means their effective width is measured on the y-axis instead of the x-axis.

- Because processing-time windowing is sensitive to the order that input data are encountered, the results for each of the "windows" differs for each of the two observation orders, even though the events themselves technically happened at the same times in each version. On the left we get 12, 18, 18, whereas on the right we get 7, 36, 5.

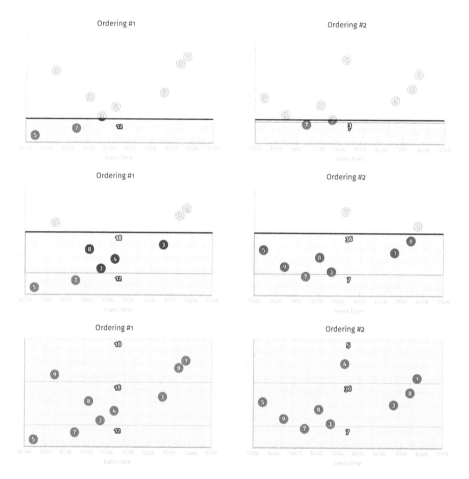

Figure 4-3. Processing-time "windowing" via triggers, over two different processing-time orderings of the same inputs (http://streamingbook.net/fig/4-3)

Processing-Time Windowing via Ingress Time

Lastly, let's look at processing-time windowing achieved by mapping the event times of input data to be their ingress times. Code-wise, there are four aspects worth mentioning here:

Time-shifting

When elements arrive, their event times need to be overwritten with the time of ingress. We can do this in Beam by providing a new DoFn that sets the timestamp of the element to the current time via the outputWithTimestamp method.

Windowing

Return to using standard event-time fixed windowing.

Triggering

Because ingress time affords the ability to calculate a perfect watermark, we can use the default trigger, which in this case implicitly fires exactly once when the watermark passes the end of the window.

Accumulation mode

Because we only ever have one output per window, the accumulation mode is irrelevant.

The actual code might thus look something like that in Example 4-2.

Example 4-2. Processing-time windowing via repeated, discarding panes of a global event-time window

```
PCollection<String> raw = IO.read().apply(ParDo.of(
  new DoFn<String, String>() {
    public void processElement(ProcessContext c) {
      c.outputWithTimestmap(new Instant());
    }
  });
PCollection<KV<Team, Integer>> input =
  raw.apply(ParDo.of(new ParseFn()));
PCollection<KV<Team, Integer>> totals = input
  .apply(Window.info(FixedWindows.of(TWO_MINUTES))
  .apply(Sum.integersPerKey());
```

Execution on a streaming engine would look like Figure 4-4. As data arrive, their event times are updated to match their ingress times (i.e., the processing times at arrival), resulting in a rightward horizontal shift onto the ideal watermark line. Here are some interesting notes about this figure:

- As with the other processing-time windowing example, we get different results when the ordering of inputs changes, even though the values and event times for the input stay constant.

- Unlike the other example, the windows are once again delineated in the event-time domain (and thus along the x-axis). Despite this, they aren't bonafide event-time windows; we've simply mapped processing time onto the event-time domain, erasing the original record of occurrence for each input and replacing it with a new one that instead represents the time the datum was first observed by the pipeline.

- Despite this, thanks to the watermark, trigger firings still happen at exactly the same time as in the previous processing-time example. Furthermore, the output values produced are identical to that example, as predicted: 12, 18, 18 on the left, and 7, 36, 5 on the right.

- Because perfect watermarks are possible when using ingress time, the actual watermark matches the ideal watermark, ascending up and to the right with a slope of one.

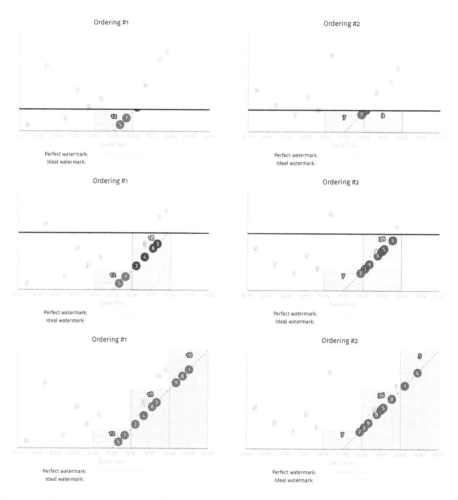

Figure 4-4. Processing-time windowing via the use of ingress time, over two different processing-time orderings of the same inputs (http://streamingbook.net/fig/4-4)

Although it's interesting to see the different ways you can implement processing-time windowing, the big takeaway here is the one I've been harping on since the first chapter: event-time windowing is order-agnostic, at least in the limit (actual panes along the way might differ until the input becomes complete); processing-time windowing is not. *If you care about the times at which your events actually happened, you must use event-time windowing or your results will be meaningless.* I will get off my soapbox now.

Where: Session Windows

Enough with processing-time windowing. Let's now go back to tried-and-true event-time windowing, but now we're going to look at one of my favorite features: the dynamic, data-driven windows called *sessions*.

Sessions are a special type of window that captures a period of activity in the data that is terminated by a gap of inactivity. They're particularly useful in data analysis because they can provide a view of the activities for a specific user over a specific period of time during which they were engaged in some activity. This allows for the correlation of activities within the session, drawing inferences about levels of engagement based on the lengths of the sessions, and so on.

From a windowing perspective, sessions are particularly interesting in two ways:

- They are an example of a *data-driven window*: the location and sizes of the windows are a direct consequence of the input data themselves, rather than being based on some predefined pattern within time, as are fixed and sliding windows.

- They are also an example of an *unaligned window*; that is, a window that does not apply uniformly across the data, but instead only to a specific subset of the data (e.g., per user). This is in contrast to aligned windows like fixed and sliding windows, which typically apply uniformly across the data.

For some use cases, it's possible to tag the data within a single session with a common identifier ahead of time (e.g., a video player that emits heartbeat pings with quality-of-service information; for any given viewing, all of the pings can be tagged ahead of time with a single session ID). In this case, sessions are much easier to construct because it's basically just a form of grouping by key.

However, in the more general case (i.e., where the actual session itself is not known ahead of time), the sessions must be constructed from the locations of the data within time alone. When dealing with out-of-order data, this becomes particularly tricky.

Figure 4-5 shows an example of this, with five independent records grouped together into session windows with a gap timeout of 60 minutes. Each record starts out in a 60-minute window of its own (a proto-session). Merging together overlapping proto-sessions yields the two larger session windows containing three and two records, respectively.

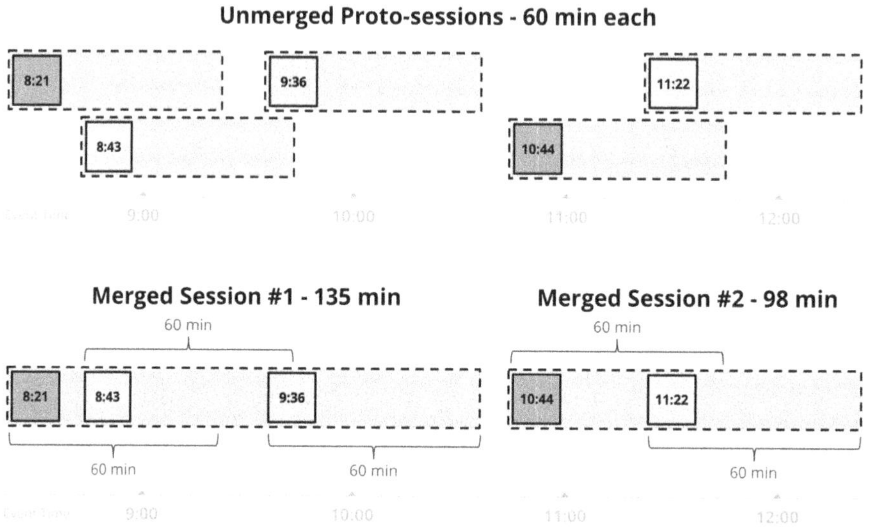

| 8:21 | | 9:36 | | 11:22 |
| 8:43 | | | 10:44 | |

9:00   10:00   11:00   12:00

Merged Session #1 - 135 min

60 min

| 8:21 | 8:43 | | 9:36 |

60 min   60 min

Merged Session #2 - 98 min

60 min

| 10:44 | | 11:22 |

60 min

9:00   10:00   11:00   12:00

Figure 4-5. Unmerged proto-session windows, and the resultant merged sessions

They key insight in providing general session support is that a complete session window is, by definition, a composition of a set of smaller, overlapping windows, each containing a single record, with each record in the sequence separated from the next by a gap of inactivity no larger than a predefined timeout. Thus, even if we observe the data in the session out of order, we can build up the final session simply by merging together any overlapping windows for individual data as they arrive.

To look at this another way, consider the example we've been using so far. If we specify a session timeout of one minute, we would expect to identify two sessions in the data, delineated in Figure 4-6 by the dashed black lines. Each of those sessions captures a burst of activity from the user, with each event in the session separate by less than one minute from at least one other event in the session.

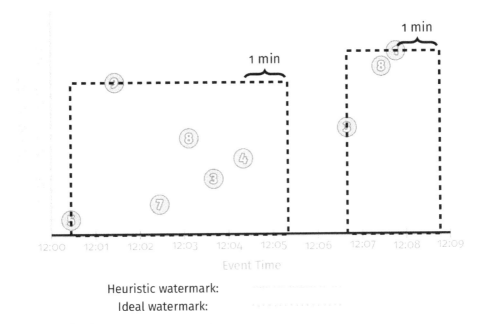

Heuristic watermark:
Ideal watermark:

Figure 4-6. Sessions we want to compute

To see how the window merging works to build up these sessions over time as events are encountered, let's look at it in action. We'll take the early/late code with retractions enabled from Example 2-10 and update the windowing to build sessions with a one-minute gap duration timeout instead. Example 4-3 illustrates what this looks like.

Example 4-3. Early/on-time/late firings with session windows and retractions

```
PCollection<KV<Team, Integer>> totals = input
  .apply(Window.into(Sessions.withGapDuration(ONE_MINUTE))
              .triggering(
                AfterWatermark()
                  .withEarlyFirings(AlignedDelay(ONE_MINUTE))
                  .withLateFirings(AfterCount(1)))
              .accumulatingAndRetractingFiredPanes())
  .apply(Sum.integersPerKey());
```

Executed on a streaming engine, you'd get something like that shown in Figure 4-7 (note that I've left in the dashed black lines annotating the expected final sessions for reference).

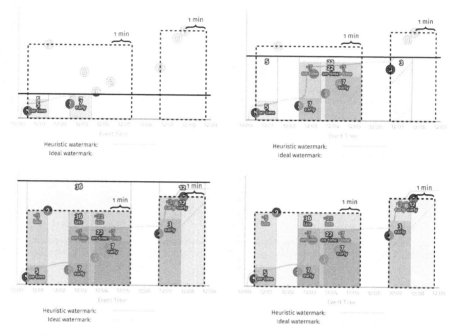

Figure 4-7. Early and late firings with session windows and retractions on a streaming engine (http://streamingbook.net/fig/4-7)

There's quite a lot going on here, so I'll walk you through some of it:

- When the first record with value 5 is encountered, it's placed into a single proto-session window that begins at that record's event time and spans the width of the session gap duration; for example, one minute beyond the point at which that datum occurred. Any windows we encounter in the future that overlap this window should be part of the same session and will be merged into it as such.

- The second record to arrive is the 7, which similarly is placed into its own proto-session window, given that it doesn't overlap with the window for the 5.

- In the meantime, the watermark has passed the end of the first window, so the value of 5 is materialized as an on-time result just before 12:06. Shortly thereafter, the second window is also materialized as a speculative result with value 7, right as processing time hits 12:06.

- We next observe a pair of records 3 and 4, the proto-sessions for which overlap. As a result, they are merged together, and by the time the early trigger for 12:07 fires, a single window with value 7 is emitted.

- When the 8 arrives shortly thereafter, it overlaps with both of the windows with value 7. All three are thus merged together, forming a new combined session with value 22. When the watermark then passes the end of this session, it materializes both the new session with value 22 as well as retractions for the two windows of value 7 that were previously emitted, but later incorporated into it.

- A similar dance occurs when the 9 arrives late, joining the proto-session with value 5 and session with value 22 into a single larger session of value 36. The 36 and the retractions for the 5 and 22 windows are all emitted immediately by the late data trigger.

This is some pretty powerful stuff. And what's really awesome is how easy it is to describe something like this within a model that breaks apart the dimensions of stream processing into distinct, composable pieces. In the end, you can focus more on the interesting business logic at hand, and less on the minutiae of shaping the data into some usable form.

If you don't believe me, check out this blog post describing how to manually build up sessions on Spark Streaming 1.x (*http://bit.ly/2sXe3vJ*) (note that this is not done to point fingers at them; the Spark folks had just done a good enough job with everything else that someone actually bothered to go to the trouble of documenting what it takes to build a specific variety of sessions support on top of Spark 1.x; you can't say the same for most other systems out there). It's quite involved, and they're not even doing proper event-time sessions, or providing speculative or late firings, or retractions.

Where: Custom Windowing

Up until now, we've talked primarily about predefined types of windowing strategies: fixed, sliding, and sessions. You can get a lot of mileage out of standard types of windows, but there are plenty of real-world use cases for which being able to define a custom windowing strategy can really save the day (three of which we're about to see now).

Most systems today don't support custom windowing to the degree that it's supported in Beam,[1] so we focus on the Beam approach. In Beam, a custom windowing strategy consists of two things:

Window assignment
    This places each element into an initial window. At the limit, this allows every element to be placed within a unique window, which is very powerful.

---

1 As far as I know, Apache Flink is the only other system to support custom windowing to the extent that Beam does. And to be fair, its support extends even beyond that of Beam's, thanks to the ability to provide a custom window evictor. Head asplode.

(Optional) window merging

This allows windows to merge at grouping times, which makes it possible for windows to evolve over time, which we saw in action earlier with session windows.

To give you a sense for how simple windowing strategies really are, and also how useful custom windows support can be, we're going to look in detail at the stock implementations of fixed windows and sessions in Beam and then consider a few real-world use cases that require custom variations on those themes. In the process, we'll see both how easy it is to create a custom windowing strategy, and how limiting the lack of custom windowing support can be when your use case doesn't quite fit into the stock approaches.

Variations on Fixed Windows

To begin, let's look at the relatively simple strategy of fixed windows. The stock fixed-windows implementation is as straightforward as you might imagine, and consists of the following logic:

Assignment

The element is placed into the appropriate fixed-window based on its timestamp and the window's size and offset parameters.

Merging

None.

An abbreviated version of the code looks like Example 4-4.

Example 4-4. Abbreviated FixedWindows implementation

```
public class FixedWindows extends WindowFn<Object, IntervalWindow> {
  private final Duration size;
  private final Duration offset;
  public Collection<IntervalWindow> assignWindow(AssignContext c) {
    long start = c.timestamp().getMillis() - c.timestamp()
                    .plus(size)
                    .minus(offset)
                    .getMillis() % size.getMillis();
    return Arrays.asList(IntervalWindow(new Instant(start), size));
  }
}
```

Keep in mind that the point of showing you the code here isn't so much to teach you how to write windowing strategies (although it's nice to demystify them and call out how simple they are). It's really to help contrast the comparative ease and difficulty of supporting some relatively basic use cases, both with and without custom windowing, respectively. Let's consider two such use cases that are variations on the fixed-windows theme now.

Unaligned fixed windows

One characteristic of the default fixed-windows implementation that we alluded to previously is that windows are aligned across all of the data. In our running example, the window from noon to 1 PM for any given team aligns with the corresponding windows for all other teams, which also extend from noon to 1 PM. And in use cases for which you want to compare like windows across another dimension, such as between teams, this alignment is very useful. However, it comes at a somewhat subtle cost. All of the active windows from noon to 1 PM become complete at around the same time, which means that once an hour the system is hit with a massive load of windows to materialize.

To see what I mean, let's look at a concrete example (Example 4-5). We'll begin with a score summation pipeline as we've used in most examples, with fixed two-minute windows, and a single watermark trigger.

Example 4-5. Watermark completeness trigger (same as Example 2-6)

```
PCollection<KV<Team, Integer>> totals = input
  .apply(Window.into(FixedWindows.of(TWO_MINUTES))
               .triggering(AfterWatermark()))
  .apply(Sum.integersPerKey());
```

But in this instance, we'll look at two different keys (see Figure 4-8) from the same dataset in parallel. What we'll see is that the outputs for those two keys are all aligned, on account of the windows being aligned across all of the keys. As a result, we end up with N panes being materialized every time the watermark passes the end of a window, where N is the number of keys with updates in that window. In this example, where N is 2, that's maybe not too painful. But when N starts to order in the thousands, millions, or more, that synchronized burstiness can become problematic.

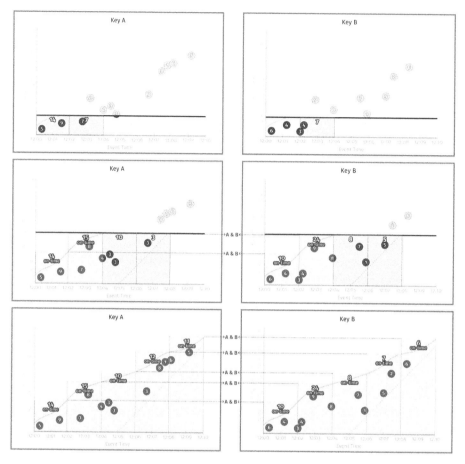

Figure 4-8. Aligned fixed windows (http://streamingbook.net/fig/4-8)

In circumstances for which comparing across windows is unnecessary, it's often more desirable to spread window completion load out evenly across time. This makes system load more predictable, which can reduce the provisioning requirements for handling peak load. In most systems, however, unaligned fixed windows are only available if the system provides support for them out of the box.[2] But with custom-windowing support, it's a relatively trivial modification to the default fixed-windows implementation to provide unaligned fixed-windows support. What we want to do is continue guaranteeing that the windows for all elements being grouped together (i.e., the ones with the same key) have the same alignment, while relaxing the alignment

---

2 And I'm not actually aware of any such systems at this time.

restriction across different keys. The code changes to the default fixed-windowing strategy and looks something like Example 4-6.

Example 4-6. Abbreviated UnalignedFixedWindows implementation

```
public class UnalignedFixedWindows
    extends WindowFn<KV<K, V>, IntervalWindow> {
  private final Duration size;
  private final Duration offset;
  public Collection<IntervalWindow> assignWindow(AssignContext c) {
    long perKeyShift = hash(c.element().key()) % size.getMillis();
    long start = perKeyShift + c.timestamp().getMillis()
                    - c.timestamp()
                      .plus(size)
                      .minus(offset)
                      .getMillis() % size.getMillis();
    return Arrays.asList(IntervalWindow(new Instant(start), size));
  }
}
```

With this change, the windows for all elements *with the same key* are aligned,[3] but the windows for elements *with different keys* will (typically) be unaligned, thus spreading window completion load out at the cost of also making comparisons across keys somewhat less meaningful. We can switch our pipeline to use our new windowing strategy, illustrated in Example 4-7.

Example 4-7. Unaligned fixed windows with a single watermark trigger

```
PCollection<KV<Team, Integer>> totals = input
  .apply(Window.into(UnalignedFixedWindows.of(TWO_MINUTES))
            .triggering(AfterWatermark()))
  .apply(Sum.integersPerKey());
```

And then you can see what this looks like in Figure 4-9 by comparing different fixed-window alignments across the same dataset as before (in this case, I've chosen a maximal phase shift between the two alignments to most clearly call out the benefits, given that randomly chosen phases across a large number of keys will result in similar effects).

---

3 This naturally implies the use of keyed data, but because windowing is intrinsically tied to grouping by key anyway, that restriction isn't particularly burdensome.

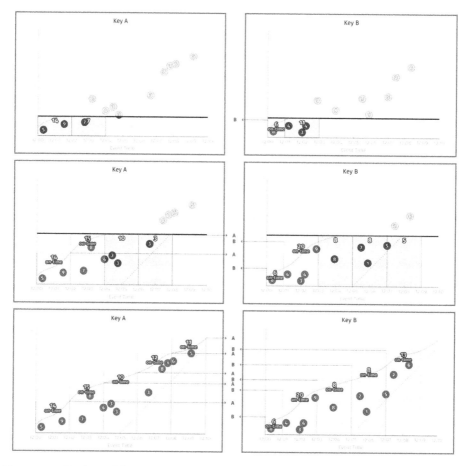

Figure 4-9. Unaligned fixed windows (http://streamingbook.net/fig/4-9)

Note how there are no instances where we emit multiple panes for multiple keys simultaneously. Instead, the panes arrive individually at a much more even cadence. This is another example of being able to make trade-offs in one dimension (ability to compare across keys) in exchange for benefits in another dimension (reduced peak resource provisioning requirements) when the use case allows. Such flexibility is critical when you're trying to process massive quantities of data as efficiently as possible.

Let's now look at a second variation on fixed windows, one which is more intrinsically tied to the data being processed.

Per-element/key fixed windows

Our second example comes courtesy of one of the early adopters of Cloud Dataflow. This company generates analytics data for its customers, but each customer is allowed to configure the window size over which it wants to aggregate its metrics. In other words, each customer gets to define the specific size of its fixed windows.

Supporting a use case like this isn't too difficult as long the number of available window sizes is itself fixed. For example, you could imagine offering the option of choosing 30-minute, 60-minute, and 90-minute fixed windows and then running a separate pipeline (or fork of the pipeline) for each of those options. Not ideal, but not too horrible. However, that rapidly becomes intractable as the number of options increases, and in the limit of providing support for truly arbitrary window sizes (which is what this customer's use case required) is entirely impractical.

Fortunately, because each record the customer processes is already annotated with metadata describing the desired size of window for aggregation, supporting arbitrary, per-user fixed-window size was as simple as changing a couple of lines from the stock fixed-windows implementation, as demonstrated in Example 4-8.

Example 4-8. Modified (and abbreviated) FixedWindows implementation that supports per-element window sizes

```
public class PerElementFixedWindows<T extends HasWindowSize>
    extends WindowFn<T, IntervalWindow> {
  private final Duration offset;
  public Collection<IntervalWindow> assignWindow(AssignContext c) {
    long perElementSize = c.element().getWindowSize();
    long start = perKeyShift + c.timestamp().getMillis()
                 - c.timestamp()
                   .plus(size)
                   .minus(offset)
                   .getMillis() % size.getMillis();
    return Arrays.asList(IntervalWindow(
        new Instant(start), perElementSize));
  }
}
```

With this change, each element is assigned to a fixed window with the appropriate size, as dictated by metadata carried around in the element itself.[4] Changing the pipeline code to use this new strategy is again trivial, as shown in Example 4-9.

---

4 And it's not critical that the element itself know the window size; you could just as easily look up and cache the appropriate window size for whatever the desired dimension is; for example, per-user.

Example 4-9. Per-element fixed-window sizes with a single watermark trigger

```
PCollection<KV<Team, Integer>> totals = input
  .apply(Window.into(new PerElementFixedWindows())
              .triggering(AfterWatermark()))
  .apply(Sum.integersPerKey());
```

And then looking at this pipeline in action (Figure 4-10), it's easy to see that the elements for Key A all have two minutes as their window size, whereas the elements for Key B have one-minute window sizes.

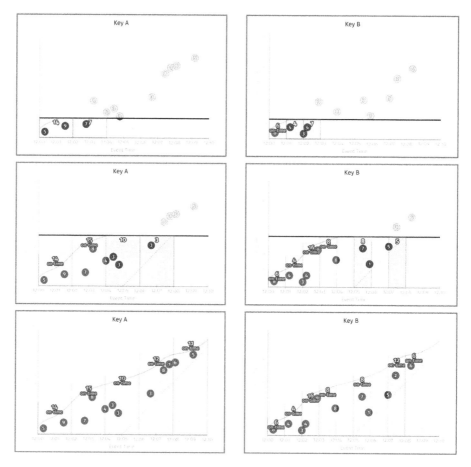

Figure 4-10. Per-key custom-sized fixed windows (http://streamingbook.net/fig/4-10)

This really isn't something you would ever reasonably expect a system to provide to you; the nature of where window size preferences are stored is too use-case specific for it to make sense to try to build into a standard API. Nevertheless, as exhibited by this customer's needs, use cases like this do exist. That's why the flexibility provided by custom windowing is so powerful.

Variations on Session Windows

To really drive home the usefulness of custom windowing, let's look at one final example, which is a variation on sessions. Session windowing is understandably a bit more complex than fixed windows. Its implementation consists of the following:

Assignment
> Each element is initially placed into a proto-session window that begins at the element's timestamp and extends for the gap duration.

Merging
> At grouping time, all eligible windows are sorted, after which any overlapping windows are merged together.

An abbreviated version of the sessions code (hand merged together from a number of helper classes) looks something like that shown in Example 4-10.

Example 4-10. Abbreviated Sessions implementation

```
public class Sessions extends WindowFn<Object, IntervalWindow> {
  private final Duration gapDuration;
  public Collection<IntervalWindow> assignWindows(AssignContext c) {
    return Arrays.asList(
      new IntervalWindow(c.timestamp(), gapDuration));
  }
  public void mergeWindows(MergeContext c) throws Exception {
    List<IntervalWindow> sortedWindows = new ArrayList<>();
    for (IntervalWindow window : c.windows()) {
      sortedWindows.add(window);
    }
    Collections.sort(sortedWindows);
    List<MergeCandidate> merges = new ArrayList<>();
    MergeCandidate current = new MergeCandidate();
    for (IntervalWindow window : sortedWindows) {
      if (current.intersects(window)) {
        current.add(window);
      } else {
        merges.add(current);
        current = new MergeCandidate(window);
      }
    }
    merges.add(current);
    for (MergeCandidate merge : merges) {
      merge.apply(c);
    }
```

```
        }
}
```

As before, the point of seeing the code isn't so much to teach you how custom windowing functions are implemented, or even what the implementation of sessions
looks like; it's really to show the ease with which you can support new use via custom
windowing.

Bounded sessions

One such custom use case I've come across multiple times is bounded sessions: sessions that are not allowed to grow beyond a certain size, either in time, element
count, or some other dimension. This can be for semantic reasons, or it can simply be
an exercise in spam protection. However, given the variations in types of limits (some
use cases care about total session size in event time, some care about total element
count, some care about element density, etc.), it's difficult to provide a clean and concise API for bounded sessions. Much more practical is allowing users to implement
their own custom windowing logic, tailored to their specific use case. An example of
one such use case, in which session windows are time-limited, might look something
like Example 4-11 (eliding some of the builder boilerplate we'll utilize here).

Example 4-11. Abbreviated Sessions implementation

```
public class BoundedSessions extends WindowFn<Object, IntervalWindow> {
  private final Duration gapDuration;
  private final Duration maxSize;
  public Collection<IntervalWindow> assignWindows(AssignContext c) {
    return Arrays.asList(
      new IntervalWindow(c.timestamp(), gapDuration));
  }
  private Duration windowSize(IntervalWindow window) {
    return window == null
      ? new Duration(0)
      : new Duration(window.start(), window.end());
  }
  public void mergeWindows(MergeContext c) throws Exception {
    List<IntervalWindow> sortedWindows = new ArrayList<>();
    for (IntervalWindow window : c.windows()) {
      sortedWindows.add(window);
    }
    Collections.sort(sortedWindows);
    List<MergeCandidate> merges = new ArrayList<>();
    MergeCandidate current = new MergeCandidate();
    for (IntervalWindow window : sortedWindows) {
      MergeCandidate next = new MergeCandidate(window);
      if (current.intersects(window)) {
        current.add(window);
        if (windowSize(current.union) <= (maxSize - gapDuration))
```

```
      continue;
    // Current window exceeds bounds, so flush and move to next
    next = new MergeCandidate();
  }
  merges.add(current);
  current = next;
}
merges.add(current);
for (MergeCandidate merge : merges) {
  merge.apply(c);
}
  }
}
}
```

As always, updating our pipeline (the early/on-time/late version of it, from Example 4-3, in this case) to use this custom windowing strategy is trivial, as you can see in Example 4-12.

Example 4-12. Early, on-time, and late firings via the early/on-time/late API

```
PCollection<KV<Team, Integer>> totals = input
  .apply(Window.into(BoundedSessions
                    .withGapDuration(ONE_MINUTE)
                    .withMaxSize(THREE_MINUTES))
              .triggering(
                AfterWatermark()
                  .withEarlyFirings(AlignedDelay(ONE_MINUTE))
                  .withLateFirings(AfterCount(1)))
              .accumulatingAndRetractingFiredPanes())
  .apply(Sum.integersPerKey());
```

And executed over our running example, it might then look something like Figure 4-11.

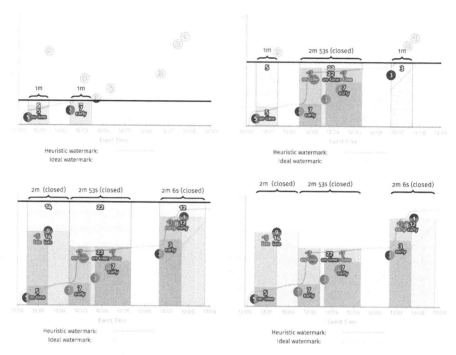

Figure 4-11. Session windows bounded to three minutes in length (http://streaming book.net/fig/4-11)

Note how the large session with value 36 that spanned [12:00.26, 12:05.20), or nearly five minutes of time, in the unbounded sessions implementation from Figure 4-7 now ends up broken apart into two shorter sessions of length 2 minutes and 2 minutes 53 seconds.

Given how few systems provide custom windowing support today, it's worth pointing out how much more effort would be required to implement such a thing using a system that supported only an unbounded sessions implementation. Your only real recourse would be to write code downstream of the session grouping logic that looked at the generated sessions and chopped them up if they exceed the length limit. This would require the ability to decompose a session after the fact, which would obviate the benefits of incremental aggregation (something we look at in more detail in Chapter 7), increasing cost. It would also eliminate any spam protection benefits one might hope to gain by limiting session lengths, because the sessions would first need to grow to their full sizes before being chopped or truncated.

One Size Does Not Fit All

We've now looked at three real-world use cases, each of which was a subtle variation on the stock types of windowing typically provided by data processing systems: unaligned fixed windows, per-element fixed windows, and bounded sessions. In all three cases, we saw how simple it was to support those use cases via custom windowing and how much more difficult (or expensive) it would be to support those use cases without it. Though custom windowing doesn't see broad support across the industry as yet, it's a feature that provides much needed flexibility for balancing trade-offs when building data processing pipelines that need to handle complex, real-world use cases over massive amounts of data as efficiently as possible.

Summary

Advanced windowing is a complex and varied topic. In this chapter, we covered three advanced concepts:

Processing-time windows
> We saw how this relates to event-time windowing, calling out the places where it's inherently useful and, most important, identifying those where it's not by specifically highlighting the stability of results that event-time windowing affords us.

Session windows
> We had our first introduction to the dynamic class of merging window strategies and seeing just how much heavy lifting the system does for us in providing such a powerful construct that you can simply drop into place.

Custom windows
> Here, we looked at three real-world examples of custom windows that are difficult or impossible to achieve in systems that provide only a static set of stock windowing strategies but relatively trivial to implement in a system with custom-windowing support:
>
> - *Unaligned fixed windows*, which provide a more even distribution of outputs over time when using a watermark trigger in conjunction with fixed windows.
>
> - *Per-element fixed windows*, which provide the flexibility to dynamically choose the size of fixed windows per element (e.g., to provide customizable per-user or per-ad-campaign window sizes), for greater customization of the pipeline semantics to the use case at hand.
>
> - *Bounded-session windows*, which limit how large a given session may grow; for example, to counteract spam attempts or to place a bound on the latency for completed sessions being materialized by the pipeline.

After deep diving through watermarks in Chapter 3 with Slava and taking a broad survey of advanced windowing here, we've now gone well beyond the basics of robust stream processing in multiple dimensions. With that, we conclude our focus on the Beam Model.

Up next is Reuven's Chapter 5 on consistency guarantees, exactly-once processing, and side effects, after which we begin our journey into Part II, *Streams and Tables* with Chapter 6.

Exactly-Once and Side Effects

We now shift from discussing programming models and APIs to the systems that implement them. A model and API allows users to describe what they want to compute. Actually running the computation accurately at scale requires a system—usually a distributed system.

In this chapter, we focus on how an implementing system can correctly implement the Beam Model to produce accurate results. Streaming systems often talk about *exactly-once processing*; that is, ensuring that every record is processed exactly one time. We will explain what we mean by this, and how it might be implemented.

As a motivating example, this chapter focuses on techniques used by Google Cloud Dataflow to efficiently guarantee exactly-once processing of records. Toward the end of the chapter, we also look at techniques used by some other popular streaming systems to guarantee exactly once.

Why Exactly Once Matters

It almost goes without saying that for many users, any risk of dropped records or data loss in their data processing pipelines is unacceptable. Even so, historically many general-purpose streaming systems made no guarantees about record processing—all processing was "best effort" only. Other systems provided at-least-once guarantees, ensuring that records were always processed at least once, but records might be duplicated (and thus result in inaccurate aggregations); in practice, many such at-least-once systems performed aggregations in memory, and thus their aggregations could still be lost when machines crashed. These systems were used for low-latency, speculative results but generally could guarantee nothing about the veracity of these results.

As Chapter 1 points out, this led to a strategy that was coined the *Lambda Architecture*—run a streaming system to get fast, but inaccurate results. Sometime later (often after end of day), a batch system runs to get the correct answer. This works only if the data stream is replayable; however, this was true for enough data sources that this strategy proved viable. Nonetheless, many people who tried this experienced a number of issues with the Lambda Architecture:

Inaccuracy

Users tend to underestimate the impact of failures. They often assume that a small percentage of records will be lost or duplicated (often based on experiments they ran), and are shocked on that one bad day when 10% (or more!) of records are lost or are duplicated. In a sense, such systems provide only "half" a guarantee—and without a full one, anything is possible.

Inconsistency

The batch system used for the end-of-day calculation often has different data semantics than the streaming system. Getting the two pipelines to produce comparable results proved more difficult than initially thought.

Complexity

By definition, Lambda requires you to write and maintain two different codebases. You also must run and maintain two complex distributed systems, each with different failure modes. For anything but the simplest of pipelines, this quickly becomes overwhelming.

Unpredictability

In many use cases, end users will see streaming results that differ from the daily results by an uncertain amount, which can change randomly. In these cases, users will stop trusting the streaming data and wait for daily batch results instead, thus destroying the value of getting low-latency results in the first place.

Latency

Some business use cases *require* low-latency correct results, which the Lambda Architecture does not provide by design.

Fortunately, many Beam runners can do much better. In this chapter, we explain how exactly-once stream processing helps users count on accurate results and avoid the risk of data loss while relying on a single codebase and API. Because a variety of issues that can affect a pipeline's output are often erroneously conflated with exactly-once guarantees, we first explain precisely which issues are in and out of scope when we refer to "exactly once" in the context of Beam and data processing.

Accuracy Versus Completeness

Whenever a Beam pipeline processes a record for a pipeline, we want to ensure that the record is never dropped or duplicated. However, the nature of streaming pipelines is such that records sometimes show up late, after aggregates for their time windows have already been processed. The Beam SDK allows the user to configure how long the system should wait for late data to arrive; any (and only) records arriving later than this deadline are dropped. This feature contributes to *completeness*, not to accuracy: all records that showed up in time for processing are accurately processed exactly once, whereas these late records are explicitly dropped.

Although late records are usually discussed in the context of streaming systems, it's worth noting that batch pipelines have similar completeness issues. For example, a common batch paradigm is to run a job at 2 AM over all the previous day's data. However, if some of yesterday's data wasn't collected until after 2 AM, it won't be processed by the batch job! Thus, batch pipelines also provide accurate but not always complete results.

Side Effects

One characteristic of Beam and Dataflow is that users inject custom code that is executed as part of their pipeline graph. Dataflow does *not* guarantee that this code is run only once per record,[1] whether by the streaming or batch runner. It might run a given record through a user transform multiple times, or it might even run the same record simultaneously on multiple workers; this is necessary to guarantee at-least-once processing in the face of worker failures. Only one of these invocations can "win" and produce output further down the pipeline.

As a result, nonidempotent side effects are not guaranteed to execute exactly once; if you write code that has side effects external to the pipeline, such as contacting an outside service, these effects might be executed more than once for a given record. This situation is usually unavoidable because there is no way to atomically commit Dataflow's processing with the side effect on the external service. Pipelines do need to eventually send results to the outside world, and such calls might not be idempotent. As you will see later in the chapter, often such sinks are able to add an extra stage to restructure the call into an idempotent operation first.

Problem Definition

So, we've given a couple of examples of what we're *not* talking about. What do we mean then by exactly-once processing? To motivate this, let's begin with a simple streaming pipeline,[2] shown in Example 5-1.

---

1 In fact, no system we are aware of that provides at-least once (or better) is able to guarantee this, including all other Beam runners.

2 Dataflow also provides an accurate batch runner; however, in this context we are focused on the streaming runner.

Example 5-1. A simple streaming pipeline

```
Pipeline p = Pipeline.create(options);
// Calculate 1-minute counts of events per user.
PCollection<..> perUserCounts =
    p.apply(ReadFromUnboundedSource.read())
     .apply(new KeyByUser())
     .Window.<..>into(FixedWindows.of(Duration.standardMinutes(1)))
     .apply(Count.perKey());
// Process these per-user counts, and write the output somewhere.
perUserCounts.apply(new ProcessPerUserCountsAndWriteToSink());
// Add up all these per-user counts to get 1-minute counts of all events.
perUserCounts.apply(Values.<..>create())
             .apply(Count.globally())
             .apply(new ProcessGlobalCountAndWriteToSink());
p.run();
```

This pipeline computes two different windowed aggregations. The first counts how many events came from each individual user over the course of a minute, and the second counts how many total events came in each minute. Both aggregations are written to unspecified streaming sinks.

Remember that Dataflow executes pipelines on many different workers in parallel. After each GroupByKey (the Count operations use GroupByKey under the covers), all records with the same key are processed on the same machine following a process called *shuffle*. The Dataflow workers shuffle data between themselves using Remote Procedure Calls (RPCs), ensuring that records for a given key all end up on the same machine.

Figure 5-1 shows the shuffles that Dataflow creates for the pipeline in Example 5-1.[3] The Count.perKey shuffles all the data for each user onto a given worker, whereas the Count.globally shuffles all these partial counts to a single worker to calculate the global sum.

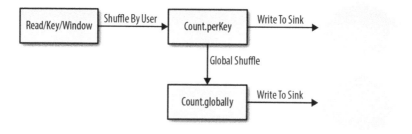

Figure 5-1. Shuffles in a pipeline

---

3 The Dataflow optimizer groups many steps together and adds shuffles only where they are needed.

For Dataflow to accurately process data, this shuffle process must ensure that every record is shuffled exactly once. As you will see in a moment, the distributed nature of shuffle makes this a challenging problem.

This pipeline also both reads and writes data from and to the outside world, so Dataflow must ensure that this interaction does not introduce any inaccuracies. Dataflow has always supported this task—what Apache Spark and Apache Flink call *end-to-end exactly once*—for sources and sinks whenever technically feasible.

The focus of this chapter will be on three things:

Shuffle
How Dataflow guarantees that every record is shuffled exactly once.

Sources
How Dataflow guarantees that every source record is processed exactly once.

Sinks
How Dataflow guarantees that every sink produces accurate output.

Ensuring Exactly Once in Shuffle

As just explained, Dataflow's streaming shuffle uses RPCs. Now, any time you have two machines communicating via RPC, you should think long and hard about data integrity. First of all, RPCs can fail for many reasons. The network might be interrupted, the RPC might time out before completing, or the receiving server might decide to fail the call. To guarantee that records are not lost in shuffle, Dataflow employs *upstream backup*. This simply means that the sender will retry RPCs until it receives positive acknowledgment of receipt. Dataflow also ensures that it will continue retrying these RPCs even if the sender crashes. This guarantees that every record is delivered *at least once*.

Now, the problem is that these retries might themselves create duplicates. Most RPC frameworks, including the one Dataflow uses, provide the sender with a status indicating success or failure. In a distributed system, you need to be aware that RPCs can sometimes succeed even when they have appeared to fail. There are many reasons for this: race conditions with the RPC timeout, positive acknowledgment from the server failing to transfer even though the RPC succeeded, and so on. The only status that a sender can really trust is a successful one.

An RPC returning a failure status generally indicates that the call might or might not have succeeded. Although specific error codes can communicate unambiguous failure, many common RPC failures, such as Deadline Exceeded, are ambiguous. In the case of streaming shuffle,[4] retrying an RPC that really succeeded means delivering a record twice! Dataflow needs some way of detecting and removing these duplicates.

At a high level, the algorithm for this task is quite simple (see Figure 5-2): every message sent is tagged with a unique identifier. Each receiver stores a catalog of all identifiers that have already been seen and processed. Every time a record is received, its identifier is looked up in this catalog. If it is found, the record is dropped as a duplicate. Because Dataflow is built on top of a scalable key/value store, this store is used to hold the deduplication catalog.

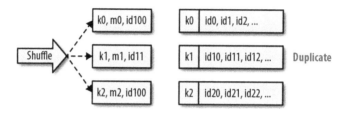

Figure 5-2. Detecting duplicates in shuffle

Addressing Determinism

Making this strategy work in the real world requires a lot of care, however. One immediate wrinkle is that the Beam Model allows for user code to produce nondeterministic output. This means that a ParDo can execute twice on the same input record (due to a retry), yet produce different output on each retry. The desired behavior is that only one of those outputs will commit into the pipeline; however, the nondeterminism involved makes it difficult to guarantee that both outputs have the same deterministic ID. Even trickier, a ParDo can output multiple records, so each of these retries might produce a different number of outputs!

So, why don't we simply require that all user processing be deterministic? Our experience is that in practice, many pipelines require nondeterministic transforms. And all too often, pipeline authors do not realize that the code they wrote is nondeterministic. For example, consider a transform that looks up supplemental data in Cloud Bigtable in order to enrich its input data. This is a nondeterministic task, as the external value might change in between retries of the transform. Any code that relies on current time is likewise not deterministic. We have also seen transforms that need to rely on random number generators. And even if the user code is purely deterministic, any event-time aggregation that allows for late data might have nondeterministic inputs.

---

4 Batch pipelines also need to guard against duplicates in shuffle. However the problem is much easier to solve in batch, which is why historical batch systems did do this and streaming systems did not. Streaming runtimes that use a microbatch architecture, such as Spark Streaming, delegate duplicate detection to a batch shuffler.

Dataflow addresses this issue by using checkpointing to make nondeterministic processing effectively deterministic. Each output from a transform is checkpointed, together with its unique ID, to stable storage *before* being delivered to the next stage.[5] Any retries in the shuffle delivery simply replay the output that has been checkpointed—the user's nondeterministic code is not run again on retry. To put it another way, the user's code may be run multiple times but only one of those runs can "win." Furthermore, Dataflow uses a consistent store that allows it to prevent duplicates from being written to stable storage.

Performance

To implement exactly-once shuffle delivery, a catalog of record IDs is stored in each receiver key. For every record that arrives, Dataflow looks up the catalog of IDs already seen to determine whether this record is a duplicate. Every output from step to step is checkpointed to storage to ensure that the generated record IDs are stable.

However, unless implemented carefully, this process would significantly degrade pipeline performance for customers by creating a huge increase in reads and writes. Thus, for exactly-once processing to be viable for Dataflow users, that I/O has to be reduced, in particular by preventing I/O on every record.

Dataflow achieves this goal via two key techniques: *graph optimization* and *Bloom filters*.

Graph Optimization

The Dataflow service runs a series of optimizations on the pipeline graph before executing it. One such optimization is *fusion*, in which the service fuses many logical steps into a single execution stage. Figure 5-3 shows some simple examples.

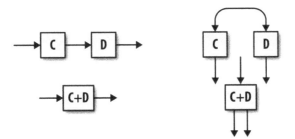

Figure 5-3. Example optimizations: fusion

---

5 A lot of care is taken to make sure this checkpointing is efficient; for example, schema and access pattern optimizations that are intimately tied to the characteristics of the underlying key/value store.

All fused steps are run as an in-process unit, so there's no need to store exactly-once data for each of them. In many cases, fusion reduces the entire graph down to a few physical steps, greatly reducing the amount of data transfer needed (and saving on state usage, as well).

Dataflow also optimizes associative and commutative Combine operations (such as Count and Sum) by performing partial combining locally before sending the data to the main grouping operation, as illustrated in Figure 5-4. This approach can greatly reduce the number of messages for delivery, consequently also reducing the number of reads and writes.

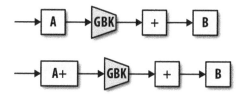

Figure 5-4. Example optimizations: combiner lifting

Bloom Filters

The aforementioned optimizations are general techniques that improve exactly-once performance as a byproduct. For an optimization aimed strictly at improving exactly-once processing, we turn to *Bloom filters.*

In a healthy pipeline, most arriving records will not be duplicates. We can use that fact to greatly improve performance via Bloom filters, which are compact data structures that allow for quick set-membership checks. Bloom filters have a very interesting property: they can return false positives but never false negatives. If the filter says "Yes, the element is in the set," we know that the element is *probably* in the set (with a probability that can be calculated). However, if the filter says an element is *not* in the set, it definitely isn't. This function is a perfect fit for the task at hand.

The implementation in Dataflow works like this: each worker keeps a Bloom filter of every ID it has seen. Whenever a new record ID shows up, it looks it up in the filter. If the filter returns false, this record is not a duplicate and the worker can skip the more expensive lookup from stable storage. It needs to do that second lookup only if the Bloom filter returns true, but as long as the filter's false-positive rate is low, that step is rarely needed.

Bloom filters tend to fill up over time, however, and as that happens, the false-positive rate increases. We also need to construct this Bloom filter anew any time a worker restarts by scanning the ID catalog stored in state. Helpfully, Dataflow attaches a system timestamp to each record.[6] Thus, instead of creating a single Bloom filter, the service creates a separate one for every 10-minute range. When a record arrives, Dataflow queries the appropriate filter based on the system timestamp.[7] This step prevents the Bloom filters from saturating because filters are garbage-collected over time, and it also bounds the amount of data that needs to be scanned at startup.[8]

Figure 5-5 illustrates this process: records arrive in the system and are delegated to a Bloom filter based on their arrival time. None of the records hitting the first filter are duplicates, and all of their catalog lookups are filtered. Record r1 is delivered a second time, so a catalog lookup is needed to verify that it is indeed a duplicate; the same is true for records r4 and r6. Record r8 is not a duplicate; however, due to a false positive in its Bloom filter, a catalog lookup is generated (which will determine that r8 is not a duplicate and should be processed).

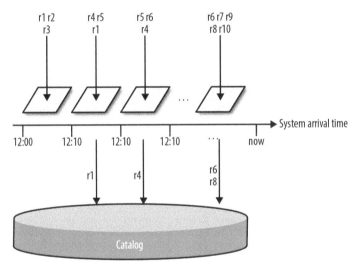

Figure 5-5. Exactly-once Bloom filters

Garbage Collection

Every Dataflow worker persistently stores a catalog of unique record IDs it has seen. As Dataflow's state and consistency model is per-key, in reality each key stores a cata-

---

6 This is not the custom user-supplied timestamp used for windowing. Rather this is a deterministic processing-time timestamp that is assigned by the sending worker.

7 Some care needs to be taken to ensure that this algorithm works. Each sender must guarantee that the system timestamps it generates are strictly increasing, and this guarantee must be maintained across worker restarts.

8 In theory, we could dispense with startup scans entirely by lazily building the Bloom filter for a bucket only when a threshold number of records show up with timestamps in that bucket.

log of records that have been delivered to that key. We can't store these identifiers for-ever, or all available storage will eventually fill up. To avoid that issue, you need garbage collection of acknowledged record IDs.

One strategy for accomplishing this goal would be for senders to tag each record with a strictly increasing sequence number in order to track the earliest sequence number still in flight (corresponding to an unacknowledged record delivery). Any identifier in the catalog with an earlier sequence number could then be garbage-collected because all earlier records have already been acknowledged.

There is a better alternative, however. As previously mentioned, Dataflow already tags each record with a system timestamp that is used for bucketing exactly-once Bloom filters. Consequently, instead of using sequence numbers to garbage-collect the exactly-once catalog, Dataflow calculates a garbage-collection watermark based on these system timestamps (this is the processing-time watermark discussed in Chap-ter 3). A nice side benefit of this approach is that because this watermark is based on the amount of physical time spent waiting in a given stage (unlike the data water-mark, which is based on custom event times), it provides intuition on what parts of the pipeline are slow. This metadata is the basis for the System Lag metric shown in the Dataflow WebUI.

What happens if a record arrives with an old timestamp and we've already garbage-collected identifiers for this point in time? This can happen due to an effect we call *network remnants*, in which an old message becomes stuck for an indefinite period of time inside the network and then suddenly shows up. Well, the low watermark that triggers garbage collection won't advance until record deliveries have been acknowl-edged, so we know that this record has already been successfully processed. Such net-work remnants are clearly duplicates and are ignored.

Exactly Once in Sources

Beam provides a source API for reading data into a Dataflow pipeline.[9] Dataflow might retry reads from a source if processing fails and needs to ensure that every unique record produced by a source is processed exactly once.

For most sources Dataflow handles this process transparently; such sources are *deter-ministic*. For example, consider a source that reads data out of files. The records in a file will always be in a deterministic order and at deterministic byte locations, no mat-ter how many times the file is read.[10] The filename and byte location uniquely identify each record, so the service can automatically generate unique IDs for each record.

---

9 At the time of this writing, a new, more-flexible API called SplittableDoFn (*http://bit.ly/2JQa7GJ*) is available for Apache Beam.

10 We assume that nobody is maliciously modifying the bytes in the file while we are reading it.

Another source that provides similar determinism guarantees is Apache Kafka; each Kafka topic is divided into a static set of partitions, and records in a partition always have a deterministic order. Such deterministic sources will work seamlessly in Dataflow with no duplicates.

However, not all sources are so simple. For example, one common source for Dataflow pipelines is Google Cloud Pub/Sub. Pub/Sub is a *nondeterministic* source: multiple subscribers can pull from a Pub/Sub topic, but which subscribers receive a given message is unpredictable. If processing fails Pub/Sub will redeliver messages but the messages might be delivered to different workers than those that processed them originally, and in a different order. This nondeterministic behavior means that Dataflow needs assistance for detecting duplicates because there is no way for the service to deterministically assign record IDs that will be stable upon retry. (We dive into a more detailed case study of Pub/Sub later in this chapter.)

Because Dataflow cannot automatically assign record IDs, nondeterministic sources are required to inform the system what the record IDs should be. Beam's Source API provides the `UnboundedReader.getCurrentRecordId`[11] method. If a source provides unique IDs per record and notifies Dataflow that it requires deduplication,[12] records with the same ID will be filtered out.

Exactly Once in Sinks

At some point, every pipeline needs to output data to the outside world, and a sink is simply a transform that does exactly that. Keep in mind that delivering data externally is a side effect, and we have already mentioned that Dataflow does not guarantee exactly-once application of side effects. So, how can a sink guarantee that outputs are delivered exactly once?

The simplest answer is that a number of built-in sinks are provided as part of the Beam SDK. These sinks are carefully designed to ensure that they do not produce duplicates, even if executed multiple times. Whenever possible, pipeline authors are encouraged to use one of these built-in sinks.

However, sometimes the built-ins are insufficient and you need to write your own. The best approach is to ensure that your side-effect operation is idempotent and therefore robust in the face of replay. However, often some component of a side-effect `DoFn` is nondeterministic and thus might change on replay. For example, in a windowed aggregation, the set of records in the window can also be nondeterministic!

---

11 Again note that the SplittableDoFn API (*http://bit.ly/2JQa7GJ*) has different methods for this.

12 Using the `requiresDedupping` override.

Specifically, the window might attempt to fire with elements e0, e1, e2, but the worker crashes before committing the window processing (but not before those elements are sent as a side effect). When the worker restarts, the window will fire again, but now a late element e3 shows up. Because this element shows up before the window is committed, it's not counted as late data, so the DoFn is called again with elements e0, e1, e2, e3. These are then sent to the side-effect operation. Idempotency does not help here, because different logical record sets were sent each time.

There are other ways nondeterminism can be introduced. The standard way to address this risk is to rely on the fact that Dataflow currently guarantees that only one version of a DoFn's output can make it past a shuffle boundary.[13]

A simple way of using this guarantee is via the built-in Reshuffle transform. The pattern presented in Example 5-2 ensures that the side-effect operation always receives a deterministic record to output.

Example 5-2. Reshuffle example

```
c.apply(Window.<..>into(FixedWindows.of(Duration.standardMinutes(1))))
 .apply(GroupByKey.<..>.create())
 .apply(new PrepareOutputData())
 .apply(Reshuffle.<..>of())
 .apply(WriteToSideEffect());
```

The preceding pipeline splits the sink into two steps: PrepareOutputData and Write ToSideEffect. PrepareOutputData outputs records corresponding to idempotent writes. If we simply ran one after the other, the entire process might be replayed on failure, PrepareOutputData might produce a different result, and both would be written as side effects. When we add the Reshuffle in between the two, Dataflow guarantees this can't happen.

Of course, Dataflow might still run the WriteToSideEffect operation multiple times. The side effects themselves still need to be idempotent, or the sink will receive duplicates. For example, an operation that sets or overwrites a value in a data store is idempotent, and will generate correct output even if it's run several times. An operation that appends to a list is not idempotent; if the operation is run multiple times, the same value will be appended each time.

While Reshuffle provides a simple way of achieving stable input to a DoFn, a GroupBy Key works just as well. However, there is currently a proposal that removes the need to add a GroupByKey to achieve stable input into a DoFn. Instead, the user could

---

13 Note that these determinism boundaries might become more explicit in the Beam Model at some point. Other Beam runners vary in their ability to handle nondeterministic user code.

annotate `WriteToSideEffect` with a special annotation, `@RequiresStableInput`, and the system would then ensure stable input to that transform.

Use Cases

To illustrate, let's examine some built-in sources and sinks to see how they implement the aforementioned patterns.

Example Source: Cloud Pub/Sub

Cloud Pub/Sub is a fully managed, scalable, reliable, and low-latency system for delivering messages from publishers to subscribers. Publishers publish data on named topics, and subscribers create named subscriptions to pull data from these topics. Multiple subscriptions can be created for a single topic, in which case each subscription receives a full copy of all data published on the topic from the time of the subscription's creation. Pub/Sub guarantees that records will continue to be delivered until they are acknowledged; however, a record might be delivered multiple times.

Pub/Sub is intended for distributed use, so many publishing processes can publish to the same topic and many subscribing processes can pull from the same subscription. After a record has been pulled, the subscriber must acknowledge it within a certain amount of time, or that pull expires and Pub/Sub will redeliver that record to another of the subscribing processes.

Although these characteristics make Pub/Sub highly scalable, they also make it a challenging source for a system like Dataflow. It's impossible to know which record will be delivered to which worker, and in which order. What's more, in the case of failure, redelivery might send the records to different workers in different orders!

Pub/Sub provides a stable message ID with each message, and this ID will be the same upon redelivery. The Dataflow Pub/Sub source will default to using this ID for removing duplicates from Pub/Sub. (The records are shuffled based on a hash of the ID, so that repeated deliveries are always processed on the same worker.) In some cases, however, this is not quite enough. The user's publishing process might retry publishes, and as a result introduce duplicates into Pub/Sub. From that service's perspective these are unique records, so they will get unique record IDs. Dataflow's Pub/Sub source allows the user to provide their own record IDs as a custom attribute. As long as the publisher sends the same ID when retrying, Dataflow will be able to detect these duplicates.

Beam (and therefore Dataflow) provides a reference source implementation for Pub/Sub. However, keep in mind that this is *not* what Dataflow uses but rather an implementation used only by non-Dataflow runners (such as Apache Spark, Apache Flink, and the DirectRunner). For a variety of reasons, Dataflow handles Pub/Sub internally and does not use the public Pub/Sub source.

Example Sink: Files

The streaming runner can use Beam's file sinks (TextIO, AvroIO, and any other sink that implements FileBasedSink) to continuously output records to files. Example 5-3 provides an example use case.

Example 5-3. Windowed file writes

```
c.apply(Window.<..>into(FixedWindows.of(Duration.standardMinutes(1))))
 .apply(TextIO.writeStrings().to(new MyNamePolicy()).withWindowedWrites());
```

The snippet in Example 5-3 writes 10 new files each minute, containing data from that window. MyNamePolicy is a user-written function that determines output file-names based on the shard and the window. You can also use triggers, in which case each trigger pane will be output as a new file.

This process is implemented using a variant on the pattern in Example 5-3. Files are written out to temporary locations, and these temporary filenames are sent to a sub-sequent transform through a GroupByKey. After the GroupByKey is a finalize transform that atomically moves the temporary files into their final location. The pseudocode in Example 5-4 provides a sketch of how a consistent streaming file sink is implemented in Beam. (For more details, see FileBasedSink and WriteFiles in the Beam codebase.)

Example 5-4. File sink

```
c
  // Tag each record with a random shard id.
  .apply("AttachShard", WithKeys.of(new RandomShardingKey(getNumShards()))))
  // Group all records with the same shard.
  .apply("GroupByShard", GroupByKey.<..>())
  // For each window, write per-shard elements to a temporary file. This is the
  // non-deterministic side effect. If this DoFn is executed multiple times, it will
  // simply write multiple temporary files; only one of these will pass on through
  // to the Finalize stage.
  .apply("WriteTempFile", ParDo.of(new DoFn<..> {
    @ProcessElement
      public void processElement(ProcessContext c, BoundedWindow window) {
        // Write the contents of c.element() to a temporary file.
        // User-provided name policy used to generate a final filename.
        c.output(new FileResult()).
    }
  }))
  // Group the list of files onto a singleton key.
  .apply("AttachSingletonKey", WithKeys.<..>of((Void)null))
  .apply("FinalizeGroupByKey", GroupByKey.<..>create())
  // Finalize the files by atomically renaming them. This operation is idempotent.
  // Once this DoFn has executed once for a given FileResult, the temporary file
```

```
    // is gone, so any further executions will have no effect.
    .apply("Finalize", ParDo.of(new DoFn<..>, Void> {
      @ProcessElement
      public void processElement(ProcessContext c)  {
        for (FileResult result : c.element()) {
          rename(result.getTemporaryFileName(), result.getFinalFilename());
        }
}})));
```

You can see how the nonidempotent work is done in `WriteTempFile`. After the `Group ByKey` completes, the `Finalize` step will always see the same bundles across retries. Because file rename is idempotent,[14] this give us an exactly-once sink.

Example Sink: Google BigQuery

Google BigQuery is a fully managed, cloud-native data warehouse. Beam provides a BigQuery sink, and BigQuery provides a streaming insert API that supports extremely low-latency inserts. This streaming insert API allows you to tag inserts with a unique ID, and BigQuery will attempt to filter duplicate inserts with the same ID.[15] To use this capability, the BigQuery sink must generate statistically unique IDs for each record. It does this by using the `java.util.UUID` package, which generates statistically unique 128-bit IDs.

Generating a random universally unique identifier (UUID) is a nondeterministic operation, so we must add a `Reshuffle` before we insert into BigQuery. After we do this, any retries by Dataflow will always use the same UUID that was shuffled. Duplicate attempts to insert into BigQuery will always have the same insert ID, so Big-Query is able to filter them. The pseudocode shown in Example 5-5 illustrates how the BigQuery sink is implemented.

Example 5-5. BigQuery sink

```
// Apply a unique identifier to each record
c
  .apply(new DoFn<> {
  @ProcessElement
  public void processElement(ProcessContext context) {
    String uniqueId = UUID.randomUUID().toString();
    context.output(KV.of(ThreadLocalRandom.current().nextInt(0, 50),
                              new RecordWithId(context.element(), uniqueId)));
  }
```

---

14 As long as you properly handle the failure when the source file no longer exists.

15 Due to the global nature of the service, BigQuery does not guarantee that all duplicates are removed. Users can periodically run a query over their tables to remove any duplicates that were not caught by the streaming insert API. See the BigQuery documentation for more information.

```
})
// Reshuffle the data so that the applied identifiers are stable and will not change.
.apply(Reshuffle.<Integer, RecordWithId>of())
// Stream records into BigQuery with unique ids for deduplication.
.apply(ParDo.of(new DoFn<..> {
  @ProcessElement
  public void processElement(ProcessContext context) {
    insertIntoBigQuery(context.element().record(), context.element().id());
  }
});
```

Again we split the sink into a nonidempotent step (generating a random number), followed by a step that is idempotent.

Other Systems

Now that we have explained Dataflow's exactly once in detail, let us contrast this with some brief overviews of other popular streaming systems. Each implements exactly-once guarantees in a different way and makes different trade-offs as a result.

Apache Spark Streaming

Spark Streaming uses a microbatch architecture for continuous data processing. Users logically deal with a stream object; however, under the covers, Spark represents this stream as a continuous series of RDDs.[16] Each RDD is processed as a batch, and Spark relies on the exactly-once nature of batch processing to ensure correctness; as mentioned previously, techniques for correct batch shuffles have been known for some time. This approach can cause increased latency to output—especially for deep pipelines and high input volumes—and often careful tuning is required to achieve desired latency.

Spark does assume that operations are all idempotent and might replay the chain of operations up the current point in the graph. A checkpoint primitive is provided, however, that causes an RDD to be materialized, guaranteeing that history prior to that RDD will not be replayed. This checkpoint feature is intended for performance reasons (e.g., to prevent replaying an expensive operation); however, you can also use it to implement nonidempotent side effects.

Apache Flink

Apache Flink also provides exactly-once processing for streaming pipelines but does so in a manner different than either Dataflow or Spark. Flink streaming pipelines periodically compute consistent snapshots, each representing the consistent point-in-

---

16 Resilient Distributed Datasets; Spark's abstraction of a distributed dataset, similar to PCollection in Beam.

time state of an entire pipeline. Flink snapshots are computed progressively, so there is no need to halt all processing while computing a snapshot. This allows records to continue flowing through the system while taking a snapshot, alleviating some of the latency issues with the Spark Streaming approach.

Flink implements these snapshots by inserting special numbered snapshot markers into the data streams flowing from sources. As each operator receives a snapshot marker, it executes a specific algorithm allowing it to copy its state to an external location and propagate the snapshot marker to downstream operators. After all operators have executed this snapshot algorithm, a complete snapshot is made available. Any worker failures will cause the entire pipeline to roll back its state from the last complete snapshot. In-flight messages do not need to be included in the snapshot. All message delivery in Flink is done via an ordered TCP-based channel. Any connection failures can be handled by resuming the connection from the last good sequence number;[17] unlike Dataflow, Flink tasks are statically allocated to workers, so it can assume that the connection will resume from the same sender and replay the same payloads.

Because Flink might roll back to the previous snapshot at any time, any state modifications not yet in a snapshot must be considered tentative. A sink that sends data to the world outside the Flink pipeline must wait until a snapshot has completed, and then send only the data that is included in that snapshot. Flink provides a `notifySnap shotComplete` callback that allows sinks to know when each snapshot is completed, and send the data onward. Even though this does affect the output latency of Flink pipelines,[18] this latency is introduced only at sinks. In practice, this allows Flink to have lower end-to-end latency than Spark for deep pipelines because Spark introduces batch latency at each stage in the pipeline.

Flink's distributed snapshots are an elegant way of dealing with consistency in a streaming pipeline; however, a number of assumptions are made about the pipeline. Failures are assumed to be rare,[19] as the impact of a failure (rolling back to the previous snapshot) is substantial. To maintain low-latency output, it is also assumed that snapshots can complete quickly. It remains to be seen whether this causes issues on very large clusters where the failure rate will likely increase, as will the time needed to complete a snapshot.

Implementation is also simplified by assuming that tasks are statically allocated to workers (at least within a single snapshot epoch). This assumption allows Flink to

---

17 These sequence numbers are per connection and are unrelated to the snapshot epoch number.

18 Only for nonidempotent sinks. Completely idempotent sinks do not need to wait for the snapshot to complete.

19 Specifically, Flink assumes that the mean time to worker failure is more than the time to snapshot; otherwise, the pipeline would be unable to make progress.

provide a simple exactly-once transport between workers because it knows that if a connection fails, the same data can be pulled in order from the same worker. In contrast, tasks in Dataflow are constantly load balanced between workers (and the set of workers is constantly growing and shrinking), so Dataflow is unable to make this assumption. This forces Dataflow to implement a much more complex transport layer in order to provide exactly-once processing.

Summary

In summary, exactly-once data processing, which was once thought to be incompatible with low-latency results, is quite possible—Dataflow does it efficiently without sacrificing latency. This enables far richer uses for stream processing.

Although this chapter has focused on Dataflow-specific techniques, other streaming systems also provide exactly-once guarantees. Apache Spark Streaming runs streaming pipelines as a series of small batch jobs, relying on exactly-once guarantees in the Spark batch runner. Apache Flink uses a variation on Chandy Lamport distributed snapshots to get a running consistent state and can use these snapshots to ensure exactly-once processing. We encourage you to learn about these other systems, as well, for a broad understanding of how different stream-processing systems work!

PART II

Streams and Tables

CHAPTER 6

Streams and Tables

You have reached the part of the book where we talk about streams and tables. If you recall, back in Chapter 1, we briefly discussed two important but orthogonal dimensions of data: *cardinality* and *constitution*. Until now, we've focused strictly on the cardinality aspects (bounded versus unbounded) and otherwise ignored the constitution aspects (stream versus table). This has allowed us to learn about the challenges brought to the table by the introduction of unbounded datasets, without worrying too much about the lower-level details that really drive the way things work. We're now going to expand our horizons and see what the added dimension of constitution brings to the mix.

Though it's a bit of a stretch, one way to think about this shift in approach is to compare the relationship of classical mechanics to quantum mechanics. You know how in physics class they teach you a bunch of classical mechanics stuff like Newtonian theory and so on, and then after you think you've more or less mastered that, they come along and tell you it was all bunk, and classical physics gives you only part of the picture, and there's actually this other thing called quantum mechanics that really explains how things work at a lower level, but it didn't make sense to complicate matters up front by trying to teach you both at once, and...oh wait...we also haven't fully reconciled everything between the two yet, so just squint at it and trust us that it all makes sense somehow? Well this is a lot like that, except your brain will hurt less because physics is way harder than data processing, and you won't have to squint at anything and pretend it makes sense because it actually does come together beautifully in the end, which is really cool.

So, with the stage appropriately set, the point of this chapter is twofold:

- To try to describe the relationship between the Beam Model (as we've described it in the book up to this point) and the theory of "streams and tables" (as popularized by Martin Kleppmann (*http://bit.ly/2LO0cik*) and Jay Kreps (*http://bit.ly/*

2sX0bl8), among others, but essentially originating out of the database world). It turns out that stream and table theory does an illuminating job of describing the low-level concepts that underlie the Beam Model. Additionally, a clear understanding of how they relate is particularly informative when considering how robust stream processing concepts might be cleanly integrated into SQL (something we consider in Chapter 8).

- To bombard you with bad physics analogies for the sheer fun of it. Writing a book is a lot of work; you have to find little joys here and there to keep you going.

Stream-and-Table Basics Or: a Special Theory of Stream and Table Relativity

The basic idea of streams and tables derives from the database world. Anyone familiar with SQL is likely familiar with tables and their core properties, roughly summarized as: tables contain rows and columns of data, and each row is uniquely identified by some sort of key, either explicit or implicit.

If you think back to your database systems class in college,[1] you'll probably recall the data structure underlying most databases is an *append-only log*. As transactions are applied to a table in the database, those transactions are recorded in a log, the contents of which are then serially applied to the table to materialize those updates. In streams and tables nomenclature, that log is effectively the stream.

From that perspective, we now understand how to create a table from a stream: the table is just the result of applying the transaction log of updates found in the stream. But how do we create a stream from a table? It's essentially the inverse: a stream is a changelog for a table. The motivating example typically used for table-to-stream conversion is *materialized views*. Materialized views in SQL let you specify a query on a table, which itself is then manifested by the database system as another first-class table. This materialized view is essentially a cached version of that query, which the database system ensures is always up to date as the contents of the source table evolve over time. Perhaps unsurprisingly, materialized views are implemented via the changelog for the original table; any time the source table changes, that change is logged. The database then evaluates that change within the context of the materialized view's query and applies any resulting change to the destination materialized view table.

---

1 If you didn't go to college for computer science and you've made it this far in the book, you are likely either 1) my parents, 2) masochistic, or 3) very smart (and for the record, I'm not implying these groups are necessarily mutually exclusive; figure that one out if you can, Mom and Dad! <winky-smiley/>).

Combining these two points together and employing yet another questionable physics analogy, we arrive at what one might call the Special Theory of Stream and Table Relativity:

Streams → tables
>   The aggregation of a stream of updates over time yields a table.

Tables → streams
>   The observation of changes to a table over time yields a stream.

This is a very powerful pair of concepts, and their careful application to the world of stream processing is a big reason for the massive success of Apache Kafka, the ecosystem that is built around these underlying principles. However, those statements themselves are not quite general enough to allow us to tie streams and tables to all of the concepts in the Beam Model. For that, we must go a little bit deeper.

Toward a General Theory of Stream and Table Relativity

If we want to reconcile stream/table theory with everything we know of the Beam Model, we'll need to tie up some loose ends, specifically:

- How does batch processing fit into all of this?
- What is the relationship of streams to bounded and unbounded datasets?
- How do the four *what*, *where*, *when*, *how* questions map onto a streams/tables world?

As we attempt to do so, it will be helpful to have the right mindset about streams and tables. In addition to understanding them in relation to each other, as captured by the previous definition, it can be illuminating to define them independent of each other. Here's a simple way of looking at it that will underscore some of our future analyses:

- Tables are data *at rest*.

  This isn't to say tables are static in any way; nearly all useful tables are continuously changing over time in some way. But at any given time, a snapshot of the table provides some sort of picture of the dataset contained together as a whole.[2] In that way, tables act as a conceptual resting place for data to accumulate and be observed over time. Hence, data at rest.

- Streams are data *in motion*.

---

2 And note that in some cases, the tables themselves can accept time as a query parameter, allowing you to peer backward in time to snapshots of the table as it existed in the past.

Whereas tables capture a view of the dataset as a whole at a *specific point in time*, streams capture the evolution of that data *over time*. Julian Hyde is fond of saying streams are like the derivatives of tables, and tables the integrals of streams, which is a nice way of thinking about it for you math-minded individuals out there. Regardless, the important feature of streams is that they capture the inherent movement of data within a table as it changes. Hence, data in motion.

Though tables and streams are intimately related, it's important to keep in mind that they are very much *not* the same thing, even if there are many cases in which one might be fully derived from the other. The differences are subtle but important, as we'll see.

Batch Processing Versus Streams and Tables

With our proverbial knuckles now cracked, let's start to tie up some loose ends. To begin, we tackle the first one, regarding batch processing. At the end, we'll discover that the resolution to the second issue, regarding the relationship of streams to bounded and unbounded data, will fall out naturally from the answer for the first. Score one for serendipity.

A Streams and Tables Analysis of MapReduce

To keep our analysis relatively simple, but solidly concrete, as it were, let's look at how a traditional MapReduce (*http://bit.ly/2uvKRe6*) job fits into the streams/tables world. As alluded to by its name, a MapReduce job superficially consists of two phases: Map and Reduce. For our purposes, though, it's useful to look a little deeper and treat it more like six:

MapRead
> This consumes the input data and preprocesses them a bit into a standard key/value form for mapping.

Map
> This repeatedly (and/or in parallel) consumes a single key/value pair[3] from the preprocessed input and outputs zero or more key/value pairs.

---

3 Note that no guarantees are made about the keys of two successive records observed by a single mapper, because no key-grouping has occurred yet. The existence of the key here is really just to allow keyed datasets to be consumed in a natural way, and if there are no obvious keys for the input data, they'll all just share what is effectively a global null key.

MapWrite

This clusters together sets of Map-phase output values having identical keys and writes those key/value-list groups to (temporary) persistent storage. In this way, the MapWrite phase is essentially a group-by-key-and-checkpoint operation.

ReduceRead

This consumes the saved shuffle data and converts them into a standard key/value-list form for reduction.

Reduce

This repeatedly (and/or in parallel) consumes a single key and its associated value-list of records and outputs zero or more records, all of which may optionally remain associated with that same key.

ReduceWrite

This writes the outputs from the Reduce phase to the output datastore.

Note that the MapWrite and ReduceRead phases sometimes are referred to in aggregate as the Shuffle phase, but for our purposes, it's better to consider them independently. It's perhaps also worth noting that the functions served by the MapRead and ReduceWrite phases are more commonly referred to these days as sources and sinks. Digressions aside, however, let's now see how this all relates to streams and tables.

Map as streams/tables

Because we start and end with static[4] datasets, it should be clear that we begin with a table and end with a table. But what do we have in between? Naively, one might assume that it's tables all the way down; after all, batch processing is (conceptually) known to consume and produce tables. And if you think of a batch processing job as a rough analog of executing a classic SQL query, that feels relatively natural. But let's look a little more closely at what's really happening, step by step.

First up, MapRead consumes a table and produces *something*. That something is consumed next by the Map phase, so if we want to understand its nature, a good place to start would be with the Map phase API, which looks something like this in Java:

```
void map(KI key, VI value, Emit<KO, VO> emitter);
```

The map call will be repeatedly invoked for each key/value pair in the input table. If you think this sounds suspiciously like the input table is being consumed as a stream

---

4 Calling the inputs to a batch job "static" might be a bit strong. In reality, the dataset being consumed can be constantly changing as it's processed; that is, if you're reading directly from an HBase/Bigtable table within a timestamp range in which the data aren't guaranteed to be immutable. But in most cases, the recommended approach is to ensure that you're somehow processing a static snapshot of the input data, and any deviation from that assumption is at your own peril.

of records, you'd be right. We look more closely at how the table is being converted into a stream later, but for now, suffice it to say that the MapRead phase is iterating over the data at rest in the input table and putting them into motion in the form of a stream that is then consumed by the Map phase.

Next up, the Map phase consumes that stream, and then does what? Because the map operation is an element-wise transformation, it's not doing anything that will halt the moving elements and put them to rest. It might change the effective cardinality of the stream by either filtering some elements out or exploding some elements into multiple elements, but those elements all remain independent from one another after the Map phase concludes. So, it seems safe to say that the Map phase both consumes a stream as well as produces a stream.

After the Map phase is done, we enter the MapWrite phase. As I noted earlier, the MapWrite groups records by key and then writes them in that format to persistent storage. The *persistent* part of the write actually isn't strictly necessary at this point as long as there's persistence *somewhere* (i.e., if the upstream inputs are saved and one can recompute the intermediate results from them in cases of failure, similar to the approach Spark takes with Resilient Distributed Datasets [RDDs]). What *is* important is that the records are grouped together into some kind of datastore, be it in memory, on disk, or what have you. This is important because, as a result of this grouping operation, records that were previously flying past one-by-one in the stream are now brought to rest in a location dictated by their key, thus allowing per-key groups to accumulate as their like-keyed brethren and sistren arrive. Note how similar this is to the definition of stream-to-table conversion provided earlier: *the aggregation of a stream of updates over time yields a table*. The MapWrite phase, by virtue of grouping the stream of records by their keys, has put those data to rest and thus converted the stream back into a table.[5] Cool!

We're now halfway through the MapReduce, so, using Figure 6-1, let's recap what we've seen so far.

We've gone from table to stream and back again across three operations. MapRead converted the table into a stream, which was then transformed into a new stream by Map (via the user's code), which was then converted back into a table by MapWrite. We're going to find that the next three operations in the MapReduce look very similar, so I'll go through them more quickly, but I still want to point out one important detail along the way.

---

5 Note that grouping a stream by key is importantly distinct from simply *partitioning* that stream by key, which ensures that all records with the same key end up being processed by the same machine but doesn't do anything to put the records to rest. They instead remain in motion and thus continue on as a stream. A grouping operation is more like a partition-by-key followed by a write to the appropriate group for that partition, which is what puts them to rest and turns the stream into a table.

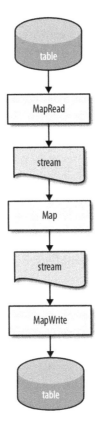

Figure 6-1. Map phases in a MapReduce. Data in a table are converted to a stream and back again.

Reduce as streams/tables

Picking up where we left off after the MapWrite phase, ReduceRead itself is relatively uninteresting. It's basically identical to MapRead, except that the values being read are singleton lists of values instead of singleton values, because the data stored by Map-Write were key/value-list pairs. But it's still just iterating over a snapshot of a table to convert it into a stream. Nothing new here.

And even though it *sounds* like it might be interesting, Reduce in this context is really just a glorified Map phase that happens to receive a list of values for each key instead of a single value. So it's still just mapping single (composite) records into zero or more new records. Nothing particularly new here, either.

ReduceWrite is the one that's a bit noteworthy. We know already that this phase must convert a stream to a table, given that Reduce produces a stream and the final output is a table. But how does that happen? If I told you it was a direct result of key-grouping the outputs from the previous phase into persistent storage, just like we saw with MapWrite, you might believe me, until you remembered that I noted earlier that key-association was an *optional* feature of the Reduce phase. With that feature enabled, ReduceWrite *is* essentially identical to MapWrite.[6] But if that feature is disabled and the outputs from Reduce have no associated keys, what exactly is happening to bring those data to rest?

To understand what's going on, it's useful to think again of the semantics of a SQL table. Though often recommended, it's not strictly required for a SQL table to have a primary key uniquely identifying each row. In the case of keyless tables, each row that is inserted is considered to be a new, independent row (even if the data therein are identical to one or more extant rows in the table), much as though there were an implicit AUTO_INCREMENT field being used as the key (which incidentally, is what's effectively happening under the covers in most implementations, even though the "key" in this case might just be some physical block location that is never exposed or expected to be used as a logical identifier). This implicit unique key assignment is precisely what's happening in ReduceWrite with unkeyed data. Conceptually, there's still a group-by-key operation happening; that's what brings the data to rest. But lacking a user-supplied key, the ReduceWrite is treating each record as though it has a new, never-before-seen key, and effectively grouping each record with itself, resulting again in data at rest.[7]

Take a look at Figure 6-2, which shows the entire pipeline from the perspective of stream/tables. You can see that it's a sequence of TABLE → STREAM → STREAM → TABLE → STREAM → STREAM → TABLE. Even though we're processing bounded data and even though we're doing what we traditionally think of as batch processing, it's really just streams and tables under the covers.

---

6 One giant difference, from an implementation perspective at least, being that ReduceWrite, knowing that keys have already been grouped together by MapWrite, and further knowing that Reduce is unable to alter keys for the case in which its outputs remain keyed, can simply accumulate the outputs generated by reducing the values for a single key in order to group them together, which is much simpler than the full-blown shuffle implementation required for a MapWrite phase.

7 Another way of looking at it is that there are two types of tables: updateable and appendable; this is the way the Flink folks have framed it for their Table API. But even though that's a great intuitive way of capturing the observed semantics of the two situations, I think it obscures the underlying nature of what's actually happening that causes a stream to come to rest as a table; that is, grouping.

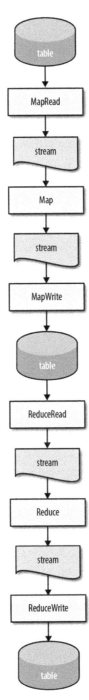

Figure 6-2. Map and Reduce phases in a MapReduce, viewed from the perspective of streams and tables

Reconciling with Batch Processing

So where does this leave us with respect to our first two questions?

1. **Q:** How does batch processing fit into stream/table theory?

    A: Quite nicely. The basic pattern is as follows:

    a. Tables are read in their entirety to become streams.

    b. Streams are processed into new streams until a grouping operation is hit.

    c. Grouping turns the stream into a table.

    d. Steps a through c repeat until you run out of stages in the pipeline.

2. **Q:** How do streams relate to bounded/unbounded data?

    A: As we can see from the MapReduce example, streams are simply the in-motion form of data, regardless of whether they're bounded or unbounded.

Taken from this perspective, it's easy to see that stream/table theory isn't remotely at odds with batch processing of bounded data. In fact, it only further supports the idea I've been harping on that batch and streaming really aren't that different: at the end of the of day, it's streams and tables all the way down.

With that, we're well on our way toward a general theory of streams and tables. But to wrap things up cleanly, we last need to revisit the four *what*/*where*/*when*/*how* questions within the streams/tables context, to see how they all relate.

What, *Where*, *When*, and *How* in a Streams and Tables World

In this section, we look at each of the four questions and see how they relate to streams and tables. We'll also answer any questions that may be lingering from the previous section, one big one being: if grouping is the thing that brings data to rest, what precisely is the "ungrouping" inverse that puts them in motion? More on that later. But for now, on to transformations.

What: Transformations

In Chapter 3, we learned that transformations tell us *what* the pipeline is computing; that is, whether it's building models, counting sums, filtering spam, and so on. We saw in the earlier MapReduce example that four of the six stages answered *what* questions:

- Map and Reduce both applied the pipeline author's element-wise transformation on each key/value or key/value-list pair in the input stream, respectively, yielding a new, transformed stream.

- MapWrite and ReduceWrite both grouped the outputs from the previous stage according to the key assigned by that stage (possibly implicitly, in the optional Reduce case), and in doing so transformed the input stream into an output table.

Viewed in that light, you can see that there are essentially two types of *what* transforms from the perspective of stream/table theory:

Nongrouping

These operations (as we saw in Map and Reduce) simply accept a stream of records and produce a new, transformed stream of records on the other side. Examples of nongrouping transformations are filters (e.g., removing spam messages), exploders (i.e., splitting apart a larger composite record into its constituent parts), and mutators (e.g., divide by 100), and so on.

Grouping

These operations (as we saw in MapWrite and ReduceWrite) accept a stream of records and group them together in some way, thereby transforming the stream into a table. Examples of grouping transformations are joins, aggregations, list/set accumulation, changelog application, histogram creation, machine learning model training, and so forth.

To get a better sense for how all of this ties together, let's look at an updated version of Figure 2-2, where we first began to look at transformations. To save you jumping back there to see what we were talking about, Example 6-1 contains the code snippet we were using.

Example 6-1. Summation pipeline

```
PCollection<String> raw = IO.read(...);
PCollection<KV<Team, Integer>> input = raw.apply(new ParseFn());
PCollection<KV<Team, Integer>> totals =
  input.apply(Sum.integersPerKey());
```

This pipeline is simply reading in input data, parsing individual team member scores, and then summing those scores per team. The event-time/processing-time visualization of it looks like the diagram presented in Figure 6-3.

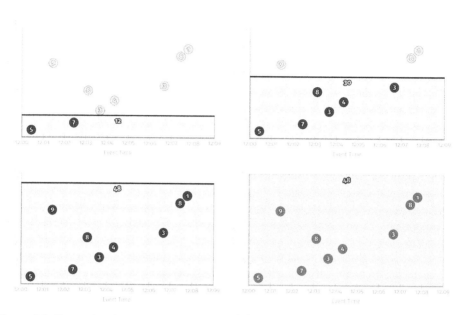

Figure 6-3. Event-time/processing-time view of classic batch processing (http://streaming book.net/fig/6-3)

Figure 6-4 depicts a more topological view of this pipeline over time, rendered from a streams-and-tables perspective.

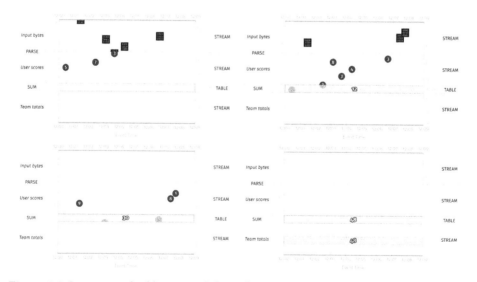

Figure 6-4. Streams and tables view of classic batch processing (http://streaming book.net/fig/6-4)

In the streams and tables version of this visualization, the passage of time is manifested by scrolling the graph area downward in the processing-time dimension (y-axis) as time advances. The nice thing about rendering things this way is that it very clearly calls out the difference between nongrouping and grouping operations. Unlike our previous diagrams, in which I elided all initial transformations in the pipeline other than the Sum.integersByKey, I've included the initial parsing operation here, as well, because the nongrouping aspect of the parsing operation provides a nice contrast to the grouping aspect of the summation. Viewed in this light, it's very easy to see the difference between the two. The nongrouping operation does nothing to halt the motion of the elements in the stream, and as a result yields another stream on the other side. In contrast, the grouping operation brings all the elements in the stream to rest as it adds them together into the final sum. Because this example was running on a batch processing engine over bounded data, the final results are emitted only after the end of the input is reached. As we noted in Chapter 2 this example is sufficient for bounded data, but is too limiting in the context of unbounded data because the input will theoretically never end. But is it really insufficient?

Looking at the new streams/tables portion of the diagram, if all we're doing is calculating sums as our final results (and not actually transforming those sums in any additional way further downstream within the pipeline), the table we created with our grouping operation has our answer sitting right there, evolving over time as new data arrive. Why don't we just read our results from there?

This is exactly the point being made by the folks championing stream processors as a database[8] (primarily the Kafka and Flink crews): anywhere you have a grouping operation in your pipeline, you're creating a table that includes what is effectively the output values of that portion of the stage. If those output values happen to be the final thing your pipeline is calculating, you don't need to rematerialize them somewhere else if you can read them directly out of that table. Besides providing quick and easy access to results as they evolve over time, this approach saves on compute resources by not requiring an additional sink stage in the pipeline to materialize the outputs, yields disk savings by eliminating redundant data storage, and obviates the need for any engineering work building the aforementioned sink stages.[9] The only major caveat is that you need to take care to ensure that only the data processing pipeline has the ability to make modifications to the table. If the values in the table can change out from under the pipeline due to external modification, all bets are off regarding consistency guarantees.

---

8 Though as we can clearly see from this example, it's not just a streaming thing; you can get the same effect with a batch system if its state tables are world readable.

9 This is particularly painful if a sink for your storage system of choice doesn't exist yet; building proper sinks that can uphold consistency guarantees is a surprisingly subtle and difficult task.

A number of folks in the industry have been recommending this approach for a while now, and it's being put to great use in a variety of scenarios. We've seen MillWheel customers within Google do the same thing by serving data directly out of their Bigtable-based state tables, and we're in the process of adding first-class support for accessing state from outside of your pipeline in the C++–based Apache Beam equivalent we use internally at Google (Google Flume); hopefully those concepts will make their way to Apache Beam proper someday soon, as well.

Now, reading from the state tables is great if the values therein are your final results. But, if you have more processing to perform downstream in the pipeline (e.g., imagine our pipeline was actually computing the top scoring team), we still need some better way to cope with unbounded data, allowing us to transform the table back into a stream in a more incremental fashion. For that, we'll want to journey back through the remaining three questions, beginning with windowing, expanding into triggering, and finally tying it all together with accumulation.

Where: Windowing

As we know from Chapter 3, windowing tells us *where* in event time grouping occurs. Combined with our earlier experiences, we can thus also infer it must play a role in stream-to-table conversion because grouping is what drives table creation. There are really two aspects of windowing that interact with stream/table theory:

Window assignment
   This effectively just means placing a record into one or more windows.

Window merging
   This is the logic that makes dynamic, data-driven types of windows, such as sessions, possible.

The effect of window assignment is quite straightforward. When a record is conceptually placed into a window, the definition of the window is essentially combined with the user-assigned key for that record to create an implicit composite key used at grouping time.[10] Simple.

For completeness, let's take another look at the original windowing example from Chapter 3, but from a streams and tables perspective. If you recall, the code snippet looked something like Example 6-2 (with parsing *not* elided this time).

---

10 This also means that if you place a value into multiple windows—for example, sliding windows—the value must conceptually be duplicated into multiple, independent records, one per window. Even so, it's possible in some cases for the underlying system to be smart about how it treats certain types of overlapping windows, thus optimize away the need for actually duplicating the value. Spark, for example, does this for sliding windows.

Example 6-2. Summation pipeline

```
PCollection<String> raw = IO.read(...);
PCollection<KV<Team, Integer>> input = raw.apply(new ParseFn());
PCollection<KV<Team, Integer>> totals = input
  .apply(Window.into(FixedWindows.of(TWO_MINUTES)))
  .apply(Sum.integersPerKey());
```

And the original visualization looked like that shown in Figure 6-5.

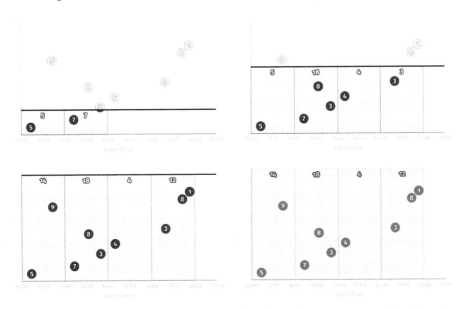

Figure 6-5. Event-time/processing-time view of windowed summation on a batch engine (http://streamingbook.net/fig/6-5)

And now, Figure 6-6 shows the streams and tables version.

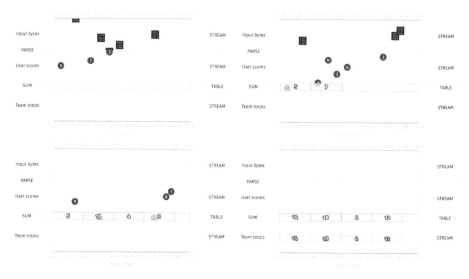

Figure 6-6. Streams and tables view of windowed summation on a batch engine (http://streamingbook.net/fig/6-6)

As you might expect, this looks remarkably similar to Figure 6-4, but with four groupings in the table (corresponding to the four windows occupied by the data) instead of just one. But as before, we must wait until the end of our bounded input is reached before emitting results. We look at how to address this for unbounded data in the next section, but first let's touch briefly on merging windows.

Window merging

Moving on to merging, we'll find that the effect of window merging is more complicated than window assignment, but still straightforward when you think about the logical operations that would need to happen. When grouping a stream into windows that can merge, that grouping operation has to take into account all of the windows that could possibly merge together. Typically, this is limited to windows whose data all have the same key (because we've already established that windowing modifies grouping to not be just by key, but also key and window). For this reason, the system doesn't really treat the key/window pair as a flat composite key, but rather as a hierarchical key, with the user-assigned key as the root, and the window a child component of that root. When it comes time to actually group data together, the system first groups by the root of the hierarchy (the key assigned by the user). After the data have been grouped by key, the system can then proceed with grouping by window within that key (using the child components of the hierarchical composite keys). This act of grouping by window is where window merging happens.

What's interesting from a streams and tables perspective is how this window merging changes the mutations that are ultimately applied to a table; that is, how it modifies the changelog that dictates the contents of the table over time. With nonmerging windows, each new element being grouped results in a single mutation to the table (to add that element to the group for the element's key+window). With merging windows, the act of grouping a new element can result in one or more existing windows being merged with the new window. So, the merging operation must inspect all of the existing windows for the current key, figure out which windows can merge with this new window, and then atomically commit deletes for the old unmerged windows in conjunction with an insert for the new merged window into the table. This is why systems that support merging windows typically define the unit of atomicity/parallelization as key, rather than key+window. Otherwise, it would be impossible (or at least much more expensive) to provide the strong consistency needed for correctness guarantees. When you begin to look at it in this level of detail, you can see why it's so nice to have the system taking care of the nasty business of dealing with window merges. For an even closer view of window merging semantics, I refer you to section 2.2.2 of "The Dataflow Model" (*http://bit.ly/2sXgVJ3*).

At the end of the day, windowing is really just a minor alteration to the semantics of grouping, which means it's a minor alteration to the semantics of stream-to-table conversion. For window assignment, it's as simple as incorporating the window into an implicit composite key used at grouping time. When window merging becomes involved, that composite key is treated more like a hierarchical key, allowing the system to handle the nasty business of grouping by key, figuring out window merges within that key, and then atomically applying all the necessary mutations to the corresponding table for us. Hooray for layers of abstraction!

All that said, we still haven't actually addressed the problem of converting a table to a stream in a more incremental fashion in the case of unbounded data. For that, we need to revisit triggers.

When: Triggers

We learned in Chapter 3 that we use triggers to dictate *when* the contents of a window will be materialized (with watermarks providing a useful signal of input completeness for certain types of triggers). After data have been grouped together into a window, we use triggers to dictate when that data should be sent downstream. In streams/ tables terminology, we understand that grouping means stream-to-table conversion. From there, it's a relatively small leap to see that triggers are the complement to grouping; in other words, that "ungrouping" operation we were grasping for earlier. Triggers are what drive table-to-stream conversion.

In streams/tables terminology, triggers are special procedures applied to a table that allow for data within that table to be materialized in response to relevant events. Stated that way, they actually sound suspiciously similar to classic database triggers. And indeed, the choice of name here was no coincidence; they are essentially the same thing. When you specify a trigger, you are in effect writing code that then is evaluated for every row in the state table as time progresses. When that trigger fires, it takes the corresponding data that are currently at rest in the table and puts them into motion, yielding a new stream.

Let's return to our examples. We'll begin with the simple per-record trigger from Chapter 2, which simply emits a new result every time a new record arrives. The code and event-time/processing-time visualization for that example is shown in Example 6-3. Figure 6-7 presents the results.

Example 6-3. Triggering repeatedly with every record

```
PCollection<String>> raw = IO.read(...);
PCollection<KV<Team, Integer>> input = raw.apply(new ParseFn());
PCollection<KV<Team, Integer>> totals = input
  .apply(Window.into(FixedWindows.of(TWO_MINUTES))
              .triggering(Repeatedly(AfterCount(1))));
  .apply(Sum.integersPerKey());
```

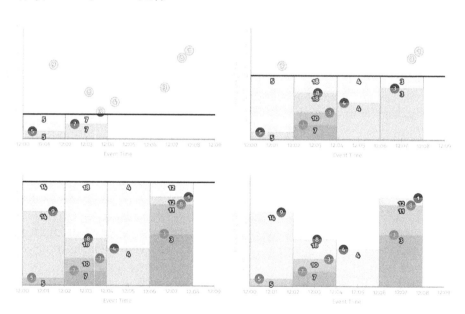

Figure 6-7. Per-record triggering on a streaming engine (http://streamingbook.net/fig/6-7)

As before, new results are materialized every time a new record is encountered. Rendered in a streams and tables type of view, this diagram would look like Figure 6-8.

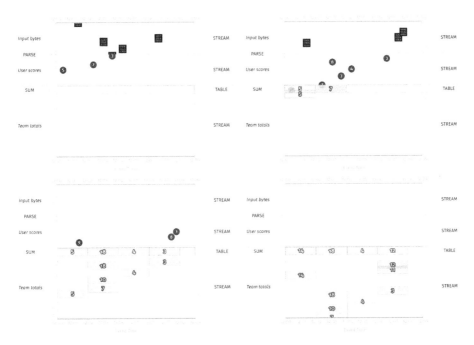

Figure 6-8. Streams and tables view of windowed summation with per-record triggering on a streaming engine (http://streamingbook.net/fig/6-8)

An interesting side effect of using per-record triggers is how it somewhat masks the effect of data being brought to rest, given that they are then immediately put back into motion again by the trigger. Even so, the aggregate artifact from the grouping remains at rest in the table, as the ungrouped stream of values flows away from it.

To get a better sense of the at-rest/in-motion relationship, let's skip forward in our triggering examples to the basic watermark completeness streaming example from Chapter 2, which simply emitted results when complete (due to the watermark passing the end of the window). The code and event-time/processing-time visualization for that example are presented in Example 6-4 (note that I'm only showing the heuristic watermark version here, for brevity and ease of comparison) and Figure 6-9 illustrates the results.

Example 6-4. Watermark completeness trigger

```
PCollection<String> raw = IO.read(...);
PCollection<KV<Team, Integer>> input = raw.apply(new ParseFn());
PCollection<KV<Team, Integer>> totals = input
  .apply(Window.into(FixedWindows.of(TWO_MINUTES))
              .triggering(AfterWatermark()))
  .apply(Sum.integersPerKey());
```

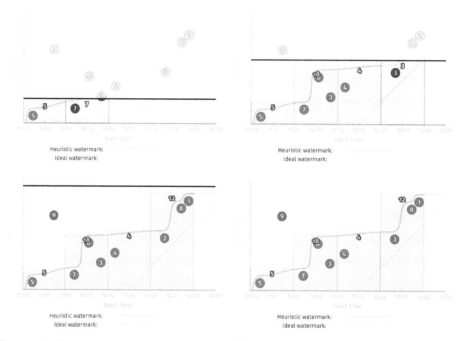

Figure 6-9. Event-time/processing-time view of windowed summation with a heuristic watermark on a streaming engine (http://streamingbook.net/fig/6-9)

Thanks to the trigger specified in Example 6-4, which declares that windows should be materialized when the watermark passes them, the system is able to emit results in a progressive fashion as the otherwise unbounded input to the pipeline becomes more and more complete. Looking at the streams and tables version in Figure 6-10, it looks as you might expect.

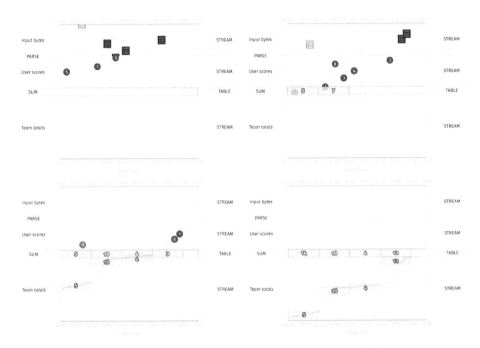

Figure 6-10. Streams and tables view of windowed summation with a heuristic watermark on a streaming engine (http://streamingbook.net/fig/6-10)

In this version, you can see very clearly the ungrouping effect triggers have on the state table. As the watermark passes the end of each window, it pulls the result for that window out of the table and sets it in motion downstream, separate from all the other values in the table. We of course still have the late data issue from before, which we can solve again with the more comprehensive trigger shown in Example 6-5.

Example 6-5. Early, on-time, and late firings via the early/on-time/late API

```
PCollection<String> raw = IO.read(...);
PCollection<KV<Team, Integer>> input = raw.apply(new ParseFn());
PCollection<KV<Team, Integer>> totals = input
  .apply(Window.into(FixedWindows.of(TWO_MINUTES))
               .triggering(
                 AfterWatermark()
                   .withEarlyFirings(AlignedDelay(ONE_MINUTE))
                   .withLateFirings(AfterCount(1))))
  .apply(Sum.integersPerKey());
```

The event-time/processing-time diagram looks like Figure 6-11.

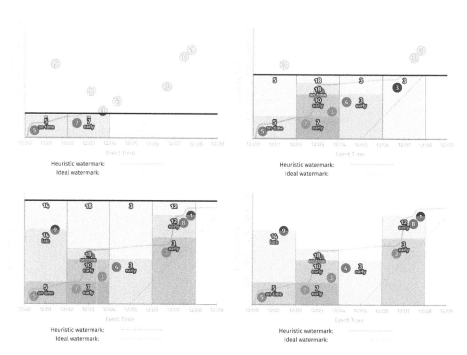

Figure 6-11. Event-time/processing-time view of windowed summation on a streaming engine with early/on-time/late trigger (http://streamingbook.net/fig/6-11)

Whereas the streams and tables version looks like that shown in Figure 6-12.

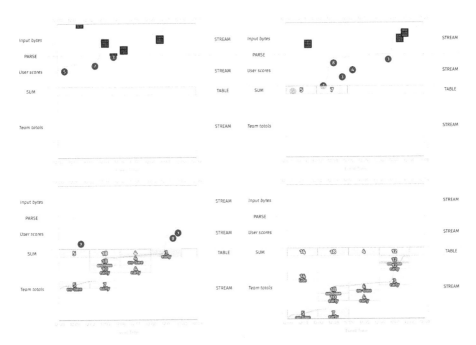

Figure 6-12. Streams and tables view of windowed summation on a streaming engine with early/on-time/late trigger (http://streamingbook.net/fig/6-12)

This version makes even more clear the ungrouping effect triggers have, rendering an evolving view of the various independent pieces of the table into a stream, as dictated by the triggers specified in Example 6-6.

The semantics of all the concrete triggers we've talked about so far (event-time, processing-time, count, composites like early/on-time/late, etc.) are just as you would expect when viewed from the streams/tables perspective, so they aren't worth further discussion. However, we haven't yet spent much time talking about what triggers look like in a classic batch processing scenario. Now that we understand what the underlying streams/tables topology of a batch pipeline looks like, this is worth touching upon briefly.

At the end of the day, there's really only one type of trigger used in classic batch scenarios: one that fires when the input is complete. For the initial MapRead stage of the MapReduce job we looked at earlier, that trigger would conceptually fire for all of the data in the input table as soon as the pipeline launched, given that the input for a batch job is assumed to be complete from the get go.[11] That input source table would thus be converted into a stream of individual elements, after which the Map stage could begin processing them.

For table-to-stream conversions in the middle of the pipeline, such as the Reduce-Read stage in our example, the same type of trigger is used. In this case, however, the trigger must actually wait for all of the data in the table to be complete (i.e., what is more commonly referred to as all of the data being written to the shuffle), much as our example batch pipelines in Figures 6-4 and 6-6 waited for the end of the input before emitting their final results.

Given that classic batch processing effectively always makes use of the input-data-complete trigger, you might ask what any custom triggers specified by the author of the pipeline might mean in a batch scenario. The answer here really is: it depends. There are two aspects worth discussing:

Trigger guarantees (or lack thereof)

Most existing batch processing systems have been designed with this lock-step read-process-group-write-repeat sequence in mind. In such circumstances, it's difficult to provide any sort of finer-grained trigger abilities, because the only place they would manifest any sort of change would be at the final shuffle stage of the pipeline. This doesn't mean that the triggers specified by the user aren't honored, however; the semantics of triggers are such that it's possible to resort to lower common denominators when appropriate.

For example, an `AfterWatermark` trigger is meant to trigger *after* the watermark passes the end of a window. It makes no guarantees how *far* beyond the end of the window the watermark may be when it fires. Similarly, an `AfterCount(N)` trigger only guarantees that *at least* N elements have been processed before triggering; N might very well be all of the elements in the input set.

Note that this clever wording of trigger names wasn't chosen simply to accommodate classic batch systems within the model; it's a very necessary part of the model itself, given the natural asynchronicity and nondeterminism of triggering. Even in a finely tuned, low-latency, true-streaming system, it's essentially impossible to guarantee that an `AfterWatermark` trigger will fire while the watermark is precisely *at* the end of any given window, except perhaps under the most extremely limited circumstances (e.g., a single machine processing all of the data for the pipeline with a relatively modest load). And even if you could guarantee

---

11 Note that this high-level conceptual view of how things work in batch pipelines belies the complexity of efficiently triggering an entire table of data at once, particularly when that table is sizeable enough to require a plurality of machines to process. The SplittableDoFn API (*https://s.apache.org/splittable-do-fn*) recently added to Beam provides some insight into the mechanics involved.

it, what really would be the point? Triggers provide a means of controlling the flow of data from a table into a stream, nothing more.

The blending of batch and streaming

Given what we've learned in this writeup, it should be clear that the main semantic difference between batch and streaming systems is the ability to trigger tables incrementally. But even that isn't really a semantic difference, but more of a latency/throughput trade-off (because batch systems typically give you higher throughput at the cost of higher latency of results).

This goes back to something I said in "Batch and Streaming Efficiency Differences" on page 7: there's really not that much difference between batch and streaming systems today except for an efficiency delta (in favor of batch) and a natural ability to deal with unbounded data (in favor of streaming). I argued then that much of that efficiency delta comes from the combination of larger bundle sizes (an explicit compromise of latency in favor of throughput) and more efficient shuffle implementations (i.e., stream → table → stream conversions). From that perspective, it should be possible to provide a system that seamlessly integrates the best of both worlds: one which provides the ability to handle unbounded data naturally but can also balance the tensions between latency, throughput, and cost across a broad spectrum of use cases by transparently tuning the bundle sizes, shuffle implementations, and other such implementation details under the covers.

This is precisely what Apache Beam already does at the API level.[12] The argument being made here is that there's room for unification at the execution-engine level, as well. In a world like that, batch and streaming will no longer be a thing, and we'll be able to say goodbye to both batch *and* streaming as independent concepts once and for all. We'll just have general data processing systems that combine the best ideas from both branches in the family tree to provide an optimal experience for the specific use case at hand. Some day.

At this point, we can stick a fork in the trigger section. It's done. We have only one more brief stop on our way to having a holistic view of the relationship between the Beam Model and streams-and-tables theory: *accumulation*.

How: Accumulation

In Chapter 2, we learned that the three accumulation modes (discarding, accumulating, accumulating and retracting[13]) tell us how refinements of results relate when a

---

12 And yes, if you blend batch and streaming together you get Beam, which is where that name came from originally. For reals.

13 This is why you should always use an Oxford comma.

window is triggered multiple times over the course of its life. Fortunately, the relationship to streams and tables here is pretty straightforward:

- *Discarding mode* requires the system to either throw away the previous value for the window when triggering or keep around a copy of the previous value and compute the delta the next time the window triggers.[14] (This mode might have better been called Delta mode.)

- *Accumulating mode* requires no additional work; the current value for the window in the table at triggering time is what is emitted. (This mode might have better been called Value mode.)

- *Accumulating and retracting mode* requires keeping around copies of all previously triggered (but not yet retracted) values for the window. This list of previous values can grow quite large in the case of merging windows like sessions, but is vital to cleanly reverting the effects of those previous trigger firings in cases where the new value cannot simply be used to overwrite a previous value. (This mode might have better been called Value and Retractions mode.)

The streams-and-tables visualizations of accumulation modes add little additional insight into their semantics, so we won't investigate them here.

A Holistic View of Streams and Tables in the Beam Model

Having addressed the four questions, we can now take a holistic view of streams and tables in a Beam Model pipeline. Let's take our running example (the team scores calculation pipeline) and see what its structure looks like at the streams-and-table level. The full code for the pipeline might look something like Example 6-6 (repeating Example 6-5).

Example 6-6. Our full score-parsing pipeline

```
PCollection<String> raw = IO.read(...);
PCollection<KV<Team, Integer>> input = raw.apply(new ParseFn());
PCollection<KV<Team, Integer>> totals = input
  .apply(Window.into(FixedWindows.of(TWO_MINUTES))
            .triggering(
               AfterWatermark()
                 .withEarlyFirings(AlignedDelay(ONE_MINUTE))
                 .withLateFirings(AfterCount(1))))
  .apply(Sum.integersPerKey());
```

---

14 Note that in the case of merging windows, in addition to merging the current values for the two windows to yield a merged current value, the previous values for those two windows would need to be merged, as well, to allow for the later calculation of a merged delta come triggering time.

Breaking that apart into stages separated by the intermediate `PCollection` types (where I've used more semantic "type" names like `Team` and `User Score` than real types for clarity of what is happening at each stage), you would arrive at something like that depicted in Figure 6-13.

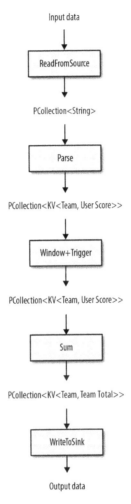

Figure 6-13. Logical phases of a team score summation pipeline, with intermediate PCollection types

When you actually run this pipeline, it first goes through an optimizer, whose job is to convert this logical execution plan into an optimized, physical execution plan. Each execution engine is different, so actual physical execution plans will vary between runners. But a believable strawperson plan might look something like Figure 6-14.

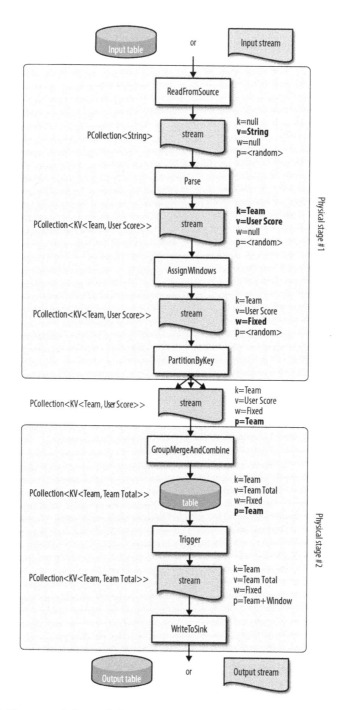

Figure 6-14. Theoretical physical phases of a team score summation pipeline, with intermediate PCollection types

There's a lot going on here, so let's walk through all of it. There are three main differences between Figures 6-13 and 6-14 that we'll be discussing:

Logical versus physical operations

As part of building a physical execution plan, the underlying engine must convert the logical operations provided by the user into a sequence of primitive operations supported by the engine. In some cases, those physical equivalents look essentially the same (e.g., Parse), and in others, they're very different.

Physical stages and fusion

It's often inefficient to execute each logical phase as a fully independent physical stage in the pipeline (with attendant serialization, network communication, and deserialization overhead between each). As a result, the optimizer will typically try to fuse as many physical operations as possible into a single physical stage.

Keys, values, windows, and partitioning

To make it more evident what each physical operation is doing, I've annotated the intermediate PCollections with the type of key, value, window, and data partitioning in effect at each point.

Let's now walk through each logical operation in detail and see what it translated to in the physical plan and how they all relate to streams and tables:

ReadFromSource

Other than being fused with the physical operation immediately following it (Parse), not much interesting happens in translation for ReadFromSource. As far as the characteristics of our data at this point, because the read is essentially consuming raw input bytes, we basically have raw strings with no keys, no windows, and no (or random) partitioning. The original data source can be either a table (e.g., a Cassandra table) or a stream (e.g., RabbitMQ) or something a little like both (e.g., Kafka in log compaction mode). But regardless, the end result of reading from the input source is a stream.

Parse

The logical Parse operation also translates in a relatively straightforward manner to the physical version. Parse takes the raw strings and extracts a key (team ID) and value (user score) from them. It's a nongrouping operation, and thus the stream it consumed remains a stream on the other side.

Window+Trigger

This logical operation is spread out across a number of distinct physical operations. The first is window assignment, in which each element is assigned to a set of windows. That happens immediately in the AssignWindows operation, which is a nongrouping operation that simply annotates each element in the stream with the window(s) it now belongs to, yielding another stream on the other side.

The second is window merging, which we learned earlier in the chapter happens as part of the grouping operation. As such, it gets sunk down into the `GroupMer geAndCombine` operation later in the pipeline. We discuss that operation when we talk about the logical `Sum` operation next.

And finally, there's triggering. Triggering happens after grouping and is the way that we'll convert the table created by grouping back into a stream. As such, it gets sunk into its own operation, which follows `GroupMergeAndCombine`.

Sum

Summation is really a composite operation, consisting of a couple pieces: partitioning and aggregation. Partitioning is a nongrouping operation that redirects the elements in the stream in such a way that elements with the same keys end up going to the same physical machine. Another word for partitioning is shuffling, though that term is a bit overloaded because "Shuffle" in the MapReduce sense is often used to mean both partitioning *and* grouping (*and* sorting, for that matter). Regardless, partitioning physically alters the stream in a way that makes it groupable but doesn't do anything to actually bring the data to rest. As a result, it's a nongrouping operation that yields another stream on the other side.

After partitioning comes grouping. Grouping itself is a composite operation. First comes grouping by key (enabled by the previous partition-by-key operation). Next comes window merging and grouping by window, as we described earlier. And finally, because summation is implemented as a `CombineFn` in Beam (essentially an incremental aggregation operation), there's combining, where individual elements are summed together as they arrive. The specific details are not terribly important for our purposes here. What is important is the fact that, since this is (obviously) a grouping operation, our chain of streams now comes to rest in a table containing the summed team totals as they evolve over time.

WriteToSink

Lastly, we have the write operation, which takes the stream yielded by triggering (which was sunk below the `GroupMergeAndCombine` operation, as you might recall) and writes it out to our output data sink. That data itself can be either a table or stream. If it's a table, `WriteToSink` will need to perform some sort of grouping operation as part of writing the data into the table. If it's a stream, no grouping will be necessary (though partitioning might still be desired; for example, when writing into something like Kafka).

The big takeaway here is not so much the precise details of everything that's going on in the physical plan, but more the overall relationship of the Beam Model to the world of streams and tables. We saw three types of operations: nongrouping (e.g., `Parse`), grouping (e.g., `GroupMergeAndCombine`), and ungrouping (e.g., `Trigger`). The nongrouping operations always consumed streams and produced streams on the other side. The grouping operations always consumed streams and yielded tables. And the ungrouping operations consumed tables and yielded streams. These insights, along with everything else we've learned along the way, are enough for us to formulate a more general theory about the relationship of the Beam Model to streams and tables.

A General Theory of Stream and Table Relativity

Having surveyed how stream processing, batch processing, the four *what*/*where*/*when*/*how* questions, and the Beam Model as a whole relate to stream and table theory, let's now attempt to articulate a more general definition of stream and table relativity.

A general theory of stream and table relativity:

- *Data processing pipelines* (both batch and streaming) consist of *tables*, *streams*, and *operations* upon those tables and streams.

- *Tables* are *data at rest*, and act as a container for data to accumulate and be observed over time.

- *Streams* are *data in motion*, and encode a discretized view of the evolution of a table over time.

- *Operations* act upon a stream or table and yield a new stream or table. They are categorized as follows:

  — stream → stream: Nongrouping (element-wise) operations

    Applying *nongrouping* operations to a stream alters the data in the stream while leaving them in motion, yielding a new stream with possibly different cardinality.

  — stream → table: Grouping operations

    Grouping data within a stream brings those data to rest, yielding a *table* that evolves over time.

      — *Windowing* incorporates the dimension of event time into such groupings.

      — *Merging windows* dynamically combine over time, allowing them to reshape themselves in response to the data observed and dictating that key remain the unit of atomicity/parallelization, with window being a child component of grouping within that key.

  — table → stream: Ungrouping (triggering) operations

    Triggering data within a table ungroups them into motion, yielding a *stream* that captures a view of the table's evolution over time.

- *Watermarks* provide a notion of input completeness relative to event time, which is a useful reference point when triggering event-timestamped data, particularly data grouped into event-time windows from unbounded streams.

- The *accumulation mode* for the trigger determines the nature of the stream, dictating whether it contains deltas or values, and whether retractions for previous deltas/values are provided.

— table → table: (none)

There are no operations that consume a table and yield a table, because it's not possible for data to go from rest and back to rest without being put into motion. As a result, all modifications to a table are via conversion to a stream and back again.

What I love about these rules is that they just make sense. They have a very natural and intuitive feeling about them, and as a result they make it so much easier to understand how data flow (or don't) through a sequence of operations. They codify the fact that data exist in one of two constitutions at any given time (streams or tables), and they provide simple rules for reasoning about the transitions between those states. They demystify windowing by showing how it's just a slight modification of a thing everyone already innately understands: grouping. They highlight why grouping operations in general are always such a sticking point for streaming (because they bring data in streams to rest as tables) but also make it very clear what sorts of operations are needed to get things unstuck (triggers; i.e., ungrouping operations). And they underscore just how unified batch and stream processing really are, at a conceptual level.

When I set out to write this chapter, I wasn't entirely sure what I was going to end up with, but the end result was much more satisfying than I'd imagined it might be. In the chapters to come, we use this theory of stream and table relativity again and again to help guide our analyses. And every time, its application will bring clarity and insight that would otherwise have been much harder to gain. Streams and tables are the best.

Summary

In this chapter, we first established the basics of stream and table theory. We first defined streams and tables relatively:

streams → tables
    The aggregation of a stream of updates over time yields a table.

tables → streams
    The observation of changes to a table over time yields a stream.

We next defined them independently:

- Tables are data *at rest*.
- Streams are data *in motion*.

We then assessed the classic MapReduce model of batch computation from a streams and tables perspective and came to the conclusion that the following four steps describe batch processing from that perspective:

1. Tables are read in their entirety to become streams.
2. Streams are processed into new streams until a grouping operation is hit.
3. Grouping turns the stream into a table.
4. Steps 1 through 3 repeat until you run out of operations in the pipeline.

From this analysis, we were able to see that streams are just as much a part of batch processing as they are stream processing, and also that the idea of data being a stream is an orthogonal one from whether the data in question are bounded or unbounded.

Next, we spent a good deal of time considering the relationship between streams and tables and the robust, out-of-order stream processing semantics afforded by the Beam Model, ultimately arriving at the general theory of stream and table relativity we enumerated in the previous section. In addition to the basic definitions of streams and tables, the key insight in that theory is that there are four (really, just three) types of operations in a data processing pipeline:

stream → stream
Nongrouping (element-wise) operations

stream → table
Grouping operations

table → stream
Ungrouping (triggering) operations

table → table
(nonexistent)

By classifying operations in this way, it becomes trivial to understand how data flow through (and linger within) a given pipeline over time.

Finally, and perhaps most important of all, we learned this: when you look at things from the streams-and-tables point of view, it becomes abundantly clear how batch and streaming really are just the same thing conceptually. Bounded or unbounded, it doesn't matter. It's streams and tables from top to bottom.

</bad-physics-jokes>

CHAPTER 7

The Practicalities of Persistent State

Why do people write books? When you factor out the joy of creativity, a certain fondness for grammar and punctuation, and perhaps the occasional touch of narcissism, you're basically left with the desire to capture an otherwise ephemeral idea so that it can be revisited in the future. At a very high level, I've just motivated and explained persistent state in data processing pipelines.

Persistent state is, quite literally, the tables we just talked about in Chapter 6, with the additional requirement that the tables be robustly stored in a media relatively immune to loss. Stored on local disk counts, as long as you don't ask your Site Reliability Engineers. Stored on a replicated set of disks is better. Stored on a replicated set of disks in distinct physical locations is better still. Stored in memory once definitely doesn't count. Stored in replicated memory across multiple machines with UPS power backup and generators onsite maybe does. You get the picture.

In this chapter, our objective is to do the following:

- Motivate the need for persistent state within pipelines
- Look at two forms of implicit state often found within pipelines
- Consider a real-world use case (advertising conversion attribution) that lends itself poorly to implicit state, use that to motivate the salient features of a general, explicit form of persistent state management
- Explore a concrete manifestation of one such state API, as found in Apache Beam

Motivation

To begin, let's more precisely motivate persistent state. We know from Chapter 6 that grouping is what gives us tables. And the core of what I postulated at the beginning of this chapter was correct: the point of persisting these tables is to capture the otherwise ephemeral data contained therein. But why is that necessary?

The Inevitability of Failure

The answer to that question is most clearly seen in the case of processing unbounded input data, so we'll start there. The main issue is that pipelines processing unbounded data are effectively intended to run forever. But running forever is a far more demanding Service-Level Objective than can be achieved by the environments in which these pipelines typically execute. Long-running pipelines will inevitably see interruptions thanks to machine failures, planned maintenance, code changes, and the occasional misconfigured command that takes down an entire cluster of production pipelines. To ensure that they can resume where they left off when these kinds of things happen, long-running pipelines need some sort of durable recollection of where they were before the interruption. That's where persistent state comes in.

Let's expand on that idea a bit beyond unbounded data. Is this only relevant in the unbounded case? Do batch pipelines use persistent state, and why or why not? As with nearly every other batch-versus-streaming question we've come across, the answer has less to do with the nature of batch and streaming systems themselves (perhaps unsurprising given what we learned in Chapter 6), and more to do with the types of datasets they historically have been used to process.

Bounded datasets by nature are finite in size. As a result, systems that process bounded data (historically batch systems) have been tailored to that use case. They often assume that the input can be reprocessed in its entirety upon failure. In other words, if some piece of the processing pipeline fails and if the input data are still available, we can simply restart the appropriate piece of the processing pipeline and let it read the same input again. This is called *reprocessing the input*.

They might also assume failures are infrequent and thus optimize for the common case by persisting as little as possible, accepting the extra cost of recomputation upon failure. For particularly expensive, multistage pipelines, there might be some sort of per-stage global checkpointing that allows for more efficiently resuming execution (typically as part of a shuffle), but it's not a strict requirement and might not be present in many systems.

Unbounded datasets, on the other hand, must be assumed to have infinite size. As a result, systems that process unbounded data (historically streaming systems) have been built to match. They never assume that all of the data will be available for reprocessing, only some known subset of it. To provide at-least-once or exactly-once semantics, any data that are no longer available for reprocessing must be accounted for in durable checkpoints. And if at-most-once is all you're going for, you don't need checkpointing.

At the end of the day, there's nothing batch- or streaming-specific about persistent state. State can be useful in both circumstances. It just happens to be critical when processing unbounded data, so you'll find that streaming systems typically provide more sophisticated support for persistent state.

Correctness and Efficiency

Given the inevitability of failures and the need to cope with them, persistent state can be seen as providing two things:

- A *basis for correctness* in light of ephemeral inputs. When processing bounded data, it's often safe to assume inputs stay around forever;[1] with unbounded data, this assumption typically falls short of reality. Persistent state allows you to keep around the intermediate bits of information necessary to allow processing to continue when the inevitable happens, even after your input source has moved on and forgotten about records it gave you previously.

- A way to *minimize work duplicated and data persisted* as part of coping with failures. Regardless of whether your inputs are ephemeral, when your pipeline experiences a machine failure, any work on the failed machine that wasn't checkpointed somewhere must be redone. Depending upon the nature of the pipeline and its inputs, this can be costly in two dimensions: the amount of work performed during reprocessing, and the amount of input data stored to support reprocessing.

Minimizing duplicated work is relatively straightforward. By checkpointing partial progress within a pipeline (both the intermediate results computed as well as the current location within the input as of checkpointing time), it's possible to greatly reduce the amount of work repeated when failures occur because none of the operations that came before the checkpoint need to be replayed from durable inputs. Most commonly, this involves data at rest (i.e., tables), which is why we typically refer to persistent state in the context of tables and grouping. But there are persistent forms of streams (e.g., Kafka and its relatives) that serve this function, as well.

Minimizing the amount of data persisted is a larger discussion, one that will consume a sizeable chunk of this chapter. For now, at least, suffice it to say that, for many real-world use cases, rather than remembering all of the raw inputs within a checkpoint for any given stage in the pipeline, it's often practical to instead remember some partial, intermediate form of the ongoing calculation that consumes less space than all of the original inputs (for example, when computing a

---

1 For some definition of "forever," typically at least "until we successfully complete execution of our batch pipeline and no longer require the inputs."

mean, the total sum and the count of values seen are much more compact than the complete list of values contributing to that sum and count). Not only can checkpointing these intermediate data drastically reduce the amount of data that you need to remember at any given point in the pipeline, it also commensurately reduces the amount of reprocessing needed for that specific stage to recover from a failure.

Furthermore, by intelligently garbage-collecting those bits of persistent state that are no longer needed (i.e., state for records which are known to have been processed completely by the pipeline already), the amount of data stored in persistent state for a given pipeline can be kept to a manageable size over time, even when the inputs are technically infinite. This is how pipelines processing unbounded data can continue to run effectively forever, while still providing strong consistency guarantees but without a need for complete recall of the original inputs to the pipeline.

At the end of the day, persistent state is really just a means of providing correctness and efficient fault tolerance in data processing pipelines. The amount of support needed in either of those dimensions depends greatly upon the natures of the inputs to the pipeline and the operations being performed. Unbounded inputs tend to require more correctness support than bounded inputs. Computationally expensive operations tend to demand more efficiency support than computationally cheap operations.

Implicit State

Let's now begin to talk about the practicalities of persistent state. In most cases, this essentially boils down to finding the right balance between always persisting everything (good for consistency, bad for efficiency) and never persisting anything (bad for consistency, good for efficiency). We'll begin at the always-persisting-everything end of the spectrum, and work our way in the other direction, looking at ways of trading off complexity of implementation for efficiency without compromising consistency (because compromising consistency by never persisting anything is the easy way out for cases in which consistency doesn't matter, and a nonoption, otherwise). As before, we use the Apache Beam APIs to concretely ground our discussions, but the concepts we discuss are applicable across most systems in existence today.

Also, because there isn't much you can do to reduce the size of raw inputs, short of perhaps compressing the data, our discussion centers around the ways data are persisted within the intermediate state tables created as part of grouping operations within a pipeline. The inherent nature of grouping multiple records together into some sort of composite will provide us with opportunities to eke out gains in efficiency at the cost of implementation complexity.

Raw Grouping

The first step in our exploration, at the always-persisting-everything end of the spectrum, is the most straightforward implementation of grouping within a pipeline: raw grouping of the inputs. The grouping operation in this case is typically akin to list appending: any time a new element arrives in the group, it's appended to the list of elements seen for that group.

In Beam, this is exactly what you get when you apply a `GroupByKey` transform to a `PCollection`. The stream representing that `PCollection` in motion is grouped by key to yield a table at rest containing the records from the stream,[2] grouped together as lists of values with identical keys. This shows up in the `PTransform` signature for `GroupByKey`, which declares the input as a `PCollection` of K/V pairs, and the output as a collection of K/Iterable<V> pairs:

```
class GroupByKey<K, V> extends PTransform<
    PCollection<KV<K, V>>, PCollection<KV<K, Iterable<V>>>>
```

Every time a trigger fires for a key+window in that table, it will emit a new pane for that key+window, with the value being the `Iterable<V>` we see in the preceding signature.

Let's look at an example in action in Example 7-1. We'll take the summation pipeline from Example 6-5 (the one with fixed windowing and early/on-time/late triggers) and convert it to use raw grouping instead of incremental combination (which we discuss a little later in this chapter). We do this by first applying a `GroupByKey` transformation to the parsed user/score key/value pairs. The `GroupByKey` operation performs raw grouping, yielding a `PCollection` with key/value pairs of users and `Iterable<Integer>` groups of scores. We then sum up all of the `Integers` in each iterable by using a simple `MapElements` lambda that converts the `Iterable<Integer>` into an `IntStream<Integer>` and calls `sum` on it.

Example 7-1. Early, on-time, and late firings via the early/on-time/late API

```
PCollection<String> raw = IO.read(...);
PCollection<KV<Team, Integer>> input = raw.apply(new ParseFn());
PCollection<KV<Team, Integer>> groupedScores = input
  .apply(Window.into(FixedWindows.of(TWO_MINUTES))
              .triggering(
                AfterWatermark()
                  .withEarlyFirings(AlignedDelay(ONE_MINUTE))
                  .withLateFirings(AfterCount(1))))
```

---

2 Recall that Beam doesn't currently expose these state tables directly; you must trigger them back into a stream to observe their contents as a new PCollection.

```
   .apply(GroupBy.<String, Integer>create());
PCollection<KV<Team, Integer>> totals = input
   .apply(MapElements.via((KV<String, Iterable<Integer>> kv) ->
      StreamSupport.intStream(
         kv.getValue().spliterator(), false).sum()));
```

Looking at this pipeline in action, we would see something like that depicted in Figure 7-1.

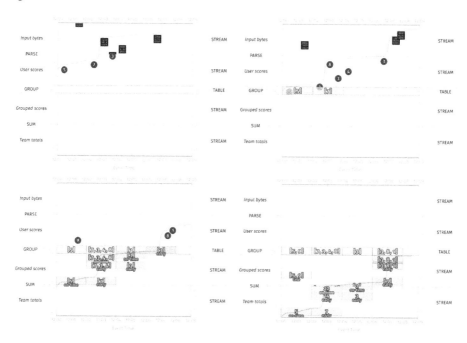

Figure 7-1. Summation via raw grouping of inputs with windowing and early/on-time/ late triggering. The raw inputs are grouped together and stored in the table via the GroupByKey transformation. After being triggered, the MapElements lambda sums the raw inputs within a single pane together to yield per-team scores. (http://streaming book.net/fig/7-1)

Comparing this to Figure 6-10 (which was using incremental combining, discussed shortly), it's clear to see this is a lot worse. First, we're storing a lot more data: instead of a single integer per window, we now store all the inputs for that window. Second, if we have multiple trigger firings, we're duplicating effort by re-summing inputs we already added together for previous trigger firings. And finally, if the grouping operation is the point at which we checkpoint our state to persistent storage, upon machine failure we again must recompute the sums for any retriggerings of the table. That's a lot of duplicated data and computation. Far better would be to incrementally compute and checkpoint the actual sums, which is an example of *incremental combining*.

Incremental Combining

The first step in our journey of trading implementation complexity for efficiency is incremental combining. This concept is manifested in the Beam API via the CombineFn class. In a nutshell, incremental combining is a form of automatic state built upon a user-defined associative and commutative combining operator (if you're not sure what I mean by these two terms, I define them more precisely in a moment). Though not strictly necessary for the discussion that follows, the important parts of the CombineFn API look like Example 7-2.

Example 7-2. Abbreviated CombineFn API from Apache Beam

```
class CombineFn<InputT, AccumT, OutputT> {
    // Returns an accumulator representing the empty value.
    AccumT createAccumulator();

    // Adds the given input value into the given accumulator
    AccumT addInput(AccumT accumulator, InputT input);

    // Merges the given accumulators into a new, combined accumulator
    AccumT mergeAccumulators(Iterable<AccumT> accumulators);

    // Returns the output value for the given accumulator
    OutputT extractOutput(AccumT accumulator);
}
```

A CombineFn accepts inputs of type InputT, which can be combined together into partial aggregates called *accumulators*, of type AccumT. These accumulators themselves can also be combined together into new accumulators. And finally, an accumulator can be transformed into an output value of type OutputT. For something like an average, the inputs might be integers, the accumulators pairs of integers (i.e., Pair<sum of inputs, count of inputs>), and the output a single floating-point value representing the mean value of the combined inputs.

But what does all this structure buy us? Conceptually, the basic idea with incremental combining is that many types of aggregations (sum, mean, etc.) exhibit the following properties:

- Incremental aggregations possess an *intermediate form* that captures the *partial progress* of combining a set of N inputs *more compactly* than the full list of those inputs themselves (i.e., the AccumT type in CombineFn). As discussed earlier, for mean, this is a sum/count pair. Basic summation is even simpler, with a single number as its accumulator. A histogram would have a relatively complex accumulator composed of buckets, where each bucket contains a count for the number of values seen within some specific range. In all three cases, however, the amount of space consumed by an accumulator that represents the aggregation of

N elements remains significantly smaller than the amount of space consumed by the original N elements themselves, particularly as the size of N grows.

- Incremental aggregations are *indifferent to ordering* across two dimensions:

    — *Individual elements*, meaning:

    ```
    COMBINE(a, b) == COMBINE(b, a)
    ```

    — *Groupings of elements*, meaning:

    ```
    COMBINE(COMBINE(a, b), c) == COMBINE(a, COMBINE(b, c))
    ```

These properties are known as *commutativity* and *associativity*, respectively. In concert,[3] they effectively mean that we are free to combine elements and partial aggregates in any arbitrary order and with any arbitrary subgrouping. This allows us to optimize the aggregation in two ways:

Incrementalization

Because the order of individual inputs doesn't matter, we don't need to buffer all of the inputs ahead of time and then process them in some strict order (e.g., in order of event time; note, however, that this remains independent of *shuffling* elements by event time into proper event-time windows before aggregating); we can simply combine them one-by-one as they arrive. This not only greatly reduces the amount of data that must be buffered (thanks to the first property of our operation, which stated the intermediate form was a more compact representation of partial aggregation than the raw inputs themselves), but also spreads the computation load more evenly over time (versus aggregating a burst of inputs all at once after the full input set has been buffered).

Parallelization

Because the order in which partial subgroups of inputs are combined doesn't matter, we're free to arbitrarily distribute the computation of those subgroups. More specifically, we're free to spread the computation of those subgroups across a plurality of machines. This optimization is at the heart of MapReduce's Combiners (the genesis of Beam's CombineFn).

MapReduce's Combiner optimization is essential to solving the hot-key problem, where some sort of grouping computation is performed on an input stream that is too large to be reasonably processed by a single physical machine. A canonical example is breaking down high-volume analytics data

---

3 Or, as my colleague Kenn Knowles points out, if you take the definition as being commutativity across sets, the three-parameter version of commutativity is actually sufficient to also imply associativity: `COMBINE(a, b, c) == COMBINE(a, c, b) == COMBINE(b, a, c) == COMBINE(b, c, a) == COMBINE(c, a, b) == COMBINE(c, b, a)`. Math is fun.

(e.g., web traffic to a popular website) across a relatively low number of dimensions (e.g., by web browser family: Chrome, Firefox, Safari, etc.). For websites with a particularly high volume of traffic, it's often intractable to calculate stats for any single web browser family on a single machine, even if that's the only thing that machine is dedicated to doing; there's simply too much traffic to keep up with. But with an associative and commutative operation like summation, it's possible to spread the initial aggregation across multiple machines, each of which computes a partial aggregate. The set of partial aggregates generated by those machines (whose size is now many of orders magnitude smaller than the original inputs) might then be further combined together on a single machine to yield the final aggregate result.

As an aside, this ability to parallelize also yields one additional benefit: the aggregation operation is naturally compatible with merging windows. When two windows merge, their values must somehow be merged, as well. With raw grouping, this means merging the two full lists of buffered values together, which has a cost of O(N). But with a CombineFn, it's a simple combination of two partial aggregates, typically an O(1) operation.

For the sake of completeness, consider again Example 6-5, shown in Example 7-3, which implements a summation pipeline using incremental combination.

Example 7-3. Grouping and summation via incremental combination, as in Example 6-5

```
PCollection<String> raw = IO.read(...);
PCollection<KV<Team, Integer>> input = raw.apply(new ParseFn());
PCollection<KV<Team, Integer>> totals = input
  .apply(Window.into(FixedWindows.of(TWO_MINUTES))
              .triggering(
                AfterWatermark()
                  .withEarlyFirings(AlignedDelay(ONE_MINUTE))
                  .withLateFirings(AfterCount(1))))
  .apply(Sum.integersPerKey());
```

When executed, we get what we saw in Figure 6-10 (shown here in Figure 7-2). Compared to Figure 7-1, this is clearly a big improvement, with much greater efficiency in terms of amount of data stored and amount of computation performed.

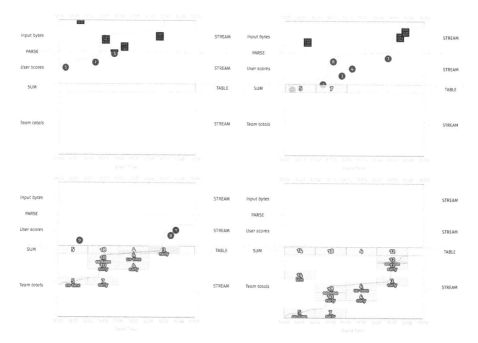

Figure 7-2. Grouping and summation via incremental combination. In this version, incremental sums are computed and stored in the table rather than lists of inputs, which must later be summed together independently. (http://streamingbook.net/fig/7-2)

By providing a more compact intermediate representation for a grouping operation, and by relaxing requirements on ordering (both at the element and subgroup levels), Beam's `CombineFn` trades off a certain amount of implementation complexity in exchange for increases in efficiency. In doing so, it provides a clean solution for the hot-key problem and also plays nicely with the concept of merging windows.

One shortcoming, however, is that your grouping operation must fit within a relatively restricted structure. This is all well and good for sums, means, and so on, but there are plenty of real-world use cases in which a more general approach, one which allows precise control over trade-offs of complexity and efficiency, is needed. We'll look next at what such a general approach entails.

Generalized State

Though both of the implicit approaches we've looked at so far have their merits, they each fall short in one dimension: flexibility. The raw grouping method requires you to always buffer up the raw inputs to the grouping operation before processing the group in whole, so there's no way to partially process some of the data along the way; it's all or nothing. The incremental combining approach specifically allows for partial processing but with the restriction that the processing in question be commutative and associative and happen as records arrive one-by-one.

If we want to support a more generalized approach to streaming persistent state, we need something more flexible. Specifically, we need flexibility in three dimensions:

- Flexibility in data structures; that is, an ability to structure the data we write and read in ways that are most appropriate and efficient for the task at hand. Raw grouping essentially provides an appendable list, and incremental combination essentially provides a single value that is always written and read in its entirety. But there are myriad other ways in which we might want to structure our persistent data, each with different types of access patterns and associated costs: maps, trees, graphs, sets, and so on. Supporting a variety of persistent data types is critical for efficiency.

  Beam supports flexibility in data types by allowing a single DoFn to declare multiple state fields, each of a specific type. In this way, logically independent pieces of state (e.g., visits and impressions) can be stored separately, and semantically different types of state (e.g., maps and lists) can be accessed in ways that are natural given their types of access patterns.

- Flexibility in write and read granularity; that is, an ability to tailor the amount and type of data written or read at any given time for optimal efficiency. What this boils down to is the ability to write and read precisely the necessary amount of data at any given point of time: no more, and no less (and in parallel as much as possible).

  This goes hand in hand with the previous point, given that dedicated data types allow for focused types of access patterns (e.g., a set-membership operation that can use something like a Bloom filter under the covers to greatly minimize the amount of data read in certain circumstances). But it goes beyond it, as well; for example, allowing multiple large reads to be dispatched in parallel (e.g., via futures).

  In Beam, flexibly granular writes and reads are enabled via datatype-specific APIs that provide fine-grained access capabilities, combined with an asynchronous I/O mechanism that allows for writes and reads to be batched together for efficiency.

- Flexibility in scheduling of processing; that is, an ability to bind the time at which specific types of processing occur to the progress of time in either of the two time domains we care about: event-time completeness and processing time. Triggers provide a restricted set of flexibility here, with completeness triggers providing a way to bind processing to the watermark passing the end of the window, and repeated update triggers providing a way to bind processing to periodic progress in the processing-time domain. But for certain use cases (e.g., certain types of joins, for which you don't necessarily care about input completeness of the entire window, just input completeness up to the event-time of a specific record in the join), triggers are insufficiently flexible. Hence, our need for a more general solution.

In Beam, flexible scheduling of processing is provided via *timers*.[4] A timer is a special type of state that binds a specific point in time in either supported time domain (event time or processing time) with a method to be called when that point in time is reached. In this way, specific bits of processing can be delayed until a more appropriate time in the future.

The common thread among these three characteristics is *flexibility*. A specific subset of use cases are served very well by the relatively inflexible approaches of raw grouping or incremental combination. But when tackling anything outside their relatively narrow domain of expertise, those options often fall short. When that happens, you need the power and flexibility of a fully general-state API to let you tailor your utilization of persistent state optimally.

To think of it another way, raw grouping and incremental combination are relatively high-level abstractions that enable the pithy expression of pipelines with (in the case of combiners, at least) some good properties for automatic optimizations. But sometimes you need to go low level to get the behavior or performance you need. That's what generalized state lets you do.

Case Study: Conversion Attribution

To see this in action, let's now look at a use case that is poorly served by both raw grouping and incremental combination: *conversion attribution*. This is a technique that sees widespread use across the advertising world to provide concrete feedback on the effectiveness of advertisements. Though relatively easy to understand, its somewhat diverse set of requirements doesn't fit nicely into either of the two types of implicit state we've considered so far.

Imagine that you have an analytics pipeline that monitors traffic to a website in conjunction with advertisement impressions that directed traffic to that site. The goal is to provide attribution of specific advertisements shown to a user toward the achievement of some goal on the site itself (which often might lie many steps beyond the initial advertisement landing page), such as signing up for a mailing list or purchasing an item.

---

4 And indeed, timers are the underlying feature used to implement most of the completeness and repeated updated triggers we discussed in Chapter 2 as well as garbage collection based on allowed lateness.

Figure 7-3 shows an example set of website visits, goals, and ad impressions, with one attributed conversion highlighted in red. Building up conversion attributions over an unbounded, out-of-order stream of data requires keeping track of impressions, visits, and goals seen so far. That's where persistent state comes in.

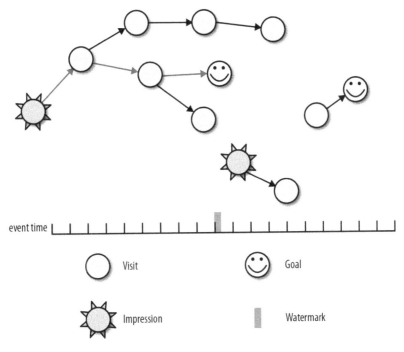

Figure 7-3. Example conversion attribution

In this diagram, a user's traversal of various pages on a website is represented as a graph. Impressions are advertisements that were shown to the user and clicked, resulting in the user visiting a page on the site. Visits represent a single page viewed on the site. Goals are specific visited pages that have been identified as a desired destination for users (e.g., completing a purchase, or signing up for a mailing list). The goal of conversion attribution is to identify ad impressions that resulted in the user achieving some goal on the site. In this figure, there is one such conversion highlighted in red. Note that events might arrive out of order, hence the event-time axis in the diagram and the watermark reference point indicating the time up to which input is believed to be correct.

A lot goes into building a robust, large-scale attribution pipeline, but there are a few aspects worth calling out explicitly. Any such pipeline we attempt to build must do the following:

Handle out-of-order data

Because the website traffic and ad impression data come from separate systems, both of which are implemented as distributed collection services themselves, the data might arrive wildly out of order. Thus, our pipeline must be resilient to such disorder.

Handle high volumes of data

Not only must we assume that this pipeline will be processing data for a large number of independent users, but depending upon the volume of a given ad campaign and the popularity of a given website, we might need to store a large amount of impression and/or traffic data as we attempt to build evidence of attribution. For example, it would not be unheard of to store 90 days worth of visit, impression, and goal tree[5] data per user to allow us to build up attributions that span multiple months' worth of activity.

Protect against spam

Given that money is involved, correctness is paramount. Not only must we ensure that visits and impressions are accounted for exactly once (something we'll get more or less for free by simply using an execution engine that supports effectively-once processing), but we must also guard our advertisers against spam attacks that attempt to charge advertisers unfairly. For example, a single ad that is clicked multiple times in a row by the same user will arrive as multiple impressions, but as long as those clicks occur within a certain amount of time of one another (e.g., within the same day), they must be attributed only once. In other words, even if the system guarantees we'll see every individual *impression* once, we must also perform some manual deduplication across impressions that are technically different events but which our business logic dictates we interpret as duplicates.

Optimize for performance

Above all, because of the potential scale of this pipeline, we must always keep an eye toward optimizing the performance of our pipeline. Persistent state, because of the inherent costs of writing to persistent storage, can often be the performance bottleneck in such a pipeline. As such, the flexibility characteristics we discussed earlier will be critical in ensuring our design is as performant as possible.

---

5 Thanks to the nature of web browsing, the visit trails we'll be analyzing are trees of URLs linked by HTTP referrer fields. In reality, they would end up being directed graphs, but for the sake of simplicity, we'll assume each page on our website has incoming links from exactly one other referring page on the site, thus yielding a simpler tree structure. Generalizing to graphs is a natural extension of the tree-based implementation, and only further drives home the points being made.

Conversion Attribution with Apache Beam

Now that we understand the basic problem that we're trying to solve and have some of the important requirements squarely in mind, let's use Beam's State and Timers API to build a basic conversion attribution transformation. We'll write this just like we would any other DoFn in Beam, but we'll make use of state and timer extensions that allow us to write and read persistent state and timer fields. Those of you that want to follow along in real code can find the full implementation on GitHub (*http:// bit.ly/2yeAGAQ*).

Note that, as with all grouping operations in Beam, usage of the State API is scoped to the current key and window, with window lifetimes dictated by the specified allowed lateness parameter; in this example, we'll be operating within a single global window. Parallelism is linearized per key, as with most DoFns. Also note that, for simplicity, we'll be eliding the manual garbage collection of visits and impressions falling outside of our 90-day horizon that would be necessary to keep the persisted state from growing forever.

To begin, let's define a few POJO classes for visits, impressions, a visit/impression union (used for joining), and completed attributions, as shown in Example 7-4.

Example 7-4. POJO definitions of Visit, Impression, VisitOrImpression, and Attribution objects

```
@DefaultCoder(AvroCoder.class)
class Visit {
    @Nullable private String url;
    @Nullable private Instant timestamp;
    // The referring URL. Recall that we've constrained the problem in this
    // example to assume every page on our website has exactly one possible
    // referring URL, to allow us to solve the problem for simple trees
    // rather than more general DAGs.
    @Nullable private String referer;
    @Nullable private boolean isGoal;

    @SuppressWarnings("unused")
    public Visit() {
    }

    public Visit(String url, Instant timestamp, String referer,
                 boolean isGoal) {
        this.url = url;
        this.timestamp = timestamp;
        this.referer = referer;
        this.isGoal = isGoal;
    }

    public String url() { return url; }
```

```java
    public Instant timestamp() { return timestamp; }
    public String referer() { return referer; }
    public boolean isGoal() { return isGoal; }

    @Override
    public String toString() {
        return String.format("{ %s %s from:%s%s }", url, timestamp, referer,
                             isGoal ? " isGoal" : "");
    }
}

@DefaultCoder(AvroCoder.class)
class Impression {
    @Nullable private Long id;
    @Nullable private String sourceUrl;
    @Nullable private String targetUrl;
    @Nullable private Instant timestamp;

    public static String sourceAndTarget(String source, String target) {
        return source + ":" + target;
    }

    @SuppressWarnings("unused")
    public Impression() {
    }

    public Impression(Long id, String sourceUrl, String targetUrl,
                      Instant timestamp) {
        this.id = id;
        this.sourceUrl = sourceUrl;
        this.targetUrl = targetUrl;
        this.timestamp = timestamp;
    }

    public Long id() { return id; }
    public String sourceUrl() { return sourceUrl; }
    public String targetUrl() { return targetUrl; }
    public String sourceAndTarget() {
        return sourceAndTarget(sourceUrl, targetUrl);
    }
    public Instant timestamp() { return timestamp; }

    @Override
    public String toString() {
        return String.format("{ %s source:%s target:%s %s }",
                             id, sourceUrl, targetUrl, timestamp);
    }
}

@DefaultCoder(AvroCoder.class)
class VisitOrImpression {
    @Nullable private Visit visit;
```

```java
    @Nullable private Impression impression;

    @SuppressWarnings("unused")
    public VisitOrImpression() {
    }

    public VisitOrImpression(Visit visit, Impression impression) {
        this.visit = visit;
        this.impression = impression;
    }

    public Visit visit() { return visit; }
    public Impression impression() { return impression; }
}

@DefaultCoder(AvroCoder.class)
class Attribution {
    @Nullable private Impression impression;
    @Nullable private List<Visit> trail;
    @Nullable private Visit goal;

    @SuppressWarnings("unused")
    public Attribution() {
    }

    public Attribution(Impression impression, List<Visit> trail, Visit goal) {
        this.impression = impression;
        this.trail = trail;
        this.goal = goal;
    }

    public Impression impression() { return impression; }
    public List<Visit> trail() { return trail; }
    public Visit goal() { return goal; }

    @Override
    public String toString() {
        StringBuilder builder = new StringBuilder();
        builder.append("imp=" + impression.id() + " " + impression.sourceUrl());
        for (Visit visit : trail) {
            builder.append(" → " + visit.url());
        }
        builder.append(" → " + goal.url());
        return builder.toString();
    }
}
```

We next define a Beam DoFn to consume a flattened collection of Visits and Impressions, keyed by the user. In turn, it will yield a collection of Attributions. Its signature looks like Example 7-5.

Example 7-5. DoFn signature for our conversion attribution transformation

```
class AttributionFn extends DoFn<KV<String, VisitOrImpression>, Attribution>
```

Within that DoFn, we need to implement the following logic:

1. Store all visits in a map keyed by their URL so that we can easily look them up when tracing visit trails backward from a goal.

2. Store all impressions in a map keyed by the URL they referred to, so we can identify impressions that initiated a trail to a goal.

3. Any time we see a visit that happens to be a goal, set an event-time timer for the timestamp of the goal. Associated with this timer will be a method that performs goal attribution for the pending goal. This will ensure that attribution only happens once the input leading up to the goal is complete.

4. Because Beam lacks support for a dynamic set of timers (currently all timers must be declared at pipeline definition time, though each individual timer can be set and reset for different points in time at runtime), we also need to keep track of the timestamps for all of the goals we still need to attribute. This will allow us to have a single attribution timer set for the minimum timestamp of all pending goals. After we attribute the goal with the earliest timestamp, we set the timer again with the timestamp of the next earliest goal.

Let's now walk through the implementation in pieces. First up, we need to declare specifications for all of our state and timer fields within the DoFn. For state, the specification dictates the type of data structure for the field itself (e.g., map or list) as well as the type(s) of data contained therein, and their associated coder(s); for timers, it dictates the associated time domain. Each specification is then assigned a unique ID string (via the @StateID/@TimerId annotations), which will allow us to dynamically associate these specifications with parameters and methods later on. For our use case, we'll define (in Example 7-6) the following:

- Two MapState specifications for visits and impressions
- A single SetState specification for goals
- A ValueState specification for keeping track of the minimum pending goal timestamp
- A Timer specification for our delayed attribution logic

Example 7-6. State field specifications

```
class AttributionFn extends DoFn<KV<String, VisitOrImpression>, Attribution> {
    @StateId("visits")
    private final StateSpec<MapState<String, Visit>> visitsSpec =
        StateSpecs.map(StringUtf8Coder.of(), AvroCoder.of(Visit.class));

    // Impressions are keyed by both sourceUrl (i.e., the query) and targetUrl
    // (i.e., the click), since a single query can result in multiple impressions.
    // The source and target are encoded together into a single string by the
    // Impression.sourceAndTarget method.
    @StateId("impressions")
    private final StateSpec<MapState<String, Impression>> impSpec =
        StateSpecs.map(StringUtf8Coder.of(), AvroCoder.of(Impression.class));

    @StateId("goals")
    private final StateSpec<SetState<Visit>> goalsSpec =
        StateSpecs.set(AvroCoder.of(Visit.class));

    @StateId("minGoal")
    private final StateSpec<ValueState<Instant>> minGoalSpec =
        StateSpecs.value(InstantCoder.of());

    @TimerId("attribution")
    private final TimerSpec timerSpec =
        TimerSpecs.timer(TimeDomain.EVENT_TIME);
```

... continued in Example 7-7 below ...

Next up, we implement our core `@ProcessElement` method. This is the processing logic that will run every time a new record arrives. As noted earlier, we need to record visits and impressions to persistent state as well as keep track of goals and manage the timer that will bind our attribution logic to the progress of event-time completeness as tracked by the watermark. Access to state and timers is provided via parameters passed to our `@ProcessElement` method, and the Beam runtime invokes our method with appropriate parameters indicated by `@StateId` and `@TimerId` annotations. The logic itself is then relatively straightforward, as demonstrated in Example 7-7.

Example 7-7. @ProcessElement implementation

```
... continued from Example 7-6 above ...

@ProcessElement
public void processElement(
        @Element KV<String, VisitOrImpression> kv,
        @StateId("visits") MapState<String, Visit> visitsState,
        @StateId("impressions") MapState<String, Impression> impressionsState,
        @StateId("goals") SetState<Visit> goalsState,
```

```
            @StateId("minGoal") ValueState<Instant> minGoalState,
            @TimerId("attribution") Timer attributionTimer) {
    Visit visit = kv.getValue().visit();
    Impression impression = kv.getValue().impression();

    if (visit != null) {
        if (!visit.isGoal()) {
            LOG.info("Adding visit: {}", visit);
            visitsState.put(visit.url(), visit);
        } else {
            LOG.info("Adding goal (if absent): {}", visit);
            goalsState.addIfAbsent(visit);
            Instant minTimestamp = minGoalState.read();
            if (minTimestamp == null || visit.timestamp().isBefore(minTimestamp)) {
                LOG.info("Setting timer from {} to {}",
                        Utils.formatTime(minTimestamp),
                        Utils.formatTime(visit.timestamp()));
                attributionTimer.set(visit.timestamp());
                minGoalState.write(visit.timestamp());
            }
            LOG.info("Done with goal");
        }
    }
    if (impression != null) {
        // Dedup logical impression duplicates with the same source and target URL.
        // In this case, first one to arrive (in processing time) wins. A more
        // robust approach might be to pick the first one in event time, but that
        // would require an extra read before commit, so the processing-time
        // approach may be slightly more performant.
        LOG.info("Adding impression (if absent): {} → {}",
                impression.sourceAndTarget(), impression);
        impressionsState.putIfAbsent(impression.sourceAndTarget(), impression);
    }
}
```

... continued in Example 7-8 below ...

Note how this ties back to our three desired capabilities in a general state API:

Flexibility in data structures

> We have maps, a set, a value, and a timer. They allow us to efficiently manipulate our state in ways that are effective for our algorithm.

Flexibility in write and read granularity

> Our @ProcessElement method is called for every single visit and impression we process. As such, we need it to be as efficient as possible. We take advantage of the ability to make fine-grained, blind writes only to the specific fields we need. We also only ever read from state within our @ProcessElement method in the uncommon case of encountering a new goal. And when we do, we read only a

single integer value, without touching the (potentially much larger) maps and list.

Flexibility in scheduling of processing

Thanks to timers, we're able to delay our complex goal attribution logic (defined next) until we're confident we've received all the necessary input data, minimizing duplicated work and maximizing efficiency.

Having defined the core processing logic, let's now look at our final piece of code, the goal attribution method. This method is annotated with an `@TimerId` annotation to identify it as the code to execute when the corresponding attribution timer fires. The logic here is significantly more complicated than the `@ProcessElement` method:

1. First, we need to load the entirety of our visit and impression maps, as well as our set of goals. We need the maps to piece our way backward through the attribution trail we'll be building, and we need the goals to know which goals we're attributing as a result of the current timer firing, as well as the next pending goal we want to schedule for attribution in the future (if any).

2. After we've loaded our state, we process goals for this timer one at a time in a loop, repeatedly:

   - Checking to see if any impressions referred the user to the current visit in the trail (beginning with the goal). If so, we've completed attribution of this goal and can break out of the loop and emit the attribution trail.

   - Checking next to see if any visits were the referrer for the current visit. If so, we've found a back pointer in our trail, so we traverse it and start the loop over.

   - If no matching impressions or visits are found, we have a goal that was reached organically, with no associated impression. In this case, we simply break out of the loop and move on to the next goal, if any.

3. After we've exhausted our list of goals ready for attribution, we set a timer for the next pending goal in the list (if any) and reset the corresponding `ValueState` tracking the minimum pending goal timestamp.

To keep things concise, we first look at the core goal attribution logic, shown in Example 7-8, which roughly corresponds to point 2 in the preceding list.

Example 7-8. Goal attribution logic

```
... continued from Example 7-7 above ...

private Impression attributeGoal(Visit goal,
                                 Map<String, Visit> visits,
                                 Map<String, Impression> impressions,
```

```
                        List<Visit> trail) {
    Impression impression = null;
    Visit visit = goal;
    while (true) {
        String sourceAndTarget = Impression.sourceAndTarget(
            visit.referer(), visit.url());
        LOG.info("attributeGoal: visit={} sourceAndTarget={}",
                visit, sourceAndTarget);
        if (impressions.containsKey(sourceAndTarget)) {
            LOG.info("attributeGoal: impression={}", impression);
            // Walked entire path back to impression. Return success.
            return impressions.get(sourceAndTarget);
        } else if (visits.containsKey(visit.referer())) {
            // Found another visit in the path, continue searching.
            visit = visits.get(visit.referer());
            trail.add(0, visit);
        } else {
            LOG.info("attributeGoal: not found");
            // Referer not found, trail has gone cold. Return failure.
            return null;
        }
    }
}
}

... continued in Example 7-9 below ...
```

The rest of the code (eliding a few simple helper methods), which handles initializing and fetching state, invoking the attribution logic, and handling cleanup to schedule any remaining pending goal attribution attempts, looks like Example 7-9.

Example 7-9. Overall @TimerId handling logic for goal attribution

```
... continued from Example 7-8 above ...

@OnTimer("attribution")
public void attributeGoal(
        @Timestamp Instant timestamp,
        @StateId("visits") MapState<String, Visit> visitsState,
        @StateId("impressions") MapState<String, Impression> impressionsState,
        @StateId("goals") SetState<Visit> goalsState,
        @StateId("minGoal") ValueState<Instant> minGoalState,
        @TimerId("attribution") Timer attributionTimer,
        OutputReceiver<Attribution> output) {
    LOG.info("Processing timer: {}", Utils.formatTime(timestamp));

    // Batch state reads together via futures.
    ReadableState<Iterable<Map.Entry<String, Visit> > > visitsFuture
        = visitsState.entries().readLater();
    ReadableState<Iterable<Map.Entry<String, Impression> > > impressionsFuture
        = impressionsState.entries().readLater();
    ReadableState<Iterable<Visit>> goalsFuture = goalsState.readLater();
```

```java
    // Accessed the fetched state.
    Map<String, Visit> visits = buildMap(visitsFuture.read());
    Map<String, Impression> impressions = buildMap(impressionsFuture.read());
    Iterable<Visit> goals = goalsFuture.read();

    // Find the matching goal
    Visit goal = findGoal(timestamp, goals);

    // Attribute the goal
    List<Visit> trail = new ArrayList<>();
    Impression impression = attributeGoal(goal, visits, impressions, trail);
    if (impression != null) {
        output.output(new Attribution(impression, trail, goal));
        impressions.remove(impression.sourceAndTarget());
    }
    goalsState.remove(goal);

    // Set the next timer, if any.
    Instant minGoal = minTimestamp(goals, goal);
    if (minGoal != null) {
        LOG.info("Setting new timer at {}", Utils.formatTime(minGoal));
        minGoalState.write(minGoal);
        attributionTimer.set(minGoal);
    } else {
        minGoalState.clear();
    }
}
```

This code block ties back to the three desired capabilities of a general state API in very similar ways as the `@ProcessElement` method, with one noteworthy difference:

Flexibility in write and read granularity

We were able to make a single, coarse-grained read up front to load all of the data in the maps and set. This is typically much more efficient than loading each field separately, or even worse loading each field element by element. It also shows the importance of being able to traverse the spectrum of access granularities, from fine-grained to coarse-grained.

And that's it! We've implemented a basic conversion attribution pipeline, in a way that's efficient enough to be operated at respectable scales using a reasonable amount of resources. And importantly, it functions properly in the face of out-of-order data. If you look at the dataset used for the unit test (*http://bit.ly/2sY4goW*) in Example 7-10, you can see it presents a number of challenges, even at this small scale:

- Tracking and attributing multiple distinct conversions across a shared set of URLs.

- Data arriving out of order, and in particular, goals arriving (in processing time) before visits and impressions that lead to them, as well as other goals which occurred earlier.

- Source URLs that generate multiple distinct impressions to different target URLs.

- Physically distinct impressions (e.g., multiple clicks on the same advertisement) that must be deduplicated to a single logical impression.

Example 7-10. Example dataset for validating conversion attribution logic

```
private static TestStream<KV<String, VisitOrImpression>> createStream() {
    // Impressions and visits, in event-time order, for two (logical) attributable
    // impressions and one unattributable impression.
    Impression signupImpression = new Impression(
        123L, "http://search.com?q=xyz",
        "http://xyz.com/", Utils.parseTime("12:01:00"));
    Visit signupVisit = new Visit(
        "http://xyz.com/", Utils.parseTime("12:01:10"),
        "http://search.com?q=xyz", false/*isGoal*/);
    Visit signupGoal = new Visit(
        "http://xyz.com/join-mailing-list", Utils.parseTime("12:01:30"),
        "http://xyz.com/", true/*isGoal*/);

    Impression shoppingImpression = new Impression(
        456L, "http://search.com?q=thing",
        "http://xyz.com/thing", Utils.parseTime("12:02:00"));
    Impression shoppingImpressionDup = new Impression(
        789L, "http://search.com?q=thing",
        "http://xyz.com/thing", Utils.parseTime("12:02:10"));
    Visit shoppingVisit1 = new Visit(
        "http://xyz.com/thing", Utils.parseTime("12:02:30"),
        "http://search.com?q=thing", false/*isGoal*/);
    Visit shoppingVisit2 = new Visit(
        "http://xyz.com/thing/add-to-cart", Utils.parseTime("12:03:00"),
        "http://xyz.com/thing", false/*isGoal*/);
    Visit shoppingVisit3 = new Visit(
        "http://xyz.com/thing/purchase", Utils.parseTime("12:03:20"),
        "http://xyz.com/thing/add-to-cart", false/*isGoal*/);
    Visit shoppingGoal = new Visit(
        "http://xyz.com/thing/receipt", Utils.parseTime("12:03:45"),
        "http://xyz.com/thing/purchase", true/*isGoal*/);

    Impression unattributedImpression = new Impression(
        000L, "http://search.com?q=thing",
        "http://xyz.com/other-thing", Utils.parseTime("12:04:00"));
    Visit unattributedVisit = new Visit(
```

```
        "http://xyz.com/other-thing", Utils.parseTime("12:04:20"),
        "http://search.com?q=other thing", false/*isGoal*/);

    // Create a stream of visits and impressions, with data arriving out of order.
    return TestStream.create(
        KvCoder.of(StringUtf8Coder.of(), AvroCoder.of(VisitOrImpression.class)))
        .advanceWatermarkTo(Utils.parseTime("12:00:00"))
        .addElements(visitOrImpression(shoppingVisit2, null))
        .addElements(visitOrImpression(shoppingGoal, null))
        .addElements(visitOrImpression(shoppingVisit3, null))
        .addElements(visitOrImpression(signupGoal, null))
        .advanceWatermarkTo(Utils.parseTime("12:00:30"))
        .addElements(visitOrImpression(null, signupImpression))
        .advanceWatermarkTo(Utils.parseTime("12:01:00"))
        .addElements(visitOrImpression(null, shoppingImpression))
        .addElements(visitOrImpression(signupVisit, null))
        .advanceWatermarkTo(Utils.parseTime("12:01:30"))
        .addElements(visitOrImpression(null, shoppingImpressionDup))
        .addElements(visitOrImpression(shoppingVisit1, null))
        .advanceWatermarkTo(Utils.parseTime("12:03:45"))
        .addElements(visitOrImpression(null, unattributedImpression))
        .advanceWatermarkTo(Utils.parseTime("12:04:00"))
        .addElements(visitOrImpression(unattributedVisit, null))
        .advanceWatermarkToInfinity();
}
```

And remember, we're working here on a relatively constrained version of conversion attribution. A full-blown impelementation would have additional challenges to deal with (e.g., garbage collection, DAGs of visits instead of trees). Regardless, this pipeline provides a nice contrast to the oftentimes insufficiently flexible approaches provided by raw grouping an incremental combination. By trading off some amount of implementation complexity, we were able to find the necessary balance of efficiency, without compromising on correctness. Additionally, this pipeline highlights the more imperative approach towards stream processing that state and timers afford (think C or Java), which is a nice complement to the more functional approach afforded by windowing and triggers (think Haskell).

Summary

In this chapter, we've looked closely at why persistent state is important, coming to the conclusion that it provides a basis for correctness and efficiency in long-lived pipelines. We then looked at the two most common types of implicit state encountered in data processing systems: raw grouping and incremental combination. We learned that raw grouping is straightforward but potentially inefficient and that incremental combination greatly improves efficiency for operations that are commutative and associative. Finally, we looked a relatively complex, but very practical use case (and implementation via Apache Beam Java) grounded in real-world experience, and used that to highlight the important characteristics needed in a general state abstraction:

- *Flexibility in data structures*, allowing for the use of data types tailored to specific use cases at hand.
- *Flexibility in write and read granularity*, allowing the amount of data written and read at any point to be tailored to the use case, minimizing or maximizing I/O as appropriate.
- *Flexibility in scheduling of processing*, allowing certain portions of processing to be delayed until a more appropriate point in time, such as when the input is believed to be complete up to a specific point in event time.

CHAPTER 8

Streaming SQL

Let's talk SQL. In this chapter, we're going to start somewhere in the middle with the punchline, jump back in time a bit to establish additional context, and finally jump back to the future to wrap everything up with a nice bow. Imagine Quentin Tarantino held a degree in computer science and was super pumped to tell the world about the finer points of streaming SQL, and so he offered to ghostwrite this chapter with me; it's sorta like that. Minus the violence.

What Is Streaming SQL?

I would argue that the answer to this question has eluded our industry for decades. In all fairness, the database community has understood maybe 99% of the answer for quite a while now. But I have yet to see a truly cogent and comprehensive definition of streaming SQL that encompasses the full breadth of robust streaming semantics. That's what we'll try to come up with here, although it would be hubris to assume we're 100% of the way there now. Maybe 99.1%? Baby steps.

Regardless, I want to point out up front that most of what we'll discuss in this chapter is still purely hypothetical as of the time of writing. This chapter and the one that follows (covering streaming joins) both describe an idealistic vision for what streaming SQL could be. Some pieces are already implemented in systems like Apache Calcite, Apache Flink, and Apache Beam. Many others aren't implemented anywhere. Along the way, I'll try to call out a few of the things that do exist in concrete form, but given what a moving target that is, your best bet is to simply consult the documentation for your specific system of interest.

On that note, it's also worth highlighting that the vision for streaming SQL presented here is the result of a collaborative discussion between the Calcite, Flink, and Beam communities. Julian Hyde, the lead developer on Calcite, has long pitched (*http://bit.ly/2JTzR4V*) his vision for what streaming SQL might look like. In 2016, members of the Flink community integrated Calcite SQL support into Flink itself, and began adding streaming-specific features such as windowing constructs to the Calcite SQL dialect. Then, in 2017, all three communities began a discussion (*http://s.apache.org/streaming-sql-spec*) to try to come to agreement on what language extensions and semantics for robust stream processing in Calcite SQL should look like. This chapter attempts to distill the ideas from that discussion down into a clear and cohesive narrative about integrating streaming concepts into SQL, regardless of whether it's Calcite or some other dialect.

Relational Algebra

When talking about what streaming means for SQL, it's important to keep in mind the theoretical foundation of SQL: relational algebra. Relational algebra is simply a mathematical way of describing relationships between data that consist of named, typed tuples. At the heart of relational algebra is the relation itself, which is a set of these tuples. In classic database terms, a relation is something akin to a table, be it a physical database table, the result of a SQL query, a view (materialized or otherwise), and so on; it's a set of rows containing named and typed columns of data.

One of the more critical aspects of relational algebra is its closure property: applying any operator from the relational algebra to any valid relation[1] always yields another relation. In other words, relations are the common currency of relational algebra, and all operators consume them as input and produce them as output.

Historically, many attempts to support streaming in SQL have fallen short of satisfying the closure property. They treat streams separately from classic relations, providing new operators to convert between the two, and restricting the operations that can be applied to one or the other. This significantly raises the bar of adoption for any such streaming SQL system: would-be users must learn the new operators and understand the places where they're applicable, where they aren't, and similarly relearn the rules of applicability in this new world for any old operators. What's worse, most of these systems still fall short of providing the full suite of streaming semantics that we would want, such as support for robust out-of-order processing and strong temporal join support (the latter of which we cover in Chapter 9). As a result, I would argue that it's basically impossible to name any existing streaming SQL implementation that has achieved truly broad adoption. The additional cognitive overhead and restricted

---

[1] What I mean by "valid relation" here is simply a relation for which the application of a given operator is well formed. For example, for the SQL query SELECT x FROM y, a valid relation y would be any relation containing an attribute/column named x. Any relation not containing a such-named attribute would be invalid and, in the case of a real database system, would yield a query execution error.

capabilities of such streaming SQL systems have ensured that they remain a niche enterprise.

To change that, to truly bring streaming SQL to the forefront, what we need is a way for streaming to become a first-class citizen within the relational algebra itself, such that the entire standard relational algebra can apply naturally in both streaming and nonstreaming use cases. That isn't to say that streams and tables should be treated as exactly the same thing; they most definitely are not the same, and recognizing that fact lends clarity to understanding and power to navigating the stream/table relationship, as we'll see shortly. But the core algebra should apply cleanly and naturally to both worlds, with minimal extensions beyond the standard relational algebra only in the cases where absolutely necessary.

Time-Varying Relations

To cut to the chase, the punchline I referred to at the beginning of the chapter is this: the key to naturally integrating streaming into SQL is to extend relations, the core data objects of relational algebra, to represent a set of data *over time* rather than a set of data at a *specific point* in time. More succinctly, instead of *point-in-time* relations, we need *time-varying relations*.[2]

But what are time-varying relations? Let's first define them in terms of classic relational algebra, after which we'll also consider their relationship to stream and table theory.

In terms of relational algebra, a time-varying relation is really just the evolution of a classic relation over time. To understand what I mean by that, imagine a raw dataset consisting of user events. Over time, as users generate new events, the dataset continues to grow and evolve. If you observe that set at a specific point in time, that's a classic relation. But if you observe the holistic evolution of the set *over time*, that's a time-varying relation.

Put differently, if classic relations are like two-dimensional tables consisting of named, typed columns in the x-axis and rows of records in the y-axis, time-varying relations are like three-dimensional tables with x- and y-axes as before, but an additional z-axis capturing different versions of the two-dimensional table over time. As the relation changes, new snapshots of the relation are added in the z dimension.

Let's look at an example. Imagine our raw dataset is users and scores; for example, per-user scores from a mobile game as in most of the other examples throughout the book. And suppose that our example dataset here ultimately ends up looking like this when observed at a specific point in time, in this case 12:07:

---

2 Much credit to Julian Hyde for this name and succinct rendering of the concept.

```
12:07> SELECT * FROM UserScores;
-----------------------
| Name  | Score | Time  |
-----------------------
| Julie | 7     | 12:01 |
| Frank | 3     | 12:03 |
| Julie | 1     | 12:03 |
| Julie | 4     | 12:07 |
-----------------------
```

In other words, it recorded the arrivals of four scores over time: Julie's score of 7 at
12:01, both Frank's score of 3 and Julie's second score of 1 at 12:03, and, finally, Julie's
third score of 4 at 12:07 (note that the Time column here contains processing-time
timestamps representing the *arrival time* of the records within the system; we get into
event-time timestamps a little later on). Assuming these were the only data to ever
arrive for this relation, it would look like the preceding table any time we observed it
after 12:07. But if instead we had observed the relation at 12:01, it would have looked
like the following, because only Julie's first score would have arrived by that point:

```
12:01> SELECT * FROM UserScores;
-----------------------
| Name  | Score | Time  |
-----------------------
| Julie | 7     | 12:01 |
-----------------------
```

If we had then observed it again at 12:03, Frank's score and Julie's second score would
have also arrived, so the relation would have evolved to look like this:

```
12:03> SELECT * FROM UserScores;
-----------------------
| Name  | Score | Time  |
-----------------------
| Julie | 7     | 12:01 |
| Frank | 3     | 12:03 |
| Julie | 1     | 12:03 |
-----------------------
```

From this example we can begin to get a sense for what the *time-varying* relation for
this dataset must look like: it would capture the entire evolution of the relation over
time. Thus, if we observed the time-varying relation (or TVR) at or after 12:07, it
would thus look like the following (note the use of a hypothetical TVR keyword to signal that we want the query to return the full time-varying relation, not the standard
point-in-time snapshot of a classic relation):

```
12:07> SELECT TVR * FROM UserScores;
------------------------------------------------------------
|      [-inf, 12:01)       |      [12:01, 12:03)       |
| ----------------------- | ----------------------- |
| | Name  | Score | Time  | | | Name  | Score | Time  | |
| ----------------------- | ----------------------- |
```

```
| |          |         |         | | | Julie | 7    | 12:01 | |
| |          |         |         | | | |       |      |       | |
| |          |         |         | | | |       |      |       | |
| |          |         |         | | | |       |      |       | |
| ------------------------ | ------------------------ |
------------------------------------------------------------
|      [12:03, 12:07)      |       [12:07, now)        |
| ------------------------ | ------------------------ |
| | Name  | Score | Time  | | | Name  | Score | Time  | |
| ------------------------ | ------------------------ |
| | Julie | 7     | 12:01 | | | Julie | 7     | 12:01 | |
| | Frank | 3     | 12:03 | | | Frank | 3     | 12:03 | |
| | Julie | 1     | 12:03 | | | Julie | 1     | 12:03 | |
| |       |       |       | | | Julie | 4     | 12:07 | |
| ------------------------ | ------------------------ |
------------------------------------------------------------
```

Because the printed/digital page remains constrained to two dimensions, I've taken the liberty of flattening the third dimension into a grid of two-dimensional relations. But you can see how the time-varying relation essentially consists of a sequence of classic relations (ordered left to right, top to bottom), each capturing the full state of the relation for a specific range of time (all of which, by definition, are contiguous).

What's important about defining time-varying relations this way is that they really are, for all intents and purposes, just a sequence of classic relations that each exist independently within their own disjointed (but adjacent) time ranges, with each range capturing a period of time during which the relation did not change. This is important, because it means that the application of a relational operator to a time-varying relation is equivalent to individually applying that operator to each classic relation in the corresponding sequence. And taken one step further, the result of individually applying a relational operator to a sequence of relations, each associated with a time interval, will always yield a corresponding sequence of relations with the same time intervals. In other words, the result is a corresponding time-varying relation. This definition gives us two very important properties:

- The *full set of operators* from classic relational algebra *remain valid* when applied to time-varying relations, and furthermore continue to behave exactly as you'd expect.

- The *closure property* of relational algebra *remains intact* when applied to time-varying relations.

Or more succinctly, *all the rules of classic relational algebra continue to hold when applied to time-varying relations*. This is huge, because it means that our substitution of time-varying relations for classic relations hasn't altered the parameters of the game in any way. Everything continues to work the way it did back in classic relational land, just on sequences of classic relations instead of singletons. Going back to our examples, consider two more time-varying relations over our raw dataset, both observed at some time after 12:07. First a simple filtering relation using a WHERE clause:

```
12:07> SELECT TVR * FROM UserScores WHERE Name = "Julie";
------------------------------------------------------------
|        [-inf, 12:01)       |       [12:01, 12:03)       |
| ------------------------ | ------------------------ |
| | Name  | Score | Time  | | | Name  | Score | Time  | |
| ------------------------ | ------------------------ |
| |       |       |       | | | Julie | 7     | 12:01 | |
| |       |       |       | | | |     |       |       | |
| |       |       |       | | | |     |       |       | |
| ------------------------ | ------------------------ |
------------------------------------------------------------
|        [12:03, 12:07)      |       [12:07, now)         |
| ------------------------ | ------------------------ |
| | Name  | Score | Time  | | | Name  | Score | Time  | |
| ------------------------ | ------------------------ |
| | Julie | 7     | 12:01 | | | Julie | 7     | 12:01 | |
| | Julie | 1     | 12:03 | | | Julie | 1     | 12:03 | |
| |       |       |       | | | Julie | 4     | 12:07 | |
| ------------------------ | ------------------------ |
------------------------------------------------------------
```

As you would expect, this relation looks a lot like the preceding one, but with Frank's scores filtered out. Even though the time-varying relation captures the added dimension of time necessary to record the evolution of this dataset over time, the query behaves exactly as you would expect, given your understanding of SQL.

For something a little more complex, let's consider a grouping relation in which we're summing up all the per-user scores to generate a total overall score for each user:

```
12:07> SELECT TVR Name, SUM(Score) as Total, MAX(Time) as Time
       FROM UserScores GROUP BY Name;
------------------------------------------------------------
|        [-inf, 12:01)       |       [12:01, 12:03)       |
| ------------------------ | ------------------------ |
| | Name  | Total | Time  | | | Name  | Total | Time  | |
| ------------------------ | ------------------------ |
| |       |       |       | | | Julie | 7     | 12:01 | |
| |       |       |       | | | |     |       |       | |
| ------------------------ | ------------------------ |
------------------------------------------------------------
|        [12:03, 12:07)      |       [12:07, now)         |
| ------------------------ | ------------------------ |
| | Name  | Total | Time  | | | Name  | Total | Time  | |
| ------------------------ | ------------------------ |
| | Julie | 8     | 12:03 | | | Julie | 12    | 12:07 | |
| | Frank | 3     | 12:03 | | | Frank | 3     | 12:03 | |
| ------------------------ | ------------------------ |
------------------------------------------------------------
```

Again, the time-varying version of this query behaves exactly as you would expect, with each classic relation in the sequence simply containing the sum of the scores for each user. And indeed, no matter how complicated a query we might choose, the results are always identical to applying that query independently to the commensurate classic relations composing the input time-varying relation. I cannot stress enough how important this is!

All right, that's all well and good, but time-varying relations themselves are more of a theoretical construct than a practical, physical manifestation of data; it's pretty easy to see how they could grow to be quite huge and unwieldy for large datasets that change frequently. To see how they actually tie into real-world stream processing, let's now explore the relationship between time-varying relations and stream and table theory.

Streams and Tables

For this comparison, let's consider again our grouped time-varying relation that we looked at earlier:

```
12:07> SELECT TVR Name, SUM(Score) as Total, MAX(Time) as Time
       FROM UserScores GROUP BY Name;
-----------------------------------------------------------
|       [-inf, 12:01)      |       [12:01, 12:03)       |
| ------------------------ | -------------------------- |
| | Name  | Total | Time | | | Name  | Total | Time | |
| ------------------------ | -------------------------- |
| |       |       |      | | | Julie | 7     | 12:01 | |
| |       |       |      | | |       |       |       | |
| ------------------------ | -------------------------- |
-----------------------------------------------------------
|       [12:03, 12:07)     |       [12:07, now)         |
| ------------------------ | -------------------------- |
| | Name  | Total | Time | | | Name  | Total | Time | |
| ------------------------ | -------------------------- |
| | Julie | 8     | 12:03 | | | Julie | 12    | 12:07 | |
| | Frank | 3     | 12:03 | | | Frank | 3     | 12:03 | |
| ------------------------ | -------------------------- |
-----------------------------------------------------------
```

We understand that this sequence captures the full history of the relation over time. Given our understanding of tables and streams from Chapter 6, it's not too difficult to understand how time-varying relations relate to stream and table theory.

Tables are quite straightforward: because a time-varying relation is essentially a sequence of classic relations (each capturing a snapshot of the relation at a specific point in time), and classic relations are analogous to tables, observing a time-varying relation as a table simply yields the point-in-time relation snapshot for the time of observation.

For example, if we were to observe the previous grouped time-varying relation as a table at 12:01, we'd get the following (note the use of another hypothetical keyword, TABLE, to explicitly call out our desire for the query to return a table):

```
12:01> SELECT TABLE Name, SUM(Score) as Total, MAX(Time) as Time
       FROM UserScores GROUP BY Name;
-------------------------
| Name  | Total | Time  |
-------------------------
| Julie | 7     | 12:01 |
-------------------------
```

And observing at 12:07 would yield the expected:

```
12:07> SELECT TABLE Name, SUM(Score) as Total, MAX(Time) as Time
       FROM UserScores GROUP BY Name;
-------------------------
| Name  | Total | Time  |
-------------------------
| Julie | 12    | 12:07 |
| Frank | 3     | 12:03 |
-------------------------
```

What's particularly interesting here is that there's actually support for the idea of time-varying relations within SQL, even as it exists today. The SQL 2011 standard provides "temporal tables," which store a versioned history of the table over time (in essence, time-varying relations) as well as an AS OF SYSTEM TIME construct that allows you to explicitly query and receive a snapshot of the temporal table/time-varying relation at whatever point in time you specified. For example, even if we performed our query at 12:07, we could still see what the relation looked like back at 12:03:

```
12:07> SELECT TABLE Name, SUM(Score) as Total, MAX(Time) as Time
       FROM UserScores GROUP BY Name AS OF SYSTEM TIME '12:03';
-------------------------
| Name  | Total | Time  |
-------------------------
| Julie | 8     | 12:03 |
| Frank | 3     | 12:03 |
-------------------------
```

So there's some amount of precedent for time-varying relations in SQL already. But I digress. The main point here is that tables capture a snapshot of the time-varying relation at a specific point in time. Most real-world table implementations simply track real time as we observe it; others maintain some additional historical information, which in the limit is equivalent to a full-fidelity time-varying relation capturing the entire history of a relation over time.

Streams are slightly different beasts. We learned in Chapter 6 that they too capture the evolution of a table over time. But they do so somewhat differently than the time-varying relations we've looked at so far. Instead of holistically capturing snapshots of the entire relation each time it changes, they capture the *sequence of changes* that result in those snapshots within a time-varying relation. The subtle difference here becomes more evident with an example.

As a refresher, recall again our baseline example TVR query:

```
12:07> SELECT TVR Name, SUM(Score) as Total, MAX(Time) as Time
         FROM UserScores GROUP BY Name;
------------------------------------------------------------
|      [-inf, 12:01)      |       [12:01, 12:03)      |
| ----------------------- | ------------------------- |
| | Name  | Total | Time  | | | Name  | Total | Time  | |
| ----------------------- | ------------------------- |
| |       |       |       | | | Julie | 7     | 12:01 | |
| |       |       |       | | | |       |       |       | |
| ----------------------- | ------------------------- |
------------------------------------------------------------
|      [12:03, 12:07)     |       [12:07, now)        |
| ----------------------- | ------------------------- |
| | Name  | Total | Time  | | | Name  | Total | Time  | |
| ----------------------- | ------------------------- |
| | Julie | 8     | 12:03 | | | Julie | 12    | 12:07 | |
| | Frank | 3     | 12:03 | | | Frank | 3     | 12:03 | |
| ----------------------- | ------------------------- |
------------------------------------------------------------
```

Let's now observe our time-varying relation as a stream as it exists at a few distinct points in time. At each step of the way, we'll compare the original table rendering of the TVR at that point in time with the evolution of the stream up to that point. To see what stream renderings of our time-varying relation look like, we'll need to introduce two new hypothetical keywords:

- A STREAM keyword, similar to the TABLE keyword I've already introduced, that indicates we want our query to return an event-by-event stream capturing the evolution of the time-varying relation over time. You can think of this as applying a per-record trigger to the relation over time.

- A special Sys.Undo[3] column that can be referenced from a STREAM query, for the sake of identifying rows that are retractions. More on this in a moment.

---

3 Note that the Sys.Undo name used here is riffing off the concise undo/redo nomenclature from Apache Flink (*https://flink.apache.org/news/2017/04/04/dynamic-tables.html*), which I think is a very clean way to capture the ideas of retraction and nonretraction rows.

Thus, starting out from 12:01, we'd have the following:

```
                                      12:01> SELECT STREAM Name,
12:01> SELECT TABLE Name,                         SUM(Score) as Total,
           SUM(Score) as Total,                   MAX(Time) as Time,
           MAX(Time) as Time                      Sys.Undo as Undo
       FROM UserScores GROUP BY Name;         FROM UserScores GROUP BY Name;
------------------------                ----------------------------------
| Name  | Total | Time  |               | Name  | Total | Time  | Undo |
------------------------                ----------------------------------
| Julie | 7     | 12:01 |               | Julie | 7     | 12:01 |      |
------------------------                ........ [12:01, 12:01] ........
```

The table and stream renderings look almost identical at this point. Mod the Undo column (discussed in more detail in the next example), there's only one difference: whereas the table version is complete as of 12:01 (signified by the final line of dashes closing off the bottom end of the relation), the stream version remains incomplete, as signified by the final ellipsis-like line of periods marking both the open tail of the relation (where additional data might be forthcoming in the future) as well as the processing-time range of data observed so far. And indeed, if executed on a real implementation, the STREAM query would wait indefinitely for additional data to arrive. Thus, if we waited until 12:03, three new rows would show up for the STREAM query. Compare that to a fresh TABLE rendering of the TVR at 12:03:

```
                                      12:01> SELECT STREAM Name,
12:03> SELECT TABLE Name,                         SUM(Score) as Total,
           SUM(Score) as Total,                   MAX(Time) as Time,
           MAX(Time) as Time                      Sys.Undo as Undo
       FROM UserScores GROUP BY Name;         FROM UserScores GROUP BY Name;
------------------------                ----------------------------------
| Name  | Total | Time  |               | Name  | Total | Time  | Undo |
------------------------                ----------------------------------
| Julie | 8     | 12:03 |               | Julie | 7     | 12:01 |      |
| Frank | 3     | 12:03 |               | Frank | 3     | 12:03 |      |
------------------------                | Julie | 7     | 12:03 | undo |
                                        | Julie | 8     | 12:03 |      |
                                        ........ [12:01, 12:03] ........
```

Here's an interesting point worth addressing: why are there *three* new rows in the stream (Frank's 3 and Julie's undo-7 and 8) when our original dataset contained only *two* rows (Frank's 3 and Julie's 1) for that time period? The answer lies in the fact that here we are observing the stream of changes to an *aggregation* of the original inputs; in particular, for the time period from 12:01 to 12:03, the stream needs to capture two important pieces of information regarding the change in Julie's aggregate score due to the arrival of the new 1 value:

- The previously reported total of 7 was incorrect.
- The new total is 8.

That's what the special Sys.Undo column allows us to do: distinguish between normal rows and rows that are a *retraction* of a previously reported value.[4]

A particularly nice feature of STREAM queries is that you can begin to see how all of this relates to the world of classic Online Transaction Processing (OLTP) tables: the STREAM rendering of this query is essentially capturing a sequence of INSERT and DELETE operations that you could use to materialize this relation over time in an OLTP world (and really, when you think about it, OLTP tables themselves are essentially time-varying relations mutated over time via a stream of INSERTs, UPDATEs, and DELETEs).

Now, if we don't care about the retractions in the stream, it's also perfectly fine not to ask for them. In that case, our STREAM query would look like this:

```
12:01> SELECT STREAM Name,
         SUM(Score) as Total,
         MAX(Time) as Time
         FROM UserScores GROUP BY Name;
------------------------
| Name  | Total | Time  |
------------------------
| Julie | 7     | 12:01 |
| Frank | 3     | 12:03 |
| Julie | 8     | 12:03 |
.... [12:01, 12:03] .....
```

But there's clearly value in understanding what the full stream looks like, so we'll go back to including the Sys.Undo column for our final example. Speaking of which, if we waited another four minutes until 12:07, we'd be greeted by two additional rows in the STREAM query, whereas the TABLE query would continue to evolve as before:

```
12:07> SELECT TABLE Name,
         SUM(Score) as Total,
         MAX(Time) as Time
         FROM UserScores GROUP BY Name;
--------------------------
| Name  | Total | Time  |
--------------------------
| Julie | 12    | 12:07 |
| Frank | 3     | 12:03 |
--------------------------
```

```
12:01> SELECT STREAM Name,
         SUM(Score) as Total,
         MAX(Time) as Time,
         Sys.Undo as Undo
         FROM UserScores GROUP BY Name;
-------------------------------
| Name  | Total | Time  | Undo |
-------------------------------
| Julie | 7     | 12:01 |      |
| Frank | 3     | 12:03 |      |
| Julie | 7     | 12:03 | undo |
| Julie | 8     | 12:03 |      |
| Julie | 8     | 12:07 | undo |
```

---

4 Now, in this example, it's not too difficult to figure out that the new value of 8 should replace the old value of 7, given that the mapping is 1:1. But we'll see a more complicated example later on when we talk about sessions that is much more difficult to handle without having retractions as a guide.

```
                                | Julie | 12    | 12:07 |      |
                                ........ [12:01, 12:07] ........
```

And by this time, it's quite clear that the STREAM version of our time-varying relation is a very different beast from the table version: the table captures a snapshot of the entire relation *at a specific point in time*, whereas the stream captures a view of the individual changes to the relation *over time*.[5] Interestingly though, that means that the STREAM rendering has more in common with our original, table-based TVR rendering:

```
12:07> SELECT TVR Name, SUM(Score) as Total, MAX(Time) as Time
       FROM UserScores GROUP BY Name;
--------------------------------------------------------------
|      [-inf, 12:01)      |         [12:01, 12:03)         |
| ----------------------- | -----------------------------  |
| | Name  | Total | Time  | | | Name  | Total | Time  | |
| ----------------------- | -----------------------------  |
| |       |       |       | | | Julie | 7     | 12:01 | |
| |       |       |       | | | |     |       |       | |
| ----------------------- | -----------------------------  |
|                                                            |
--------------------------------------------------------------
|      [12:03, 12:07)      |         [12:07, now)           |
| ----------------------- | -----------------------------  |
| | Name  | Total | Time  | | | Name  | Total | Time  | |
| ----------------------- | -----------------------------  |
| | Julie | 8     | 12:03 | | | Julie | 12    | 12:07 | |
| | Frank | 3     | 12:03 | | | Frank | 3     | 12:03 | |
| ----------------------- | -----------------------------  |
--------------------------------------------------------------
```

Indeed, it's safe to say that the STREAM query simply provides an alternate rendering of the entire history of data that exists in the corresponding table-based TVR query. The value of the STREAM rendering is its conciseness: it captures only the delta of changes between each of the point-in-time relation snapshots in the TVR. The value of the sequence-of-tables TVR rendering is the clarity it provides: it captures the evolution of the relation over time in a format that highlights its natural relationship to classic relations, and in doing so provides for a simple and clear definition of relational semantics within the context of streaming as well as the additional dimension of time that streaming brings.

---

5 And indeed, this is a key point to remember. There are some systems that advocate treating streams and tables as identical, claiming that we can simply treat streams like never-ending tables. That statement is accurate inasmuch as the true underlying primitive is the time-varying relation, and all relational operations may be applied equally to any time-varying relation, regardless of whether the actual physical manifestation is a stream or a table. But that sort of approach conflates the two very different types of views that tables and streams provide for a given time-varying relation. Pretending that two very different things are the same might seem simple on the surface, but it's not a road toward understanding, clarity, and correctness.

Another important aspect of the similarities between the STREAM and table-based TVR renderings is the fact that they are essentially equivalent in the overall data they encode. This gets to the core of the stream/table duality that its proponents have long preached: streams and tables[6] are really just two different sides of the same coin. Or to resurrect the bad physics analogy from Chapter 6, streams and tables are to time-varying relations as waves and particles are to light:[7] a complete time-varying relation is both a table and a stream at the same time; tables and streams are simply different physical manifestations of the same concept, depending upon the context.

Now, it's important to keep in mind that this stream/table duality is true only as long as both versions encode the same information; that is, when you have full-fidelity tables or streams. In many cases, however, full fidelity is impractical. As I alluded to earlier, encoding the full history of a time-varying relation, no matter whether it's in stream or table form, can be rather expensive for a large data source. It's quite common for stream and table manifestations of a TVR to be lossy in some way. Tables typically encode only the most recent version of a TVR; those that support temporal or versioned access often compress the encoded history to specific point-in-time snapshots, and/or garbage-collect versions that are older than some threshold. Similarly, streams typically encode only a limited duration of the evolution of a TVR, often a relatively recent portion of that history. Persistent streams like Kafka afford the ability to encode the entirety of a TVR, but again this is relatively uncommon, with data older than some threshold typically thrown away via a garbage-collection process.

The main point here is that streams and tables are absolutely duals of one another, each a valid way of encoding a time-varying relation. But in practice, it's common for the physical stream/table manifestations of a TVR to be lossy in some way. These partial-fidelity streams and tables trade off a decrease in total encoded information for some benefit, usually decreased resource costs. And these types of trade-offs are important because they're often what allow us to build pipelines that operate over data sources of truly massive scale. But they also complicate matters, and require a deeper understanding to use correctly. We discuss this topic in more detail later on when we get to SQL language extensions. But before we try to reason about SQL extensions, it will be useful to understand a little more concretely the biases present in both the SQL and non-SQL data processing approaches common today.

---

6 Here referring to tables in the sense of tables that can vary over time; that is, the table-based TVRs we've been looking at.

7 This one courtesy Julian Hyde.

Looking Backward: Stream and Table Biases

In many ways, the act of adding robust streaming support to SQL is largely an exercise in attempting to merge the *where*, *when*, and *how* semantics of the Beam Model with the *what* semantics of the classic SQL model. But to do so cleanly, and in a way that remains true to the look and feel of classic SQL, requires an understanding of how the two models relate to each other. Thus, much as we explored the relationship of the Beam Model to stream and table theory in Chapter 6, we'll now explore the relationship of the Beam Model to the classic SQL model, using stream and table theory as the underlying framework for our comparison. In doing so, we'll uncover the inherent biases present in each model, which will provide us some insights in how to best marry the two in a clean, natural way.

The Beam Model: A Stream-Biased Approach

Let's begin with the Beam Model, building upon the discussion in Chapter 6. To begin, I want to discuss the inherent stream bias in the Beam Model as it exists today relative to streams and tables.

If you think back to Figures 6-11 and 6-12, they showed two different views of the same score-summation pipeline that we've used as an example throughout the book: in Figure 6-11 a logical, Beam-Model view, and in Figure 6-12 a physical, streams and tables–oriented view. Comparing the two helped highlight the relationship of the Beam Model to streams and tables. But by overlaying one on top of the other, as I've done in Figure 8-1, we can see an additional interesting aspect of the relationship: the Beam Model's inherent stream bias.

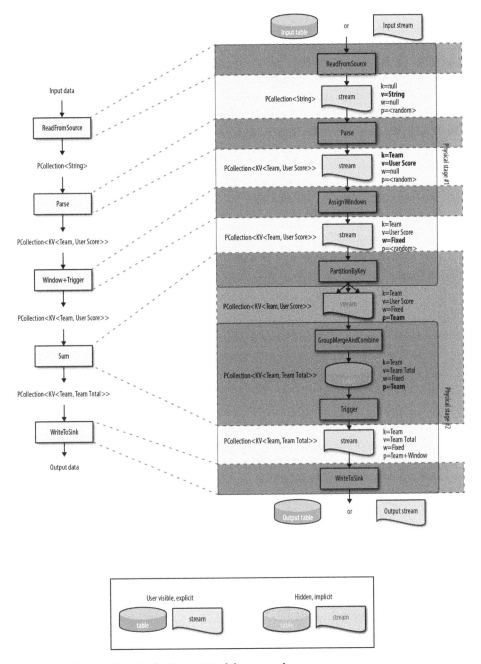

Figure 8-1. Stream bias in the Beam Model approach

In this figure, I've drawn dashed red lines connecting the transforms in the logical view to their corresponding components in the physical view. The thing that stands out when observed this way is that all of the logical transformations are connected by *streams*, even the operations that involve grouping (which we know from Chapter 6 results in a table being created *somewhere*). In Beam parlance, these transformations are `PTransforms`, and they are always applied to `PCollections` to yield new `PCollections`. The important takeaway here is that `PCollections` in Beam are *always* streams. As a result, the Beam Model is an inherently stream-biased approach to data processing: streams are the common currency in a Beam pipeline (even batch pipelines), and tables are always treated specially, either abstracted behind sources and sinks at the edges of the pipeline or hidden away beneath a grouping and triggering operation somewhere in the pipeline.

Because Beam operates in terms of streams, anywhere a table is involved (sources, sinks, and any intermediate groupings/ungroupings), some sort of conversion is necessary to keep the underlying table hidden. Those conversions in Beam look something like this:

- *Sources* that *consume* tables typically hardcode the manner in which those tables are *triggered*; there is no way for a user to specify custom triggering of the table they want to consume. The source may be written to trigger every new update to the table as a record, it might batch groups of updates together, or it might provide a single, bounded snapshot of the data in the table at some point in time. It really just depends on what's practical for a given source, and what use case the author of the source is trying to address.

- *Sinks* that *write* tables typically hardcode the manner in which they *group* their input streams. Sometimes, this is done in a way that gives the user a certain amount of control; for example, by simply grouping on a user-assigned key. In other cases, the grouping might be implicitly defined; for example, by grouping on a random physical partition number when writing input data with no natural key to a sharded output source. As with sources, it really just depends on what's practical for the given sink and what use case the author of the sink is trying to address.

- For *grouping/ungrouping operations*, in contrast to sources and sinks, Beam provides users complete flexibility in how they group data into tables and ungroup them back into streams. This is by design. Flexibility in grouping operations is necessary because the way data are grouped is a key ingredient of the algorithms that define a pipeline. And flexibility in ungrouping is important so that the application can shape the generated streams in ways that are appropriate for the use case at hand.[8]

However, there's a wrinkle here. Remember from Figure 8-1 that the Beam Model is inherently biased toward streams. As a result, although it's possible to cleanly apply a grouping operation directly to a stream (this is Beam's GroupByKey operation), the model never provides first-class table objects to which a trigger can be directly applied. As a result, triggers must be applied somewhere else. There are basically two options here:

Predeclaration of triggers
> This is where triggers are specified at a point in the pipeline *before* the table to which they are actually applied. In this case, you're essentially prespecifying behavior you'd like to see later on in the pipeline after a grouping operation is encountered. When declared this way, triggers are *forward-propagating*.

Post-declaration of triggers
> This is where triggers are specified at a point in the pipeline *following* the table to which they are applied. In this case, you're specifying the behavior you'd like to see at the point where the trigger is declared. When declared this way, triggers are *backward-propagating*.

Because post-declaration of triggers allows you to specify the behavior you want at the actual place you want to observe it, it's much more intuitive. Unfortunately, Beam as it exists today (2.x and earlier) uses predeclaration of triggers (similar to how windowing is also predeclared).

Even though Beam provides a number of ways to cope with the fact that tables are hidden, we're still left with the fact that tables must always be triggered before they can be observed, even if the contents of that table are really the final data that you want to consume. This is a shortcoming of the Beam Model as it exists today, one which could be addressed by moving away from a stream-centric model and toward one that treats both streams and tables as first-class entities.

Let's now look at the Beam Model's conceptual converse: classic SQL.

---

8 Though there are a number of efforts in flight across various projects that are trying to simplify the specification of triggering/ungrouping semantics. The most compelling proposal, made independently within both the Flink and Beam communities, is that triggers should simply be specified at the outputs of a pipeline and automatically propagated up throughout the pipeline. In this way, one would describe only the desired shape of the streams that actually create materialized output; the shape of all other streams in the pipeline would be implicitly derived from there.

The SQL Model: A Table-Biased Approach

In contrast to the Beam Model's stream-biased approach, SQL has historically taken a table-biased approach: queries are applied to tables, and always result in new tables. This is similar to the batch processing model we looked at in Chapter 6 with Map-Reduce,[9] but it will be useful to consider a concrete example like the one we just looked at for the Beam Model.

Consider the following denormalized SQL table:

`UserScores (user, team, score, timestamp)`

It contains user scores, each annotated with the IDs of the corresponding user and their corresponding team. There is no primary key, so you can assume that this is an append-only table, with each row being identified implicitly by its unique physical offset. If we want to compute team scores from this table, we could use a query that looks something like this:

```
SELECT team, SUM(score) as total
FROM UserScores
GROUP BY team;
```

When executed by a query engine, the optimizer will probably break this query down into roughly three steps:

1. Scanning the input table (i.e., triggering a snapshot of it)
2. Projecting the fields in that table down to team and score
3. Grouping rows by team and summing the scores

If we look at this using a diagram similar to Figure 8-1, it would look like Figure 8-2.

The SCAN operation takes the input table and triggers it into a bounded stream that contains a snapshot of the contents of that table at query execution time. That stream is consumed by the SELECT operation, which projects the four-column input rows down to two-column output rows. Being a nongrouping operation, it yields another stream. Finally, that two-column stream of teams and user scores enters the GROUP BY and is grouped by team into a table, with scores for the same team SUM'd together, yielding our output table of teams and their corresponding team score totals.

---

9 Though, of course, a single SQL query has vastly more expressive power than a single MapReduce, given the far less-confining set of operations and composition options available.

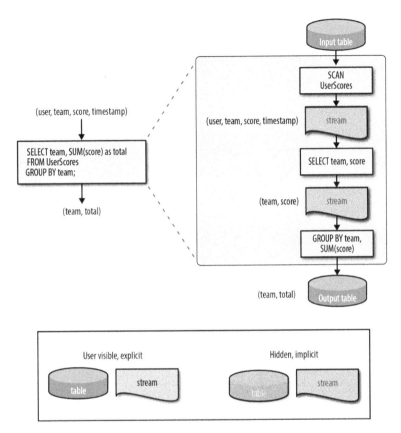

Figure 8-2. Table bias in a simple SQL query

This is a relatively simple example that naturally ends in a table, so it really isn't sufficient to highlight the table-bias in classic SQL. But we can tease out some more evidence by simply splitting the main pieces of this query (projection and grouping) into two separate queries:

```
SELECT team, score
INTO TeamAndScore
FROM UserScores;

SELECT team, SUM(score) as total
INTO TeamTotals
FROM TeamAndScore
GROUP BY team;
```

In these queries, we first project the UserScores table down to just the two columns we care about, storing the results in a temporary TeamAndScore table. We then group that table by team, summing up the scores as we do so. After breaking things out into a pipeline of two queries, our diagram looks like that shown in Figure 8-3.

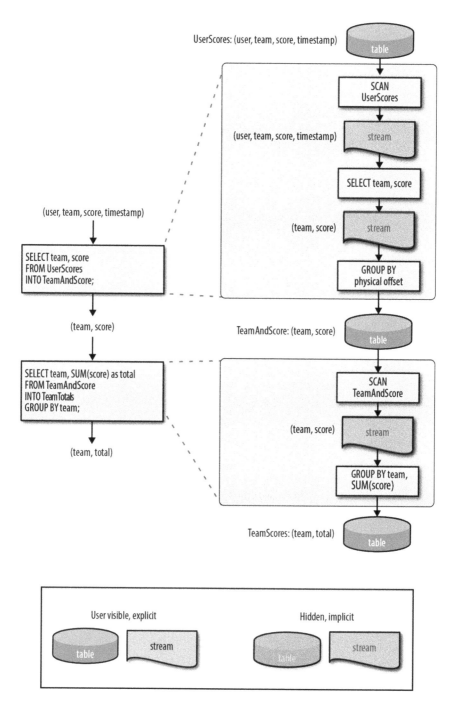

Figure 8-3. Breaking the query into two to reveal more evidence of table bias

If classic SQL exposed streams as first-class objects, you would expect the result from the first query, TeamAndScore, to be a stream because the SELECT operation consumes a stream and produces a stream. But because SQL's common currency is tables, it must first convert the projected stream into a table. And because the user hasn't specified any explicit key for grouping, it must simply group keys by their identity (i.e., append semantics, typically implemented by grouping by the physical storage offset for each row).

Because TeamAndScore is now a table, the second query must then prepend an additional SCAN operation to scan the table back into a stream to allow the GROUP BY to then group it back into a table again, this time with rows grouped by team and with their individual scores summed together. Thus, we see the two implicit conversions (from a stream and back again) that are inserted due to the explicit materialization of the intermediate table.

That said, tables in SQL are not *always* explicit; implicit tables can exist, as well. For example, if we were to add a HAVING clause to the end of the query with the GROUP BY statement, to filter out teams with scores less than a certain threshold, the diagram would change to look something like Figure 8-4.

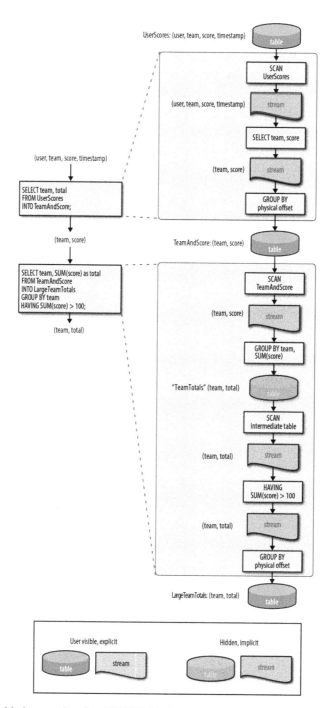

UserScores: (user, team, score, timestamp)

SCAN
UserScores

(user, team, score, timestamp) stream

SELECT team, score

(team, score) stream

GROUP BY
physical offset

(user, team, score, timestamp)

```
SELECT team, total
FROM UserScores
INTO TeamAndScore;
```

(team, score)

TeamAndScore: (team, score)

SCAN
TeamAndScore

(team, score) stream

GROUP BY team,
SUM(score)

"TeamTotals" (team, total) table

```
SELECT team, SUM(score) as total
FROM TeamAndScore
INTO LargeTeamTotals
GROUP BY team
HAVING SUM(score) > 100;
```

(team, total)

SCAN
intermediate table

(team, total) stream

HAVING
SUM(score) > 100

(team, total) stream

GROUP BY
physical offset

LargeTeamTotals: (team, total) table

User visible, explicit   Hidden, implicit

table   stream   table   stream

Figure 8-4. Table bias with a final HAVING clause

With the addition of the HAVING clause, what used to be the user-visible TeamTotals table is now an implicit, intermediate table. To filter the results of the table according to the rules in the HAVING clause, that table must be triggered into a stream that can be filtered and then that stream must be implicitly grouped back into a table to yield the new output table, LargeTeamTotals.

The important takeaway here is the clear table bias in classic SQL. Streams are always implicit, and thus for any materialized stream a conversion from/to a table is required. The rules for such conversions can be categorized roughly as follows:

Input tables (i.e., sources, in Beam Model terms)
These are always implicitly triggered in their entirety at a specific point in time[10] (generally query execution time) to yield a bounded stream containing a snapshot of the table at that time. This is identical to what you get with classic batch processing, as well; for example, the MapReduce case we looked at in Chapter 6.

Output tables (i.e., sinks, in Beam Model terms)
These tables are either direct manifestations of a table created by a final grouping operation in the query, or are the result of an implicit grouping (by some unique identifier for the row) applied to a query's terminal stream, for queries that do not end in a grouping operation (e.g., the projection query in the previous examples, or a GROUP BY followed by a HAVING clause). As with inputs, this matches the behavior seen in classic batch processing.

Grouping/ungrouping operations
Unlike Beam, these operations provide complete flexibility in one dimension only: grouping. Whereas classic SQL queries provide a full suite of grouping operations (GROUP BY, JOIN, CUBE, etc.), they provide only a single type of implicit ungrouping operation: trigger an intermediate table in its entirety after all of the upstream data contributing to it have been incorporated (again, the exact same implicit trigger provided in MapReduce as part of the shuffle operation). As a result, SQL offers great flexibility in shaping algorithms via grouping but essentially zero flexibility in shaping the implicit streams that exist under the covers during query execution.

Materialized views

Given how analogous classic SQL queries are to classic batch processing, it might be tempting to write off SQL's inherent table bias as nothing more than an artifact of SQL not supporting stream processing in any way. But to do so would be to ignore

---

10 Note that we're speaking conceptually here; there are of course a multitude of optimizations that can be applied in actual execution; for example, looking up specific rows via an index rather than scanning the entire table.

the fact that databases have supported a specific type of stream processing for quite some time: *materialized views*. A materialized view is a view that is physically materialized as a table and kept up to date *over* time by the database as the source table(s) evolve. Note how this sounds remarkably similar to our definition of a time-varying relation. What's fascinating about materialized views is that they add a very useful form of stream processing to SQL *without* significantly altering the way it operates, including its inherent table bias.

For example, let's consider the queries we looked at in Figure 8-4. We can alter those queries to instead be CREATE MATERIALIZED VIEW[11] statements:

```
CREATE MATERIALIZED VIEW TeamAndScoreView AS
SELECT team, score
FROM UserScores;

CREATE MATERIALIZED VIEW LargeTeamTotalsView AS
SELECT team, SUM(score) as total
FROM TeamAndScoreView
GROUP BY team
HAVING SUM(score) > 100;
```

In doing so, we transform them into continuous, standing queries that process the updates to the UserScores table continuously, in a streaming manner. Even so, the resulting physical execution diagram for the views *looks almost exactly the same* as it did for the one-off queries; nowhere are streams made into explicit first-class objects in order to support this idea of streaming materialized views. The *only* noteworthy change in the physical execution plan is the substitution of a different trigger: SCAN-AND-STREAM instead of SCAN, as illustrated in Figure 8-5.

---

11 It's been brought to my attention multiple times that the "MATERIALIZED" aspect of these queries is just an optimization: semantically speaking, these queries could just as easily be replaced with generic CREATE VIEW statements, in which case the database might instead simply rematerialize the entire view each time it is referenced. This is true. The reason I use the MATERIALIZED variant here is that the semantics of a materialized view are to incrementally update the view table in response to a stream of changes, which is indicative of the streaming nature behind them. That said, the fact that you can instead provide a similar experience by reexecuting a bounded query each time a view is accessed provides a nice link between streams and tables as well as a link between streaming systems and the way batch systems have been historically used for processing data that evolves over time. You can either incrementally process changes as they occur or you can reprocess the entire input dataset from time to time. Both are valid ways of processing an evolving table of data.

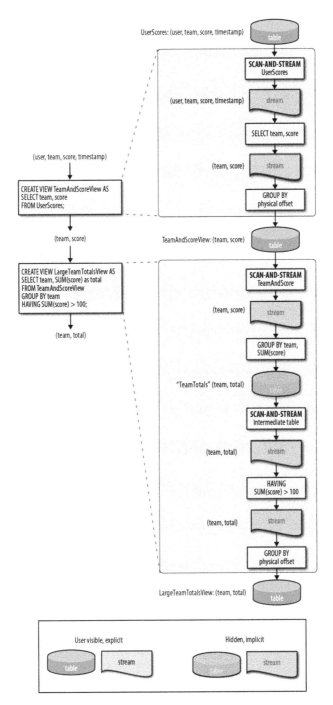

Figure 8-5. Table bias in materialized views

What is this SCAN-AND-STREAM trigger? SCAN-AND-STREAM starts out like a SCAN trigger, emitting the full contents of the table at a point in time into a stream. But instead of stopping there and declaring the stream to be done (i.e., bounded), it continues to also trigger all subsequent modifications to the input table, yielding an unbounded stream that captures the evolution of the table over time. In the general case, these modifications include not only INSERTs of new values, but also DELETEs of previous values and UPDATEs to existing values (which, practically speaking, are treated as a simultaneous DELETE/INSERT pair, or undo/redo values as they are called in Flink).

Furthermore, if we consider the table/stream conversion rules for materialized views, the only real difference is the trigger used:

- *Input tables* are implicitly triggered via a SCAN-AND-STREAM trigger instead of a SCAN trigger. Everything else is the same as classic batch queries.
- *Output tables* are treated the same as classic batch queries.
- *Grouping/ungrouping operations* function the same as classic batch queries, with the only difference being the use of a SCAN-AND-STREAM trigger instead of a SNAP SHOT trigger for implicit ungrouping operations.

Given this example, it's clear to see that SQL's inherent table bias is not just an artifact of SQL being limited to batch processing:[12] materialized views lend SQL the ability to perform a specific type of stream processing without any significant changes in approach, including the inherent bias toward tables. Classic SQL is just a table-biased model, regardless of whether you're using it for batch or stream processing.

Looking Forward: Toward Robust Streaming SQL

We've now looked at time-varying relations, the ways in which tables and streams provide different renderings of a time-varying relation, and what the inherent biases of the Beam and SQL models are with respect to stream and table theory. So where does all of this leave us? And perhaps more to the point, what do we need to change or add within SQL to support robust stream processing? The surprising answer is: not much if we have good defaults.

We know that the key conceptual change is to replace classic, point-in-time relations with time-varying relations. We saw earlier that this is a very seamless substitution, one which applies across the full breadth of relational operators already in existence, thanks to maintaining the critical closure property of relational algebra. But we also saw that dealing in time-varying relations directly is often impractical; we need the

---

12 Though it's probably fair to say that SQL's table bias is likely an artifact of SQL's *roots* in batch processing.

ability to operate in terms of our two more-common physical manifestations: tables and streams. This is where some simple extensions with good defaults come in.

We also need some tools for robustly reasoning about time, specifically event time. This is where things like timestamps, windowing, and triggering come into play. But again, judicious choice of defaults will be important to minimize how often these extensions are necessary in practice.

What's great is that we don't really need anything more than that. So let's now finally spend some time looking in detail at these two categories of extensions: *stream/table selection* and *temporal operators*.

Stream and Table Selection

As we worked through time-varying relation examples, we already encountered the two key extensions related to stream and table selection. They were those TABLE and STREAM keywords we placed after the SELECT keyword to dictate our desired physical view of a given time-varying relation:

```
12:07> SELECT TABLE Name,           12:01> SELECT STREAM Name
           SUM(Score) as Total,                SUM(Score) as Total,
           MAX(Time)                           MAX(Time)
       FROM UserScores                    FROM UserScores
       GROUP BY Name;                     GROUP BY Name;
-----------------------------        -----------------------------
| Name  | Total | Time  |            | Name  | Total | Time  |
-----------------------------        -----------------------------
| Julie | 12    | 12:07 |            | Julie | 7     | 12:01 |
| Frank | 3     | 12:03 |            | Frank | 3     | 12:03 |
-----------------------------        | Julie | 8     | 12:03 |
                                     | Julie | 12    | 12:07 |
                                     ..... [12:01, 12:07] ....
```

These extensions are relatively straightforward and easy to use when necessary. But the really important thing regarding stream and table selection is the choice of good defaults for times when they aren't explicitly provided. Such defaults should honor the classic, table-biased behavior of SQL that everyone is accustomed to, while also operating intuitively in a world that includes streams. They should also be easy to remember. The goal here is to help maintain a natural feel to the system, while also greatly decreasing the frequency with which we must use explicit extensions. A good choice of defaults that satisfies all of these requirements is:

- If *all* of the inputs are tables, the output is a TABLE.
- If *any* of the inputs are streams, the output is a STREAM.

What's additionally important to call out here is that these physical renderings of a time-varying relation are really only necessary when you want to materialize the TVR in some way, either to view it directly or write it to some output table or stream. Given a SQL system that operates under the covers in terms of full-fidelity time-varying relations, intermediate results (e.g., WITH AS or SELECT INTO statements) can remain as full-fidelity TVRs in whatever format the system naturally deals in, with no need to render them into some other, more limited concrete manifestation.

And that's really it for stream and table selection. Beyond the ability to deal in streams and tables directly, we also need some better tools for reasoning about time if we want to support robust, out-of-order stream processing within SQL. Let's now look in more detail about what those entail.

Temporal Operators

The foundation of robust, out-of-order processing is the event-time timestamp: that small piece of metadata that captures the time at which an event occurred rather than the time at which it is observed. In a SQL world, event time is typically just another column of data for a given TVR, one which is natively present in the source data themselves.[13] In that sense, this idea of materializing a record's event time within the record itself is something SQL already handles naturally by putting a timestamp in a regular column.

Before we go any further, let's look at an example. To help tie all of this SQL stuff together with the concepts we've explored previously in the book, we resurrect our running example of summing up nine scores from various members of a team to arrive at that team's total score. If you recall, those scores look like Figure 8-6 when plotted on X = event-time/Y = processing-time axes.

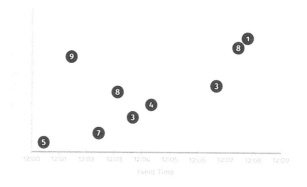

Figure 8-6. Data points in our running example

---

13 For some use cases, capturing and using the current processing time for a given record as its event time going forward can be useful (for example, when logging events directly into a TVR, where the time of ingress is the natural event time for that record).

If we were to imagine these data as a classic SQL table, they might look something like this, ordered by event time (left-to-right in Figure 8-6):

```
12:10> SELECT TABLE *, Sys.MTime as ProcTime
       FROM UserScores ORDER BY EventTime;
-------------------------------------------------
| Name  | Team  | Score | EventTime | ProcTime |
-------------------------------------------------
| Julie | TeamX |     5 | 12:00:26  | 12:05:19 |
| Frank | TeamX |     9 | 12:01:26  | 12:08:19 |
| Ed    | TeamX |     7 | 12:02:26  | 12:05:39 |
| Julie | TeamX |     8 | 12:03:06  | 12:07:06 |
| Amy   | TeamX |     3 | 12:03:39  | 12:06:13 |
| Fred  | TeamX |     4 | 12:04:19  | 12:06:39 |
| Naomi | TeamX |     3 | 12:06:39  | 12:07:19 |
| Becky | TeamX |     8 | 12:07:26  | 12:08:39 |
| Naomi | TeamX |     1 | 12:07:46  | 12:09:00 |
-------------------------------------------------
```

If you recall, we saw this table way back in Chapter 2 when I first introduced this dataset. This rendering provides a little more detail on the data than we've typically shown, explicitly highlighting the fact that the nine scores themselves belong to seven different users, each a member of the same team. SQL provides a nice, concise way to see the data laid out fully before we begin diving into examples.

Another nice thing about this view of the data is that it fully captures the event time and processing time for each record. You can imagine the event-time column as being just another piece of the original data, and the processing-time column as being something supplied by the system (in this case, using a hypothetical Sys.MTime column that records the processing-time modification timestamp of a given row; that is, the time at which that row arrived in the source table), capturing the ingress time of the records themselves into the system.

The fun thing about SQL is how easy it is to view your data in different ways. For example, if we instead want to see the data in processing-time order (bottom-to-top in Figure 8-6), we could simply update the ORDER BY clause:

```
12:10> SELECT TABLE *, Sys.MTime as ProcTime
       FROM UserScores ORDER BY ProcTime;
-------------------------------------------------
| Name  | Team  | Score | EventTime | ProcTime |
-------------------------------------------------
| Julie | TeamX |     5 | 12:00:26  | 12:05:19 |
| Ed    | TeamX |     7 | 12:02:26  | 12:05:39 |
| Amy   | TeamX |     3 | 12:03:39  | 12:06:13 |
| Fred  | TeamX |     4 | 12:04:19  | 12:06:39 |
| Julie | TeamX |     8 | 12:03:06  | 12:07:06 |
| Naomi | TeamX |     3 | 12:06:39  | 12:07:19 |
| Frank | TeamX |     9 | 12:01:26  | 12:08:19 |
| Becky | TeamX |     8 | 12:07:26  | 12:08:39 |
```

```
| Naomi | TeamX |    1 |  12:07:46 | 12:09:00 |
-------------------------------------------------
```

As we learned earlier, these table renderings of the data are really a partial-fidelity view of the complete underlying TVR. If we were to instead query the full table-oriented TVR (but only for the three most important columns, for the sake of brevity), it would expand to something like this:

```
12:10> SELECT TVR Score, EventTime, Sys.MTime as ProcTime
       FROM UserScores ORDER BY ProcTime;
----------------------------------------------------------------------
|         [-inf, 12:05:19)        |     [12:05:19, 12:05:39)        |
| ------------------------------- | ------------------------------- |
| | Score | EventTime | ProcTime || | Score | EventTime | ProcTime ||
| ------------------------------- | ------------------------------- |
| ------------------------------- || |    5 |  12:00:26 | 12:05:19 ||
|                                 | ------------------------------- |
|                                 |                                 |
|                                 |                                 |
----------------------------------------------------------------------
|      [12:05:39, 12:06:13)       |     [12:06:13, 12:06:39)        |
| ------------------------------- | ------------------------------- |
| | Score | EventTime | ProcTime || | Score | EventTime | ProcTime ||
| ------------------------------- | ------------------------------- |
| |    5 |  12:00:26 | 12:05:19 || |    5 |  12:00:26 | 12:05:19 ||
| |    7 |  12:02:26 | 12:05:39 || |    7 |  12:02:26 | 12:05:39 ||
| ------------------------------- || |    3 |  12:03:39 | 12:06:13 ||
|                                 | ------------------------------- |
----------------------------------------------------------------------
|      [12:06:39, 12:07:06)       |     [12:07:06, 12:07:19)        |
| ------------------------------- | ------------------------------- |
| | Score | EventTime | ProcTime || | Score | EventTime | ProcTime ||
| ------------------------------- | ------------------------------- |
| |    5 |  12:00:26 | 12:05:19 || |    5 |  12:00:26 | 12:05:19 ||
| |    7 |  12:02:26 | 12:05:39 || |    7 |  12:02:26 | 12:05:39 ||
| |    3 |  12:03:39 | 12:06:13 || |    3 |  12:03:39 | 12:06:13 ||
| |    4 |  12:04:19 | 12:06:39 || |    4 |  12:04:19 | 12:06:39 ||
| ------------------------------- || |    8 |  12:03:06 | 12:07:06 ||
|                                 | ------------------------------- |
----------------------------------------------------------------------
|      [12:07:19, 12:08:19)       |     [12:08:19, 12:08:39)        |
| ------------------------------- | ------------------------------- |
| | Score | EventTime | ProcTime || | Score | EventTime | ProcTime ||
| ------------------------------- | ------------------------------- |
| |    5 |  12:00:26 | 12:05:19 || |    5 |  12:00:26 | 12:05:19 ||
| |    7 |  12:02:26 | 12:05:39 || |    7 |  12:02:26 | 12:05:39 ||
| |    3 |  12:03:39 | 12:06:13 || |    3 |  12:03:39 | 12:06:13 ||
| |    4 |  12:04:19 | 12:06:39 || |    4 |  12:04:19 | 12:06:39 ||
| |    8 |  12:03:06 | 12:07:06 || |    8 |  12:03:06 | 12:07:06 ||
| |    3 |  12:06:39 | 12:07:19 || |    3 |  12:06:39 | 12:07:19 ||
| ------------------------------- || |    9 |  12:01:26 | 12:08:19 ||
|                                 | ------------------------------- |
|                                 |                                 |
```

```
----------------------------------------------------------------
|      [12:08:39, 12:09:00)       |       [12:09:00, now)         |
| ------------------------------- | ----------------------------- |
| | Score | EventTime | ProcTime | | | Score | EventTime | ProcTime | |
| ------------------------------- | ----------------------------- |
| |     5 |  12:00:26 |  12:05:19 | | |     5 |  12:00:26 |  12:05:19 | |
| |     7 |  12:02:26 |  12:05:39 | | |     7 |  12:02:26 |  12:05:39 | |
| |     3 |  12:03:39 |  12:06:13 | | |     3 |  12:03:39 |  12:06:13 | |
| |     4 |  12:04:19 |  12:06:39 | | |     4 |  12:04:19 |  12:06:39 | |
| |     8 |  12:03:06 |  12:07:06 | | |     8 |  12:03:06 |  12:07:06 | |
| |     3 |  12:06:39 |  12:07:19 | | |     3 |  12:06:39 |  12:07:19 | |
| |     9 |  12:01:26 |  12:08:19 | | |     9 |  12:01:26 |  12:08:19 | |
| |     8 |  12:07:26 |  12:08:39 | | |     8 |  12:07:26 |  12:08:39 | |
| ------------------------------- | |     1 |  12:07:46 |  12:09:00 | |
|                                   | ----------------------------- |
----------------------------------------------------------------
```

That's a lot of data. Alternatively, the STREAM version would render much more compactly in this instance; thanks to there being no explicit grouping in the relation, it looks essentially identical to the point-in-time TABLE rendering earlier, with the addition of the trailing footer describing the range of processing time captured in the stream so far, plus the note that the system is still waiting for more data in the stream (assuming we're treating the stream as unbounded; we'll see a bounded version of the stream shortly):

```
12:00> SELECT STREAM Score, EventTime, Sys.MTime as ProcTime FROM UserScores;
-------------------------------
| Score | EventTime | ProcTime |
-------------------------------
|     5 |  12:00:26 |  12:05:19 |
|     7 |  12:02:26 |  12:05:39 |
|     3 |  12:03:39 |  12:06:13 |
|     4 |  12:04:19 |  12:06:39 |
|     8 |  12:03:06 |  12:07:06 |
|     3 |  12:06:39 |  12:07:19 |
|     9 |  12:01:26 |  12:08:19 |
|     8 |  12:07:26 |  12:08:39 |
|     1 |  12:07:46 |  12:09:00 |
........ [12:00, 12:10] ........
```

But this is all just looking at the raw input records without any sort of transformations. Much more interesting is when we start altering the relations. When we've explored this example in the past, we've always started with classic batch processing to sum up the scores over the entire dataset, so let's do the same here. The first example pipeline (previously provided as Example 6-1) looked like Example 8-1 in Beam.

Example 8-1. Summation pipeline

```
PCollection<String> raw = IO.read(...);
PCollection<KV<Team, Integer>> input = raw.apply(new ParseFn());
PCollection<KV<Team, Integer>> totals =
  input.apply(Sum.integersPerKey());
```

And rendered in the streams and tables view of the world, that pipeline's execution looked like Figure 8-7.

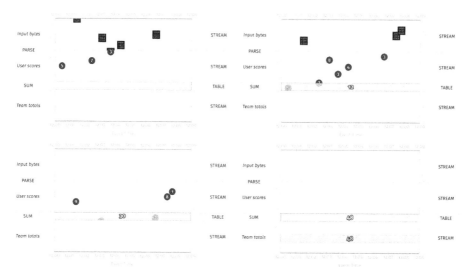

Figure 8-7. Streams and tables view of classic batch processing (http://streaming book.net/fig/8-7)

Given that we already have our data placed into an appropriate schema, we won't be doing any parsing in SQL; instead, we focus on everything in the pipeline after the parse transformation. And because we're going with the classic batch model of retrieving a single answer only after all of the input data have been processed, the TABLE and STREAM views of the summation relation would look essentially identical (recall that we're dealing with bounded versions of our dataset for these initial, batch-style examples; as a result, this STREAM query actually terminates with a line of dashes and an END-OF-STREAM marker):

```
12:10> SELECT TABLE SUM(Score) as Total, MAX(EventTime),
       MAX(Sys.MTime) as "MAX(ProcTime)" FROM UserScores GROUP BY Team;
-------------------------------------------
| Total | MAX(EventTime) | MAX(ProcTime) |
-------------------------------------------
|    48 |       12:07:46 |      12:09:00 |
-------------------------------------------

12:00> SELECT STREAM SUM(Score) as Total, MAX(EventTime),
       MAX(Sys.MTime) as "MAX(ProcTime)" FROM UserScores GROUP BY Team;
-------------------------------------------
| Total | MAX(EventTime) | MAX(ProcTime) |
-------------------------------------------
|    48 |       12:07:46 |      12:09:00 |
------ [12:00, 12:10] END-OF-STREAM ------
```

More interesting is when we start adding windowing into the mix. That will give us a chance to begin looking more closely at the temporal operations that need to be added to SQL to support robust stream processing.

Where: **windowing**

As we learned in Chapter 6, windowing is a modification of grouping by key, in which the window becomes a secondary part of a hierarchical key. As with classic programmatic batch processing, you can window data into more simplistic windows quite easily within SQL as it exists now by simply including time as part of the GROUP BY parameter. Or, if the system in question provides it, you can use a built-in windowing operation. We look at SQL examples of both in a moment, but first, let's revisit the programmatic version from Chapter 3. Thinking back to Example 6-2, the windowed Beam pipeline looked like that shown in Example 8-2.

Example 8-2. Summation pipeline

```
PCollection<String> raw = IO.read(...);
PCollection<KV<Team, Integer>> input = raw.apply(new ParseFn());
PCollection<KV<Team, Integer>> totals = input
  .apply(Window.into(FixedWindows.of(TWO_MINUTES)))
  .apply(Sum.integersPerKey());
```

And the execution of that pipeline (in streams and tables rendering from Figure 6-5), looked like the diagrams presented in Figure 8-8.

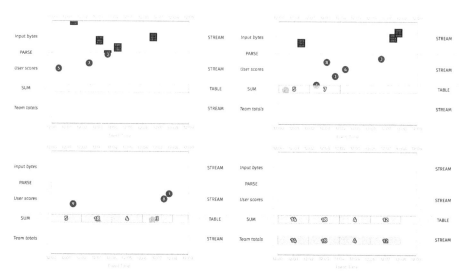

Figure 8-8. Streams and tables view of windowed summation on a batch engine (http://streamingbook.net/fig/8-8)

As we saw before, the only material change from Figure 8-7 to 8-8 is that the table created by the SUM operation is now partitioned into fixed, two-minute windows of time, yielding four windowed answers at the end rather than the single global sum that we had previously.

To do the same thing in SQL, we have two options: implicitly window by including some unique feature of the window (e.g., the end timestamp) in the GROUP BY statement, or use a built-in windowing operation. Let's look at both.

First, ad hoc windowing. In this case, we perform the math of calculating windows ourselves in our SQL statement:

```
12:10> SELECT TABLE SUM(Score) as Total,
         "[" || EventTime / INTERVAL '2' MINUTES || ", " ||
         (EventTime / INTERVAL '2' MINUTES) + INTERVAL '2' MINUTES ||
         ")" as Window,
       MAX(Sys.MTime) as "MAX(ProcTime)"
     FROM UserScores
     GROUP BY Team, EventTime / INTERVAL '2' MINUTES;
-------------------------------------------------
| Total | Window                | MAX(ProcTime) |
-------------------------------------------------
| 14    | [12:00:00, 12:02:00)  | 12:08:19      |
| 18    | [12:02:00, 12:04:00)  | 12:07:06      |
| 4     | [12:04:00, 12:06:00)  | 12:06:39      |
| 12    | [12:06:00, 12:08:00)  | 12:09:00      |
-------------------------------------------------
```

We can also achieve the same result using an explicit windowing statement such as those supported by Apache Calcite:

```
12:10> SELECT TABLE SUM(Score) as Total,
          TUMBLE(EventTime, INTERVAL '2' MINUTES) as Window,
          MAX(Sys.MTime) as 'MAX(ProcTime)'
       FROM UserScores
       GROUP BY Team, TUMBLE(EventTime, INTERVAL '2' MINUTES);
-------------------------------------------------
| Total | Window              | MAX(ProcTime) |
-------------------------------------------------
| 14    | [12:00:00, 12:02:00) | 12:08:19      |
| 18    | [12:02:00, 12:04:00) | 12:07:06      |
| 4     | [12:04:00, 12:06:00) | 12:06:39      |
| 12    | [12:06:00, 12:08:00) | 12:09:00      |
-------------------------------------------------
```

This then begs the question: if we can implicitly window using existing SQL constructs, why even bother supporting explicit windowing constructs? There are two reasons, only the first of which is apparent in this example (we'll see the other one in action later on in the chapter):

1. Windowing takes care of the window-computation math for you. It's a lot easier to consistently get things right when you specify basic parameters like width and slide directly rather than computing the window math yourself.[14]

2. Windowing allows the concise expression of more complex, dynamic groupings such as sessions. Even though SQL is technically able to express the every-element-within-some-temporal-gap-of-another-element relationship that defines session windows, the corresponding incantation is a tangled mess of analytic functions, self joins, and array unnesting that no mere mortal could be reasonably expected to conjure on their own.

Both are compelling arguments for providing first-class windowing constructs in SQL, in addition to the ad hoc windowing capabilities that already exist.

At this point, we've seen what windowing looks like from a classic batch/classic relational perspective when consuming the data as a table. But if we want to consume the data as a stream, we get back to that third question from the Beam Model: when in processing time do we materialize outputs?

When: triggers

The answer to that question, as before, is triggers and watermarks. However, in the context of SQL, there's a strong argument to be made for having a different set of

---

14 Maths are easy to get wrong.

defaults than those we introduced with the Beam Model in Chapter 3: rather than defaulting to using a single watermark trigger, a more SQL-ish default would be to take a cue from materialized views and trigger on every element. In other words, any time a new input arrives, we produce a corresponding new output.

A SQL-ish default: per-record triggers. There are two compelling benefits to using trigger-every-record as the default:

Simplicity

> The semantics of per-record updates are easy to understand; materialized views have operated this way for years.

Fidelity

> As in change data capture systems, per-record triggering yields a full-fidelity stream rendering of a given time-varying relation; no information is lost as part of the conversion.

The downside is primarily cost: triggers are always applied after a grouping operation, and the nature of grouping often presents an opportunity to reduce the cardinality of data flowing through the system, thus commensurately reducing the cost of further processing those aggregate results downstream. Even so, the benefits in clarity and simplicity for use cases where cost is not prohibitive arguably outweigh the cognitive complexity of defaulting to a non-full-fidelity trigger up front.

Thus, for our first take at consuming aggregate team scores as a stream, let's see what things would look like using a per-record trigger. Beam itself doesn't have a precise per-record trigger, so, as demonstrated in Example 8-3, we instead use a repeated AfterCount(1) trigger, which will fire immediately any time a new record arrives.

Example 8-3. Per-record trigger

```
PCollection<String> raw = IO.read(...);
PCollection<KV<Team, Integer>> input = raw.apply(new ParseFn());
PCollection<KV<Team, Integer>> totals = input
  .apply(Window.into(FixedWindows.of(TWO_MINUTES))
              .triggering(Repeatedly(AfterCount(1)))
  .apply(Sum.integersPerKey());
```

A streams and tables rendering of this pipeline would then look something like that depicted in Figure 8-9.

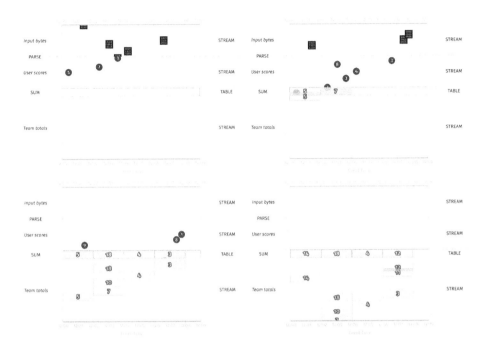

Figure 8-9. Streams and tables view of windowed summation on a streaming engine with per-record triggering (http://streamingbook.net/fig/8-9)

An interesting side effect of using per-record triggers is how it somewhat masks the effect of data being brought to rest because they are then immediately put back into motion again by the trigger. Even so, the aggregate artifact from the grouping remains at rest in the table, as the ungrouped stream of values flows away from it.

Moving back to SQL, we can see now what the effect of rendering the corresponding time-value relation as a stream would be. It (unsurprisingly) looks a lot like the stream of values in the animation in Figure 8-9:

```
12:00> SELECT STREAM SUM(Score) as Total,
          TUMBLE(EventTime, INTERVAL '2' MINUTES) as Window,
          MAX(Sys.MTime) as 'MAX(ProcTime)''
       FROM UserScores
       GROUP BY Team, TUMBLE(EventTime, INTERVAL '2' MINUTES);
-------------------------------------------------
| Total | Window                 | MAX(ProcTime) |
-------------------------------------------------
| 5     | [12:00:00, 12:02:00)   | 12:05:19      |
| 7     | [12:02:00, 12:04:00)   | 12:05:39      |
| 10    | [12:02:00, 12:04:00)   | 12:06:13      |
| 4     | [12:04:00, 12:06:00)   | 12:06:39      |
| 18    | [12:02:00, 12:04:00)   | 12:07:06      |
| 3     | [12:06:00, 12:08:00)   | 12:07:19      |
```

```
| 14    | [12:00:00, 12:02:00) | 12:08:19    |
| 11    | [12:06:00, 12:08:00) | 12:08:39    |
| 12    | [12:06:00, 12:08:00) | 12:09:00    |
............... [12:00, 12:10] ...............
```

But even for this simple use case, it's pretty chatty. If we're building a pipeline to process data for a large-scale mobile application, we might not want to pay the cost of processing downstream updates for each and every upstream user score. This is where custom triggers come in.

Watermark triggers. If we were to switch the Beam pipeline to use a watermark trigger, for example, we could get exactly one output per window in the stream version of the TVR, as demonstrated in Example 8-4 and shown in Figure 8-10.

Example 8-4. Watermark trigger

```
PCollection<String> raw = IO.read(...);
PCollection<KV<Team, Integer>> input = raw.apply(new ParseFn());
PCollection<KV<Team, Integer>> totals = input
  .apply(Window.into(FixedWindows.of(TWO_MINUTES))
              .triggering(AfterWatermark()))
  .apply(Sum.integersPerKey());
```

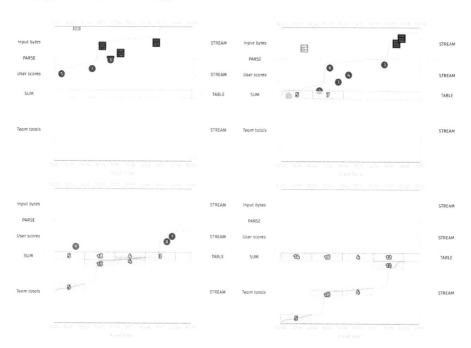

Figure 8-10. Windowed summation with watermark triggering (http://streaming book.net/fig/8-10)

To get the same effect in SQL, we'd need language support for specifying a custom trigger. Something like an EMIT <when> statement, such as EMIT WHEN WATERMARK PAST <column>. This would signal to the system that the table created by the aggregation should be triggered into a stream exactly once per row, when the input watermark for the table exceeds the timestamp value in the specified column (which in this case happens to be the end of the window).

Let's look at this relation rendered as a stream. From the perspective of understanding when trigger firings occur, it's also handy to stop relying on the MTime values from the original inputs and instead capture the current timestamp at which rows in the stream are emitted:

```
12:00> SELECT STREAM SUM(Score) as Total,
          TUMBLE(EventTime, INTERVAL '2' MINUTES) as Window,
          CURRENT_TIMESTAMP as EmitTime
       FROM UserScores
       GROUP BY Team, TUMBLE(EventTime, INTERVAL '2' MINUTES)
       EMIT WHEN WATERMARK PAST WINDOW_END(Window);
-------------------------------------------
| Total | Window                | EmitTime |
-------------------------------------------
| 5     | [12:00:00, 12:02:00)  | 12:06:00 |
| 18    | [12:02:00, 12:04:00)  | 12:07:30 |
| 4     | [12:04:00, 12:06:00)  | 12:07:41 |
| 12    | [12:06:00, 12:08:00)  | 12:09:22 |
............. [12:00, 12:10] .............
```

The main downside here is the late data problem due to the use of a heuristic watermark, as we encountered in previous chapters. In light of late data, a nicer option might be to also immediately output an update any time a late record shows up, using a variation on the watermark trigger that supported repeated late firings, as shown in Example 8-5 and Figure 8-11.

Example 8-5. Watermark trigger with late firings

```
PCollection<String> raw = IO.read(...);
PCollection<KV<Team, Integer>> input = raw.apply(new ParseFn());
PCollection<KV<Team, Integer>> totals = input
  .apply(Window.into(FixedWindows.of(TWO_MINUTES))
             .triggering(AfterWatermark()
                 .withLateFirings(AfterCount(1))))
  .apply(Sum.integersPerKey());
```

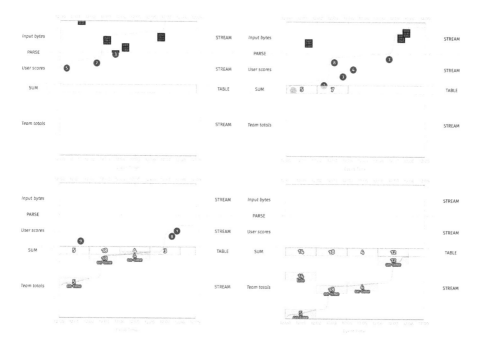

Figure 8-11. Windowed summation with on-time/late triggering (http://streaming book.net/fig/8-11)

We can do the same thing in SQL by allowing the specification of two triggers:

- A watermark trigger to give us an initial value: `WHEN WATERMARK PAST <column>`, with the end of the window used as the timestamp `<column>`.

- A repeated delay trigger for late data: `AND THEN AFTER <duration>`, with a `<dura tion>` of 0 to give us per-record semantics.

Now that we're getting multiple rows per window, it can also be useful to have another two system columns available: the timing of each row/pane for a given window relative to the watermark (`Sys.EmitTiming`), and the index of the pane/row for a given window (`Sys.EmitIndex`, to identify the sequence of revisions for a given row/window):

```
12:00> SELECT STREAM SUM(Score) as Total,
         TUMBLE(EventTime, INTERVAL '2' MINUTES) as Window,
         CURRENT_TIMESTAMP as EmitTime,
         Sys.EmitTiming, Sys.EmitIndex
       FROM UserScores
       GROUP BY Team, TUMBLE(EventTime, INTERVAL '2' MINUTES)
       EMIT WHEN WATERMARK PAST WINDOW_END(Window)
         AND THEN AFTER 0 SECONDS;
```

```
-----------------------------------------------------------------
| Total | Window                  | EmitTime | Sys.EmitTiming | Sys.EmitIndex |
-----------------------------------------------------------------
| 5     | [12:00:00, 12:02:00) | 12:06:00 | on-time        | 0             |
| 18    | [12:02:00, 12:04:00) | 12:07:30 | on-time        | 0             |
| 4     | [12:04:00, 12:06:00) | 12:07:41 | on-time        | 0             |
| 14    | [12:00:00, 12:02:00) | 12:08:19 | late           | 1             |
| 12    | [12:06:00, 12:08:00) | 12:09:22 | on-time        | 0             |
.......................... [12:00, 12:10] .............................
```

For each pane, using this trigger, we're able to get a single on-time answer that is likely to be correct, thanks to our heuristic watermark. And for any data that arrives late, we can get an updated version of the row amending our previous results.

Repeated delay triggers. The other main temporal trigger use case you might want is repeated delayed updates; that is, trigger a window one minute (in processing time) after any new data for it arrive. Note that this is different than triggering on aligned boundaries, as you would get with a microbatch system. As Example 8-6 shows, triggering via a delay relative to the most recent new record arriving for the window/row helps spread triggering load out more evenly than a bursty, aligned trigger would. It also does not require any sort of watermark support. Figure 8-12 presents the results.

Example 8-6. Repeated triggering with one-minute delays

```
PCollection<String> raw = IO.read(...);
PCollection<KV<Team, Integer>> input = raw.apply(new ParseFn());
PCollection<KV<Team, Integer>> totals = input
  .apply(Window.into(FixedWindows.of(TWO_MINUTES))
             .triggering(Repeatedly(UnalignedDelay(ONE_MINUTE))))
  .apply(Sum.integersPerKey());
```

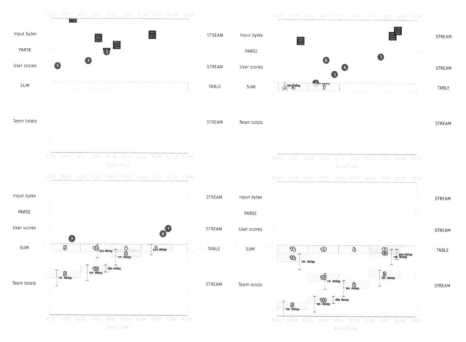

*Figure 8-12. Windowed summation with repeated one-minute-delay triggering (http://
streamingbook.net/fig/8-12)*

The effect of using such a trigger is very similar to the per-record triggering we
started out with but slightly less chatty thanks to the additional delay introduced in
triggering, which allows the system to elide some number of the rows being produced. Tweaking the delay allows us to tune the volume of data generated, and thus
balance the tensions of cost and timeliness as appropriate for the use case.

Rendered as a SQL stream, it would look something like this:

```
12:00> SELECT STREAM SUM(Score) as Total,
         TUMBLE(EventTime, INTERVAL '2' MINUTES) as Window,
         CURRENT_TIMESTAMP as EmitTime,
         Sys.EmitTiming, SysEmitIndex
       FROM UserScores
       GROUP BY Team, TUMBLE(EventTime, INTERVAL '2' MINUTES)
       EMIT AFTER 1 MINUTE;
```

Total	Window	EmitTime	Sys.EmitTiming	Sys.EmitIndex
5	[12:00:00, 12:02:00)	12:06:19	n/a	0
10	[12:02:00, 12:04:00)	12:06:39	n/a	0
4	[12:04:00, 12:06:00)	12:07:39	n/a	0
18	[12:02:00, 12:04:00)	12:08:06	n/a	1
3	[12:06:00, 12:08:00)	12:08:19	n/a	0

```
| 14    | [12:00:00, 12:02:00) | 12:09:19 | n/a    | 1    |        |
| 12    | [12:06:00, 12:08:00) | 12:09:22 | n/a    | 1    |        |
............................ [12:00, 12:10] ............................
```

Data-driven triggers.   Before moving on to the final question in the Beam Model, it's worth briefly discussing the idea of *data-driven triggers*. Because of the dynamic way types are handled in SQL, it might seem like data-driven triggers would be a very natural addition to the proposed EMIT *<when>* clause. For example, what if we want to trigger our summation any time the total score exceeds 10? Wouldn't something like EMIT WHEN Score > 10 work very naturally?

Well, yes and no. Yes, such a construct would fit very naturally. But when you think about what would actually be happening with such a construct, you essentially would be triggering on every record, and then executing the Score > 10 predicate to decide whether the triggered row should be propagated downstream. As you might recall, this sounds a lot like what happens with a HAVING clause. And, indeed, you can get the exact same effect by simply prepending HAVING Score > 10 to the end of the query. At which point, it begs the question: is it worth adding explicit data-driven triggers? Probably not. Even so, it's still encouraging to see just how easy it is to get the desired effect of data-driven triggers using standard SQL and well-chosen defaults.

How: accumulation

So far in this section, we've been ignoring the Sys.Undo column that I introduced toward the beginning of this chapter. As a result, we've defaulted to using *accumulating mode* to answer the question of *how* refinements for a window/row relate to one another. In other words, any time we observed multiple revisions of an aggregate row, the later revisions built upon the previous revisions, accumulating new inputs together with old ones. I opted for this approach because it matches the approach used in an earlier chapter, and it's a relatively straightforward translation from how things work in a table world.

That said, accumulating mode has some major drawbacks. In fact, as we discussed in Chapter 2, it's plain broken for any query/pipeline with a sequence of two or more grouping operations due to over counting. The only sane way to allow for the consumption of multiple revisions of a row within a system that allows for queries containing more than one serial grouping operation is if it operates by default in *accumulating and retracting* mode. Otherwise, you run into issues where a given input record is included multiple times in a single aggregation due to the blind incorporation of multiple revisions for a single row.

So, when we come to the question of incorporating accumulation mode semantics into a SQL world, the option that fits best with our goal of providing an intuitive and natural experience is if the system uses retractions by default under the covers.[15] As noted when I introduced the Sys.Undo column earlier, if you don't care about the retractions (as in the examples in this section up until now), you don't need to ask for them. But if you do ask for them, they should be there.

Retractions in a SQL world. To see what I mean, let's look at another example. To motivate the problem appropriately, let's look at a use case that's relatively impractical without retractions: building session windows and writing them incrementally to a key/value store like HBase. In this case, we'll be producing incremental sessions from our aggregation as they are built up. But in many cases, a given session will simply be an evolution of one or more previous sessions. In that case, you'd really like to delete the previous session(s) and replace it/them with the new one. But how do you do that? The only way to tell whether a given session replaces another one is to compare them to see whether the new one overlaps the old one. But that means duplicating some of the session-building logic in a separate part of your pipeline. And, more important, it means that you no longer have idempotent output, and you'll thus need to jump through a bunch of extra hoops if you want to maintain end-to-end exactly-once semantics. Far better would be for the pipeline to simply tell you which sessions were removed and which were added in their place. This is what retractions give you.

To see this in action (and in SQL), let's modify our example pipeline to compute session windows with a gap duration of one minute. For simplicity and clarity, we go back to using the default per-record trigger. Note that I've also shifted a few of the data points within processing time for these session examples to make the diagram cleaner; event-time timestamps remain the same. The updated dataset looks like this (with shifted processing-time timestamps highlighted in yellow):

```
12:00> SELECT STREAM Score, EventTime, Sys.MTime as ProcTime
       FROM UserScoresForSessions;
-----------------------------------
| Score | EventTime | ProcTime |
-----------------------------------
|     5 |  12:00:26 | 12:05:19 |
|     7 |  12:02:26 | 12:05:39 |
|     3 |  12:03:39 | 12:06:13 |
|     4 |  12:04:19 | 12:06:46 |   # Originally 12:06:39
|     3 |  12:06:39 | 12:07:19 |
|     8 |  12:03:06 | 12:07:33 |   # Originally 12:07:06
|     8 |  12:07:26 | 12:08:13 |   # Originally 12:08:39
|     9 |  12:01:26 | 12:08:19 |
```

---

15 It's sufficient for retractions to be used by default and not simply always because the system only needs the *option* to use retractions. There are specific use cases; for example, queries with a single grouping operation whose results are being written into an external storage system that supports per-key updates, where the system can detect retractions are not needed and disable them as an optimization.

```
|    1 |  12:07:46 | 12:09:00 |
........ [12:00, 12:10] ........
```

To begin with, let's look at the pipeline without retractions. After it's clear why that pipeline is problematic for the use case of writing incremental sessions to a key/value store, we'll then look at the version with retractions.

The Beam code for the nonretracting pipeline would look something like Example 8-7. Figure 8-13 shows the results.

Example 8-7. Session windows with per-record triggering and accumulation but no retractions

```
PCollection<String> raw = IO.read(...);
PCollection<KV<Team, Integer>> input = raw.apply(new ParseFn());
PCollection<KV<Team, Integer>> totals = input
  .apply(Window.into(Sessions.withGapDuration(ONE_MINUTE))
             .triggering(Repeatedly(AfterCount(1)))
             .accumulatingFiredPanes())
  .apply(Sum.integersPerKey());
```

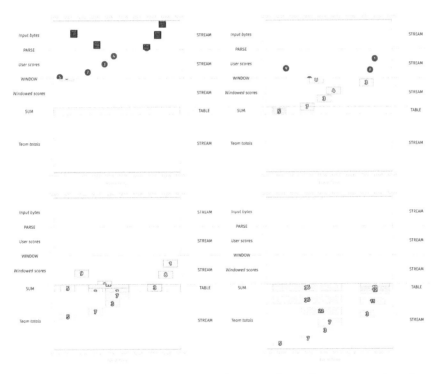

Figure 8-13. Session window summation with accumulation but no retractions (http://streamingbook.net/fig/8-13)

And finally, rendered in SQL, the output stream would look like this:

```
12:00> SELECT STREAM SUM(Score) as Total,
          SESSION(EventTime, INTERVAL '1' MINUTE) as Window,
          CURRENT_TIMESTAMP as EmitTime
       FROM UserScoresForSessions
       GROUP BY Team, SESSION(EventTime, INTERVAL '1' MINUTE);
-------------------------------------------
| Total | Window                | EmitTime |
-------------------------------------------
| 5     | [12:00:26, 12:01:26)  | 12:05:19 |
| 7     | [12:02:26, 12:03:26)  | 12:05:39 |
| 3     | [12:03:39, 12:04:39)  | 12:06:13 |
| 7     | [12:03:39, 12:05:19)  | 12:06:46 |
| 3     | [12:06:39, 12:07:39)  | 12:07:19 |
| 22    | [12:02:26, 12:05:19)  | 12:07:33 |
| 11    | [12:06:39, 12:08:26)  | 12:08:13 |
| 36    | [12:00:26, 12:05:19)  | 12:08:19 |
| 12    | [12:06:39, 12:08:46)  | 12:09:00 |
............. [12:00, 12:10] .............
```

The important thing to notice in here (in the animation as well as the SQL rendering) is what the stream of incremental sessions looks like. From our holistic viewpoint, it's pretty easy to visually identify in the animation which later sessions supersede those that came before. But imagine receiving elements in this stream one by one (as in the SQL listing) and needing to write them to HBase in a way that eventually results in the HBase table containing only the two final sessions (with values 36 and 12). How would you do that? Well, you'd need to do a bunch of read-modify-write operations to read all of the existing sessions for a key, compare them with the new session, determine which ones overlap, issue deletes for the obsolete sessions, and then finally issue a write for the new session—all at significant additional cost, and with a loss of idempotence, which would ultimately leave you unable to provide end-to-end, exactly-once semantics. It's just not practical.

Contrast this then with the same pipeline, but with retractions enabled, as demonstrated in Example 8-8 and depicted in Figure 8-14.

Example 8-8. Session windows with per-record triggering, accumulation, and retractions

```
PCollection<String> raw = IO.read(...);
PCollection<KV<Team, Integer>> input = raw.apply(new ParseFn());
PCollection<KV<Team, Integer>> totals = input
  .apply(Window.into(Sessions.withGapDuration(ONE_MINUTE))
              .triggering(Repeatedly(AfterCount(1))
              .accumulatingAndRetractingFiredPanes())
  .apply(Sum.integersPerKey());
```

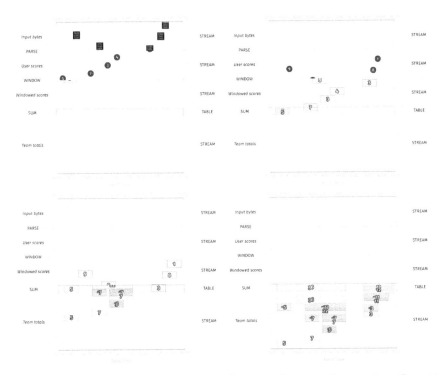

Figure 8-14. Session window summation with accumulation and retractions (http://streamingbook.net/fig/8-14)

And, lastly, in SQL form. For the SQL version, we're assuming that the system is using retractions under the covers by default, and individual retraction rows are then materialized in the stream any time we request the special Sys.Undo column.[16] As I described originally, the value of that column is that it allows us to distinguish retraction rows (labeled undo in the Sys.Undo column) from normal rows (unlabeled in the Sys.Undo column here for clearer contrast, though they could just as easily be labeled redo, instead):

```
12:00> SELECT STREAM SUM(Score) as Total,
         SESSION(EventTime, INTERVAL '1' MINUTE) as Window,
         CURRENT_TIMESTAMP as EmitTime,
         Sys.Undo as Undo
       FROM UserScoresForSessions
       GROUP BY Team, SESSION(EventTime, INTERVAL '1' MINUTE);
-------------------------------------------------
```

---

16 Note that it's a little odd for the simple addition of a new column in the SELECT statement to result in a new rows appearing in a query. A fine alternative approach would be to require Sys.Undo rows to be filtered out via a WHERE clause when not needed.

```
| Total | Window                   | EmitTime | Undo |
-------------------------------------------------------
| 5     | [12:00:26, 12:01:26)     | 12:05:19 |      |
| 7     | [12:02:26, 12:03:26)     | 12:05:39 |      |
| 3     | [12:03:39, 12:04:39)     | 12:06:13 |      |
| 3     | [12:03:39, 12:04:39)     | 12:06:46 | undo |
| 7     | [12:03:39, 12:05:19)     | 12:06:46 |      |
| 3     | [12:06:39, 12:07:39)     | 12:07:19 |      |
| 7     | [12:02:26, 12:03:26)     | 12:07:33 | undo |
| 7     | [12:03:39, 12:05:19)     | 12:07:33 | undo |
| 22    | [12:02:26, 12:05:19)     | 12:07:33 |      |
| 3     | [12:06:39, 12:07:39)     | 12:08:13 | undo |
| 11    | [12:06:39, 12:08:26)     | 12:08:13 |      |
| 5     | [12:00:26, 12:01:26)     | 12:08:19 | undo |
| 22    | [12:02:26, 12:05:19)     | 12:08:19 | undo |
| 36    | [12:00:26, 12:05:19)     | 12:08:19 |      |
| 11    | [12:06:39, 12:08:26)     | 12:09:00 | undo |
| 12    | [12:06:39, 12:08:46)     | 12:09:00 |      |
................ [12:00, 12:10] .................
```

With retractions included, the sessions stream no longer just includes new sessions, but also retractions for the old sessions that have been replaced. With this stream, it's trivial[17] to properly build up the set of sessions in HBase over time: you simply write new sessions as they arrive (unlabeled redo rows) and delete old sessions as they're retracted (undo rows). Much better!

Discarding mode, or lack thereof.   With this example, we've shown how simply and naturally you can incorporate retractions into SQL to provide both *accumulating mode* and *accumulating and retracting mode* semantics. But what about *discarding mode*?

For specific use cases such as very simple pipelines that partially aggregate high-volume input data via a single grouping operation and then write them into a storage system, which itself supports aggregation (e.g., a database-like system), discarding mode can be extremely valuable as a resource-saving option. But outside of those relatively narrow use cases, discarding mode is confusing and error-prone. As such, it's probably not worth incorporating directly into SQL. Systems that need it can provide it as an option outside of the SQL language itself. Those that don't can simply provide the more natural default of *accumulating and retracting mode*, with the option to ignore retractions when they aren't needed.

---

17 Note that this triviality applies only in cases for which eventual consistency is sufficient. If you need to always have a globally coherent view of all sessions at any given time, you must 1) be sure to write/delete (via tombstones) each session at its emit time, and 2) only ever read from the HBase table at a timestamp that is less than the output watermark from your pipeline (to synchronize reads against the multiple, independent writes/deletes that happen when sessions merge). Or better yet, cut out the middle person and serve the sessions from your state tables directly.

Summary

This has been a long journey but a fascinating one. We've covered a ton of information in this chapter, so let's take a moment to reflect on it all.

First, we reasoned that the key difference between streaming and nonstreaming data processing is the *added dimension of time*. We observed that relations (the foundational data object from relational algebra, which itself is the basis for SQL) themselves evolve over time, and from that derived the notion of a *TVR*, which captures the evolution of a relation as a sequence of classic snapshot relations over time. From that definition, we were able to see that the *closure property* of relational algebra *remains intact* in a world of TVRs, which means that the entire suite of relational operators (and thus SQL constructs) continues to function as one would expect as we move from a world of point-in-time snapshot relations into a streaming-compatible world of TVRs.

Second, we explored the biases inherent in both the Beam Model and the classic SQL model as they exist today, coming to the conclusion that Beam has a stream-oriented approach, whereas SQL takes a table-oriented approach.

And finally, we looked at the hypothetical language extensions needed to add support for robust stream processing to SQL,[18] as well as some carefully chosen defaults that can greatly decrease the need for those extensions to be used:

Table/stream selection
> Given that any time-varying relation can be rendered in two different ways (table or stream), we need the ability to choose which rendering we want when materializing the results of a query. We introduced the TABLE, STREAM, and TVR keywords to provide a nice explicit way to choose the desired rendering.

> Even better is not needing to explicitly specify a choice, and that's where good defaults come in. If all the inputs are tables, a good default is for the output to be a table, as well; this gives you the classic relational query behavior everyone is accustomed to. Conversely, if any of the inputs are streams, a reasonable default is for the output to be a stream, as well.

Windowing
> Though you can declare some types of simple windows declaratively using existing SQL constructs, there is still value in having explicit windowing operators:

---

18 To be clear, they're not all hypothetical. Calcite has support for the windowing constructs described in this chapter.

- Windowing operators encapsulate the window-computation math.

- Windowing allows the concise expression of complex, dynamic groupings like sessions.

Thus, the addition of simple windowing constructs for use in grouping can help make queries less error prone while also providing capabilities (like sessions) that are impractical to express in declarative SQL as it exists today.

Watermarks

This isn't so much a SQL extension as it is a system-level feature. If the system in question integrates watermarks under the covers, they can be used in conjunction with triggers to generate streams containing a single, authoritative version of a row only after the input for that row is believed to be complete. This is critical for use cases in which it's impractical to poll a materialized view table for results, and instead the output of the pipeline must be consumed directly as a stream. Examples are notifications and anomaly detection.

Triggers

Triggers define the shape of a stream as it is created from a TVR. If unspecified, the default should be per-record triggering, which provides straightforward and natural semantics matching those of materialized views. Beyond the default, there are essentially two main types of useful triggers:

- *Watermark triggers*, for yielding a single output per window when the inputs to that window are believed to be complete.

- *Repeated delay triggers*, for providing periodic updates.

Combinations of those two can also be useful, especially in the case of heuristic watermarks, to provide the early/on-time/late pattern we saw earlier.

Special system columns

When consuming a TVR as a stream, there are some interesting metadata that can be useful and which are most easily exposed as system-level columns. We looked at four:

Sys.MTime

The processing time at which a given row was last modified in a TVR.

Sys.EmitTiming

The timing of the row emit relative to the watermark (early, on-time, late).

`Sys.EmitIndex`

The zero-based index of the emit version for this row.[19]

`Sys.Undo`

Whether the row is a normal row or a retraction (undo). By default, the system should operate with retractions under the covers, as is necessary any time a series of more than one grouping operation might exist. If the `Sys.Undo` column is not projected when rendering a TVR as a stream, only normal rows will be returned, providing a simple way to toggle between *accumulating* and *accumulating and retracting* modes.

Stream processing with SQL doesn't need to be difficult. In fact, stream processing in SQL is quite common already in the form of materialized views. The important pieces really boil down to capturing the evolution of datasets/relations over time (via time-varying relations), providing the means of choosing between physical table or stream representations of those time-varying relations, and providing the tools for reasoning about time (windowing, watermarks, and triggers) that we've been talking about throughout this book. And, critically, you need good defaults to minimize how often these extensions need to be used in practice.

---

19 Note that the definition of "index" becomes complicated in the case of merging windows like sessions. A reasonable approach is to take the maximum of all of the previous sessions being merged together and increment by one.

CHAPTER 9

Streaming Joins

When I first began learning about joins, it was an intimidating topic; LEFT, OUTER, SEMI, INNER, CROSS: the language of joins is expressive and expansive. Add on top of that the dimension of time that streaming brings to the table, and you're left with what appears to be a challengingly complex topic. The good news is that joins really aren't the frightening beast with nasty, pointy teeth that they might initially appear to be. As is the case with so many other complex topics, after you understand the central ideas and themes of joins, the broader landscape that's built on top of these basics suddenly becomes so much more accessible. So please join me now as we explore the fascinating topic of...well, joins.

All Your Joins Are Belong to Streaming

What does it mean to join two datasets? We understand intuitively that joins are just a specific type of grouping operation: by joining together data that share some property (i.e., key), we collect together some number of previously unrelated individual data elements into a *group* of related elements. And as we learned in Chapter 6, grouping operations always consume a stream and yield a table. Knowing these two things, it's only a small leap to then arrive at the conclusion that forms the basis for this entire chapter: *at their hearts, all joins are streaming joins*.

What's great about this fact is that it actually makes the topic of streaming joins that much more tractable. All of the tools we've learned for reasoning about time within the context of streaming grouping operations (windowing, watermarks, triggers, etc.) continue to apply in the case of streaming joins. What's perhaps intimidating is that adding streaming to the mix seems like it could only serve to complicate things. But as you'll see in the examples that follow, there's a certain elegant simplicity and consistency to modeling all joins as streaming joins. Instead of feeling like there are a confounding multitude of different join approaches, it becomes clear that nearly all types of joins really boil down to minor variations on the same pattern. In the end, that clarity of insight helps makes joins (streaming or otherwise) much less intimidating.

To give us something concrete to reason about, let's consider a number of different types of joins as they're applied to the following datasets, conveniently named `Left` and `Right` to match the common nomenclature:

```
12:10> SELECT TABLE * FROM Left;        12:10> SELECT TABLE * FROM Right;
--------------------                    --------------------
| Num | Id | Time |                     | Num | Id | Time |
--------------------                    --------------------
| 1   | L1 | 12:02 |                    | 2   | R2 | 12:01 |
| 2   | L2 | 12:06 |                    | 3   | R3 | 12:04 |
| 3   | L3 | 12:03 |                    | 4   | R4 | 12:05 |
--------------------                    --------------------
```

Each contains three columns:

Num

A single number.

Id

A portmanteau of the first letter in the name of the corresponding table ("L" or "R") and the Num, thus providing a way to uniquely identify the source of a given cell in join results.

Time

The arrival time of the given record in the system, which becomes important when considering streaming joins.

To keep things simple, note that our initial datasets will have strictly unique join keys. When we get to SEMI joins, we'll introduce some more complicated datasets to highlight join behavior in the presence of duplicate keys.

We first look at *unwindowed joins* in a great deal of depth because windowing often affects join semantics in only a minor way. After we exhaust our appetite for unwindowed joins, we then touch upon some of the more interesting points of joins in a windowed context.

Unwindowed Joins

It's a popular myth that streaming joins over unbounded data always require windowing. But by applying the concepts we learned in Chapter 6, we can see that's simply not true. Joins (both windowed and unwindowed) are simply another type of grouping operation, and grouping operations yield tables. Thus, if we want to consume the table created by an unwindowed join (or, equivalently, joins within a single global window covering all of time) as a stream, we need only apply an ungrouping (or trigger) operation that isn't of the "wait until we've seen all the input" variety. Windowing the join into a nonglobal window and using a watermark trigger (i.e., a "wait until we've seen all the input in a finite temporal chunk of the stream" trigger) is indeed one option, but so is triggering on every record (i.e., materialized view semantics) or periodically as processing time advances, regardless of whether the join is windowed or not. Because it makes the examples easy to follow, we assume the use of an implicit default per-record trigger in all of the following unwindowed join examples that observe the join results as a stream.

Now, onto joins themselves. ANSI SQL defines five types of joins: FULL OUTER, LEFT OUTER, RIGHT OUTER, INNER, and CROSS. We look at the first four in depth, and discuss the last only briefly in the next paragraph. We also touch on two other interesting, but less-often encountered (and less well supported, at least using standard syntax) variations: ANTI and SEMI joins.

On the surface, it sounds like a lot of variations. But as you'll see, there's really only one type of join at the core: the FULL OUTER join. A CROSS join is just a FULL OUTER join with a vacuously true join predicate; that is, it returns every possible pairing of a row from the left table with a row from the right table. All of the other join variations simply reduce down to some logical subset of the FULL OUTER join.[1] As a result, after you understand the commonality between all the different join types, it becomes a lot easier to keep them all in your head. It also makes reasoning about them in the context of streaming all that much simpler.

One last note here before we get started: we'll be primarily considering equi joins with at most 1:1 cardinality, by which I mean joins in which the join predicate is an equality statement and there is at most one matching row on each side of the join. This keeps the examples simple and concise. When we get to SEMI joins, we'll expand our example to consider joins with arbitrary N:M cardinality, which will let us observe the behavior of more arbitrary predicate joins.

FULL OUTER

Because they form the conceptual foundation for each of the other variations, we first look at FULL OUTER joins. Outer joins embody a rather liberal and optimistic interpretation of the word "join": the result of FULL OUTER–joining two datasets is essentially

---

1 From a conceptual perspective, at least. There are many different ways to implement each of these types of joins, some of which are likely much more efficient than performing an actual FULL OUTER join and then filtering down its results, especially when the rest of the query and the distribution of the data are taken into consideration.

the full list of rows in both datasets,[2] with rows in the two datasets that share the same join key combined together, but unmatched rows for either side included unjoined.

For example, if we FULL OUTER–join our two example datasets into a new relation containing only the joined IDs, the result would look something like this:

```
12:10> SELECT TABLE
         Left.Id as L,
          Right.Id as R,
        FROM Left FULL OUTER JOIN Right
        ON L.Num = R.Num;
----------------
| L    | R    |
----------------
| L1   | null |
| L2   | R2   |
| L3   | R3   |
| null | R4   |
----------------
```

We can see that the FULL OUTER join includes both rows that satisfied the join predicate (e.g., "L2, R2" and "L3, R3"), but it also includes partial rows that failed the predicate (e.g., "L1, null" and "null, R4", where the null is signaling the unjoined portion of the data).

Of course, that's just a point-in-time snapshot of this FULL OUTER–join relation, taken after all of the data have arrived in the system. We're here to learn about streaming joins, and streaming joins by definition involve the added dimension of time. As we know from Chapter 8, if we want to understand how a given dataset/relation changes over time, we want to speak in terms of time-varying relations (TVRs). So to best understand how the join evolves over time, let's look now at the full TVR for this join (with changes between each snapshot relation highlighted in yellow):

```
12:10> SELECT TVR
         Left.Id as L,
          Right.Id as R,
        FROM Left FULL OUTER JOIN Right
        ON L.Num = R.Num;
---------------------------------------------------------------------------
| [-inf, 12:01) | [12:01, 12:02) | [12:02, 12:03) | [12:03, 12:04) |
| -------------- | -------------- | -------------- | -------------- |
| | L    | R    | | | L    | R    | | | L    | R    | | | L    | R    | |
| -------------- | -------------- | -------------- | -------------- |
| -------------- | | null | R2   | | | L1   | null | | | L1   | null | |
|                | -------------- | | null | R2   | | | null | R2   | |
|                |                | -------------- | | L3   | null | |
|                |                |                | -------------- |
```

---

2 Again, ignoring what happens when there are duplicate join keys; more on this when we get to SEMI joins.

```
-----------------------------------------------------------------
|  [12:04, 12:05) |  [12:05, 12:06) |  [12:06, 12:07) |
| --------------- | --------------- | --------------- |
| | L    | R    | | | L    | R    | | | L    | R    | |
| --------------- | --------------- | --------------- |
| | L1   | null | | | L1   | null | | | L1   | null | |
| | null | R2   | | | null | R2   | | | L2   | R2   | |
| | L3   | R3   | | | L3   | R3   | | | L3   | R3   | |
| | --------------- | | null | R4   | | | null | R4   | |
|                 | | --------------- | | --------------- |
-----------------------------------------------------
```

And, as you might then expect, the stream rendering of this TVR would capture the
specific deltas between each of those snapshots:

```
12:00> SELECT STREAM
         Left.Id as L,
         Right.Id as R,
         CURRENT_TIMESTAMP as Time,
         Sys.Undo as Undo
       FROM Left FULL OUTER JOIN Right
       ON L.Num = R.Num;
-----------------------------------
| L    | R    | Time  | Undo |
-----------------------------------
| null | R2   | 12:01 |      |
| L1   | null | 12:02 |      |
| L3   | null | 12:03 |      |
| L3   | null | 12:04 | undo |
| L3   | R3   | 12:04 |      |
| null | R4   | 12:05 |      |
| null | R2   | 12:06 | undo |
| L2   | R2   | 12:06 |      |
....... [12:00, 12:10] .......
```

Note the inclusion of the Time and Undo columns, to highlight the times when given
rows materialize in the stream, and also call out instances when an update to a given
row first results in a retraction of the previous version of that row. The undo/retrac-
tion rows are critical if this stream is to capture a full-fidelity view of the TVR over
time.

So, although each of these three renderings of the join (table, TVR, stream) are distinct from one another, it's also pretty clear how they're all just different views on the
same data: the table snapshot shows us the overall dataset as it exists after all the data
have arrived, and the TVR and stream versions capture (in their own ways) the evolution of the entire relation over the course of its existence.

With that basic familiarity of FULL OUTER joins in place, we now understand all of the
core concepts of joins in a streaming context. No windowing needed, no custom triggers, nothing particularly painful or unintuitive. Just a per-record evolution of the
join over time, as you would expect. Even better, all of the other types of joins are just

variations on this theme (conceptually, at least), essentially just an additional filtering operation performed on the per-record stream of the FULL OUTER join. Let's now look at each of them in more detail.

LEFT OUTER

LEFT OUTER joins are a just a FULL OUTER join with any unjoined rows from the right dataset removed. This is most clearly seen by taking the original FULL OUTER join and graying out the rows that would be filtered. For a LEFT OUTER join, that would look like the following, where every row with an unjoined left side is filtered out of the original FULL OUTER join:

```
12:10> SELECT TABLE
          Left.Id as L,
          Right.Id as R
       FROM Left LEFT OUTER JOIN Right
       ON L.Num = R.Num;
------------------
| L    | R    |
------------------
| L1   | null |
| L2   | R2   |
| L3   | R3   |
| null | R4   |
------------------
```

```
12:00> SELECT STREAM Left.Id as L,
          Right.Id as R,
          Sys.EmitTime as Time,
          Sys.Undo as Undo
       FROM Left LEFT OUTER JOIN Right
       ON L.Num = R.Num;
-----------------------------------
| L    | R    | Time  | Undo |
-----------------------------------
| null | R2   | 12:01 |      |
| L1   | null | 12:02 |      |
| L3   | null | 12:03 |      |
| L3   | null | 12:04 | undo |
| L3   | R3   | 12:04 |      |
| null | R4   | 12:05 |      |
| null | R2   | 12:06 | undo |
| L2   | R2   | 12:06 |      |
....... [12:00, 12:10] .......
```

To see what the table and stream would actually look like in practice, let's look at the same queries again, but this time with the grayed-out rows omitted entirely:

```
12:10> SELECT TABLE
          Left.Id as L,
          Right.Id as R
       FROM Left LEFT OUTER JOIN Right
       ON L.Num = R.Num;
------------------
| L    | R    |
------------------
| L1   | null |
| L2   | R2   |
| L3   | R3   |
------------------
```

```
12:00> SELECT STREAM Left.Id as L,
          Right.Id as R,
          Sys.EmitTime as Time,
          Sys.Undo as Undo
       FROM Left LEFT OUTER JOIN Right
       ON L.Num = R.Num;
-----------------------------------
| L    | R    | Time  | Undo |
-----------------------------------
| L1   | null | 12:02 |      |
| L3   | null | 12:03 |      |
| L3   | null | 12:04 | undo |
| L3   | R3   | 12:04 |      |
| L2   | R2   | 12:06 |      |
....... [12:00, 12:10] .......
```

RIGHT OUTER

RIGHT OUTER joins are the converse of a left join: all unjoined rows from the left data-set in the full outer join are right out, *cough*, removed:

```
12:10> SELECT TABLE
          Left.Id as L,
          Right.Id as R
       FROM Left RIGHT OUTER JOIN Right
       ON L.Num = R.Num;
       ---------------
       | L    | R    |
       ---------------
       | L1   | null |
       | L2   | R2   |
       | L3   | R3   |
       | null | R4   |
       ---------------
```

```
12:00> SELECT STREAM Left.Id as L,
          Right.Id as R,
          Sys.EmitTime as Time,
          Sys.Undo as Undo
       FROM Left RIGHT OUTER JOIN Right
       ON L.Num = R.Num;
       ---------------------------------
       | L    | R    | Time  | Undo |
       ---------------------------------
       | null | R2   | 12:01 |      |
       | L1   | null | 12:02 |      |
       | L3   | null | 12:03 |      |
       | L3   | null | 12:04 | undo |
       | L3   | R3   | 12:04 |      |
       | null | R4   | 12:05 |      |
       | null | R2   | 12:06 | undo |
       | L2   | R2   | 12:06 |      |
       ....... [12:00, 12:10] .......
```

And here we see how the queries rendered as the actual RIGHT OUTER join would appear:

```
12:10> SELECT TABLE
          Left.Id as L,
          Right.Id as R
       FROM Left RIGHT OUTER JOIN Right
       ON L.Num = R.Num;
       ---------------
       | L    | R    |
       ---------------
       | L2   | R2   |
       | L3   | R3   |
       | null | R4   |
       ---------------
```

```
12:00> SELECT STREAM Left.Id as L,
          Right.Id as R,
          Sys.EmitTime as Time,
          Sys.Undo as Undo
       FROM Left RIGHT OUTER JOIN Right
       ON L.Num = R.Num;
       ---------------------------------
       | L    | R    | Time  | Undo |
       ---------------------------------
       | null | R2   | 12:01 |      |
       | L3   | R3   | 12:04 |      |
       | null | R4   | 12:05 |      |
       | null | R2   | 12:06 | undo |
       | L2   | R2   | 12:06 |      |
       ....... [12:00, 12:10] .......
```

INNER

INNER joins are essentially the intersection of the LEFT OUTER and RIGHT OUTER joins. Or, to think of it subtractively, the rows removed from the original FULL OUTER join to create an INNER join are the union of the rows removed from the LEFT OUTER and RIGHT OUTER joins. As a result, all rows that remain unjoined on either side are absent from the INNER join:

```
12:10> SELECT TABLE                  12:00> SELECT STREAM Left.Id as L,
          Left.Id as L,                        Right.Id as R,
          Right.Id as R                        Sys.EmitTime as Time,
       FROM Left INNER JOIN Right              Sys.Undo as Undo
       ON L.Num = R.Num;                    FROM Left INNER JOIN Right
-----------------                           ON L.Num = R.Num;
| L    | R    |                     ----------------------------
-----------------                   | L    | R    | Time  | Undo |
| L1   | null |                     ----------------------------
| L2   | R2   |                     | null | R2   | 12:01 |      |
| L3   | R3   |                     | L3   | null | 12:02 |      |
| null | R4   |                     | L3   | null | 12:03 |      |
-----------------                   | L3   | null | 12:04 | undo |
                                    | L3   | R3   | 12:04 |      |
                                    | null | R4   | 12:05 |      |
                                    | null | R2   | 12:06 | undo |
                                    | L2   | R2   | 12:06 |      |
                                    ....... [12:00, 12:10] .......
```

And again, more succinctly rendered as the INNER join would look in reality:

```
12:10> SELECT TABLE                  12:00> SELECT STREAM Left.Id as L,
          Left.Id as L,                        Right.Id as R,
          Right.Id as R                        Sys.EmitTime as Time,
       FROM Left INNER JOIN Right              Sys.Undo as Undo
       ON L.Num = R.Num;                    FROM Left INNER JOIN Right
-----------------                           ON L.Num = R.Num;
| L    | R    |                     ----------------------------
-----------------                   | L    | R    | Time  | Undo |
| L2   | R2   |                     ----------------------------
| L3   | R3   |                     | L3   | R3   | 12:04 |      |
-----------------                   | L2   | R2   | 12:06 |      |
                                    ....... [12:00, 12:10] .......
```

Given this example, you might be inclined to think retractions never play a part in INNER join streams because they were all filtered out in this example. But imagine if the value in the Left table for the row with a Num of 3 were updated from "L3" to "L3v2" at 12:07. In addition to resulting in a different value on the left side for our final TABLE query (again performed at 12:10, which is after the update to row 3 on the Left arrived), it would also result in a STREAM that captures both the removal of the old value via a retraction and the addition of the new value:

```
12:10> SELECT TABLE                  12:00> SELECT STREAM Left.Id as L,
          Left.Id as L,                        Right.Id as R,
          Right.Id as R                        Sys.EmitTime as Time,
       FROM LeftV2 INNER JOIN Right            Sys.Undo as Undo
       ON L.Num = R.Num;                    FROM LeftV2 INNER JOIN Right
-----------------                           ON L.Num = R.Num;
| L    | R    |                     ----------------------------
-----------------                   | L    | R    | Time  | Undo |
| L2   | R2   |                     ----------------------------
                                    | L3   | R3   | 12:04 |      |
```

```
| L3v2 | R3   |
--------------
```

```
| L2   | R2  | 12:06 |      |
| L3   | R3  | 12:07 | undo |
| L3v2 | R3  | 12:07 |      |
....... [12:00, 12:10] .......
```

ANTI

ANTI joins are the obverse of the INNER join: they contain all of the *unjoined* rows. Not all SQL systems support a clean ANTI join syntax, but I'll use the most straightforward one here for clarity:

```
12:10> SELECT TABLE
         Left.Id as L,
         Right.Id as R
       FROM Left ANTI JOIN Right
       ON L.Num = R.Num;
---------------
| L    | R    |
---------------
| L1   | null |
| L2   | R2   |
| L3   | R3   |
| null | R4   |
---------------
```

```
12:00> SELECT STREAM Left.Id as L,
         Right.Id as R,
         Sys.EmitTime as Time,
         Sys.Undo as Undo
       FROM Left ANTI JOIN Right
       ON L.Num = R.Num;
----------------------------
| L    |  R   | Time  | Undo |
----------------------------
| null | R2   | 12:01 |      |
| L1   | null | 12:02 |      |
| L3   | null | 12:03 |      |
| L3   | null | 12:04 | undo |
| L3   | R3   | 12:04 |      |
| null | R4   | 12:05 |      |
| null | R2   | 12:06 | undo |
| L2   | R2   | 12:06 |      |
....... [12:00, 12:10] .......
```

What's slightly interesting about the stream rendering of the ANTI join is that it ends up containing a bunch of false-starts and retractions for rows which eventually do end up joining; in fact, the ANTI join is as heavy on retractions as the INNER join is light. The more concise versions would look like this:

```
12:10> SELECT TABLE
         Left.Id as L,
         Right.Id as R
       FROM Left ANTI JOIN Right
       ON L.Num = R.Num;
---------------
| L    | R    |
---------------
| L1   | null |
| null | R4   |
---------------
```

```
12:00> SELECT STREAM Left.Id as L,
         Right.Id as R,
         Sys.EmitTime as Time,
         Sys.Undo as Undo
       FROM Left ANTI JOIN Right
       ON L.Num = R.Num;
----------------------------
| L    | R    | Time  | Undo |
----------------------------
| null | R2   | 12:01 |      |
| L1   | null | 12:02 |      |
| L3   | null | 12:03 |      |
| L3   | null | 12:04 | undo |
| null | R4   | 12:05 |      |
| null | R2   | 12:06 | undo |
....... [12:00, 12:10] .......
```

SEMI

We now come to SEMI joins, and SEMI joins are kind of weird. At first glance, they basically look like inner joins with one side of the joined values being dropped. And, indeed, in cases for which the cardinality relationship of <side-being-kept>:<side-being-dropped> is N:M with M ≤ 1, this works (note that we'll be using kept=Left, dropped=Right for all the examples that follow). For example, on the Left and Right datasets we've used so far (which had cardinalities of 0:1, 1:0, and 1:1 for the joined data), the INNER and SEMI join variations look identical:

```
12:10> SELECT TABLE          12:10> SELECT TABLE
  Left.Id as L                 Left.Id as L
FROM Left INNER JOIN         FROM Left SEMI JOIN
Right ON L.Num = R.Num;      Right ON L.Num = R.Num;
--------                     --------
| L    | R    |              | L    | R    |
--------                     --------
| L1   | null |              | L1   | null |
| L2   | R2   |              | L2   | R2   |
| L3   | R3   |              | L3   | R3   |
| null | R4   |              | null | R4   |
--------                     --------
```

However, there's an additional subtlety to SEMI joins in the case of N:M cardinality with M > 1: because the *values* on the M side are not being returned, the SEMI join simply predicates the join condition on there being *any* matching row on the right, rather than repeatedly yielding a new result for *every* matching row.

To see this clearly, let's switch to a slightly more complicated pair of input relations that highlight the N:M join cardinality of the rows contained therein. In these relations, the N_M column states what the cardinality relationship of rows is between the left and right sides, and the Id column (as before) provides an identifier that is unique for each row in each of the input relations:

```
12:15> SELECT TABLE * FROM LeftNM;      12:15> SELECT TABLE * FROM RightNM;
---------------------                   ---------------------
| N_M | Id  | Time  |                   | N_M | Id  | Time  |
---------------------                   ---------------------
| 1:0 | L2  | 12:07 |                   | 0:1 | R1  | 12:02 |
| 1:1 | L3  | 12:01 |                   | 1:1 | R3  | 12:14 |
| 1:2 | L4  | 12:05 |                   | 1:2 | R4A | 12:03 |
| 2:1 | L5A | 12:09 |                   | 1:2 | R4B | 12:04 |
| 2:1 | L5B | 12:08 |                   | 2:1 | R5  | 12:06 |
| 2:2 | L6A | 12:12 |                   | 2:2 | R6A | 12:11 |
| 2:2 | L6B | 12:10 |                   | 2:2 | R6B | 12:13 |
---------------------                   ---------------------
```

With these inputs, the FULL OUTER join expands to look like these:

```
12:15> SELECT TABLE
       COALESCE(LeftNM.N_M,
                RightNM.N_M) as N_M,
       LeftNM.Id as L,
       RightNM.Id as R,
       FROM LeftNM
       FULL OUTER JOIN RightNM
       ON LeftNM.N_M = RightNM.N_M;
--------------------------
| N_M | L    | R    |
--------------------------
| 0:1 | null | R1   |
| 1:0 | L2   | null |
| 1:1 | L3   | R3   |
| 1:2 | L4   | R4A  |
| 1:2 | L4   | R4B  |
| 2:1 | L5A  | R5   |
| 2:1 | L5B  | R5   |
| 2:2 | L6A  | R6A  |
| 2:2 | L6A  | R6B  |
| 2:2 | L6B  | R6A  |
| 2:2 | L6B  | R6B  |
--------------------------
```

```
12:00> SELECT STREAM
       COALESCE(LeftNM.N_M,
                RightNM.N_M) as N_M,
       LeftNM.Id as L,
       RightNM.Id as R,
       Sys.EmitTime as Time,
       Sys.Undo as Undo
       FROM LeftNM
       FULL OUTER JOIN RightNM
       ON LeftNM.N_M = RightNM.N_M;
------------------------------------------
| N_M | L    | R    | Time  | Undo |
------------------------------------------
| 1:1 | L3   | null | 12:01 |      |
| 0:1 | null | R1   | 12:02 |      |
| 1:2 | null | R4A  | 12:03 |      |
| 1:2 | null | R4B  | 12:04 |      |
| 1:2 | null | R4A  | 12:05 | undo |
| 1:2 | null | R4B  | 12:05 | undo |
| 1:2 | L4   | R4A  | 12:05 |      |
| 1:2 | L4   | R4B  | 12:05 |      |
| 2:1 | null | R5   | 12:06 |      |
| 1:0 | L2   | null | 12:07 |      |
| 2:1 | null | R5   | 12:08 | undo |
| 2:1 | L5B  | R5   | 12:08 |      |
| 2:1 | L5A  | R5   | 12:09 |      |
| 2:2 | L6B  | null | 12:10 |      |
| 2:2 | L6B  | null | 12:11 | undo |
| 2:2 | L6B  | R6A  | 12:11 |      |
| 2:2 | L6A  | R6A  | 12:12 |      |
| 2:2 | L6A  | R6B  | 12:13 |      |
| 2:2 | L6B  | R6B  | 12:13 |      |
| 1:1 | L3   | null | 12:14 | undo |
| 1:1 | L3   | R3   | 12:14 |      |
.......... [12:00, 12:15] ..........
```

As a side note, one additional benefit of these more complicated datasets is that the multiplicative nature of joins when there are multiple rows on each side matching the same predicate begins to become more clear (e.g., the "2:2" rows, which expand from two rows in each the inputs to four rows in the output; if the dataset had a set of "3:3" rows, they'd expand from three rows in each of the inputs to nine rows in the output, and so on).

But back to the subtleties of SEMI joins. With these datasets, it becomes much clearer what the difference between the filtered INNER join and the SEMI join is: the INNER join yields duplicate values for any of the rows where the N:M cardinality has M > 1, whereas the SEMI join doesn't (note that I've highlighted the duplicate rows in the

INNER join version in red, and included in gray the portions of the full outer join that are omitted in the respective INNER and SEMI versions):

```
12:15> SELECT TABLE
         COALESCE(LeftNM.N_M,
                 RightNM.N_M) as N_M,
         LeftNM.Id as L
       FROM LeftNM INNER JOIN RightNM
       ON LeftNM.N_M = RightNM.N_M;
--------------------
| N_M | L   | R     |
--------------------
| 0:1 | null | R1    |
| 1:0 | L2   | null  |
| 1:1 | L3   | R3    |
| 1:2 | L4   | R5A   |
| 1:2 | L4   | R5B   |
| 2:1 | L5A  | R5    |
| 2:1 | L5B  | R5    |
| 2:2 | L6A  | R6A   |
| 2:2 | L6A  | R6B   |
| 2:2 | L6B  | R6A   |
| 2:2 | L6B  | R6B   |
--------------------
```

```
12:15> SELECT TABLE
         COALESCE(LeftNM.N_M,
                 RightNM.N_M) as N_M,
         LeftNM.Id as L
       FROM LeftNM SEMI JOIN RightNM
       ON LeftNM.N_M = RightNM.N_M;
-----------------
| N_M | L   | R     |
-----------------
| 0:1 | null | R1    |
| 1:0 | L2   | null  |
| 1:1 | L3   | R3    |
| 1:2 | L4   | R5A   |
| 1:2 | L4   | R5B   |
| 2:1 | L5A  | R5    |
| 2:1 | L5B  | R5    |
| 2:2 | L6A  | R6A   |
| 2:2 | L6A  | R6B   |
| 2:2 | L6B  | R6A   |
| 2:2 | L6B  | R6B   |
-----------------
```

Or, rendered more succinctly:

```
12:15> SELECT TABLE
         COALESCE(LeftNM.N_M,
                 RightNM.N_M) as N_M,
         LeftNM.Id as L
       FROM LeftNM INNER JOIN RightNM
       ON LeftNM.N_M = RightNM.N_M;
-------------
| N_M | L  |
-------------
| 1:1 | L3 |
| 1:2 | L4 |
| 1:2 | L4 |
| 2:1 | L5A |
| 2:1 | L5B |
| 2:2 | L6A |
| 2:2 | L6A |
| 2:2 | L6B |
| 2:2 | L6B |
-------------
```

```
12:15> SELECT TABLE
         COALESCE(LeftNM.N_M,
                 RightNM.N_M) as N_M,
         LeftNM.Id as L
       FROM LeftNM SEMI JOIN RightNM
       ON LeftNM.N_M = RightNM.N_M;
-------------
| N_M | L  |
-------------
| 1:1 | L3 |
| 1:2 | L4 |
| 2:1 | L5A |
| 2:1 | L5B |
| 2:2 | L6A |
| 2:2 | L6B |
-------------
```

The STREAM renderings then provide a bit of context as to which rows are filtered out —they are simply the later-arriving duplicate rows (from the perspective of the columns being projected):

```
12:00> SELECT STREAM
          COALESCE(LeftNM.N_M,
                 RightNM.N_M) as N_M,
          LeftNM.Id as L
          Sys.EmitTime as Time,
          Sys.Undo as Undo,
          FROM LeftNM INNER JOIN RightNM
          ON LeftNM.N_M = RightNM.N_M;
```

N_M	L	R	Time	Undo
1:1	L3	null	12:01	
0:1	null	R1	12:02	
1:2	null	R4A	12:03	
1:2	null	R4B	12:04	
1:2	null	R4A	12:05	undo
1:2	null	R4B	12:05	undo
1:2	L4	R4A	12:05	
1:2	L4	R4B	12:05	
2:1	null	R5	12:06	
1:0	L2	null	12:07	
2:1	null	R5	12:08	undo
2:1	L5B	R5	12:08	
2:1	L5A	R5	12:09	
2:2	L6B	null	12:10	
2:2	L6B	null	12:10	undo
2:2	L6B	R6A	12:11	
2:2	L6A	R6A	12:12	
2:2	L6A	R6B	12:13	
2:2	L6B	R6B	12:13	
1:1	L3	null	12:14	undo
1:1	L3	R3	12:14	

.... [12:00, 12:15] ....

```
12:00> SELECT STREAM
          COALESCE(LeftNM.N_M,
                 RightNM.N_M) as N_M,
          LeftNM.Id as L
          Sys.EmitTime as Time,
          Sys.Undo as Undo,
          FROM LeftNM SEMI JOIN RightNM
          ON LeftNM.N_M = RightNM.N_M;
```

N_M	L	R	Time	Undo
1:1	L3	null	12:01	
0:1	null	R1	12:02	
1:2	null	R4A	12:03	
1:2	null	R4B	12:04	
1:2	null	R4A	12:05	undo
1:2	null	R4B	12:05	undo
1:2	L4	R4A	12:05	
1:2	L4	R4B	12:05	
2:1	null	R5	12:06	
1:0	L2	null	12:07	
2:1	null	R5	12:08	undo
2:1	L5B	R5	12:08	
2:1	L5A	R5	12:09	
2:2	L6B	null	12:10	
2:2	L6B	null	12:10	undo
2:2	L6B	R6A	12:11	
2:2	L6A	R6A	12:12	
2:2	L6A	R6B	12:13	
2:2	L6B	R6B	12:13	
1:1	L3	null	12:14	undo
1:1	L3	R3	12:14	

.... [12:00, 12:15] ....

And again, rendered succinctly:

```
12:00> SELECT STREAM
          COALESCE(LeftNM.N_M,
                 RightNM.N_M) as N_M,
          LeftNM.Id as L
          Sys.EmitTime as Time,
          Sys.Undo as Undo,
          FROM LeftNM INNER JOIN RightNM
          ON LeftNM.N_M = RightNM.N_M;
```

N_M	L	Time	Undo
1:2	L4	12:05	
1:2	L4	12:05	
2:1	L5B	12:08	
2:1	L5A	12:09	
2:2	L6B	12:11	
2:2	L6A	12:12	

```
12:00> SELECT STREAM
          COALESCE(LeftNM.N_M,
                 RightNM.N_M) as N_M,
          LeftNM.Id as L
          Sys.EmitTime as Time,
          Sys.Undo as Undo,
          FROM LeftNM SEMI JOIN RightNM
          ON LeftNM.N_M = RightNM.N_M;
```

N_M	L	Time	Undo
1:2	L4	12:05	
2:1	L5B	12:08	
2:1	L5A	12:09	
2:2	L6B	12:11	
2:2	L6A	12:12	
1:1	L3	12:14	

```
| 2:2 || L6A || 12:13 ||        |
| 2:2 || L6B || 12:13 ||        |
| 1:1 | L3  | 12:14 |        |
...... [12:00, 12:15] ......
```
```
...... [12:00, 12:15] ......
```

As we've seen over the course of a number of examples, there's really nothing special about streaming joins. They function exactly as we might expect given our knowledge of streams and tables, with join streams capturing the history of the join over time as it evolves. This is in contrast to join tables, which simply capture a snapshot of the entire join as it exists at a specific point in time, as we're perhaps more accustomed.

But, even more important, viewing joins through the lens of stream-table theory has lent some additional clarity. The core underlying join primitive is the FULL OUTER join, which is a stream → table grouping operation that collects together all the joined and unjoined rows in a relation. All of the other variants we looked at in detail (LEFT OUTER, RIGHT OUTER, INNER, ANTI, and SEMI) simply add an additional layer of filtering on the joined stream following the FULL OUTER join.[3]

Windowed Joins

Having looked at a variety of unwindowed joins, let's next explore what windowing adds to the mix. I would argue that there are two motivations for windowing your joins:

To partition time in some meaningful way
An obvious case is fixed windows; for example, daily windows, for which events that occurred in the same day should be joined together for some business reason (e.g., daily billing tallies). Another might be limiting the range of time within a join for performance reasons. However, it turns out there are even more sophisticated (and useful) ways of partitioning time in joins, including one particularly interesting use case that no streaming system I'm aware of today supports natively: *temporal validity joins*. More on this in just a bit.

To provide a meaningful reference point for timing out a join
This is useful for a number of unbounded join situations, but it is perhaps most obviously beneficial for use cases like outer joins, for which it is unknown a priori if one side of the join will ever show up. For classic batch processing (including standard interactive SQL queries), outer joins are timed out only when the bounded input dataset has been fully processed. But when processing unbounded data, we can't wait for all data to be processed. As we discussed in Chapters 2 and

---

3 From a conceptual perspective, at least. There are, of course, many different ways to implement each of these types of joins, some of which might be much more efficient than performing an actual FULL OUTER join and then filtering down its results, depending on the rest of the query and the distribution of the data.

3, watermarks provide a progress metric for gauging the completeness of an input source in event time. But to make use of that metric for timing out a join, we need some reference point to compare against. Windowing a join provides that reference by bounding the extent of the join to the end of the window. After the watermark passes the end of the window, the system may consider the input for the window complete. At that point, just as in the bounded join case, it's safe to time out any unjoined rows and materialize their partial results.

That said, as we saw earlier, windowing is absolutely not a requirement for streaming joins. It makes a lot of sense in a many cases, but by no means is it a necessity.

In practice, most of the use cases for windowed joins (e.g., daily windows) are relatively straightforward and easy to extrapolate from the concepts we've learned up until now. To see why, we look briefly at what it means to apply fixed windows to some of the join examples we already encountered. After that, we spend the rest of this chapter investigating the much more interesting (and mind-bending) topic of *temporal validity joins*, looking first in detail at what I mean by temporal validity windows, and then moving on to looking at what joins mean within the context of such windows.

Fixed Windows

Windowing a join adds the dimension of time into the join criteria themselves. In doing so, the window serves to scope the set of rows being joined to only those contained within the window's time interval. This is perhaps more clearly seen with an example, so let's take our original Left and Right tables and window them into five-minute fixed windows:

```
12:10> SELECT TABLE *,
       TUMBLE(Time, INTERVAL '5' MINUTE)
       as Window FROM Left;
-----------------------------------
| Num | Id | Time  | Window        |
-----------------------------------
| 1   | L1 | 12:02 | [12:00, 12:05) |
| 2   | L2 | 12:06 | [12:05, 12:10) |
| 3   | L3 | 12:03 | [12:00, 12:05) |
-----------------------------------
```

```
12:10> SELECT TABLE *,
       TUMBLE(Time, INTERVAL '5' MINUTE)
       as Window FROM Right
-----------------------------------
| Num | Id | Time  | Window        |
-----------------------------------
| 2   | R2 | 12:01 | [12:00, 12:05) |
| 3   | R3 | 12:04 | [12:00, 12:05) |
| 4   | R4 | 12:05 | [12:05, 12:10) |
-----------------------------------
```

In our previous Left and Right examples, the join criterion was simply Left.Num = Right.Num. To turn this into a windowed join, we would expand the join criteria to include window equality, as well: Left.Num = Right.Num AND Left.Window = Right.Window. Knowing that, we can already infer from the preceding windowed tables how our join is going to change (highlighted for clarity): because the L2 and R2 rows do not fall within the same five-minute fixed window, they will not be joined together in the windowed variant of our join.

And indeed, if we compare the unwindowed and windowed variants side-by-side as tables, we can see this clearly (with the corresponding L2 and R2 rows highlighted on each side of the join):

```
                                    12:10> SELECT TABLE
                                             Left.Id as L,
                                             Right.Id as R,
                                             COALESCE(
                                                 TUMBLE(Left.Time, INTERVAL '5' MINUTE),
                                                 TUMBLE(Right.Time, INTERVAL '5' MINUTE)
12:10> SELECT TABLE                          ) AS Window
         Left.Id as L,                     FROM Left
         Right.Id as R,                      FULL OUTER JOIN Right
       FROM Left                             ON L.Num = R.Num AND
         FULL OUTER JOIN Right                 TUMBLE(Left.Time, INTERVAL '5' MINUTE) =
         ON L.Num = R.Num;                     TUMBLE(Right.Time, INTERVAL '5' MINUTE);
       ----------------            -----------------------------------------
       | L    | R    |             | L    | R    | Window         |
       ----------------            -----------------------------------------
       | L1   | null |             | L1   | null | [12:00, 12:05) |
       | L2   | R2   |             | null | R2   | [12:00, 12:05) |
       | L3   | R3   |             | L3   | R3   | [12:00, 12:05) |
       | null | R4   |             | L2   | null | [12:05, 12:10) |
       ----------------            | null | R4   | [12:05, 12:10) |
                                   -----------------------------------------
```

The difference is also readily apparent when comparing the unwindowed and windowed joins as streams. As I've highlighted in the example that follows, they differ primarily in their final rows. The unwindowed side completes the join for Num = 2, yielding a retraction for the unjoined R2 row in addition to a new row for the completed L2, R2 join. The windowed side, on the other hand, simply yields an unjoined L2 row because L2 and R2 fall within different five-minute windows:

```
                                    12:10> SELECT STREAM
                                             Left.Id as L,
                                             Right.Id as R,
                                             Sys.EmitTime as Time,
                                             COALESCE(
                                                 TUMBLE(Left.Time, INTERVAL '5' MINUTE),
                                                 TUMBLE(Right.Time, INTERVAL '5' MINUTE)
12:10> SELECT STREAM                         ) AS Window,
         Left.Id as L,                       Sys.Undo as Undo
         Right.Id as R,                    FROM Left
         Sys.EmitTime as Time,               FULL OUTER JOIN Right
         Sys.Undo as Undo                    ON L.Num = R.Num AND
       FROM Left                               TUMBLE(Left.Time, INTERVAL '5' MINUTE) =
         FULL OUTER JOIN Right                 TUMBLE(Right.Time, INTERVAL '5' MINUTE);
         ON L.Num = R.Num;
       -------------------------------  ------------------------------------------------
       | L    | R    | Time  | Undo |   | L    | R    | Time  | Window         | Undo |
       -------------------------------  ------------------------------------------------
       | null | R2   | 12:01 |      |   | null | R2   | 12:01 | [12:00, 12:05) |      |
```

```
| L1   | null | 12:02 |      |            | L1   | null | 12:02 | [12:00, 12:05) |      |
| L3   | null | 12:03 |      |            | L3   | null | 12:03 | [12:00, 12:05) |      |
| L3   | null | 12:04 | undo |            | L3   | null | 12:04 | [12:00, 12:05) | undo |
| L3   | R3   | 12:04 |      |            | L3   | R3   | 12:04 | [12:00, 12:05) |      |
| null | R4   | 12:05 |      |            | null | R4   | 12:05 | [12:05, 12:10) |      |
| null | R2   | 12:06 | undo |            | L2   | null | 12:06 | [12:05, 12:10) |      |
| L2   | R2   | 12:06 |      |        .............. [12:00, 12:10] ...............
....... [12:00, 12:10] .......
```

And with that, we now understand the effects of windowing on a FULL OUTER join. By applying the rules we learned in the first half of the chapter, it's then easy to derive the windowed variants of LEFT OUTER, RIGHT OUTER, INNER, ANTI, and SEMI joins, as well. I will leave most of these derivations as an exercise for you to complete, but to give a single example, LEFT OUTER join, as we learned, is just the FULL OUTER join with null columns on the left side of the join removed (again, with L2 and R2 rows highlighted to compare the differences):

```
12:10> SELECT TABLE
          Left.Id as L,
          Right.Id as R,
          COALESCE(
            TUMBLE(Left.Time, INTERVAL '5' MINUTE),
            TUMBLE(Right.Time, INTERVAL '5' MINUTE)
          ) AS Window
       FROM Left
          LEFT OUTER JOIN Right
          ON L.Num = R.Num AND
12:10> SELECT TABLE                             TUMBLE(Left.Time, INTERVAL '5' MINUTE) =
          Left.Id as L,                         TUMBLE(Right.Time, INTERVAL '5' MINUTE);
          Right.Id as R,
       FROM Left
          LEFT OUTER JOIN Right
          ON L.Num = R.Num;
---------------                         -----------------------------------
| L    | R    |                         | L    | R    | Window         |
---------------                         -----------------------------------
| L1   | null |                         | L1   | null | [12:00, 12:05) |
| L2   | R2   |                         | L2   | null | [12:05, 12:10) |
| L3   | R3   |                         | L3   | R3   | [12:00, 12:05) |
---------------                         -----------------------------------
```

By scoping the region of time for the join into fixed five-minute intervals, we chopped our datasets into two distinct windows of time: [12:00, 12:05) and [12:05, 12:10). The exact same join logic we observed earlier was then applied within those regions, yielding a slightly different outcome for the case in which the L2 and R2 rows fell into separate regions. And at a basic level, that's really all there is to windowed joins.

Temporal Validity

Having looked at the basics of windowed joins, we now spend the rest of the chapter looking at a somewhat more advanced approach: temporal validity windowing.

Temporal validity windows

Temporal validity windows apply in situations in which the rows in a relation effectively slice time into regions wherein a given value is valid. More concretely, imagine a financial system for performing currency conversions.[4] Such a system might contain a time-varying relation that captured the current conversion rates for various types of currency. For example, there might be a relation for converting from different currencies to Yen, like this:

```
12:10> SELECT TABLE * FROM YenRates;
-----------------------------------------
| Curr | Rate | EventTime | ProcTime |
-----------------------------------------
| USD  | 102  | 12:00:00  | 12:04:13 |
| Euro | 114  | 12:00:30  | 12:06:23 |
| Yen  | 1    | 12:01:00  | 12:05:18 |
| Euro | 116  | 12:03:00  | 12:09:07 |
| Euro | 119  | 12:06:00  | 12:07:33 |
-----------------------------------------
```

To highlight what I mean by saying that temporal validity windows "effectively slice time into regions wherein a given value is valid," consider only the Euro-to-Yen conversion rates in that relation:

```
12:10> SELECT TABLE * FROM YenRates WHERE Curr = "Euro";
-----------------------------------------
| Curr | Rate | EventTime | ProcTime |
-----------------------------------------
| Euro | 114  | 12:00:30  | 12:06:23 |
| Euro | 116  | 12:03:00  | 12:09:07 |
| Euro | 119  | 12:06:00  | 12:07:33 |
-----------------------------------------
```

From a database engineering perspective, we understand that these values don't mean that the rate for converting Euros to Yen is 114 ¥/€ at precisely 12:00, 116 ¥/€ at 12:03, 119 ¥/€ at 12:06, and undefined at all other times. Instead, we know that the intent of this table is to capture the fact that the conversion rate for Euros to Yen is undefined until 12:00, 114 ¥/€ from 12:00 to 12:03, 116 ¥/€ from 12:03 to 12:06, and 119 ¥/€ from then on. Or drawn out in a timeline:

```
       Undefined              114 ¥/€              116 ¥/€              119 ¥/€
|----[-inf, 12:00)----|----[12:00, 12:03)----|----[12:03, 12:06)----|----[12:06, now)----→
```

Now, if we knew all of the rates ahead of time, we could capture these regions explicitly in the row data themselves. But if we instead need to build up these regions incrementally, based only upon the start times at which a given rate becomes valid, we

---

4 Note that the example data and the temporal join use case motivating it are lifted almost wholesale from Julian Hyde's excellent "Streams, joins, and temporal tables" (*http://bit.ly/2MoNqaS*) document.

have a problem: the region for a given row will change over time depending on the rows that come after it. This is a problem even if the data arrive in order (because every time a new rate arrives, the previous rate changes from being valid forever to being valid until the arrival time of the new rate), but is further compounded if they can arrive *out of order*. For example, using the processing-time ordering in the preceding YenRates table, the sequence of timelines our table would effectively represent over time would be as follows:

```
Range of processing time | Event-time validity timeline during that range of processing-time
========================= |======================================================================
                          |
                          |      Undefined
       [-inf, 12:06:23)   |  |--[-inf, +inf)-------------------------------------------------→
                          |
                          |      Undefined          114 ¥/€
   [12:06:23, 12:07:33)   |  |--[-inf, 12:00)--|--[12:00, +inf)------------------------------→
                          |
                          |      Undefined          114 ¥/€                      119 ¥/€
   [12:07:33, 12:09:07)   |  |--[-inf, 12:00)--|--[12:00, 12:06)-------------------|--[12:06, +inf)→
                          |
                          |      Undefined          114 ¥/€          116 ¥/€       119 ¥/€
      [12:09:07, now)     |  |--[-inf, 12:00)--|--[12:00, 12:03)--|--[12:03, 12:06)--|--[12:06, +inf)→
```

Or, if we wanted to render this as a time-varying relation (with changes between each snapshot relation highlighted in yellow):

```
12:10> SELECT TVR * FROM YenRatesWithRegion ORDER BY EventTime;
-----------------------------------------------------------------------------------------
|               [-inf, 12:06:23)               |               [12:06:23, 12:07:33)        |
| ------------------------------------------   | ----------------------------------------  |
| | Curr | Rate |  Region        | ProcTime |  | | Curr | Rate |  Region       | ProcTime | |
| ------------------------------------------   | ----------------------------------------  |
| ------------------------------------------   | | Euro | 114  | [12:00, +inf) | 12:06:23 | |
|                                              | ----------------------------------------  |
|                                              |                                           |
-----------------------------------------------------------------------------------------
|               [12:07:33, 12:09:07)           |               [12:09:07, +inf)            |
| ------------------------------------------   | ----------------------------------------  |
| | Curr | Rate |  Region        | ProcTime |  | | Curr | Rate |  Region       | ProcTime | |
| ------------------------------------------   | ----------------------------------------  |
| | Euro | 114  | [12:00, 12:06) | 12:06:23 |  | | Euro | 114  | [12:00, 12:03) | 12:06:23 | |
| | Euro | 119  | [12:06, +inf)  | 12:07:33 |  | | Euro | 116  | [12:03, 12:06) | 12:09:07 | |
| ------------------------------------------   | | Euro | 119  | [12:06, +inf)  | 12:07:33 | |
|                                              | ----------------------------------------  |
-----------------------------------------------------------------------------------------
```

What's important to note here is that half of the changes involve updates to multiple rows. That maybe doesn't sound so bad, until you recall that the difference between each of these snapshots is the arrival of exactly one new row. In other words, the arrival of a single new input row results in transactional modifications to multiple output rows. That sounds less good. On the other hand, it also sounds a lot like the multirow transactions involved in building up session windows. And indeed, this is yet another example of windowing providing benefits beyond simple partitioning of time: it also affords the ability to do so in ways that involve complex, multirow transactions.

To see this in action, let's look at an animation. If this were a Beam pipeline, it would probably look something like the following:

```
PCollection<Currency, Decimal> yenRates = ...;
PCollection<Decimal> validYenRates = yenRates
    .apply(Window.into(new ValidityWindows())
    .apply(GroupByKey.<Currency, Decimal>create());
```

Rendered in a streams/tables animation, that pipeline would look like that shown in Figure 9-1.

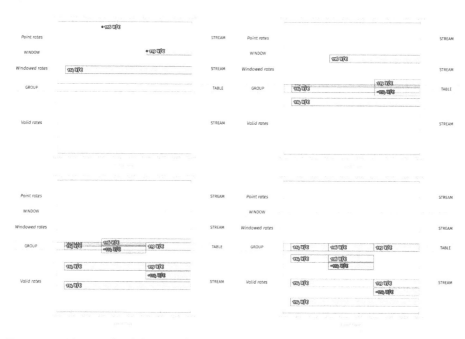

Figure 9-1. Temporal validity windowing over time (http://streamingbook.net/fig/9-1)

This animation highlights a critical aspect of temporal validity: shrinking windows. Validity windows must be able to shrink over time, thereby diminishing the reach of their validity and splitting any data contained therein across the two new windows. See the code snippets on GitHub (*http://bit.ly/2N7Nn3A*) for an example partial implementation.[5]

---

5 It's a partial implementation because it only works if the windows exist in isolation, as in Figure 9-1. As soon as you mix the windows with other data, such as the joining examples below, you would need some mechanism for splitting the data from the shrunken window into two separate windows, which Beam does not currently provide.

In SQL terms, the creation of these validity windows would look something like the following (using a hypothetical VALIDITY_WINDOW construct), viewed as a table:

```
12:10> SELECT TABLE
         Curr,
         MAX(Rate) as Rate,
         VALIDITY_WINDOW(EventTime) as Window
       FROM YenRates
       GROUP BY
         Curr,
         VALIDITY_WINDOW(EventTime)
       HAVING Curr = "Euro";
-------------------------------
| Curr | Rate | Window         |
-------------------------------
| Euro | 114  | [12:00, 12:03) |
| Euro | 116  | [12:03, 12:06) |
| Euro | 119  | [12:06, +inf)  |
-------------------------------
```

Validity Windows in Standard SQL

Note that it's possible to describe validity windows in standard SQL using a three-way self-join:

```
SELECT
  r1.Curr,
  MAX(r1.Rate) AS Rate,
  r1.EventTime AS WindowStart,
  r2.EventTime AS WIndowEnd
FROM YenRates r1
LEFT JOIN YenRates r2
  ON r1.Curr = r2.Curr
     AND r1.EventTime < r2.EventTime
LEFT JOIN YenRates r3
  ON r1.Curr = r3.Curr
     AND r1.EventTime < r3.EventTime
     AND r3.EventTime < r2.EventTime
WHERE r3.EventTime IS NULL
GROUP BY r1.Curr, WindowStart, WindowEnd
HAVING r1.Curr = 'Euro';
```

Thanks to Martin Kleppmann for pointing this out.

Or, perhaps more interestingly, viewed as a stream:

```
12:00> SELECT STREAM
         Curr,
         MAX(Rate) as Rate,
         VALIDITY_WINDOW(EventTime) as Window,
         Sys.EmitTime as Time,
         Sys.Undo as Undo,
       FROM YenRates
       GROUP BY
         Curr,
         VALIDITY_WINDOW(EventTime)
       HAVING Curr = "Euro";
-----------------------------------------------------
| Curr | Rate | Window         | Time     | Undo |
-----------------------------------------------------
| Euro | 114  | [12:00, +inf)  | 12:06:23 |      |
| Euro | 114  | [12:00, +inf)  | 12:07:33 | undo |
| Euro | 114  | [12:00, 12:06) | 12:07:33 |      |
| Euro | 119  | [12:06, +inf)  | 12:07:33 |      |
| Euro | 114  | [12:00, 12:06) | 12:09:07 | undo |
| Euro | 114  | [12:00, 12:03) | 12:09:07 |      |
| Euro | 116  | [12:03, 12:06) | 12:09:07 |      |
................ [12:00, 12:10] .................
```

Great, we have an understanding of how to use point-in-time values to effectively slice up time into ranges within which those values are valid. But the real power of these temporal validity windows is when they are applied in the context of joining them with other data. That's where temporal validity joins come in.

Temporal validity joins

To explore the semantics of temporal validity joins, suppose that our financial application contains another time-varying relation, one that tracks currency-conversion orders from various currencies to Yen:

```
12:10> SELECT TABLE * FROM YenOrders;
-----------------------------------------------
| Curr | Amount | EventTime | ProcTime |
-----------------------------------------------
| Euro | 2      | 12:02:00  | 12:05:07 |
| USD  | 1      | 12:03:00  | 12:03:44 |
| Euro | 5      | 12:05:00  | 12:08:00 |
| Yen  | 50     | 12:07:00  | 12:10:11 |
| Euro | 3      | 12:08:00  | 12:09:33 |
| USD  | 5      | 12:10:00  | 12:10:59 |
-----------------------------------------------
```

And for simplicity, as before, let's focus on the Euro conversions:

```
12:10> SELECT TABLE * FROM YenOrders WHERE Curr = "Euro";
----------------------------------------
| Curr | Amount | EventTime | ProcTime |
----------------------------------------
| Euro | 2      | 12:02:00  | 12:05:07 |
| Euro | 5      | 12:05:00  | 12:08:00 |
| Euro | 3      | 12:08:00  | 12:09:33 |
----------------------------------------
```

We'd like to robustly join these orders to the YenRates relation, treating the rows in YenRates as defining validity windows. As such, we'll actually want to join to the validity-windowed version of the YenRates relation we constructed at the end of the last section:

```
12:10> SELECT TABLE
         Curr,
         MAX(Rate) as Rate,
         VALIDITY_WINDOW(EventTime) as Window
       FROM YenRates
       GROUP BY
         Curr,
         VALIDITY_WINDOW(EventTime)
       HAVING Curr = "Euro";
------------------------------
| Curr | Rate | Window       |
------------------------------
| Euro | 114  | [12:00, 12:03) |
| Euro | 116  | [12:03, 12:06) |
| Euro | 119  | [12:06, +inf) |
------------------------------
```

Fortunately, after we have our conversion rates placed into validity windows, a windowed join between those rates and the YenOrders relation gives us exactly what we want:

```
12:10> WITH ValidRates AS
         (SELECT
            Curr,
            MAX(Rate) as Rate,
            VALIDITY_WINDOW(EventTime) as Window
          FROM YenRates
          GROUP BY
            Curr,
            VALIDITY_WINDOW(EventTime))
       SELECT TABLE
         YenOrders.Amount as "E",
         ValidRates.Rate as "Y/E",
         YenOrders.Amount * ValidRates.Rate as "Y",
         YenOrders.EventTime as Order,
         ValidRates.Window as "Rate Window"
```

```
    FROM YenOrders FULL OUTER JOIN ValidRates
      ON YenOrders.Curr = ValidRates.Curr
        AND WINDOW_START(ValidRates.Window) <= YenOrders.EventTime
        AND YenOrders.EventTime < WINDOW_END(ValidRates.Window)
      HAVING Curr = "Euro";
------------------------------------------
| E | Y/E |  Y  | Order | Rate Window    |
------------------------------------------
| 2 | 114 | 228 | 12:02 | [12:00, 12:03) |
| 5 | 116 | 580 | 12:05 | [12:03, 12:06) |
| 3 | 119 | 357 | 12:08 | [12:06, +inf)  |
------------------------------------------
```

Thinking back to our original YenRates and YenOrders relations, this joined relation indeed looks correct: each of the three conversions ended up with the (eventually) appropriate rate for the given window of event time within which their corresponding order fell. So we have a decent sense that this join is doing what we want in terms of providing us the eventual correctness we want.

That said, this simple snapshot view of the relation, taken after all the values have arrived and the dust has settled, belies the complexity of this join. To really understand what's going on here, we need to look at the full TVR. First, recall that the validity-windowed conversion rate relation was actually much more complex than the previous simple table snapshot view might lead you to believe. For reference, here's the STREAM version of the validity windows relation, which better highlights the evolution of those conversion rates over time:

```
12:00> SELECT STREAM
          Curr,
          MAX(Rate) as Rate,
          VALIDITY_WINDOW(EventTime) as Window,
          Sys.EmitTime as Time,
          Sys.Undo as Undo,
       FROM YenRates
       GROUP BY
          Curr,
          VALIDITY_WINDOW(EventTime)
       HAVING Curr = "Euro";
-----------------------------------------------------
| Curr | Rate | Window          | Time     | Undo |
-----------------------------------------------------
| Euro | 114  | [12:00, +inf)   | 12:06:23 |      |
| Euro | 114  | [12:00, +inf)   | 12:07:33 | undo |
| Euro | 114  | [12:00, 12:06)  | 12:07:33 |      |
| Euro | 119  | [12:06, +inf)   | 12:07:33 |      |
| Euro | 114  | [12:00, 12:06)  | 12:09:07 | undo |
| Euro | 114  | [12:00, 12:03)  | 12:09:07 |      |
| Euro | 116  | [12:03, 12:06)  | 12:09:07 |      |
.................. [12:00, 12:10] ...................
```

As a result, if we look at the full TVR for our validity-windowed join, you can see that the corresponding evolution of this join over time is much more complicated, due to the out-of-order arrival of values on both sides of the join:

```
12:10> WITH ValidRates AS
         (SELECT
            Curr,
            MAX(Rate) as Rate,
            VALIDITY_WINDOW(EventTime) as Window
          FROM YenRates
          GROUP BY
            Curr,
            VALIDITY_WINDOW(EventTime))
       SELECT TVR
         YenOrders.Amount as "E",
         ValidRates.Rate as "Y/E",
         YenOrders.Amount * ValidRates.Rate as "Y",
         YenOrders.EventTime as Order,
         ValidRates.Window as "Rate Window"
       FROM YenOrders FULL OUTER JOIN ValidRates
         ON YenOrders.Curr = ValidRates.Curr
           AND WINDOW_START(ValidRates.Window) <= YenOrders.EventTime
           AND YenOrders.EventTime < WINDOW_END(ValidRates.Window)
       HAVING Curr = "Euro";
--------------------------------------------------------------------------------
|            [-inf, 12:05:07)            |        [12:05:07, 12:06:23)           |
| -------------------------------------  | ------------------------------------- |
| | E | Y/E | Y   | Order | Rate Window |  | | E | Y/E | Y   | Order | Rate Window | |
| -------------------------------------  | ------------------------------------- |
| -------------------------------------  | | 2 |     |     | 12:02 |             | |
|                                        | ------------------------------------- |
--------------------------------------------------------------------------------
|          [12:06:23, 12:07:33)          |        [12:07:33, 12:08:00)           |
| -------------------------------------  | ------------------------------------- |
| | E | Y/E | Y   | Order | Rate Window |  | | E | Y/E | Y   | Order | Rate Window | |
| -------------------------------------  | ------------------------------------- |
| | 2 | 114 | 228 | 12:02 | [12:00, +inf) | | | 2 | 114 | 228 | 12:02 | [12:00, 12:06) | |
| -------------------------------------  | |   | 119 |     |       | [12:06, +inf) | |
|                                        | ------------------------------------- |
--------------------------------------------------------------------------------
|          [12:08:00, 12:09:07)          |        [12:09:07, 12:09:33)           |
| -------------------------------------  | ------------------------------------- |
| | E | Y/E | Y   | Order | Rate Window |  | | E | Y/E | Y   | Order | Rate Window | |
| -------------------------------------  | ------------------------------------- |
| | 2 | 114 | 228 | 12:02 | [12:00, 12:06) | | | 2 | 114 | 228 | 12:02 | [12:00, 12:03) | |
| | 5 | 114 | 570 | 12:05 | [12:00, 12:06) | | | 5 | 116 | 580 | 12:05 | [12:03, 12:06) | |
| |   | 119 |     |       | [12:06, +inf) | | |   | 119 |     | 12:08 | [12:06, +inf) | |
| -------------------------------------  | ------------------------------------- |
--------------------------------------------------------------------------------
|            [12:09:33, now)             |
| -------------------------------------  |
| | E | Y/E | Y   | Order | Rate Window |  |
| -------------------------------------  |
| | 2 | 114 | 228 | 12:02 | [12:00, 12:03) | |
| | 5 | 116 | 580 | 12:05 | [12:03, 12:06) | |
| | 3 | 119 | 357 | 12:08 | [12:06, +inf) | |
```

In particular, the result for the 5 € order is originally quoted at 570 ¥ because that order (which happened at 12:05) originally falls into the validity window for the 114 ¥/€ rate. But when the 116 ¥/€ rate for event time 12:03 arrives out of order, the result for the 5 € order must be updated from 570 ¥ to 580 ¥. This is also evident if you observe the results of the join as a stream (here I've highlighted the incorrect 570 ¥ in red, and the retraction for 570 ¥ and subsequent corrected value of 580 ¥ in blue):

```
12:00> WITH ValidRates AS
         (SELECT
            Curr,
            MAX(Rate) as Rate,
            VALIDITY_WINDOW(EventTime) as Window
          FROM YenRates
          GROUP BY
            Curr,
            VALIDITY_WINDOW(EventTime))
       SELECT STREAM
         YenOrders.Amount as "E",
         ValidRates.Rate as "Y/E",
         YenOrders.Amount * ValidRates.Rate as "Y",
         YenOrders.EventTime as Order,
         ValidRates.Window as "Rate Window",
         Sys.EmitTime as Time,
         Sys.Undo as Undo
       FROM YenOrders FULL OUTER JOIN ValidRates
         ON YenOrders.Curr = ValidRates.Curr
            AND WINDOW_START(ValidRates.Window) <= YenOrders.EventTime
            AND YenOrders.EventTime < WINDOW_END(ValidRates.Window)
         HAVING Curr = "Euro";
```

E	Y/E	Y	Order	Rate Window	Time	Undo
2			12:02		12:05:07	
2			12:02		12:06:23	undo
2	114	228	12:02	[12:00, +inf)	12:06:23	
2	114	228	12:02	[12:00, +inf)	12:07:33	undo
2	114	228	12:02	[12:00, 12:06)	12:07:33	
	119			[12:06, +inf)	12:07:33	
5	114	570	12:05	[12:00, 12:06)	12:08:00	
2	114	228	12:02	[12:00, 12:06)	12:09:07	undo
5	114	570	12:05	[12:00, 12:06)	12:09:07	undo
2	114	228	12:02	[12:00, 12:03)	12:09:07	
5	116	580	12:05	[12:03, 12:06)	12:09:07	
	119			[12:06, +inf)	12:09:33	undo
3	119	357	12:08	[12:06, +inf)	12:09:33	
.... [12:00, 12:10] ....

It's worth calling out that this is a fairly messy stream due to the use of a FULL OUTER join. In reality, when consuming conversion orders as a stream, you probably don't care about unjoined rows; switching to an INNER join helps eliminate those rows. You probably also don't care about cases for which the rate window changes, but the actual conversion value isn't affected. By removing the rate window from the stream, we can further decrease its chattiness:

```
12:00> WITH ValidRates AS
         (SELECT
             Curr,
             MAX(Rate) as Rate,
             VALIDITY_WINDOW(EventTime) as Window
          FROM YenRates
          GROUP BY
             Curr,
             VALIDITY_WINDOW(EventTime))
       SELECT STREAM
          YenOrders.Amount as "E",
          ValidRates.Rate as "Y/E",
          YenOrders.Amount * ValidRates.Rate as "Y",
          YenOrders.EventTime as Order,
          ValidRates.Window as "Rate Window",
          Sys.EmitTime as Time,
          Sys.Undo as Undo
       FROM YenOrders INNER JOIN ValidRates
          ON YenOrders.Curr = ValidRates.Curr
            AND WINDOW_START(ValidRates.Window) <= YenOrders.EventTime
            AND YenOrders.EventTime < WINDOW_END(ValidRates.Window)
       HAVING Curr = "Euro";
-------------------------------------------
| E | Y/E | Y   | Order | Time     | Undo |
-------------------------------------------
| 2 | 114 | 228 | 12:02 | 12:06:23 |      |
| 5 | 114 | 570 | 12:05 | 12:08:00 |      |
| 5 | 114 | 570 | 12:05 | 12:09:07 | undo |
| 5 | 116 | 580 | 12:05 | 12:09:07 |      |
| 3 | 119 | 357 | 12:08 | 12:09:33 |      |
............ [12:00, 12:10] .............
```

Much nicer. We can now see that this query very succinctly does what we originally set out to do: join two TVRs for currency conversion rates and orders in a robust way that is tolerant of data arriving out of order. Figure 9-2 visualizes this query as an animated diagram. In it, you can also very clearly see the way the overall structure of things change as they evolve over time.

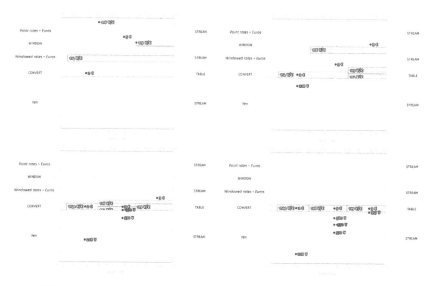

Figure 9-2. Temporal validity join, converting Euros to Yen with per-record triggering (http://streamingbook.net/fig/9-2)

Watermarks and temporal validity joins.   With this example, we've highlighted the first benefit of windowed joins called out at the beginning of this section: windowing a join allows you to partition that join within time for some practical business need. In this case, the business need was slicing time into regions of validity for our currency conversion rates.

Before we call it a day, however, it turns out that this example also provides an opportunity to highlight the second point I called out: the fact that windowing a join can provide a meaningful reference point for watermarks. To see how that's useful, imagine changing the previous query to replace the implicit default per-record trigger with an explicit watermark trigger that would fire only once when the watermark passed the end of the validity window in the join (assuming that we have a watermark available for both of our input TVRs that accurately tracks the completeness of those relations in event time as well as an execution engine that knows how to take those watermarks into consideration). Now, instead of our stream containing multiple outputs and retractions for rates arriving out of order, we could instead end up with a stream containing a single, correct converted result per order, which is clearly even more ideal than before:

```
12:00> WITH ValidRates AS
          (SELECT
              Curr,
              MAX(Rate) as Rate,
              VALIDITY_WINDOW(EventTime) as Window
```

```
      FROM YenRates
      GROUP BY
        Curr,
        VALIDITY_WINDOW(EventTime))
    SELECT STREAM
      YenOrders.Amount as "E",
      ValidRates.Rate as "Y/E",
      YenOrders.Amount * ValidRates.Rate as "Y",
      YenOrders.EventTime as Order,
      Sys.EmitTime as Time,
      Sys.Undo as Undo
    FROM YenOrders INNER JOIN ValidRates
      ON YenOrders.Curr = ValidRates.Curr
        AND WINDOW_START(ValidRates.Window) <= YenOrders.EventTime
        AND YenOrders.EventTime < WINDOW_END(ValidRates.Window)
      HAVING Curr = "Euro"
      EMIT WHEN WATERMARK PAST WINDOW_END(ValidRates.Window);
------------------------------------------
| E | Y/E |  Y  | Order | Time     | Undo |
------------------------------------------
| 2 | 114 | 228 | 12:02 | 12:08:52 |      |
| 5 | 116 | 580 | 12:05 | 12:10:04 |      |
| 3 | 119 | 357 | 12:08 | 12:10:13 |      |
............ [12:00, 12:11] .............
```

Or, rendered as an animation, which clearly shows how joined results are not emitted into the output stream until the watermark moves beyond them, as demonstrated in Figure 9-3.

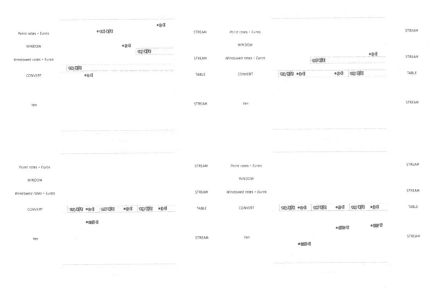

Figure 9-3. Temporal validity join, converting Euros to Yen with watermark triggering (http://streamingbook.net/fig/9-3)

Either way, it's impressive to see how this query encapsulates such a complex set of interactions into a clean and concise rendering of the desired results.

Summary

In this chapter, we analyzed the world of joins (using the join vocabulary of SQL) within the context of stream processing. We began with unwindowed joins and saw how, conceptually, all joins are streaming joins at the core. We saw how the foundation for essentially all of the other join variations is the FULL OUTER join, and discussed the specific alterations that occur as part of LEFT OUTER, RIGHT OUTER, INNER, ANTI, SEMI, and even CROSS joins. In addition, we saw how all of those different join patterns interact in a world of TVRs and streams.

We next moved on to windowed joins, and learned that windowing a join is typically motivated by one or both of the following benefits:

- The ability to *partition the join within time* for some business need
- The ability to *tie results* from the join *to the progress of a watermark*

And, finally, we explored in depth one of the more interesting and useful types of windows with respect to joining: temporal validity windows. We saw how temporal validity windows very naturally carve time into regions of validity for given values, based only on the specific points in time where those values change. We learned that joins within validity windows require a windowing framework that supports windows that can split over time, which is something no existing streaming system today supports natively. And we saw how concisely validity windows allowed us to solve the problem of joining TVRs for currency conversion rates and orders together in a robust, natural way.

Joins are often one of the more intimidating aspects of data processing, streaming or otherwise. However, by understanding the theoretical foundation of joins and how straightforwardly we can derive all the different types of joins from that basic foundation, joins become a much less frightening beast, even with the additional dimension of time that streaming adds to the mix.

CHAPTER 10

The Evolution of Large-Scale Data Processing

You have now arrived at the final chapter in the book, you stoic literate, you. Your journey will soon be complete!

To wrap things up, I'd like you to join me on a brief stroll through history, starting back in the ancient days of large-scale data processing with MapReduce and touching upon some of the highlights over the ensuing decade and a half that have brought streaming systems to the point they're at today. It's a relatively lightweight chapter in which I make a few observations about important contributions from a number of well-known systems (and a couple maybe not-so-well known), refer you to a bunch of source material you can go read on your own should you want to learn more, all while attempting not to offend or inflame the folks responsible for systems whose truly impactful contributions I'm going to either oversimplify or ignore completely for the sake of space, focus, and a cohesive narrative. Should be a good time.

On that note, keep in mind as you read this chapter that we're really just talking about specific pieces of the MapReduce/Hadoop family tree of large-scale data processing here. I'm not covering the SQL arena in any way shape or form[1]; we're not talking HPC/supercomputers, and so on. So as broad and expansive as the title of this chapter might sound, I'm really focusing on a specific vertical swath of the grand universe of large-scale data processing. Caveat literatus, and all that.

---

[1] Which means I'm skipping a ton of the academic literature around stream processing, because that's where much of it started. If you're really into hardcore academic papers on the topic, start from the references in "The Dataflow Model" paper (*http://bit.ly/2sXgVJ3*) and work backward. You should be able to find your way pretty easily.

Also note that I'm covering a disproportionate amount of Google technologies here. You would be right in thinking that this might have something to do with the fact that I've worked at Google for more than a decade. But there are two other reasons for it: 1) big data has always been important for Google, so there have been a number of worthwhile contributions created there that merit discussing in detail, and 2) my experience has been that folks outside of Google generally seem to enjoy learning more about the things we've done, because we as a company have historically been somewhat tight-lipped in that regard. So indulge me a bit while I prattle on excessively about the stuff we've been working on behind closed doors.

To ground our travels in concrete chronology, we'll be following the timeline in Figure 10-1, which shows rough dates of existence for the various systems I discuss.

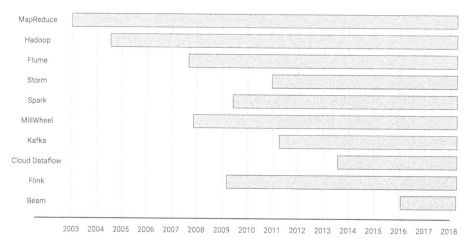

Figure 10-1. Approximate timeline of systems discussed in this chapter

At each stop, I give a brief history of the system as best I understand it and frame its contributions from the perspective of shaping streaming systems as we know them today. At the end, we recap all of the contributions to see how they've summed up to create the modern stream processing ecosystem of today.

MapReduce

We begin the journey with MapReduce (Figure 10-2).

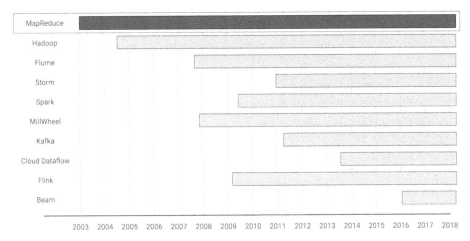

Figure 10-2. Timeline: MapReduce

I think it's safe to say that large-scale data processing as we all know it today got its start with MapReduce way back in 2003.[2] At the time, engineers within Google were building all sorts of bespoke systems to tackle data processing challenges at the scale of the World Wide Web.[3] As they did so, they noticed three things:

Data processing is hard
As the data scientists and engineers among us well know, you can build a career out of just focusing on the best ways to extract useful insights from raw data.

Scalability is hard
Extracting useful insights over massive-scale data is even more difficult yet.

Fault-tolerance is hard
Extracting useful insights from massive-scale data in a fault-tolerant, correct way on commodity hardware is brutal.

After solving all three of these challenges in tandem across a number of use cases, they began to notice some similarities between the custom systems they'd built. And they came to the conclusion that if they could build a framework that took care of the

---

2 Certainly, MapReduce itself was built upon many ideas that had been well known before, as is even explicitly stated in the MapReduce paper. That doesn't change the fact that MapReduce was the system that tied those ideas together (along with some of its own) to create something practical that solved an important and emerging problem better than anyone else before ever had, and in a way that inspired generations of data-processing systems that followed.

3 To be clear, Google was most certainly not the only company tackling data processing problems at this scale at the time. Google was just one among a number of companies involved in that first generation of attempts at taming massive-scale data processing.

latter two issues (scalability and fault-tolerance), it would make focusing on the first issue a heck of a lot simpler. Thus was born MapReduce.[4]

The basic idea with MapReduce was to provide a simple data processing API centered around two well-understood operations from the functional programming realm: map and reduce (Figure 10-3). Pipelines built with that API would then be executed on a distributed systems framework that took care of all the nasty scalability and fault-tolerance stuff that quickens the hearts of hardcore distributed-systems engineers and crushes the souls of the rest of us mere mortals.

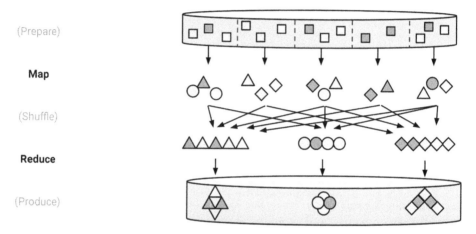

Figure 10-3. Visualization of a MapReduce job

We already discussed the semantics of MapReduce in great detail back in Chapter 6, so we won't dwell on them here. Simply recall that we broke things down into six discrete phases (MapRead, Map, MapWrite, ReduceRead, Reduce, ReduceWrite) as part of our streams and tables analysis, and we came to the conclusion in the end that there really wasn't all that much different between the overall Map and Reduce phases; at a high-level, they both do the following:

- Convert a table to a stream
- Apply a user transformation to that stream to yield another stream
- Group that stream into a table

After it was placed into service within Google, MapReduce found such broad application across a variety of tasks that the team decided it was worth sharing its ideas with

---

4 And to be clear, MapReduce actually built upon the Google File System, GFS, which itself solved the scalability and fault-tolerance issues for a specific subset of the overall problem.

the rest of the world. The result was the MapReduce paper (*https://goo.gl/Rsqr3G*), published at OSDI 2004 (see Figure 10-4).

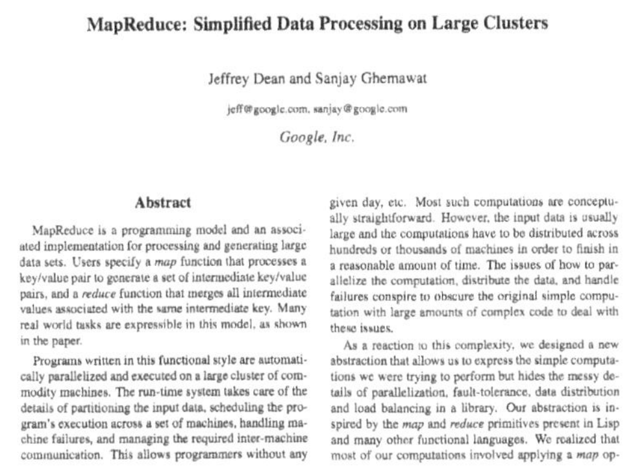

MapReduce: Simplified Data Processing on Large Clusters

Jeffrey Dean and Sanjay Ghemawat

jeff@google.com, sanjay@google.com

Google, Inc.

Abstract

MapReduce is a programming model and an associated implementation for processing and generating large data sets. Users specify a *map* function that processes a key/value pair to generate a set of intermediate key/value pairs, and a *reduce* function that merges all intermediate values associated with the same intermediate key. Many real world tasks are expressible in this model, as shown in the paper.

Programs written in this functional style are automatically parallelized and executed on a large cluster of commodity machines. The run-time system takes care of the details of partitioning the input data, scheduling the program's execution across a set of machines, handling machine failures, and managing the required inter-machine communication. This allows programmers without any

given day, etc. Most such computations are conceptually straightforward. However, the input data is usually large and the computations have to be distributed across hundreds or thousands of machines in order to finish in a reasonable amount of time. The issues of how to parallelize the computation, distribute the data, and handle failures conspire to obscure the original simple computation with large amounts of complex code to deal with these issues.

As a reaction to this complexity, we designed a new abstraction that allows us to express the simple computations we were trying to perform but hides the messy details of parallelization, fault-tolerance, data distribution and load balancing in a library. Our abstraction is inspired by the *map* and *reduce* primitives present in Lisp and many other functional languages. We realized that most of our computations involved applying a *map* op-

In it, the team described in detail the history of the project, design of the API and implementation, and details about a number of different use cases to which MapReduce had been applied. Unfortunately, they provided no actual source code, so the best that folks outside of Google at the time could do was say, "Yes, that sounds very nice indeed," and go back to building their bespoke systems.

Figure 10-4. The MapReduce paper (https://goo.gl/Rsqr3G), published at OSDI 2004

Over the course of the decade that followed, MapReduce continued to undergo heavy development within Google, with large amounts of time invested in making the system scale to unprecedented levels. For a more detailed account of some of the highlights along that journey, I recommend the post "History of massive-scale sorting experiments at Google" (*http://bit.ly/2LPvuVN*) (Figure 10-5) written by our official MapReduce historian/scalability and performance wizard, Marián Dvorský.

But for our purposes here, suffice it to say that nothing else yet has touched the magnitude of scale achieved by MapReduce, not even within Google. Considering how long MapReduce has been around, that's saying something; 14 years is an eternity in our industry.

From a streaming systems perspective, the main takeaways I want to leave you with for MapReduce are *simplicity* and *scalability*. MapReduce took the first brave steps toward taming the unruly beast that is massive-scale data processing, exposing a simple and straightforward API for crafting powerful

Figure 10-5. Marián Dvorský's "History of massive-scale sorting experiments" (http://bit.ly/2LPvuVN) blog post

data processing pipelines, its austerity belying the complex distributed systems magic happening under the covers to allow those pipelines to run at scale on large clusters of commodity hardware.

Hadoop

Next in our list is Hadoop (Figure 10-6). Fair warning: this is one of those times where I will grossly oversimplify the impact of a system for the sake of a focused narrative. The impact Hadoop has had on our industry and the world at large cannot be overstated, and it extends well beyond the relatively specific scope I discuss here.

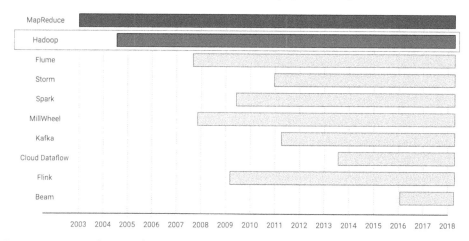

Figure 10-6. Timeline: Hadoop

Hadoop came about in 2005, when Doug Cutting and Mike Cafarella decided that the ideas from the MapReduce paper were just the thing they needed as they built a distributed version of their Nutch webcrawler. They had already built their own version of Google's distributed filesystem (originally called NDFS for Nutch Distributed File System, later renamed to HDFS, or Hadoop Distributed File System), so it was a natural next step to add a MapReduce layer on top after that paper was published. They called this layer Hadoop.

The key difference between Hadoop and MapReduce was that Cutting and Cafarella made sure the source code for Hadoop was shared with the rest of the world by open sourcing it (along with the source for HDFS) as part of what would eventually become the Apache Hadoop project. Yahoo's hiring of Cutting to help transition the Yahoo webcrawler architecture onto Hadoop gave the project an additional boost of validity and engineering oomph, and from there, an entire ecosystem of open source data processing tools grew. As with MapReduce, others have told the history of Hadoop in other fora far better than I can; one particularly good reference is Marko

Bonaci's "The history of Hadoop," (*http://bit.ly/2Kjc4fZ*) itself originally slated for inclusion in a print book (Figure 10-7).

Figure 10-7. *Marko Bonaci's "The history of Hadoop" (http://bit.ly/2Kjc4fZ)*

The main point I want you to take away from this section is the massive impact the *open source ecosystem* that flowered around Hadoop had upon the industry as a whole. By creating an open community in which engineers could improve and extend the ideas from those early GFS and MapReduce papers, a thriving ecosystem was born, yielding dozens of useful tools like Pig, Hive, HBase, Crunch, and on and on. That openness was key to incubating the diversity of ideas that exist now across our industry, and it's why I'm pigeonholing Hadoop's open source ecosystem as its single most important contribution to the world of streaming systems as we know them today.

Flume

We now return to Google territory to talk about the official successor to MapReduce within Google: Flume ([Figure 10-8] sometimes also called FlumeJava in reference to the original Java version of the system, and not to be confused with Apache Flume, which is an entirely different beast that just so happens to share the same name).

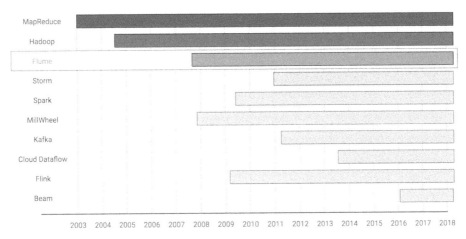

Figure 10-8. *Timeline: Flume*

The Flume project was founded by Craig Chambers when the Google Seattle office opened in 2007. It was motivated by a desire to solve some of the inherent shortcomings of MapReduce, which had become apparent over the first few years of its success. Many of these shortcomings revolved around MapReduce's rigid Map → Shuffle → Reduce structure; though refreshingly simple, it carried with it some downsides:

- Because many use cases cannot be served by the application of a single MapReduce, a number of bespoke *orchestration systems* began popping up across Google for coordinating sequences of MapReduce jobs. These systems all served essentially the same purpose (gluing together multiple MapReduce jobs to create a coherent pipeline solving a complex problem). However, having been developed independently, they were naturally incompatible and a textbook example of unnecessary duplication of effort.

- What's worse, there were numerous cases in which a clearly written sequence of MapReduce jobs would introduce *inefficiencies* thanks to the rigid structure of the API. For example, one team might write a MapReduce that simply filtered out some number of elements; that is, a map-only job with an empty reducer. It might be followed up by another team's map-only job doing some element-wise enrichment (with yet another empty reducer). The output from the second job might then finally be consumed by a final team's MapReduce performing some grouping aggregation over the data. This pipeline, consisting of essentially a single chain of Map phases followed by a single Reduce phase, would require the orchestration of three completely independent jobs, each chained together by shuffle and output phases materializing the data. But that's assuming you wanted to keep the codebase logical and clean, which leads to the final downside…

- In an effort to optimize away these inefficiencies in their MapReductions, engineers began introducing *manual optimizations* that would *obfuscate* the simple logic of the pipeline, increasing maintenance and debugging costs.

Flume addressed these issues by providing a composable, high-level API for describing data processing pipelines, essentially based around the same PCollection and PTransform concepts found in Beam, as illustrated in Figure 10-9.

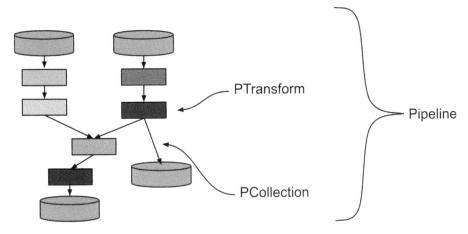

Figure 10-9. High-level pipelines in Flume (image credit: Frances Perry)

These pipelines, when launched, would be fed through an optimizer[5] to generate a plan for an optimally efficient sequence of MapReduce jobs, the execution of which was then orchestrated by the framework, which you can see illustrated in Figure 10-10.

```
PCollection<KV<String, Long>> sums =
  IO.read(...)
    .ParDo(new KeyByUser())
    .Count();
```

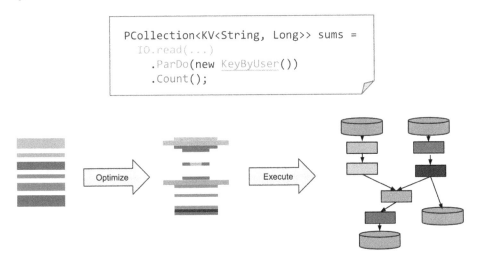

Figure 10-10. Optimization from a logical pipeline to a physical execution plan

Perhaps the most important example of an automatic optimization that Flume can perform is fusion (which Reuven discussed a bit back in Chapter 5), in which two

---

5 Not unlike the query optimizers long used in the database world.

logically independent stages can be run in the same job either sequentially (consumer-producer fusion) or in parallel (sibling fusion), as depicted in Figure 10-11.

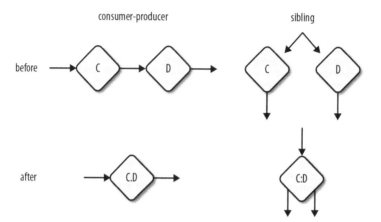

Figure 10-11. Fusion optimizations combine successive or parallel operations together into the same physical operation

Fusing two stages together eliminates serialization/deserialization and network costs, which can be significant in pipelines processing large amounts of data.

Another type of automatic optimization is *combiner lifting* (see Figure 10-12), the mechanics of which we already touched upon in Chapter 7 when we talked about incremental combining. Combiner lifting is simply the automatic application of multilevel combine logic that we discussed in that chapter: a combining operation (e.g., summation) that logically happens after a grouping operation is partially lifted into the stage preceding the group-by-key (which by definition requires a trip across the network to shuffle the data) so that it can perform partial combining before the grouping happens. In cases of very hot keys, this can greatly reduce the amount of data shuffled over the network, and also spread the load of computing the final aggregate more smoothly across multiple machines.

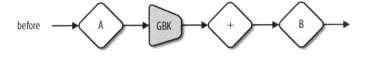

Figure 10-12. Combiner lifting applies partial aggregation on the sender side of a group-by-key operation before completing aggregation on the consumer side

As a result of its cleaner API and automatic optimizations, Flume Java was an instant hit upon its introduction at Google in early 2009. Following on the heels of that success, the team published the paper titled "Flume Java: Easy, Efficient Data-Parallel Pipelines" (*https://goo.gl/9e1nXf*) (see Figure 10-13), itself an excellent resource for learning more about the system as it originally existed.

Flume C++ followed not too much later in 2011, and in early 2012 Flume was introduced into Noogler[6] training provided to all new engineers at Google. That was the beginning of the end for Map-Reduce.

Since then, Flume has been migrated to no longer use MapReduce as its execution engine; instead, it uses a custom execution engine, called Dax, built directly into the framework itself. By freeing Flume itself from the confines of the previously underlying Map → Shuffle → Reduce structure of MapReduce, Dax enabled new optimizations, such as the dynamic work rebalancing feature described in Eugene Kirpichov and Malo Denielou's "No shard left behind" (*http://bit.ly/2JPaUnR*) blog post (Figure 10-14).

Figure 10-13. FlumeJava paper (https://goo.gl/9e1nXf)

---

6 Noogler == New + Googler == New hires at Google

No shard left behind: dynamic work rebalancing in Google Cloud Dataflow

Posted by Eugene Kirpichov, Senior Software Engineer, and Malo Denielou, Software Engineer

Introduction

Today we continue the discussion of _____ "zero-knobs" story. Previously we showcased Cloud Dataflow's capability for ____, which dynamically adjusts the number of workers to the needs of your pipeline. In this post, we discuss Dynamic Work Rebalancing (known internally at Google as Liquid Sharding), which keeps the workers busy.

We'll show how this feature addresses the problem of stragglers (workers that take a long time to finish their part of the work, delaying completion of the job and keeping other resources idle), greatly improving performance and cost in many scenarios, and how it enables and works in concert with autoscaling.

The problem of stragglers in big data processing systems

In all major distributed data processing engines — from Google's original MapReduce, to Hadoop, to modern systems such as Spark, Flink and Cloud Dataflow — one of the key operations is Map, which applies a function to all elements of an input in parallel (called ParDo in the terminology of ____ ____ programming model).

Figure 10-14. "No shard left behind" (http://bit.ly/2JPaUnR) post

Though discussed in that post in the context of Cloud Dataflow, dynamic work rebalancing (or liquid sharding, as it's colloquially known at Google) automatically rebalances extra work from straggler shards to other idle workers in the system as they complete their work early. By dynamically rebalancing the work distribution over time, it's possible to come much closer to an optimal work distribution than even the best educated initial splits could ever achieve. It also allows for adapting to variations across the pool of workers, where a slow machine that might have otherwise held up the completion of a job is simply compensated for by moving most of its tasks to other workers. When liquid sharding was rolled out at Google, it recouped significant amounts of resources across the fleet.

One last point on Flume is that it was also later extended to support streaming semantics. In addition to the batch Dax backend, Flume was extended to be able to execute pipelines on the MillWheel stream processing system (discussed in a moment). Most of the high-level streaming semantics concepts we've discussed in this book were first incorporated into Flume before later finding their way into Cloud Dataflow and eventually Apache Beam.

All that said, the primary thing to take away from Flume in this section is the introduction of a notion of *high-level pipelines*, which enabled the *automatic optimization* of clearly written, logical pipelines. This enabled the creation of much larger and complex pipelines, without the need for manual orchestration or optimization, and all while keeping the code for those pipelines logical and clear.

Storm

Next up is Apache Storm (Figure 10-15), the first real streaming system we cover. Storm most certainly wasn't the first streaming system in existence, but I would argue it was the first streaming system to see truly broad adoption across the industry, and for that reason we give it a closer look here.

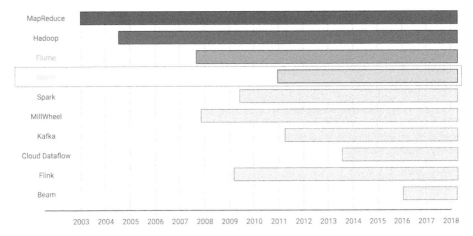

| | 2003 | 2004 | 2005 | 2006 | 2007 | 2008 | 2009 | 2010 | 2011 | 2012 | 2013 | 2014 | 2015 | 2016 | 2017 | 2018 |

Figure 10-15. Timeline: Storm

Storm was the brainchild of Nathan Marz, who later chronicled the history of its creation in a blog post titled "History of Apache Storm and lessons learned" (*http://bit.ly/2HLwSqd*) (Figure 10-16). The TL;DR version of it is that Nathan's team at the startup employing him then, BackType, had been attempting to process the Twitter firehose using a custom system of queues and workers. He came to essentially the same realization that the MapReduce folks had nearly a decade earlier: the actual data processing portion of their code was only a tiny amount of the system, and building those real-time data processing pipelines would be a lot easier if there were a framework doing all the distributed system's dirty work under the covers. Out of that was born Storm.

History of Apache Storm and lessons learned

Apache Storm recently became a top-level project, marking a huge milestone for the project and for me personally. It's crazy to think that four years ago Storm was nothing more than an idea in my head, and now it's a thriving project with a large community used by a ton of companies. In this post I want to look back at how Storm got to this point and the lessons I learned along the way.

Figure 10-16. "History of Apache Storm and lessons learned" (http://bit.ly/2HLwSqd)

The interesting thing about Storm, in comparison to the rest of the systems we've talked about so far, is that the team chose to loosen the strong consistency guarantees found in all of the other systems we've talked about so far as a way of providing lower latency. By combining at-most once or at-least once semantics with per-record processing and no integrated (i.e., no consistent) notion of persistent state, Storm was able to provide much lower latency in providing results than systems that executed over batches of data and guaranteed exactly-once correctness. And for a certain type of use cases, this was a very reasonable trade-off to make.

Unfortunately, it quickly became clear that people really wanted to have their cake and eat it, too. They didn't just want to get their answers quickly, they wanted to have both low-latency results *and* eventual correctness. But such a thing was impossible with Storm alone. Enter the Lambda Architecture.

Given the limitations of Storm, shrewd engineers began running a weakly consistent Storm streaming pipeline alongside a strongly consistent Hadoop batch pipeline. The former produced low-latency, inexact results, whereas the latter produced high-latency, exact results, both of which would then be somehow merged together in the end to provide a single low-latency, eventually consistent view of the outputs. We learned back in Chapter 1 that the Lambda Architecture was Marz's other brainchild, as detailed in his post titled "How to beat the CAP theorem" (*http://bit.ly/1ATyjbD*) (Figure 10-17).[7]

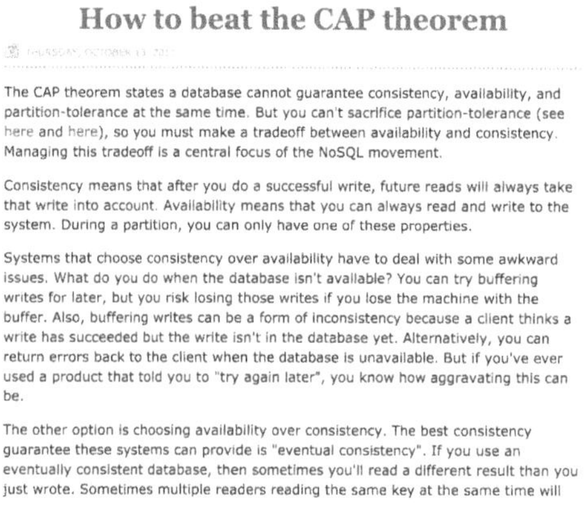

How to beat the CAP theorem

The CAP theorem states a database cannot guarantee consistency, availability, and partition-tolerance at the same time. But you can't sacrifice partition-tolerance (see here and here), so you must make a tradeoff between availability and consistency. Managing this tradeoff is a central focus of the NoSQL movement.

Consistency means that after you do a successful write, future reads will always take that write into account. Availability means that you can always read and write to the system. During a partition, you can only have one of these properties.

Systems that choose consistency over availability have to deal with some awkward issues. What do you do when the database isn't available? You can try buffering writes for later, but you risk losing those writes if you lose the machine with the buffer. Also, buffering writes can be a form of inconsistency because a client thinks a write has succeeded but the write isn't in the database yet. Alternatively, you can return errors back to the client when the database is unavailable. But if you've ever used a product that told you to "try again later", you know how aggravating this can be.

The other option is choosing availability over consistency. The best consistency guarantee these systems can provide is "eventual consistency". If you use an eventually consistent database, then sometimes you'll read a different result than you just wrote. Sometimes multiple readers reading the same key at the same time will

Figure 10-17. "How to beat the CAP theorem" (http://bit.ly/1ATyjbD)

I've already spent a fair amount of time harping on the shortcomings of the Lambda Architecture, so I won't belabor those points here. But I will reiterate this: the Lambda Architecture became quite popular, despite the costs and headaches associated with it, simply because it met a critical need that a great many businesses were otherwise having a difficult time fulfilling: that of getting low-latency, but eventually correct results out of their data processing pipelines.

From the perspective of the evolution of streaming systems, I argue that Storm was responsible for first bringing low-latency data processing to the masses. However, it did so at the cost of weak consistency, which in turn brought about the rise of the Lambda Architecture, and the years of dual-pipeline darkness that followed.

---

7 As an aside, I also highly recommend reading Martin Kleppmann's "A Critique of the CAP Theorem" (*http://bit.ly/2ybJlnt*) for very nice analysis of the shortcomings of the CAP theorem itself, as well as a more principled alternative way of looking at the same problem.

But hyperbolic dramaticism aside, Storm was the system that gave the industry its first taste of low-latency data processing, and the impact of that is reflected in the broad interest in and adoption of streaming systems today.

Before moving on, it's also worth giving a shout out to Heron. In 2015, Twitter (the largest known user of Storm in the world, and the company that originally fostered the Storm project) surprised the industry by announcing it was abandoning the Storm execution engine in favor of a new system it had developed in house, called Heron. Heron aimed to address a number of performance and maintainability issues that had plagued Storm, while remaining API compatible, as detailed in the company's paper titled "Twitter Heron: Stream Processing at Scale" (*http://bit.ly/2LNzOF4*) (Figure 10-18). Heron itself was subsequently open sourced (*http://bit.ly/2MoOpYK*) (with governance moved to its own independent foundation, not an existing one like Apache). Given the continued development on Storm, there are now two competing variants of the Storm lineage. Where things will end up is anyone's guess, but it will be exciting to watch.

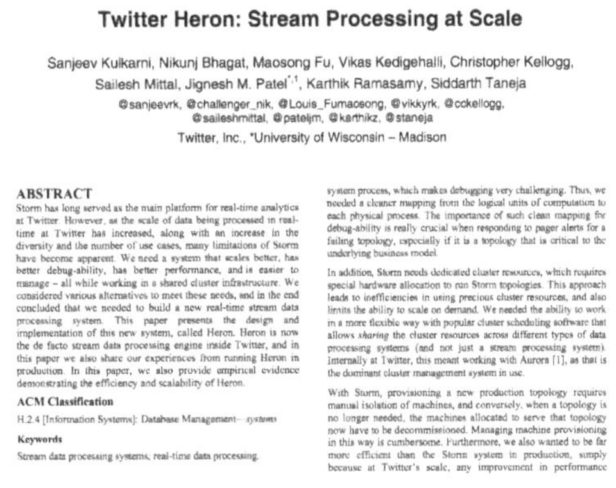

Twitter Heron: Stream Processing at Scale

Sanjeev Kulkarni, Nikunj Bhagat, Maosong Fu, Vikas Kedigehalli, Christopher Kellogg, Sailesh Mittal, Jignesh M. Patel*[,1], Karthik Ramasamy, Siddarth Taneja

@sanjeevrk, @challenger_nik, @Louis_Fumaosong, @vikkyrk, @cckellogg, @saileshmittal, @pateljm, @karthikz, @staneja

Twitter, Inc., *University of Wisconsin – Madison

ABSTRACT

Storm has long served as the main platform for real-time analytics at Twitter. However, as the scale of data being processed in real-time at Twitter has increased, along with an increase in the diversity and the number of use cases, many limitations of Storm have become apparent. We need a system that scales better, has better debug-ability, has better performance, and is easier to manage – all while working in a shared cluster infrastructure. We considered various alternatives to meet these needs, and in the end concluded that we needed to build a new real-time stream data processing system. This paper presents the design and implementation of this new system, called Heron. Heron is now the de facto stream data processing engine inside Twitter, and in this paper we also share our experiences from running Heron in production. In this paper, we also provide empirical evidence demonstrating the efficiency and scalability of Heron.

ACM Classification

H.2.4 [Information Systems]: Database Management—*systems*

Keywords

Stream data processing systems; real-time data processing.

system process, which makes debugging very challenging. Thus, we needed a cleaner mapping from the logical units of computation to each physical process. The importance of such clean mapping for debug-ability is really crucial when responding to pager alerts for a failing topology, especially if it is a topology that is critical to the underlying business model.

In addition, Storm needs dedicated cluster resources, which requires special hardware allocation to run Storm topologies. This approach leads to inefficiencies in using precious cluster resources, and also limits the ability to scale on demand. We needed the ability to work in a more flexible way with popular cluster scheduling software that allows *sharing* the cluster resources across different types of data processing systems (and not just a stream processing system). Internally at Twitter, this meant working with Aurora [1], as that is the dominant cluster management system in use.

With Storm, provisioning a new production topology requires manual isolation of machines, and conversely, when a topology is no longer needed, the machines allocated to serve that topology now have to be decommissioned. Managing machine provisioning in this way is cumbersome. Furthermore, we also wanted to be far more efficient than the Storm system in production, simply because at Twitter's scale, any improvement in performance

Figure 10-18. Heron paper (http://bit.ly/2LNzOF4)

Spark

Moving on, we now come to Apache Spark (Figure 10-19). This is another section in which I'm going to greatly oversimplify the total impact that Spark has had on the industry by focusing on a specific portion of its contributions: those within the realm of stream processing. Apologies in advance.

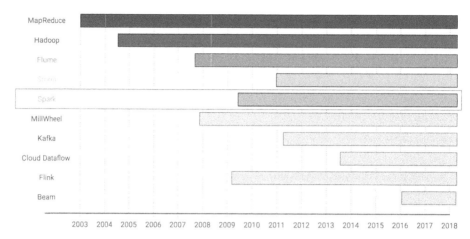

MapReduce

Hadoop

Flume

Storm

Spark

MillWheel

Kafka

Cloud Dataflow

Flink

Beam

2003 2004 2005 2006 2007 2008 2009 2010 2011 2012 2013 2014 2015 2016 2017 2018

Figure 10-19. Timeline: Spark

Spark got its start at the now famous AMPLab in UC Berkeley around 2009. The thing that initially fueled Spark's fame was its ability to oftentimes perform the bulk of a pipeline's calculations entirely in memory, without touching disk until the very end. Engineers achieved this via the Resilient Distributed Dataset (RDD) idea, which basically captured the full lineage of data at any given point in the pipeline, allowing intermediate results to be recalculated as needed on machine failure, under the assumptions that a) your inputs were always replayable, and b) your computations were deterministic. For many use cases, these preconditions were true, or at least true enough given the massive gains in performance users were able to realize over standard Hadoop jobs. From there, Spark gradually built up its eventual reputation as Hadoop's de facto successor.

A few years after Spark was created, Tathagata Das, then a graduate student in the AMPLab, came to the realization that: hey, we've got this fast batch processing engine, what if we just wired things up so we ran multiple batches one after another, and used that to process streaming data? From that bit of insight, Spark Streaming was born.

What was really fantastic about Spark Streaming was this: thanks to the strongly consistent batch engine powering things under the covers, the world now had a stream processing engine that could provide correct results all by itself without needing the help of an additional batch job. In other words, given the right use case, you could ditch your Lambda Architecture system and just use Spark Streaming. All hail Spark Streaming!

The one major caveat here was the "right use case" part. The big downside to the original version of Spark Streaming (the 1.x variants) was that it provided support for only a specific flavor of stream processing: processing-time windowing. So any use case that cared about event time, needed to deal with late data, and so on, couldn't be handled out of the box without a bunch of extra code being written by the user to implement some form of event-time handling on top of Spark's processing-time windowing architecture. This meant that Spark Streaming was best suited for in-order data or event-time-agnostic computations. And, as I've reiterated throughout this book, those conditions are not as prevalent as you would hope when dealing with the large-scale, user-centric datasets common today.

Another interesting controversy that surrounds Spark Streaming is the age-old "microbatch versus true streaming" debate. Because Spark Streaming is built upon the idea of small, repeated runs of a batch processing engine, detractors claim that Spark Streaming is not a true streaming engine in the sense that progress in the system is gated by the global barriers of each batch. There's some amount of truth there. Even though true streaming engines almost always utilize some sort of batching or bundling for the sake of throughput, they have the flexibility to do so at much finer-grained levels, down to individual keys. The fact that microbatch architectures process bundles at a global level means that it's virtually impossible to have both low per-key latency and high overall throughput, and there are a number of benchmarks that have shown this to be more or less true. But at the same time, latency on the order of minutes or multiple seconds is still quite good. And there are very few use cases that demand exact correctness and such stringent latency capabilities. So in some sense, Spark was absolutely right to target the audience it did originally; most people fall in that category. But that hasn't stopped its competitors from slamming this as a massive disadvantage for the platform. Personally, I see it as a minor complaint at best in most cases.

Shortcomings aside, Spark Streaming was a watershed moment for stream processing: the first publicly available, large-scale stream processing engine that could also provide the correctness guarantees of a batch system. And of course, as previously noted, streaming is only a very small part of Spark's overall success story, with important contributions made in the space of iterative processing and machine learning, its native SQL integration, and the aforementioned lightning-fast in-memory performance, to name a few.

If you're curious to learn more about the details of the original Spark 1.x architecture, I highly recommend Matei Zaharia's dissertation on the subject, "An Architecture for Fast and General Data Processing on Large Clusters" (*http://bit.ly/2y8rduN*) (Figure 10-20). It's 113 pages of Sparky goodness that's well worth the investment.

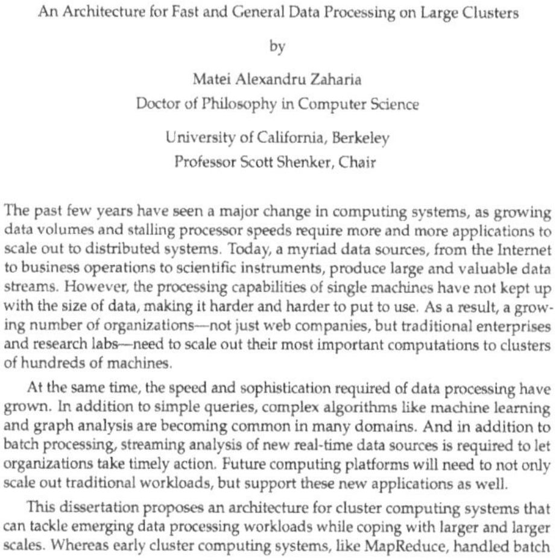

An Architecture for Fast and General Data Processing on Large Clusters

by

Matei Alexandru Zaharia

Doctor of Philosophy in Computer Science

University of California, Berkeley

Professor Scott Shenker, Chair

The past few years have seen a major change in computing systems, as growing data volumes and stalling processor speeds require more and more applications to scale out to distributed systems. Today, a myriad data sources, from the Internet to business operations to scientific instruments, produce large and valuable data streams. However, the processing capabilities of single machines have not kept up with the size of data, making it harder and harder to put to use. As a result, a growing number of organizations—not just web companies, but traditional enterprises and research labs—need to scale out their most important computations to clusters of hundreds of machines.

At the same time, the speed and sophistication required of data processing have grown. In addition to simple queries, complex algorithms like machine learning and graph analysis are becoming common in many domains. And in addition to batch processing, streaming analysis of new real-time data sources is required to let organizations take timely action. Future computing platforms will need to not only scale out traditional workloads, but support these new applications as well.

This dissertation proposes an architecture for cluster computing systems that can tackle emerging data processing workloads while coping with larger and larger scales. Whereas early cluster computing systems, like MapReduce, handled batch

Figure 10-20. Spark dissertation (http://bit.ly/ 2y8rduN)

As of today, the 2.x variants of Spark are greatly expanding upon the semantic capabilities of Spark Streaming, incorporating many parts of the model described in this book, while attempting to simplify some of the more complex pieces. And Spark is even pushing a new true streaming architecture, to try to shut down the microbatch nay-sayer arguments. But when it first came on the scene, the important contribution that Spark brought to the table was the fact that it was the *first publicly available stream processing engine with strong consistency semantics*, albeit only in the case of in-order data or event-time-

agnostic computation.

MillWheel

Next we discuss MillWheel, a project that I first dabbled with in my 20% time after joining Google in 2008, later joining the team full time in 2010 (Figure 10-21).

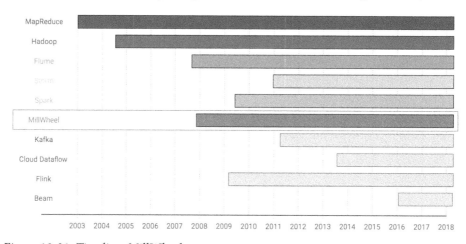

Figure 10-21. Timeline: MillWheel

MillWheel is Google's original, general-purpose stream processing architecture, and the project was founded by Paul Nordstrom around the time Google's Seattle office

---

opened. MillWheel's success within Google has long centered on an ability to provide low-latency, strongly consistent processing of unbounded, out-of-order data. Over the course of this book, we've looked at most of the bits and pieces that came together in MillWheel to make this possible:

- Reuven discussed *exactly-once guarantees* in Chapter 5. Exactly-once guarantees are essential for correctness.

- In Chapter 7 we looked at *persistent state*, the strongly consistent variations of which provide the foundation for maintaining that correctness in long-running pipelines executing on unreliable hardware.

- Slava talked about *watermarks* in Chapter 3. Watermarks provide a foundation for reasoning about disorder in input data.

- Also in Chapter 7, we looked at *persistent timers*, which provide the necessary link between watermarks and the pipeline's business logic.

It's perhaps somewhat surprising then to note that the MillWheel project was not initially focused on correctness. Paul's original vision more closely targeted the niche that Storm later espoused: low-latency data processing with weak consistency. It was the initial MillWheel customers, one building sessions over search data and another performing anomaly detection on search queries (the Zeitgeist example from the MillWheel paper), who drove the project in the direction of correctness. Both had a strong need for consistent results: sessions were used to infer user behavior, and anomaly detection was used to infer trends in search queries; the utility of both decreased significantly if the data they provided were not reliable. As a result, MillWheel's direction was steered toward one of strong consistency.

Support for out-of-order processing, which is the other core aspect of robust streaming often attributed to MillWheel, was also motivated by customers. The Zeitgeist pipeline, as a true streaming use case, wanted to generate an output stream that identified anomalies in search query traffic, and only anomalies (i.e., it was not practical for consumers of its analyses to poll all the keys in a materialized view output table waiting for an anomaly to be flagged; consumers needed a direct signal only when anomalies happened for specific keys). For anomalous spikes (i.e., *increases* in query traffic), this is relatively straightforward: when the count for a given query exceeds the expected value in your model for that query by some statistically significant amount, you can signal an anomaly. But for anomalous dips (i.e., *decreases* in query traffic), the problem is a bit trickier. It's not enough to simply see that the number of queries for a given search term has decreased, because for any period of time, the observed number always starts out at zero. What you really need to do in these cases is wait until you have reason to believe that you've seen a sufficiently representative portion of the input for a given time period, and only *then* compare the count against your model.

True Streaming

"True streaming use case" bears a bit of explanation. One recent trend in streaming systems is to try to simplify the programming models to make them more accessible by limiting the types of use cases one can address. For example, at the time of writing, both Spark's Structured Streaming and Apache Kafka's Kafka Streams systems limit themselves to what I refer to in Chapter 8 as "materialized view semantics," essentially repeated updates to an eventually consistent output table. Materialized view semantics are great when you want to consume your output as a lookup table: any time you can just lookup a value in that table and be okay with the latest result as of query time, materialized views are a good fit. They are not, however, particularly well suited for use cases in which you want to consume your output as a bonafide stream. I refer to these as true streaming use cases, with anomaly detection being one of the better examples.

As we'll discuss shortly, there are certain aspects of anomaly detection that make it unsuitable for pure materialized view semantics (i.e., record-by-record processing only), specifically the fact that it relies on reasoning about the completeness of the input data to accurately identify anomalies that are the result of an absence of data (in addition to the fact that polling an output table to see if an anomaly signal has arrived is not an approach that scales particularly well). True streaming use cases are thus the motivation for features like watermarks (Preferably *low* watermarks that pessimistically track input completeness, as described in Chapter 3, not *high* watermarks that track the event time of the newest record the system is aware of, as used by Spark Structured Streaming for garbage collecting windows, since high watermarks are more prone to incorrectly throwing away data as event time skew varies within the pipeline) and triggers. Systems that omit these features do so for the sake of simplicity but at the cost of decreased ability. There can be great value in that, most certainly, but don't be fooled if you hear such systems claim these simplifications yield equivalent or even greater generality; you can't address fewer use cases and be equally or more general.

The Zeitgeist pipeline first attempted to do this by inserting processing-time delays before the analysis logic that looked for dips. This would work reasonably decently when data arrived in order, but the pipeline's authors discovered that data could, at times, be greatly delayed and thus arrive wildly out of order. In these cases, the processing-time delays they were using weren't sufficient, because the pipeline would erroneously report a flurry of dip anomalies that didn't actually exist. What they really needed was a way to wait until the input became complete.

Watermarks were thus born out of this need for reasoning about input completeness in out-of-order data. As Slava described in Chapter 3, the basic idea was to track the known progress of the inputs being provided to the system, using as much or as little data available for the given type of data source, to construct a progress metric that could be used to quantify input completeness. For simpler input sources like a statically partitioned Kafka topic with each partition being written to in increasing event-time order (such as by web frontends logging events in real time), you can compute a perfect watermark. For more complex input sources like a dynamic set of input logs, a heuristic might be the best you can do. But either way, watermarks provide a distinct advantage over the alternative of using processing time to reason about event-time completeness, which experience has shown serves about as well as a map of London while trying to navigate the streets of Cairo.

So thanks to the needs of its customers, MillWheel ended up as a system with the right set of features for supporting robust stream processing on out-of-order data. As a result, the paper titled "MillWheel: Fault-Tolerant Stream Processing at Internet Scale" (*http://bit.ly/2yab5ZH*)[8] (Figure 10-22) spends most of its time discussing the difficulties of providing correctness in a system like this, with consistency guarantees and watermarks being the main areas of focus. It's well worth your time if you're interested in the subject.

Not long after the MillWheel paper was published, MillWheel was integrated as an alternative, streaming backend for Flume, together often referred to as Streaming Flume. Within Google today, MillWheel is in the process of being replaced by its successor, Windmill (the execution engine that also powers Cloud Dataflow, discussed in a moment), a ground-up rewrite that incorporates all the best ideas from MillWheel, along with a few new ones like better scheduling and dispatch, and a cleaner separation of user and system code.

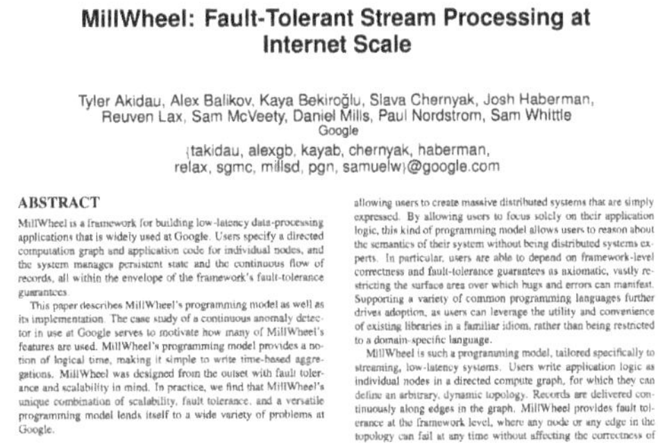

MillWheel: Fault-Tolerant Stream Processing at Internet Scale

Tyler Akidau, Alex Balikov, Kaya Bekiroğlu, Slava Chernyak, Josh Haberman, Reuven Lax, Sam McVeety, Daniel Mills, Paul Nordstrom, Sam Whittle
Google

{takidau, alexgb, kayab, chernyak, haberman, relax, sgmc, millsd, pgn, samuelw}@google.com

ABSTRACT

MillWheel is a framework for building low-latency data-processing applications that is widely used at Google. Users specify a directed computation graph and application code for individual nodes, and the system manages persistent state and the continuous flow of records, all within the envelope of the framework's fault-tolerance guarantees.

This paper describes MillWheel's programming model as well as its implementation. The case study of a continuous anomaly detector in use at Google serves to motivate how many of MillWheel's features are used. MillWheel's programming model provides a notion of logical time, making it simple to write time-based aggregations. MillWheel was designed from the outset with fault tolerance and scalability in mind. In practice, we find that MillWheel's unique combination of scalability, fault tolerance, and a versatile programming model lends itself to a wide variety of problems at Google.

allowing users to create massive distributed systems that are simply expressed. By allowing users to focus solely on their application logic, this kind of programming model allows users to reason about the semantics of their system without being distributed systems experts. In particular, users are able to depend on framework-level correctness and fault-tolerance guarantees as axiomatic, vastly restricting the surface area over which bugs and errors can manifest. Supporting a variety of common programming languages further drives adoption, as users can leverage the utility and convenience of existing libraries in a familiar idiom, rather than being restricted to a domain-specific language.

MillWheel is such a programming model, tailored specifically to streaming, low-latency systems. Users write application logic as individual nodes in a directed compute graph, for which they can define an arbitrary, dynamic topology. Records are delivered continuously along edges in the graph. MillWheel provides fault tolerance at the framework level, where any node or any edge in the topology can fail at any time without affecting the correctness of

Figure 10-22. MillWheel paper (http://bit.ly/ 2yab5ZH)

However, the big takeaway for MillWheel is that the four concepts listed earlier (exactly-once, persistent state, watermarks, persistent timers) together provided the basis for a system that was finally able to deliver on the true promise of stream processing: robust, low-latency processing of out-of-order data, even on unreliable commodity hardware.

---

8 For the record, written primarily by Sam McVeety with help from Reuven and bits of input from the rest of us on the author list; we shouldn't have alphabetized that author list, because everyone always assumes I'm the primary author on it, even though I wasn't.

Kafka

We now come to Kafka (Figure 10-23). Kafka is unique among the systems discussed in this chapter in that it's not a data processing framework,[9] but instead a transport layer. Make no mistake, however: Kafka has played one of the most influential roles in advancing stream processing out of all the system's we're discussing here.

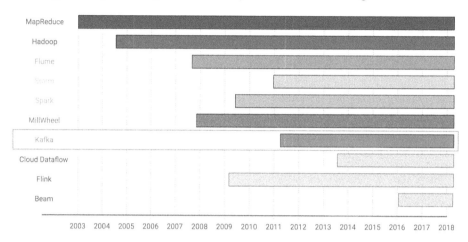

Figure 10-23. Timeline: Kafka

If you're not familiar with it, Kafka is essentially a persistent streaming transport, implemented as a set of partitioned logs. It was developed originally at LinkedIn by such industry luminaries as Neha Narkhede and Jay Kreps, and its accolades include the following:

- Providing a clean model of persistence that packaged that warm fuzzy feeling of *durable, replayable input sources* from the batch world in a streaming friendly interface.

- Providing an elastic *isolation layer* between producers and consumers.

- Embodying the relationship between *streams and tables* that we discussed in Chapter 6, revealing a foundational way of thinking about data processing in general while also providing a conceptual link to the rich and storied world of databases.

---

9 Kafka Streams and now KSQL are of course changing that, but those are relatively recent developments, and I'll be focusing primarily on the Kafka of yore.

- As a side effect of all of the above, not only becoming the *cornerstone* of a majority of stream processing installations across the industry, but also fostering the stream-processing-as-databases and microservices movements.

They must get up very early in the morning.

Of those accolades, there are two that stand out most to me. The first is the application of durability and replayability to stream data. Prior to Kafka, most stream processing systems used some sort of ephemeral queuing system like Rabbit MQ or even plain-old TCP sockets to send data around. Durability might be provided to some degree via upstream backup in the producers (i.e., the ability for upstream producers of data to resend if the downstream workers crashed), but oftentimes the upstream data was stored ephemerally, as well. And most approaches entirely ignored the idea of being able to replay input data later in cases of backfills or for prototyping, development, and regression testing.

Kafka changed all that. By taking the battle-hardened concept of a durable log from the database world and applying it to the realm of stream processing, Kafka gave us all back that sense of safety and security we'd lost when moving from the durable input sources common in the Hadoop/batch world to the ephemeral sources prevalent at the time in the streaming world. With durability and replayability, stream processing took yet another step toward being a robust, reliable replacement for the ad hoc, continuous batch processing systems of yore that were still being applied to streaming use cases.

As a streaming system developer, one of the more interesting visible artifacts of the impact that Kafka's durability and replayability features have had on the industry is how many of the stream processing engines today have grown to fundamentally rely on that replayability to provide end-to-end exactly-once guarantees. Replayability is the foundation upon which end-to-end exactly-once guarantees in Apex, Flink, Kafka Streams, Spark, and Storm are all built. When executing in exactly-once mode, each of those systems assumes/requires that the input data source be able to rewind and replay all of the data up until the most recent checkpoint. When used with an input source that does not provide such ability (even if the source can guarantee reliable delivery via upstream backup), end-to-end exactly-once semantics fall apart. That sort of broad reliance on replayability (and the related aspect of durability) is a huge testament to the amount of impact those features have had across the industry.

The second noteworthy bullet from Kafka's resume is the popularization of stream and table theory. We spent the entirety of Chapter 6 discussing streams and tables as well as much of Chapters 8 and 9. And for good reason. Streams and tables form the foundation of data processing, be it the MapReduce family tree of systems, the enormous legacy of SQL database systems, or what have you. Not all data processing approaches need speak directly in terms of streams and tables but conceptually speaking, that's how they all operate. And as both users and developers of these systems, there's great value in understanding the core underlying concepts that all of our systems build upon. We all owe a collective thanks to the folks in the Kafka community who helped shine a broader light on the streams-and-tables way of thinking.

Figure 10-24. I ❤ Logs

If you'd like to learn more about Kafka and the foundations it's built on, *I ❤ Logs* by Jay Kreps (O'Reilly; Figure 10-24) is an excellent resource.[10] Additionally, as cited originally in Chapter 6, Kreps and Martin Kleppmann have a pair of articles (Figure 10-25) that I highly recommend for reading up on the origins of streams and table theory.

Kafka has made huge contributions to the world of stream processing, arguably more than any other single system out there. In particular, the application of durability and replayability to input and output streams played a big part in helping move stream processing out of the niche realm of approximation tools and into the big leagues of general data processing. Additionally, the theory of streams and tables, popularized by the Kafka community, provides deep insight into the underlying mechanics of data processing in general.

---

10 While I recommend the book as the most comprehensive and cohesive resource, you can find much of the content from it scattered across O'Reilly's website if you just search around for Kreps' articles. Sorry, Jay...

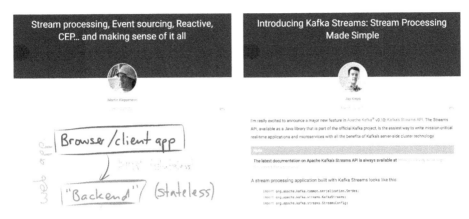

Figure 10-25. Martin's post (https://www.confluent.io/blog/making-sense-of-stream-processing/) (left) and Jay's post (https://www.confluent.io/blog/introducing-kafka-streams-stream-processing-made-simple/) (right)

Cloud Dataflow

Cloud Dataflow (Figure 10-26) is Google's fully managed, cloud-based data processing service. Dataflow launched to the world in August 2015. It was built with the intent to take the decade-plus of experiences that had gone into building MapReduce, Flume, and MillWheel, and package them up into a serverless cloud experience.

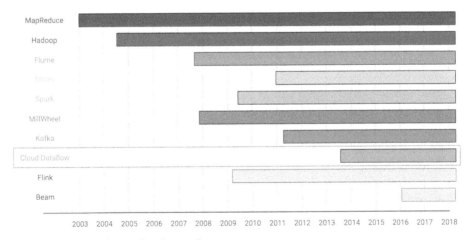

Figure 10-26. Timeline: Cloud Dataflow

Although the serverless aspect of Cloud Dataflow is perhaps its most technically challenging and distinguishing factor from a systems perspective, the primary contribution to streaming systems that I want to discuss here is its unified batch plus streaming programming model. That's all the transformations, windowing, watermarks, triggers, and accumulation goodness we've spent most of the book talking about. And all of them, of course, wrapped up the *what*/*where*/*when*/*how* way of thinking about things.

The model first arrived back in Flume, as we looked to incorporate the robust out-of-order processing support in MillWheel into the higher-level programming model Flume afforded. The combined batch and streaming approach available to Googlers internally with Flume was then the basis for the fully unified model included in Dataflow.

The key insight in the unified model—the full extent of which none of us at the time even truly appreciated—is that under the covers, batch and streaming are really not that different: they're both just minor variations on the streams and tables theme. As we learned in Chapter 6, the main difference really boils down to the ability to incrementally trigger tables into streams; everything else is conceptually the same.[11] By taking advantage of the underlying commonalities of the two approaches, it was possible to provide a single, nearly seamless experience that applied to both worlds. This was a big step forward in making stream processing more accessible.

In addition to taking advantage of the commonalities between batch and streaming, we took a long, hard look at the variety of use cases we'd encountered over the years at Google and used those to inform the pieces that went into the unified model. Key aspects we targeted included the following:

- *Unaligned, event-time windows* such as sessions, providing the ability to concisely express powerful analytic constructs and apply them to out-of-order data.

- *Custom windowing support*, because one (or even three or four) sizes rarely fit all.

- *Flexible triggering* and *accumulation modes*, providing the ability to shape the way data flow through the pipeline to match the correctness, latency, and cost needs of the given use case.

- The use of *watermarks* for reasoning about *input completeness*, which is critical for use cases like anomalous dip detection where the analysis depends upon an absence of data.

- *Logical abstraction* of the underlying execution environment, be it batch, micro-batch, or streaming, providing flexibility of choice in execution engine and

---

11 As with many broad generalizations, this one is true in a specific context, but belies the underlying complexity of reality. As I alluded to in Chapter 1, batch systems go to great lengths to optimize the cost and runtime of data processing pipelines over bounded datasets in ways that stream processing engines have yet to attempt to duplicate. To imply that modern batch and streaming systems only differ in one small way is a sizeable oversimplification in any realm beyond the purely conceptual.

avoiding system-level constructs (such as micro-batch size) from creeping into the logical API.

Taken together, these aspects provided the flexibility to balance the tensions between correctness, latency, and cost, allowing the model to be applied across a wide breadth of use cases.

Given that you've just read an entire book covering the finer points of the Dataflow/Beam Model, there's little point in trying to retread any those concepts here. However, if you're looking for a slightly more academic take on things as well as a nice overview of some of the motivating use cases alluded to earlier, you might find our 2015 Dataflow Model paper (*http://bit.ly/2sXgVJ3*) worthwhile (Figure 10-27).

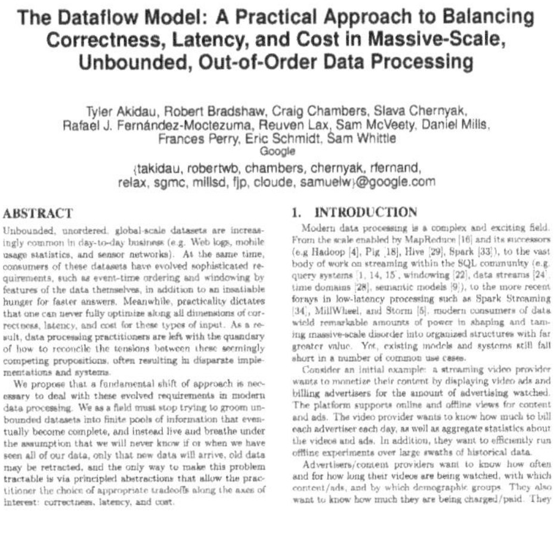

The Dataflow Model: A Practical Approach to Balancing Correctness, Latency, and Cost in Massive-Scale, Unbounded, Out-of-Order Data Processing

Tyler Akidau, Robert Bradshaw, Craig Chambers, Slava Chernyak, Rafael J. Fernández-Moctezuma, Reuven Lax, Sam McVeety, Daniel Mills, Frances Perry, Eric Schmidt, Sam Whittle
Google
{takidau, robertwb, chambers, chernyak, rfernand, relax, sgmc, millsd, fjp, cloude, samuelw}@google.com

ABSTRACT

Unbounded, unordered, global-scale datasets are increasingly common in day-to-day business (e.g. Web logs, mobile usage statistics, and sensor networks). At the same time, consumers of these datasets have evolved sophisticated requirements, such as event-time ordering and windowing by features of the data themselves, in addition to an insatiable hunger for faster answers. Meanwhile, practicality dictates that one can never fully optimize along all dimensions of correctness, latency, and cost for these types of input. As a result, data processing practitioners are left with the quandary of how to reconcile the tensions between these seemingly competing propositions, often resulting in disparate implementations and systems.

We propose that a fundamental shift of approach is necessary to deal with these evolved requirements in modern data processing. We as a field must stop trying to groom unbounded datasets into finite pools of information that eventually become complete, and instead live and breathe under the assumption that we will never know if or when we have seen all of our data, only that new data will arrive, old data may be retracted, and the only way to make this problem tractable is via principled abstractions that allow the practitioner the choice of appropriate tradeoffs along the axes of interest: correctness, latency, and cost.

1. INTRODUCTION

Modern data processing is a complex and exciting field. From the scale enabled by MapReduce [16] and its successors (e.g Hadoop [4], Pig [18], Hive [29], Spark [33]), to the vast body of work on streaming within the SQL community (e.g. query systems [1, 14, 15], windowing [22], data streams [24], time domains [28], semantic models [9]), to the more recent forays in low-latency processing such as Spark Streaming [34], MillWheel, and Storm [5], modern consumers of data wield remarkable amounts of power in shaping and taming massive-scale disorder into organized structures with far greater value. Yet, existing models and systems still fall short in a number of common use cases.

Consider an initial example: a streaming video provider wants to monetize their content by displaying video ads and billing advertisers for the amount of advertising watched. The platform supports online and offline views for content and ads. The video provider wants to know how much to bill each advertiser each day, as well as aggregate statistics about the videos and ads. In addition, they want to efficiently run offline experiments over large swaths of historical data.

Advertisers/content providers want to know how often and for how long their videos are being watched, with which content/ads, and by which demographic groups. They also want to know how much they are being charged/paid. They

Figure 10-27. Dataflow Model paper (http://bit.ly/2sXgVJ3)

Though there are many other compelling aspects to Cloud Dataflow, the important contribution from the perspective of this chapter is its *unified batch plus streaming programming model*. It brought the world a comprehensive approach to tackling unbounded, out-of-order datasets, and in a way that provided the flexibility to make the trade-offs necessary to balance the tensions between correctness, latency, and cost to match the requirements for a given use case.

Flink

Flink (Figure 10-28) burst onto the scene in 2015, rapidly transforming itself from a system that almost no one had heard of into one of the powerhouses of the streaming world, seemingly overnight.

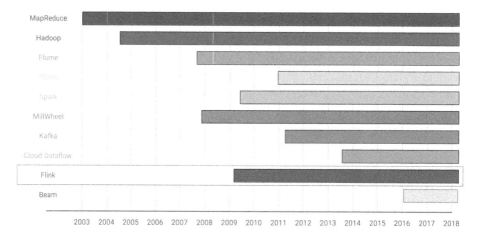

Figure 10-28. Timeline: Flink

There were two main reasons for Flink's rise to prominence:

- Its *rapid adoption of the Dataflow/Beam programming model,* which put it in the position of being the most semantically capable fully open source streaming system on the planet at the time.

- Followed shortly thereafter by its *highly efficient snapshotting* implementation (derived from research in Chandy and Lamport's original paper "Distributed Snapshots: Determining Global States of Distributed Systems" (*http://bit.ly/ 2JBCsRU*) [Figure 10-29]), which gave it the strong consistency guarantees needed for correctness.

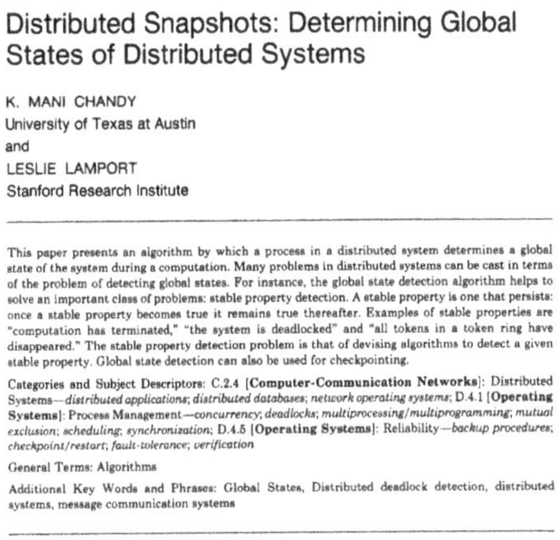
Distributed Snapshots: Determining Global States of Distributed Systems

K. MANI CHANDY
University of Texas at Austin
and
LESLIE LAMPORT
Stanford Research Institute

This paper presents an algorithm by which a process in a distributed system determines a global state of the system during a computation. Many problems in distributed systems can be cast in terms of the problem of detecting global states. For instance, the global state detection algorithm helps to solve an important class of problems: stable property detection. A stable property is one that persists: once a stable property becomes true it remains true thereafter. Examples of stable properties are "computation has terminated," "the system is deadlocked" and "all tokens in a token ring have disappeared." The stable property detection problem is that of devising algorithms to detect a given stable property. Global state detection can also be used for checkpointing.

Categories and Subject Descriptors: C.2.4 [**Computer-Communication Networks**]: Distributed Systems—*distributed applications*; *distributed databases*; *network operating systems*; D.4.1 [**Operating Systems**]: Process Management—*concurrency*; *deadlocks*; *multiprocessing/multiprogramming*; *mutual exclusion*; *scheduling*; *synchronization*; D.4.5 [**Operating Systems**]: Reliability—*backup procedures*; *checkpoint/restart*; *fault-tolerance*; *verification*

General Terms: Algorithms

Additional Key Words and Phrases: Global States, Distributed deadlock detection, distributed systems, message communication systems

Figure 10-29. Chandy-Lamport snapshots (http://bit.ly/2JBCsRU)

Reuven covered Flink's consistency mechanism briefly in Chapter 5, but to reiterate, the basic idea is that periodic barriers are propagated along the communication paths between workers in the system. The barriers act as an alignment mechanism between the various distributed workers producing data upstream from a consumer. When the consumer receives a given barrier on all of its input channels (i.e., from all of its upstream producers), it checkpoints its current progress for all active keys, at which point it is then safe to acknowledge processing of all data that came before the barrier. By tuning how frequently barriers are sent through the system, it's possible to tune the frequency of checkpointing and thus trade off increased latency (due to the need for side effects to be materialized only at checkpoint times) in exchange for higher throughput.

The simple fact that Flink now had the capability to provide exactly-once semantics along with native support for event-time processing was huge at the time. But it wasn't until Jamie Grier published his article titled "Extending the Yahoo! Streaming Benchmark" (*http://bit.ly/2LQvGnN*) (Figure 10-30) that it became clear just how performant Flink was. In that article, Jamie described two impressive achievements:

1. Building a prototype Flink pipeline that achieved greater accuracy than one of Twitter's existing Storm pipelines (thanks to Flink's exactly-once semantics) at 1% of the cost of the original.

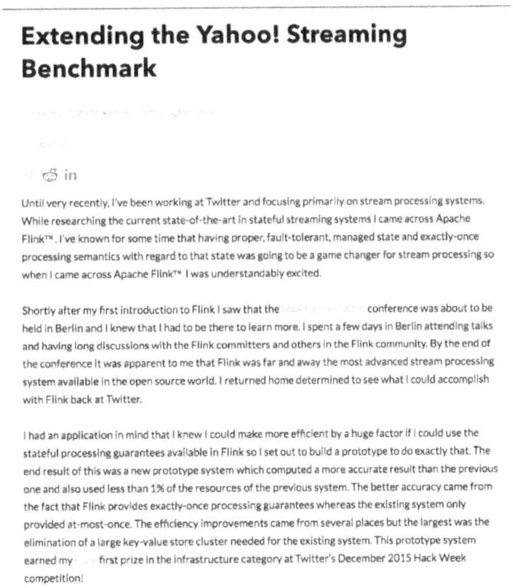
Extending the Yahoo! Streaming Benchmark

Until very recently, I've been working at Twitter and focusing primarily on stream processing systems. While researching the current state-of-the-art in stateful streaming systems I came across Apache Flink™. I've known for some time that having proper, fault-tolerant, managed state and exactly-once processing semantics with regard to that state was going to be a game changer for stream processing so when I came across Apache Flink™ I was understandably excited.

Shortly after my first introduction to Flink I saw that the conference was about to be held in Berlin and I knew that I had to be there to learn more. I spent a few days in Berlin attending talks and having long discussions with the Flink committers and others in the Flink community. By the end of the conference it was apparent to me that Flink was far and away the most advanced stream processing system available in the open source world. I returned home determined to see what I could accomplish with Flink back at Twitter.

I had an application in mind that I knew I could make more efficient by a huge factor if I could use the stateful processing guarantees available in Flink so I set out to build a prototype to do exactly that. The end result of this was a new prototype system which computed a more accurate result than the previous one and also used less than 1% of the resources of the previous system. The better accuracy came from the fact that Flink provides exactly-once processing guarantees whereas the existing system only provided at-most-once. The efficiency improvements came from several places but the largest was the elimination of a large key-value store cluster needed for the existing system. This prototype system earned my first prize in the infrastructure category at Twitter's December 2015 Hack Week competition!

Figure 10-30. "Extending the Yahoo! Streaming Benchmark" (http://bit.ly/2LQvGnN)

2. Updating the Yahoo! Streaming Benchmark (*http://bit.ly/2bhgMJd*) to show Flink (with exactly-once) achieving 7.5 times the throughput of Storm (without exactly-once). Furthermore, Flink's performance was shown to be limited due to network saturation; removing the network bottleneck allowed Flink to achieve almost 40 times the throughput of Storm.

Since then, numerous other projects (notably, Storm and Apex) have all adopted the same type of consistency mechanism.

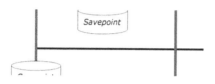

Savepoints: Turning Back Time

This post is the first in a series where the data Artisans team will highlight some of Apache Flink's® core features. By Fabian Hueske ( ) and Mike Winters ( )

Stream processing is commonly associated with 'data in motion', powering systems that make sense of and respond to data in nearly the same instant it's created. The most frequently discussed streaming topics, such as latency and throughput or watermarks and handling of late data, focus on the present rather than the past.

In reality, though, there are a number of cases where you'll need to reprocess data that your streaming application has already processed before. Some examples include:

- *Deployment of a new version of your application with a new feature, a bug fix, or a better machine learning model*
- *A/B testing different versions of an application using the same source data streams, starting the*

Figure 10-31. "Savepoints: Turning Back Time" (http://bit.ly/2JKCouO)

With the addition of a snapshotting mechanism, Flink gained the strong consistency needed for end-to-end exactly-once. But to its credit, Flink went one step further, and used the global nature of its snapshots to provide the ability to restart an entire pipeline from any point in the past, a feature known as savepoints (described in the "Savepoints: Turning Back Time" (*http://bit.ly/2JKCouO*) post by Fabian Hueske and Michael Winters [Figure 10-31]). The savepoints feature took the warm fuzziness of durable replay that Kafka had applied to the streaming transport layer and extended it to cover the breadth of an entire pipeline.

Graceful evolution of a long-running streaming pipeline over time remains an important open problem in the field, with lots of room for improvement. But Flink's savepoints feature stands as one of the first huge steps in the right direction, and one that remains unique across the industry as of this writing.

If you're interested in learning more about the system constructs underlying Flink's snapshots and savepoints, the paper "State Management in Apache Flink" (*http://bit.ly/2LLyr9O*) (Figure 10-32) discusses the implementation in good detail.

Beyond savepoints, the Flink community has continued to innovate, including bringing the first practical streaming SQL API to market for a large-scale, distributed stream processing engine, as we discussed in Chapter 8.

In summary, Flink's rapid rise to stream processing juggernaut can be attributed primarily to three characteristics of its approach: 1) incorporating the *best existing ideas* from across the industry (e.g., being the first open source adopter of the Dataflow/Beam Model), 2) *bringing its own innovations* to the table to push forward the state of the art (e.g., strong consistency via snapshots and savepoints, streaming SQL), and 3) doing both of those things *quickly* and *repeatedly*. Add in the fact that all of this is done in *open source*, and you can see why Flink has consistently continued to raise the bar for streaming processing across the industry.

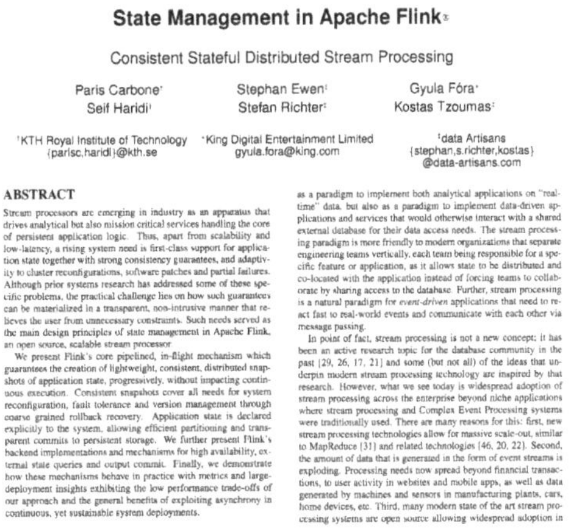

State Management in Apache Flink

Consistent Stateful Distributed Stream Processing

| Paris Carbone[*] | Stephan Ewen[†] | Gyula Fóra[*] |
| Seif Haridi[*] | Stefan Richter[†] | Kostas Tzoumas[‡] |

[*]KTH Royal Institute of Technology
{parisc,haridi}@kth.se

[†]King Digital Entertainment Limited
gyula.fora@king.com

[‡]data Artisans
{stephan,s.richter,kostas}
@data-artisans.com

ABSTRACT

Stream processors are emerging in industry as an apparatus that drives analytical but also mission critical services handling the core of persistent application logic. Thus, apart from scalability and low-latency, a rising system need is first-class support for application state together with strong consistency guarantees, and adaptivity to cluster reconfigurations, software patches and partial failures. Although prior systems research has addressed some of these specific problems, the practical challenge lies on how such guarantees can be materialized in a transparent, non-intrusive manner that relieves the user from unnecessary constraints. Such needs served as the main design principles of state management in Apache Flink, an open source, scalable stream processor.

We present Flink's core pipelined, in-flight mechanism which guarantees the creation of lightweight, consistent, distributed snapshots of application state, progressively, without impacting continuous execution. Consistent snapshots cover all needs for system reconfiguration, fault tolerance and version management through coarse grained rollback recovery. Application state is declared explicitly to the system, allowing efficient partitioning and transparent commits to persistent storage. We further present Flink's backend implementations and mechanisms for high availability, external state queries and output commits. Finally, we demonstrate how these mechanisms behave in practice with metrics and large-deployment insights exhibiting the low performance trade-offs of our approach and the general benefits of exploiting asynchrony in continuous, yet sustainable system deployments.

as a paradigm to implement both analytical applications on "real-time" data, but also as a paradigm to implement data-driven applications and services that would otherwise interact with a shared external database for their data access needs. The stream processing paradigm is more friendly to modern organizations that separate engineering teams vertically, each team being responsible for a specific feature or application, as it allows state to be distributed and co-located with the application instead of forcing teams to collaborate by sharing access to the database. Further, stream processing is a natural paradigm for *event-driven* applications that need to react fast to real-world events and communicate with each other via message passing.

In point of fact, stream processing is not a new concept; it has been an active research topic for the database community in the past [29, 26, 17, 21] and some (but not all) of the ideas that underpin modern stream processing technology are inspired by that research. However, what we see today is widespread adoption of stream processing across the enterprise beyond niche applications where stream processing and Complex Event Processing systems were traditionally used. There are many reasons for this: first, new stream processing technologies allow for massive scale-out, similar to MapReduce [31] and related technologies [46, 20, 22]. Second, the amount of data that is generated in the form of event streams is exploding. Processing needs now spread beyond financial transactions, to user activity in websites and mobile apps, as well as data generated by machines and sensors in manufacturing plants, cars, home devices, etc. Third, many modern state of the art stream processing systems are open source allowing widespread adoption in

Figure 10-32. "State Management in Apache Flink" (http://bit.ly/2LLyr9O)

Beam

The last system we talk about is Apache Beam (Figure 10-33). Beam differs from most of the other systems in this chapter in that it's primarily a programming model, API, and portability layer, not a full stack with an execution engine underneath. But that's exactly the point: just as SQL acts as a lingua franca for declarative data processing, Beam aims to be the lingua franca for programmatic data processing. Let's explore how.

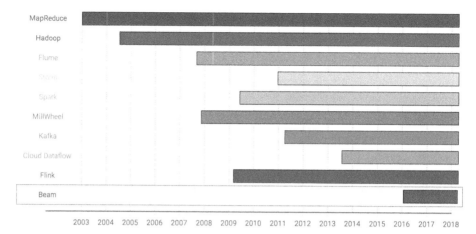

Figure 10-33. Timeline: Beam

Concretely, Beam is composed a number of components:

- A unified batch plus streaming *programming model*, inherited from Cloud Dataflow where it originated, and the finer points of which we've spent the majority of this book discussing. The model is independent of any language implementations or runtime systems. You can think of this as Beam's equivalent to SQL's relational algebra.

- A set of *SDKs (software development kits)* that implement that model, allowing pipelines to be expressed in terms of the model in idiomatic ways for a given language. Beam currently provides SDKs in Java, Python, and Go. You can think of these as Beam's programmatic equivalents to the SQL language itself.

- A set of *DSLs (domain specific languages)* that build upon the SDKs, providing specialized interfaces that capture pieces of the model in unique ways. Whereas SDKs are required to surface all aspects of the model, DSLs can expose only those pieces that make sense for the specific domain a DSL is targeting. Beam currently provides a Scala DSL called Scio and an SQL DSL, both of which layer on top of the existing Java SDK.

- A set of *runners* that can execute Beam pipelines. Runners take the logical pipeline described in Beam SDK terms, and translate them as efficiently as possible into a physical pipeline that they can then execute. Beam runners exist currently for Apex, Flink, Spark, and Google Cloud Dataflow. In SQL terms, you can think of these runners as Beam's equivalent to the various SQL database implementations, such as Postgres, MySQL, Oracle, and so on.

The core vision for Beam is built around its value as a portability layer, and one of the more compelling features in that realm is its planned support for full cross-language portability. Though not yet fully complete (but landing imminently (*http://bit.ly/ 2N0tPNL*)), the plan is for Beam to provide sufficiently performant abstraction layers between SDKs and runners that will allow for a full cross-product of SDK × runner matchups. In such a world, a pipeline written in a JavaScript SDK could seamlessly execute on a runner written in Haskell, even if the Haskell runner itself had no native ability to execute JavaScript code.

As an abstraction layer, the way that Beam positions itself relative to its runners is critical to ensure that Beam actually brings value to the community, rather than introducing just an unnecessary layer of abstraction. The key point here is that Beam aims to never be just the intersection (lowest common denominator) or union (kitchen sink) of the features found in its runners. Instead, it aims to include only the best ideas across the data processing community at large. This allows for innovation in two dimensions:

Innovation in Beam

Beam might include API support for runtime features that not all runners initially support. This is okay. Over time, we expect many runners will incorporate such features into future versions; those that don't will be a less-attractive runner choice for use cases that need such features.

An example here is Beam's SplittableDoFn API for writing composable, scalable sources (described by Eugene Kirpichov in his post "Powerful and modular I/O connectors with Splittable DoFn in Apache Beam" (*http://bit.ly/2JQa7GJ*) [Figure 10-34]). It's both unique and extremely powerful but also does not yet see broad support across all runners for some of the more innovative parts like dynamic work rebalancing. Given the value such features bring, however, we expect that will change over time.

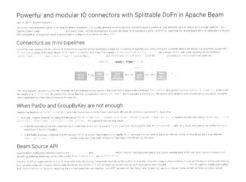

Figure 10-34. Powerful and modular I/O (http://bit.ly/2JQa7GJ)

Innovation in runners

Runners might introduce runtime features for which Beam does not initially provide API support. This is okay. Over time, runtime features that have proven their usefulness will have API support incorporated into Beam.

An example here is the state snapshotting mechanism in Flink, or savepoints, which we discussed earlier. Flink is still the only publicly available streaming system to support snapshots in this way, but there's a proposal in Beam to provide an API around snapshots because we believe graceful evolution of pipelines over time is an important feature that will be valuable across the industry. If we were to magically push out such an API today, Flink would be the only runtime system to support it. But again, that's okay. The point here is that the industry as a whole will begin to catch up over time as the value of these features becomes clear.[12] And that's better for everyone.

By encouraging innovation within both Beam itself as well as runners, we hope to push forward the capabilities of the entire industry at a greater pace over time, without accepting compromises along the way. And by delivering on the promise of portability across runtime execution engines, we hope to establish Beam as the common language for expressing programmatic data processing pipelines, similar to how SQL exists today as the common currency of declarative data processing. It's an ambitious goal, and as of writing, we're still a ways off from seeing it fully realized, but we've also come a long way so far.

Summary

We just took a whirlwind tour through a decade and a half of advances in data processing technology, with a focus on the contributions that made streaming systems what they are today. To summarize one last time, the main takeaways for each system were:

MapReduce—scalability and simplicity
> By providing a simple set of abstractions for data processing on top of a robust and scalable execution engine, MapReduce allowed data engineers to focus on the business logic of their data processing needs rather than the gnarly details of building distributed systems resilient to the failure modes of commodity hardware.

Hadoop—open source ecosystem
> By building an open source platform on the ideas of MapReduce, Hadoop created a thriving ecosystem that expanded well beyond the scope of its progenitor and allowed a multitude of new ideas to flourish.

---

12 There's an additional subtlety here that's worth calling out: even as runners adopt new semantics and tick off feature checkboxes, it's not the case that you can blindly choose any runner and have an identical experience. This is because the runners themselves can still vary greatly in their runtime and operational characteristics. Even for cases in which two given runners implement the same set of semantic features within the Beam Model, the way they go about executing those features at runtime is typically very different. As a result, when building a Beam pipeline, it's important to do your homework regarding various runners, to ensure that you choose a runtime platform that serves your use case best.

Flume—pipelines, optimization

By coupling a high-level notion of logical pipeline operations with an intelligent optimizer, Flume made it possible to write clean and maintainable pipelines whose capabilities extended beyond the Map → Shuffle → Reduce confines of MapReduce, without sacrificing any of the performance theretofore gained by contorting the logical pipeline via hand-tuned manual optimizations.

Storm—low latency with weak consistency

By sacrificing correctness of results in favor of decreased latency, Storm brought stream processing to the masses and also ushered in the era of the Lambda Architecture, where weakly consistent stream processing engines were run alongside strongly consistent batch systems to realize the true business goal of low-latency, eventually consistent results.

Spark—strong consistency

By utilizing repeated runs of a strongly consistent batch engine to provide continuous processing of unbounded datasets, Spark Streaming proved it possible to have both correctness and low-latency results, at least for in-order datasets.

MillWheel—out-of-order processing

By coupling strong consistency and exactly-once processing with tools for reasoning about time like watermarks and timers, MillWheel conquered the challenge of robust stream processing over out-of-order data.

Kafka—durable streams, streams and tables

By applying the concept of a durable log to the problem of streaming transports, Kafka brought back the warm, fuzzy feeling of replayability that had been lost by ephemeral streaming transports like RabbitMQ and TCP sockets. And by popularizing the ideas of stream and table theory, it helped shed light on the conceptual underpinnings of data processing in general.

Cloud Dataflow—unified batch plus streaming

By melding the out-of-order stream processing concepts from MillWheel with the logical, automatically optimizable pipelines of Flume, Cloud Dataflow provided a unified model for batch plus streaming data processing that provided the flexibility to balance the tensions between correctness, latency, and cost to match any given use case.

Flink—open source stream processing innovator

By rapidly bringing the power of out-of-order processing to the world of open source and combining it with innovations of their own like distributed snapshots and its related savepoints features, Flink raised the bar for open source stream processing and helped lead the current charge of stream processing innovation across the industry.

Beam—portability

By providing a robust abstraction layer that incorporates the best ideas from across the industry, Beam provides a portability layer positioned as the programmatic equivalent to the declarative lingua franca provided by SQL, while also encouraging the adoption of innovative new ideas throughout the industry.

To be certain, these 10 projects and the sampling of their achievements that I've highlighted here do not remotely encompass the full breadth of the history that has led the industry to where it exists today. But they stand out to me as important and noteworthy milestones along the way, which taken together paint an informative picture of the evolution of stream processing over the past decade and a half. We've come a long way since the early days of MapReduce, with a number of ups, downs, twists, and turns along the way. Even so, there remains a long road of open problems ahead of us in the realm of streaming systems. I'm excited to see what the future holds.

Index

A

accumulating and retracting mode, 51, 166, 243
  early/on-time/late triggers, 54
accumulating mode (accumulation), 51, 166, 243
accumulation, 27, 51-55
  accumulating and retracting mode, 51
  accumulating mode, 51
  accumulation mode in processing-time window via ingress time, 101
  discarding mode, 51
  in processsing-time windowing via triggers, 99
  in streaming SQL, 243
    discarding mode, 248
    retractions, 244-248
  in streams and tables model, 166
  side-by-side comparison of modes, 54
accumulators, 181
accuracy
  in lambda architecture processing, 122
  vs. completeness in exactly-once processing, 122-125
aggregations
  grouping and summation via incremental combination, 183
  incrementalization of, 182
  parallelization of, 182
  properties of, 181
aligned delays (processing time in triggers), 37
allowed lateness, 47-50
ANTI joins, 261
Apache Beam, 313-318
  blending of batch and streaming, 165
  code snippets for, 25
    Java SDK pseudo-code, 30
  CombineFn API, 181
  components, 314
  conversion attribution with, 189-199
  innovation in, 315
  portability layer, 315
  streaming SQL in, 201
Apache Calcite, 201
Apache Flink, 6, 201, 309-313, 317
  adoption of Dataflow/Beam programming model, 310
  consistency mechanism, 311
  end-to-end exactly once, 125
  exactly-once processing in, 136
  factors in its rapid rise to stream procesing juggernaut, 313
  highly efficient snapshotting implementation, 310
  impressive performance of, 311
  savepoints feature, 312
  snapshotting paper, 8
  watermarks in, case study, 88
Apache Kafka, 130, 304-306, 317
  application of durability and replayability to stream data, 305
  capabilities of, 304
  Kafka's Streams API, 306
  popularization of stream and table theory, 305
Apache Spark, 297-300, 317
  current developments in, 300
  end-to-end exactly once, 125
  Spark Streaming, 136, 298

ingress times as event times, 96
manually building up sessions in, 107
snapshotting paper, 8
Apache Storm, 294-297, 317
bringing low-latency data processing to the masses, 295
history of its creation, 295
append-only logs, 142
approximation algorithms, 16
AS OF SYSTEM TIME construct (SQL), 208
assignment (window), 107
in fixed windows, 108
in session windows, 115
in streams and tables model, 154
associativity, 182
at least once guarantee, 125

B

base subscription (Google Cloud Pub/Sub case study), 91
batch processing
blending with streaming, 165
commonalities between batch and streaming, 308
event-time and processing-time view of, 151
persistent state in, 176
streams and tables view, 232
streams and tables view of windowed summation on batch engine, 156
unified batch plus streaming programming model, 308, 314
vs. streams and tables, 144-150
reconciling the two, 150
batch systems, 6
bounded data processing with, 12
processing of unbounded data, 13
processing state and output in example mobile game with user scores, 31
streaming systems providing superset of, 6
Beam Model, 26, 141
(see also Apache Beam)
correct implementation to produce accurate results, 121
holistic view of streams and tables in, 166-171
relationship to streams and tables model, 170
windowing in, 55
Bloom filters, 128

bounded data, 5
processing, 12
bounded datasets
recomputation on failure, 176
bounded sessions, 116
buffering
in event-time windows, 21

C

Calcite (see Apache Calcite)
CAP theorem, 296
cardinality
in unwindowed joins, 255
SEMI join, 262
of datasets, 5, 141
reducing for a stream, 36
Chandy Lamport distributed snapshots, 138, 310
checkpointing
in bounded datasets on batch processing pipelines, 176
in Flink, 311
in processing of unbounded datasets, 176
partial progress within a pipeline, 177
persistent state over time, 7
use to make nondeterministic processing deterministic in Dataflow, 127
closure property (relational algebra), 202, 249
remaining intact when applied to time-varying relations, 205
Cloud Dataflow, 25, 307-309, 317
balancing correctness, latency, and cost, 309
Dataflow Model paper, 309
exactly-once processing in, 121
serverless aspect of, 307
unified batch and streaming programming model
key aspects of, 308
unified batch plus streaming programming model, 308
watermarks in, case study, 87-88
Cloud Pub/Sub, 66
as example source, 133
as nondeterministic source, 131
watermarks for, case study, 90-93
combination, incremental (see incremental combination)
CombineFn class (Beam), 181
combiner lifting optimization, 128, 292

commutativity, 182
completeness
    accuracy vs., in exactly-once processing, 122
    concept provided by watermarks, 62
    drawback of event-time windows in, 22
    watermarks for reasoning about input completeness, 308
    watermarks giving notion of, 41
completeness triggers, 35
    watermarks, 40
complexity in lambda architecture processing, 122
consistency
    consistency mechanism in Flink, 311
    strong consistency for exactly-once processing, 8
constitution of a dataset, 5, 141
conversion attribution, 186-188
    with Apache Beam, 189-199
correctness
    Apache Storm and, 296
    balancing with latency and cost in Cloud Dataflow, 309
    in batch and streaming systems, 7
    MillWheel and, 301
    persistent stte as basis for, 177
    supposed limitations of streaming systems, 6
custom windowing, 107-119
    benefits of, 119
    variations on fixed windows, 108-115
        per-element/key fixed windows, 113
        unaligned fixed windows, 109
    variations on session windows, 115-118
        bounded sessions, 116

D

data processing
    difficulty of, 285
    what, where, when, and how of, 25-57, 308
        what, transformations, 28-32
        when and how in streaming systems, 34-55
        where, windowing, 32-34
data processing patterns, 12-22
    bounded data, 12
    unbounded data, batch processing of, 13
    unbounded data, streaming, 14-22

data processing, large scale (see large-scale data processing, evolution of)
data types, flexibility in, 185, 194
data-driven triggers, 243
data-driven windows, sessions as example, 103
database systems, 142
Dataflow (see Google Cloud Dataflow)
Dataflow Model, 26
Dataflow Model paper, 157, 309
datasets
    cardinality of, 5
    constitution of, 5
determinism
    addressing in exactly-once processing, 126
    in sources, 130
    nondeterministic components in side effects, 131
discarding mode (accumulation), 51, 166
    early/on-time/late triggers, 53
    in streaming SQL, 248
domain specific languages (DSLs), 314
DSLs (domain specific languages), 314
duplicated work, minimizing with persistent state, 177
duplicates, detecting in shuffle, 126
dynamic windows, 52
    (see also sessions)
dynamic work rebalancing (or liquid sharding), 294

E

early/on-time/late triggers, 44-47
    accumulating and retracting mode version, 54
    discarding mode version, 53
    early panes, 44
    in bounded session window, 117
    in streams and tables model, 161
    late panes, 45
    on-time pane, 44
    watermark trigger with late firing in streaming SQL, 239
    with allowed lateness, 47-50
    with session windows and retractions, 105
efficiency
    inefficiencies in MapReduce jobs, 290
    persistent data, minimizing work duplicated and data persistend, 177
end-to-end exactly once, 125, 305

event time
  distribution of messages by, 60
  in SQL table UserScores (example), 29
  in streaming SQL, 229
  skew and watermarks, 39
  view of batch processing, 151
  vs. processing time, 9
  watermarks, 27, 85
  windowing based on, 96
  windowing by, 20
    drawbacks of, 21
event-time windowing
  over two different processing-time order-
    ings of same input, 97
  reasons for using in processing-time win-
    dowing, 102
exactly-once processing, 7, 121-138, 301
  accuracy vs. completeness, 122, 125
    problem definition, 123
    side effects, 123
  determinism and, 126
  end-to-end, 305
  ensuring exactly once in shuffles, 125
  in Apache Flink, 136, 311
  in Apache Spark Streaming, 136
  in conversion attribution pipeline, 188
  performance, 127-130
    garbage collection, 129
    graph optimization, 127
    optimization using Bloom filters, 128
  use cases
    example sink, files, 134
    example sink, Google BigQuery, 135
    example source, Cloud Pub/Sub, 133
  why exactly once matters, 121

F
failures, inevitability of, 176
fault-tolerance in large-scale data processing,
  285
files, using as sinks, 134
filtering, 15
filtering relation (WHERE clause), time-
  varying relation applied to, 206
fixed windows, 17
  unbounded data processing via in batch sys-
    tems, 13
  variations on, 108-115
    per-element/key fixed windows, 113

unaligned fixed windows, 109
  windowed joins in, 267-269
flexibility
  flexible triggering and accumulation modes,
    308
  needs in streaming persistent state, 185
    in conversion attribution using Apache
      Beam, 194
  shortcomings of implicit approaches, 184
Flume, 289-294, 317
  combined batch and streaming approach in,
    308
  combiner lifting optimization, 292
  dynamic work rebalancing (or liquid shard-
    ing), 294
  extension to support streaming semantics,
    294
  FlumeJava paper, 293
  fusion optimizations, 291
  high-level pipelines in, 290
  migration away from MapReduce to Dax
    execution engine, 293
  MillWheel integration with, 303
  optimization of MapReduce jobs, 291
FlumeJava, 289
  (see also Flume)
FULL OUTER joins, 255, 266, 278
fusion optimization on pipeline graph, 127, 291

G
garbage collection
  bits of persistent state not needed, 178
  in exactly-once processing, 129
generalized state, 184-199
  case study, conversion attribution, 186-188
  flexibility in, 200
  in conversion attribution, 186-188
  in conversion attribution using Apache
    Beam, 189-199
Google BigQuery, use as a sink, 135
Google Cloud Dataflow (see Cloud Dataflow;
  Dataflow Model)
Google Cloud Pub/Sub (see Cloud Pub/Sub)
Google technologies in large-scale data processing, 284
graph optimization in Dataflow, 127
GROUP BY statement with HAVING clause
  (SQL), 221
grouping operations

grouping via incremental combination, 183
grouping/ungrouping in Beam Model, 216
grouping/ungrouping in SQL, 223
    in materialized views, 226
grouping/ungrouping in streams and tables, 157
    in Beam Model processing, 170
    joins as, 253
    raw grouping of inputs, 179
grouping relation, time-varying relation applied to, 206
grouping transformations, 151

H

Hadoop, 288, 316
    Spark as successor to, 298
HAVING clause in GROUP BY statment (SQL), 221
HDFS (Hadoop Distributed File System), 288
Heron, 296
heuristic watermarks, 40, 62
    allowed lateness and, 50
    applying to same dataset with a perfect watermark, 41
    creation of, 65
        from dynamic sets of time-ordered logs, 65
        from Google Cloud Pub/Sub, 66
    early/on-time/late triggers and, 47
high volumes of data, handling in conversion attribution pipeline, 188
hopping windows (see sliding windows)

I

implicit state, 178, 184
implicit tables in SQL, 221
in-band watermarks, 89
inaccuracy problems in lambda architecture, 122
inconsistency in lambda architecture processing, 122
incremental combination, 181-184, 199
incrementalization of aggregations, 182
ingress time
    processing-time windowing via, 100-103
    use in achieving processing-time windowing, 96
ingress timestamping, watermark creation by, 64

inner joins, 15
INNER joins, 259, 279
input completeness, 308
input tables (SQL), 223, 226
input watermarks, 68
    for Average Session Lengths stage, 75

J

Java pseudo-code in Apache Beam examples, 30
joins, 15, 253
    (see also inner joins)
    (see also streaming joins)
    all joins as streaming joins, 253

K

kappa architecture, 6
keys, values, windows and partitioning in Beam Model, 169

L

lambda architecture, 6, 22, 296
    issues with, 121
    using Spark Streaming instead of, 298
large-scale data processing, evolution of, 283-318
    Apache Beam, 313-316
    Apache Kafka, 304-306
    Apache Storm, 294-297
    Cloud Dataflow, 307-309
    Flume, 289-294
    Hadoop, 288
    MapReduce, 284-288
    MillWheel, 300-303
    timeline of systems discussed, 284
late data
    and heuristic watermarks, 65
    and perfect watermarks, 64
late panes, 45
latency
    balancing with correctness and cost in Cloud Dataflow, 309
    improvements in Apache Storm, 295
    in lambda architecture processing, 122
    low-latency and eventually correct results with lambda architecture, 296
    system vs. data, distinguishing with processing-time watermarks, 85
lateness (allowed), 47-50

LEFT OUTER joins, 258
liquid sharding, 294
logical abstraction of execution environment, 308
logical vs. physical operations in Beam Model, 169
    and how they relate to streams and tables, 169
logs
    dymanic sets of time-ordered logs, watermark creation from, 65
    static sets of time-ordered logs, creation of watermarks, 64

M

MapReduce, 283-288, 316
    Combiners, 182
    functionality of overall Map and Reduce phases, 286
    history of massive-scale sorting experiments at Google, 287
    MapReduce paper, 287
    shortcomings of, 290
    simplicity and scalability, 287
    stages answering what questions, 150
    streams and tables analysis of, 144-150
        Map as streams/tables, 145
        Reduce as streams/tables, 147
    visualization of a job, 286
materialized views, 142, 223-226, 255
merging windows, 108, 154
    in parallelized aggregations, 183
    in session windows, 115
    in streams and tables model, 156
    no merging in fixed windows, 108
microbatch vs. true streaming debate, 299
MillWheel, 300-303, 317
    fault-tolerant stream processing at internet scale, 303
    Flume and, 294
    low-latency, strongly consistent processing of unbounded, out-of-order data, 301
MillWheel paper, 8

N

network remnants, 130
nongrouping operations, 171, 173
nongrouping transformations, 151

O

OLTP (Online Transaction Processing) tables
    STREAM queries and, 211
on-time pane, 44
open source ecosystem, Hadoop and, 289
operators (relational algebra)
    applied to time-varying relations, 205
    applying to valid relations, 202
out-of-band watermark aggregation, 90
out-of-order data
    handling in conversion attribution pipeline, 187-188
    in temporal validity windows, 271
    unbounded, processing in MillWheel, 301
outer joins, 43
output tables (SQL), 223, 226
output timestamps
    watermark propagation and, 75-80
    watermarks and
        with overlapping windows, 80
output watermarks, 68
    components of, 69
    for Mobile Sessions and Console Sessions stages, 75

P

parallelization of aggregations, 182
per-element/key fixed windows, 113
percentile watermarks, 81-83
perfect watermarks, 40, 62
    allowed lateness and, 50
    applying to same dataset with a heuristic watermark, 41
    creation of, 64
        by ingress timestamping, 64
    early/on-time/late triggers and, 47
performance
    in exactly-once shuffle delivery, 127-130
        garbage collection, 129
        graph optimization, 127
        optimizing with Bloom filters, 128
    optimizing in conversion attribution pipeline, 188
persistent state, 175-200, 301
    generalized state, 184-199
        in conversion attribution, 186-188
        in conversion attribution using Apache Beam, 189-199
    implicit state, 178-184

in incremental combining, 181
raw grouping of inputs, 179
motivation for, 175-178
correctness and efficiency, 177
inevitability of failure, 176
persistent timers, 301
physical stages and fusion in Beam Model, 169
post-declaration of triggers, 217
predeclaration of triggers, 217
processing time, 39
conversion to event time in watermarks, 40
delays in triggers, 37
event time vs., 9
in SQL table UserScores (example), 29
in streaming SQL, 229
shifting input observation order in, 96
view of batch processing, 151
watermarks, 84-86
windowing by, 18
processing-time windowing, 119
event-time windowing comparing two
processing-time orderings of same iput,
97
via ingress time, 100-103
via triggers, 98-100
processing-time windows, 95-103
downside to, 96
via ingress time, 96
via triggers, 96
Pub/Sub (see Google Cloud Pub/Sub)

Q

Questioning the Lambda Architecture post, 6

R

raw grouping, 179, 199
merging windows, 183
relational algebra, 202
defining time-varying relations in terms of,
203-207
relations (in databases), 202
repeated delay triggers, 241, 250
repeated update triggers, 35
firing with every new record, 35
reprocessing the input, 176
Reshuffle transform, 132, 135
resilient distributed datasets (RDDs), 136, 298
retractions (accumulating and retracting
mode), 51

in session window, 105
in streaming SQL, 244-248
in Sys.Undo column (hypothetical) in
streaming SQL, 211
RIGHT OUTER joins, 259
RPCs (remote procedure calls), use in shuffle
and issues with RPCs, 125
runners in Apache Beam, 314
innovation in, 315

S

savepoints, 312
scalability
in large-scale data processing, 285
in MapReduce, 287, 316
SCAN-AND-STREAM trigger, 224
scheduling of processing, flexibility in, 185, 195
SDKs (software development kits) in Apache
Beam, 314
SELECT statement (SQL), STREAM and
TABLE keywords after, 227
SEMI joins, 262-266
session windows, 103-107, 119
variations on, 115-118
bounded sessions, 116
sessions, 14, 18
calculating length per user across two input
pipelines, 70
interest from windowing standpoint, 103
manually building up on Spark Streaming
1.x (blog post), 107
retractions and, 52
shuffles in a pipeline, 124-125
ensuring exactly once in, 125
Reshuffle transform, 132
side effects
idempotent and robust in replay, 131
in exactly-once processing, 123
sinks, 223
example sink, files, 134
example sink, Google BigQuery, 135
sliding windows, 18
snapshots
Flink's highly efficient snapshotting implementation, 310, 312
in Apache Flink, 137
source watermarks, creation of, 90
sources, 223
exactly-once processing in, 130

example surce, Cloud Pub/Sub, 133
spam attacks, protecting against in conversion
    attribution pipeline, 188
Spark Streaming (see Apache Spark Streaming)
Spark Streaming paper, 8
SQL
    Spark integration with, 299
    support for time-varying relations in, 208
    table-biased approach, 218-226
    types of joins defined in ANSI SQL, 255
State Management in Apache Flink, 312
Storm (see Apache Storm)
STREAM keyword (hypothetical, in SQL), 209,
    227
STREAM queries (hypothetical, in SQL)
    providing alternate data history to table-
        based TVR query, 212
    relation to OLTP tables, 211
    Sys.Undo column referenced from, 209
streaming, 3-23
    commonalities between batch and stream-
        ing, 308
    greatly exaggerated limitations of, 6
    microbatch vs. true streaming debate, 299
    support for stream processing in SQL mate-
        rialized views, 223-226
    terminology, 4-12
    unified batch plus streaming programming
        model, 308, 314
    Zeitgeist pipeline, true streaming use case,
        301
streaming joins, 253-282
    unwindowed joins, 254-266
        FULL OUTER, 255
        INNER, 259
        LEFT OUTER, 258
        RIGHT OUTER, 259
        SEMI, 262-266
    windowed joins, 266-282
        fixed windows, 267-269
        temporal validity, 269-282
streaming SQL, 201-251
    complete definition of, 201
    looking backward, stream and table biases,
        214-226
    looking forward, toward robust streaming,
        226-248
        stream and table selection, 227
        temporal operators, 228-248

relational algebra as theoretical foundation
    of SQL, 202
temporal validity window in, 272
time-varying relations, 203-207
unwindowed joins
    ANTI, 261
streaming systems, 4
    when and how of data processing, 34-55
        how, accumulation, 51-55
        when, allowed lateness, 47-50
        when, early/on-time/late triggers, 44-47
        when, triggers, 34-39
        when, watermarks, 39-44
streams, 5
    and tables, 141-173
    as data in motion, 144
    persistent forms of, 177
    time-varying relations in, 208
streams and tables
    batch processing vs., 144-150
        how batch processing fits into stream/
            table theory, 150
        how streams relate to bounded/unboun-
            ded data, 150
        streams and tables analysis of Map-
            Reduce, 144-150
    comparing classic SQL and Beam Model,
        looking backward, 214-226
        stream-biased approch in Beam Model,
            214-217
        table-biased approach in SQL, 218-226
    conversions to and from in MapReduce, 286
    general theory of stream and table relativity,
        171-172
    holistic view of in Beam Model, 166-171
    Kafka as embodiment of relationship
        between, 304
    popularization of theory by Apache Kafka,
        305
    relationship between Beam Model and, 141
    special theory of stream and table relativity,
        142
    table/stream selection for TVRs in stream-
        ing SQL, 249
    time-varying relations in, 207-213
    toward a general theory of stream and table
        relativity, 143
    view of windowed summation, 180
    what, where, when, and how of, 150

how, accumulation, 166

what, transformations, 150-154

when, triggers, 157-165

where, windowing, 154-157

strong consistency in a streaming system, 8

subscriptions in Google Cloud Pub/Sub case study, 91

summation via incremental combination, 183

Sys.EmitIndex column (hypothetical, in SQL), 240, 251

Sys.EmitTiming column (hypothetical, in SQL), 240, 250

Sys.MTime column (hypothetical, in SQL), 229, 250

Sys.Undo column (hypothetical, in SQL), 209, 244, 251

distinguishing between normal rows and rows retracting a previous value, 211

T

TABLE keyword (hypothetical, in SQL), 208, 227

tables, 5

as data at rest, 143

conversion of streams from/to in SQL, 223

explicit and implicit in SQL, 221

persistent state, 175

table-based TVR vs. STREAM query TVR, 212

time-varying relations in, 208

tables and streams (see streams and tables)

temporal operators (in streaming SQL), 228-248

triggers, 235-243

windowing, 233-235

temporal tables (SQL), 208

temporal validity, 269-282

temporal validity joins, 274-282

watermarks and, 280

temporal validity windows, 270-274

time

event time vs. processing time, 9

partitioning in windowed joins, 266

time-agnostic processing of unbounded data, 15

filtering, 15

inner joins, 15

tools for reasoning about, 8

time-varying relations, 203-207, 227, 249

defining in terms of relational algebra, 203-207

for FULL OUTER joins, 256

in temporal validity joins, 276

in temporal validity windows, 271

relationship with stream and table theory, 207-213

timers, 186, 301

timestamps

event, 60

system timestamp for Bloom filters, 128

watermarks and, 62

timing out a join, providing reference point for, 266

tools for reasoning about time, 8

tracking subscription (Google Cloud Pub/Sub case study), 91

transformations, 28-32

in streams and tables model, 150-154

triggers, 26, 34-39

completeness, 35

watermark completeness trigger, 40

early/on-time/late, 44-47

with allowed lateness, 47-50

in processing-time window via ingress time, 101

in streaming SQL, 235-243, 250

data-driven triggers, 243

repeated delay triggers, 241

watermark triggers, 238-241

in streams and tables model, 157-165

blending of batch and streaming, 165

early/on-time/late firings, 161

per-record triggering in streaming engine, 159

trigger guarantees (or lack of), 164

windowed summation with heuristic watermark on streaming engine, 161

in unwindowed joins, 254

predeclaration or post-declaration options, Beam Model and, 217

processing-time delays in

aligned delays, 37

unaligned delays, 37

processing-time windowing via, 98-100

repeated update, 35

SCAN-AND-STREAM trigger in materialized views, 224

use in achieving processing-time windowing, 96
tumbling windows (see fixed windows)
Twitter Heron, 297

U

unaligned delays (processing time in triggers), 37
unaligned windows, 103
    unaligned fixed windows, 109
unbounded data, 5
    processing by batch systems, 13
    processing by streaming systems, 14-22
        time-agnostic processing, 15
        using approximation algorithms, 16
UnboundedReader.getCurrentRecordId method, 131
ungrouping operations, 216
    (see also grouping operations)
unified batch plus streaming programming model
    in Apache Beam, 314
unpredictability in lambda architecture processing, 122
unwindowed joins, 254-266
    ANTI, 261
    FULL OUTER, 255
    INNER, 259
    LEFT OUTER, 258
    RIGHT OUTER, 259
    SEMI, 262-266

V

visibility (watermarks), 62

W

watermark triggers
    in streaming SQL, 238-241, 250
watermarks, 27, 39-44, 59-93, 301-302
    about, 59
    allowed lateness and, 49
    and temporal validity joins, 280
    applying perfect and heuristic watermarks to same dataset, 41
    as class of functions, 41
    case study, watermarks for Google Cloud Pub/Sub, 90-93
    case study, watermarks in Apache Flink, 88

    case study, watermarks in Google Cloud Dataflow, 86-88
    for exactly-once garbage collection in Dataflow, 130
    function, converting processing time to event time, 40
    heuristic, 40
    in processing-time windowing via ingress time, 101
    in streaming SQL, 250
    percentile, 81-83
    perfect, 40
    processing-time, 84-86
    propagation, 67-81
        and output timestamps, 75-80
        with overlapping windows, 80
    source watermark creation, 62-67
        heuristic watermarks, 65
        perfect watermarks, 64
    too fast, 44
    too slow, 43
    use in Cloud Dataflow, 308
Windmill, 303
windowing, 11, 32-34, 55, 254
    (see also unwindowed joins)
    accumulation modes for a window, 27
    by event time, 20
    by processing time, 18
    custom, 107-119
        benefits of, 119
        elements of custom windowing strategy, 107
        variations on fixed windows, 108-115
        variations on session windows, 115-118
    different strategies for, 17
    dynamic windows and retractions, 52
    end of window and output timestamp, 76
    fixed windows, 17
    in Cloud Dataflow, 308
    in streaming SQL, 233-235, 249
    in streams and tables model, 154-157
    lifetime of windows, 47
    nondeterministic records in windowed aggregation, 131
    overlapping windows and output timestamp, 80
    session windows, 103-107
    sessions, 18

sessions in unbounded data processing by batch systems, 14
sliding windows, 18
summation code example, 33
summation on a batch engine, 33
summation on streaming dataset with perfect and heuristic watermarks, 41
triggers for output, 26
unbounded data processing via fixed windows in batch systems, 13

windowed file writes, 134
windowed joins, 266-282
    fixed windows, 267-269
    temporal validity, 269-282
write and read granularity, flexibility in, 185, 194

Z

Zeitgeist pipeline, true streaming use case, 301

About the Authors

Tyler Akidau is a senior staff software engineer at Google, where he is the technical lead for the Data Processing Languages & Systems group, responsible for Google's Apache Beam efforts, Google Cloud Dataflow, and internal data processing tools like Google Flume, MapReduce, and MillWheel. Tyler is also a founding member of the Apache Beam PMC. Though deeply passionate and vocal about the capabilities and importance of stream processing, he is also a firm believer in batch and streaming as two sides of the same coin, with the real endgame for data processing systems being the seamless merging between the two. He is the author of the "Dataflow Model" paper (*http://bit.ly/2sXgVJ3*) and the "Streaming 101" (*http://oreil.ly/1p1AKux*) and "Streaming 102" (*http://oreil.ly/1TV7YGU*) articles on the O'Reilly website. His preferred mode of transportation is by cargo bike, with his two young daughters in tow.

Slava Chernyak is a senior software engineer at Google Seattle. Slava spent more than six years working on Google's internal massive-scale streaming data processing systems and has since become involved with designing and building Windmill, Google Cloud Dataflow's next-generation streaming backend, from the ground up. Slava is passionate about making massive-scale stream processing available and useful to a broader audience. When he is not working on streaming systems, Slava is out enjoying the natural beauty of the Pacific Northwest.

Reuven Lax is a senior staff software engineer at Google, Seattle, and has spent the past ten years helping to shape Google's data processing and analysis strategy. For much of that time he has focused on Google's low-latency, streaming data processing efforts, first as a long-time member and lead of the MillWheel team, and more recently founding and leading the team responsible for Windmill, the next-generation stream processing engine powering Google Cloud Dataflow. He is also a Beam PMC member. He's very excited to bring Google's data processing experience to the world at large and proud to have been a part of publishing both the "MillWheel" paper (*http://bit.ly/2yab5ZH*) in 2013 and the "Dataflow Model" paper (*http://bit.ly/2sXgVJ3*) in 2015. When not at work, Reuven enjoys swing dancing, rock climbing, and exploring new parts of the world.

Colophon

The animal on the cover of *Streaming Systems* is a brown trout (*Salmo trutta*) a species of medium-sized fish native to northern Europe but now distributed across the globe. Brown trout generally weigh about 2 pounds and grow to a length of 16–31 inches. They have an overall shiny brown color with many dark spots over their upper body.

Brown trout feed mostly on aquatic invertebrates although larger members of the species have been known to prey on other fish. During spawning, the female brown trout produces thousands of eggs. It takes 3–4 years for a brown trout to reach maturity.

Popular with anglers, brown trout were introduced into lakes and rivers throughout the world during the 19th and early 20th centuries. To this day, brown trout are farmed commercially and stocked for recreational fishing. Brown trout are edible and can be prepared in several ways, including grilling, frying, and smoking.

The animal on the improved cover in Figure P-1 is a robotic tyrannosaurus rex imbued with the soul of Sean Connery. True to form, it always speaks with a Scottish accent, even when playing the role of a Russian submarine captain.

Many of the animals on O'Reilly covers are endangered; all of them are important to the world. To learn more about how you can help, go to *animals.oreilly.com*.

The cover image is from Karen Montgomery. The cover fonts are URW Typewriter and Guardian Sans. The text font is Adobe Minion Pro; the heading font is Adobe Myriad Condensed; and the code font is Dalton Maag's Ubuntu Mono.

O'REILLY®

There's much more where this came from.

Experience books, videos, live online training courses, and more from O'Reilly and our 200+ partners—all in one place.

Learn more at oreilly.com/online-learning

Milton Keynes UK
Ingram Content Group UK Ltd.
UKHW050244080924
447993UK00002B/3